FROM THE ESOTERIC SCHOOL

ESOTERIC LESSONS

1910 – 1912

RUDOLF STEINER (1916)

ESOTERIC LESSONS
1910–1912

Notes Written from Memory by the Participants
and Meditation Verses by Rudolf Steiner

VOLUME 2

TRANSLATED BY JAMES HINDES
INTRODUCTION BY CHRISTOPHER BAMFORD

RUDOLF STEINER

SteinerBooks

CW 266/2

Copyright © 2012 by SteinerBooks

SteinerBooks
Anthroposophic Press

610 Main Street
Great Barrington, Massachusetts 01230
www.steinerbooks.org

Original translation from the German by James Hindes

This book is volume 266/2 in the Collected Works (CW) of Rudolf Steiner, published by SteinerBooks, 2012. It is a translation of the *German Aus den Inhalten der esoterischen Stunden. Band II. Gedachtnisaufzeichnungen von Teilnehmern und Meditationstexte nach Niederschriften Rudolf Steiners 1910-1912*, published by Rudolf Steiner Verlag, Dornach Switzerland, 1996.

Library of Congress Cataloging-in-Publication Data is available.

ISBN 978-0-88010-617-7

All rights reserved.
No part of this book may be reproduced in any form without written permission from the publisher, except for brief quotations embodied in critical articles for review.

CONTENTS

Introduction by Christopher Bamford   xix

NOTES OF THE ESOTERIC LESSONS
1910–1912

Written from Memory by the Participants

Meditation Verses Used Repeatedly in the Esoteric Lessons
from 1910 to 1912..2

1910

FEBRUARY 6, 1910, KASSEL...11
"Sun, Earth—Meditation, Study." Esoteric training in ancient times (success or death) and today (becoming a different person); the necessity of truthfulness and patience. Use of meditation contents, with the example of the Lord's Prayer. The physical world as a parable for the spiritual (autumn/falling asleep; spring/awakening). Study as a preparation for meditation; meditation as sacrifice.

FEBRUARY 27, 1910, COLOGNE..16
Doubt, superstition, and the illusion of personality as three threatening forces.

MARCH 13, 1910, MUNICH...18
Concerning the daily verses (Sunday). "Everything around us is maya." Lucifer's influence; what is moon-like in the effects of Lucifer's work; the intervention of the good gods in like measure through what is moon-like; for example, weather catastrophes. Taking maya into meditation as the influence of Lucifer in the esoteric life; bad character traits as hindrances introduced by the good gods.

MARCH 15, 1910, MUNICH...21
Concerning the daily verses (Tuesday). The development of the human being's constituent parts (members) and the reception of theosophical teachings. The Saturn condition of the "I"; the earthly condition of the physical body.

MAY 16, 1910, HAMBURG..23
"Everything around us is maya." Example of a red object. The meditative path as a path to the true being of things (Example of the feelings called forth by colors). The feeling of shame in the dying of the plant world; the Rose Cross. The awakening of feelings not bound to external things.

MAY 19, 1910, HAMBURG..27
Concerning the daily verses (Thursday). Christ before the event of Golgotha as the spirit of the sun; thereafter as the spirit of the earth. The union with him through the imagination of the Rose Cross; the formation of complementary colors. An esotericist's faith in the good.

MAY 25, 1910, HAMBURG..30
Verse to the spirit of the day (Wednesday). An esotericist's search for balance; possible aberrations. Discordant moods: improper effects of the spirits of heaviness (leads to hypochondria and diseases of the digestive organs). Vanity, arrogance: irregular working of the spirits of light (leads to destruction of the brain, confusion, and mental illness). *In the spirit lay ...* (spirit of heaviness) *In my body ...* (spirit of light). The nine traits of the master. The five demands upon the student. Mantras. The fivefold spirit; proper and improper working. The Rose Cross.

JUNE 16, 1910, KRISTIANIA (OSLO)...37
Falling asleep and awakening; the proper preparation for sleep. The need for helpers on the external path of Druidic initiation and the inner path of Egyptian initiation. The Rosicrucian path is based upon powers acquired by the self. The task of esotericists for humanity. The return of suppressed physical pain as soul pain, as psychological pain in later incarnations.

JUNE 18, 1910, KRISTIANIA (OSLO)...40
Egyptian and Druidic initiation. The Rosicrucian path. Elucidation of the verse *In pure rays...* in view of the Spirit of Christ. The Rosicrucian verse. Dangers of illusion in meditation.

JUNE 20, 1910, KRISTIANIA (OSLO)...43
Verse to the Spirit of the day (Monday). The thoughts of the spirits of the earth as sleeping powers (sleeping in the mineral kingdom, dreaming in the plant kingdom, and waking and thinking in the animal kingdom). Changes in the interests of an esotericist during esoteric development. Dangers of esoteric development through loosening of the etheric body; deceitfulness, dishonesty, and illness.

AUGUST 24, 1910, MUNICH..48
General instructions. Consequences of entry into an esoteric training; the loosening of the bodies; waking-up experiences. The New Testament as a support in difficult times. Occult statement against illusions: "All paths into the spiritual world go through the heart." The relationship of the heart to Leo, sun, and the spirits of fire.

AUGUST 26, 1910, MUNICH..51
Duties of an esotericist upon awakening (gratitude); during meditation (pure mood); upon falling asleep (awe and reverence). Esotericists allow God to live in them consciously. Setting aside arrogance, pride, and vanity. Preparation for the appearance of Christ in the etheric. The Rosicrucian verse as a fundamental mood for meditation. *In the spirit lay...* Present incarnation: favorable for entering into an esoteric life. The future Christ event in the etheric body.

NOVEMBER 4, 1910, BERLIN..57
Learning to walk, to speak, and to understand in the esoteric sense; the meditative experiences connected to them. Inner experiences when meditating the verse *In pure rays...* The guidance of the path of training through Christ. What a human being must develop in life: walking, speaking, and thinking, in relation to Christ's words: "I am the way, the truth, and the life," and the esoteric path. Inner experiences when meditating, using the example of the verse *In pure rays ...* (stream of warmth from the East, streaming light, sounding tones; the unspeakable name of God; cold and loneliness; deceiving images). Christ as the guru for all human beings. Concerning the concept "love."

NOVEMBER 5, 1910, BERLIN..73
The need to distrust one's own esoteric experiences; sound and color experiences and their significance. The picture of the ark on the mountaintop. The squawking ravens of the lower self. Transformation of the forms of colors. The symbol of the dove. The Rose Cross as a help. Allowing the lower self to die into Christ. The lower self as the archetype of the divine that is permeated by egotism.

DECEMBER 3–4, 1910, KASSEL..87
Maya—maha-aya— the great non-being. The battle of Lucifer and Ahriman against the direct working of the divine, and its influence on the human being; egotism. The etheric brain of the human being. *Atma, Buddhi, Manas* and the symbol of the eye.

DECEMBER 11, 1910, MUNICH..89
The old path of initiation: overcoming egotism and fear. The esoteric path of modern human beings who have been weakened by materialism: maintaining the ability to understand; sense for truth and logic in the spiritual worlds. The picture of the shattered mirror. The danger of vices, illnesses, and loss of memory when starting on the esoteric path. Mission of art. The concept of blasphemy; overcoming our mistakes as a test of strength. Exoteric and the esoteric Rosicrucian verses.

DECEMBER 17and18, 1910, HANOVER..94
The vowels *i, ei, a, o, ö, u, ü*; microcosm and macrocosm.

DECEMBER 20, 1910, BERLIN..95
Consequences of loosening the connection between the physical and etheric bodies. Development of a "frontbone" (opposed to the existing human "backbone") through the development of the lotus flowers; faster healing of wounds; possible appearance of minor physical weaknesses. Supporting the loosening process through an appropriate diet. Concerning the speaking of the Rosicrucian formula.

CHRISTMAS – NEW YEAR'S EVE, 1910, STUTTGART.......................97
Intensifying the esoteric sense of responsibility. The loosening of the etheric body using exoteric and esoteric means. The formation of the "front cord" (as opposed to the spinal cord).

DECEMBER 31, 1910, STUTTGART..99
The loosening of the etheric body by exoteric means (diet, breathing exercises) and esoteric means (meditations); the destructive effects of a loosening brought about by exoteric means alone. The development of a "frontal cord" (as opposed to a spinal cord). Concerning the use of alcohol. The firm connection of the etheric body with the physical body brought about by many modern professions and present-day foods. A more conscious permeation of thinking, feeling, and willing, using the example of the verse, "I am a Christian." The Rosicrucian verse.

1911

JANUARY 1, 1911, STUTTGART...103
Maha Aya—the great non-being. The sounds *ch* and *im*. The battle against ambition, envy, curiosity, and so forth.

JANUARY 2, 1911, STUTTGART..106
The effects of certain traits in an esotericist: egotism (connection with the warmth ether, influence of Samael); untruthfulness (connection with the light ether, consequences for the nervous system, influence of Azazel); indifference and insensitivity (connection to the chemical ether, effect on the glands).

JANUARY 17, 1911, BERLIN..109
Two kinds of thoughts: through external perception and awakened through theosophy. The physical world as result of the thoughts of the divine. The constructive effects of non-sensory thoughts: formation of the lotus flowers. Practice fields for sense-free thinking: mathematics; observation of relationships, thinking processes flowing backwards. "Thought thinks the thought." "Achieve for yourself the light-permeated power of water." The Rosicrucian verse.

JANUARY 31, 1911, COLOGNE...117
The two parts of meditation. Two meditation statements: "I am an egotist." "I am not a Christian." Astral and etheric maya.

FEBRUARY 12, 1911, MUNICH..118
The esotericist today. Description of both paths into the spiritual world: the external path (imagination, study of theosophical teaching) and the inner path (meditation, inspiration). The effects of theosophy on the etheric bodies of sensitive, receptive people and on unreceptive people. The inner path of mysticism. The five steps of meditation for Molino. The Apocalypse as going forth from September 30, 395 A.D. The dangers of the external path: doubt and instability; of the inner path: egotism and illusion.

FEBRUARY 19, 1911, STRASSBURG...122
The earth as a battleground between the good spiritual powers and Lucifer and Ahriman. Lucifer gives wisdom without love; Ahriman gives power. The human stage of the archangels was on old Sun. Black magic; concerning the previous incarnation of a black magician. Victory over Lucifer and Ahriman. The redemption of Lucifer through Christ.

MARCH 5, 1911, HANOVER..124
"In your esoteric striving be careful that you do not drown." "Take care that you are not burned by the fire of your own ego." Two verses for the external and the internal paths into the spiritual world. The seals of the Apocalypse and September 30, 395 A.D. The danger of "drowning" in the external world; the danger of being "burned up" on the inner path; "occult imprisonment." Overcoming egotism

through Paul's words, "Not I, but Christ in me." Esoteric and exoteric Rosicrucian verse.

MARCH 10, 1911, MANNHEIM..132
The transformation of the esotericist, using the example of egotism. The proper feeling for an esotericist is that it is one's duty to develop. The esotericist as a fighter. Concerning disturbing thoughts during meditation.

MARCH 15, 1911, BERLIN...134
The effectiveness of frequent repetition of the same (book, exercise). The difference between subsensory (elemental) worlds and suprasensory worlds: taking hold and being taken hold of. Taking hold of the elemental world through imaginations of its symbols (earthly: three-cornered, four-cornered, five-cornered); (watery: point and circle); (air element: cancer form); (fiery: lemniscates). The danger of becoming egotistical. Working into the spiritual world through inspiration; the danger of losing oneself. The union of both directions in the Rosicrucian center; the need for an ability to distinguish between the two worlds. The Rosicrucian verse. The symbols of the forces at work in the elements in relation to minerals, plants, animals, and human beings. The work of the angels, archangels, archai, exusiai. The hierarchies and the formation of the constituent parts of the human beings (members). The connection between the higher and lower hierarchies (macrocosmic and microcosmic formation).

MARCH 29, 1911, PRAGUE..142
The proper way to immerse oneself in meditation (example: *In the pure rays of light ...*). The need for humility and devotion in order to develop discernment and to distinguish what is seen in the spiritual world; the avoidance of arrogance ("God is in me."). The acquisition of a subtle feeling for truth; review of one's own actions from time to time. Overcoming egotism through Paul's words, "Not I, but Christ in me." The esoteric Rosicrucian verse.

JUNE 12, 1911, BERLIN..149
Exoteric and esoteric knowledge. The transformation of the astral body into a "knowledge body" through spiritual-scientific knowledge. The exhalation of the "air of death" because of the influence of Lucifer. Making spiritual substance (the light of Christ) fruitful through spiritual science. Testing the wisdom given by means of one's healthy common sense.

AUGUST 23, 1911, MUNICH..154
Some comments on meditation and the significance of inner calmness of soul afterward. The tendency of the etheric body to expand in meditation and after

death. The effects of carrying sympathy and antipathy into the etheric world: appearance of deceptive pictures with the tendency to lie; arising of error from false ambition. Testing the teachings that are given by means of clear thinking.

AUGUST 26, 1911, MUNICH..169
Expansion of the etheric body in meditation. The direct influence of the third hierarchy upon the three bodies of the human being, represented by a drawing of a five-pointed star circumscribed by a circle; the work of other hierarchies around the human being. The fragmentation of certain parts of the astral body; the mastery of individual parts of the astral body by the ego with the help of spiritual science. The Rosicrucian verse, esoteric and exoteric. Christ's work in the evolution of the world and the union with the substance of Christ. Handling esoteric truths; for example, not telling others about earlier incarnations of personalities still living.

OCTOBER 10, 1911, KARLSRUHE...182
The significance of the exact sequence of words in a meditation, using the example of a recent publication of the verse *In the pure rays ...* with some incorrect words. How to handle the verses that are given. The three stages of spiritual knowledge: Imagination, Inspiration, and Intuition. Exercise for the strengthening of organs for imaginative vision: think everything backward, since everything around us is maya. Elevation of the spirits of form to the spirits of movement. The word, language, as the single real thing.

OCTOBER 14, 1911, KARLSRUHE...192
The exercise of reversed thinking, using the example of the human face: the beginning of seeing auras. The connecting bond between the physical and etheric bodies as a counterpart to the external human being. Reason for the fear of open spaces, and so forth. Deficit of justified solitude; the need for solitude. Communal prayer can lead to an experience of group-blessedness. The difficulty of distinguishing between love and egotism. The feeling of being swallowed up by higher beings. Suffering as a loving memory of earlier errors; happiness as grace. The need to be permeated by esoteric facts that have been absorbed with our reason.

OCTOBER 27, 1911, BERLIN..209
The requisite earnestness in esoteric striving. The working of Luciferic beings. The work of Samael on the warmth ether (blood) against egotism, anger and envy. The work of Azazel through the astral body upon the light ether (nervous system) against untruthfulness (example: actual and ostensible motives for attending a theosophical lecture). The work of Azael through the ego upon the chemical ether (glands and secretions) against indifference and obtuseness (example of a teacher examination in Austria).

OCTOBER 30, 1911, BERLIN..219
Meaning of illness; transformation of drives that pull us downward into drives that pull us upward. The karmic effects of materialism (softening of the brain). Our feelings and thoughts as beings within our being. The work of Mehazael (binding to the earth after intense expansion of the etheric body); Samael, Azazel, and Azael. The world as maya; future discovery of esoteric principles through science.

NOVEMBER 19, 1911, MUNICH..228
The physical world as a symbol or sign for the spiritual (example: the heart). The maya of the external world: exists only for warm-blooded beings. Effect of concentration on the heart. Verse to the spirit of Sunday. The appearance of the double (*doppelganger*). Creating a balance to certain traits through the work of Samael (fever heat); Azazel (oppressive feeling); Azael (feeling of drowning). The work of Mehazael upon human beings who wish to avoid their karma (feeling of being chained). The essence of an esoteric school.

DECEMBER 16, 1911, BERLIN...233
The work of destructive earthly powers and their strengthening through the uncompensated karma of human beings since the middle of Atlantean times. The meaning of maya. "Crossing the waters" in ancient and modern times. Finding Christ in complete freedom, without even the compelling power of human understanding. The Mystery of Golgotha actually should have taken place in the middle of Atlantean times.

DECEMBER 31, 1911, HANOVER..239
Question of the path to true reality. The meaning of maya: development of I-consciousness; the six days of creation. Penetrating into the world of reality by strengthening the self ("I"), using the example of the verse *In pure rays* ... The splitting of the personality; appearance of the double through the work of Samael.

1912

JANUARY 1, 1912, HANOVER..249
The appearance of the double; the work of the Luciferic beings Samael, Azazel, Azael, and Mehazael as a balance for certain traits that become conscious because of the training. Concerning meditation. The Rosicrucian verse.

JANUARY 6, 1912, BERLIN..254
Experiences during the splitting of the personality; the appearance of the double; feeling of loneliness, feeling of gratitude; practice keeping silent.

JANUARY 7, 1912, BERLIN..255
Mastery of the double as a necessity for the student. The transformation of the capacity to love. The value of being alone. Persisting with meditation. Elucidation of the meditation *In pure rays...* The power of keeping silent.

JANUARY 10, 1912, MUNICH..261
The fruitfulness of persisting with a meditation. Enhanced appearance of bad traits during inner development (example: critical judgment). Enduring loneliness strengthens the self (egoity). The power of keeping silent. Avoiding complaining. Handling disturbing thoughts. The gates of death. The Rosicrucian verse. Development of the feeling of loneliness; devotion; and maintaining silence. Arrival at the gate of death. Egoity and forgetting oneself.

JANUARY 16, 1912, ZURICH..268
Disturbances caused by the human being balanced by the work of Samael (form similar to the human); Azazel (form similar to that of a bird); Azael (form similar to that of a lion); Mehazael (form similar to that of a bull).

JANUARY 26, 1912, BERLIN..270
Experiences of the human soul on the path of training: crossing the threshold of death (feeling of abandonment, uselessness of abilities from the physical world for the spiritual world); descent into the underworld; vision of one's own soul-being from outside; feeling of shame; passage through the elements; recognizing the reality of thoughts. Effects of meditation: development of the lotus flowers; vision of the sun at midnight; expansion into the spiritual world.

FEBRUARY 20, 1912, STUTTGART...282
Egyptian mystery words (*I have come to the gate of death* ...) and their significance today. Death experience: feeling the physical body as a weight; splitting of the self. The relationship of the human being to the elements: experiencing Lucifer in warmth, Ahriman in the air; identifying with the fluid and the solid elements.

FEBRUARY 22, 1912, STUTTGART...287
The need for a solid esoteric standpoint. Lucifer, the community of the Beghards, and the work these souls are doing today. Confusion through ancient religions (Brahmanism and Buddhism). The penetration of Chinese culture into Europe: Ku Hung Ming; the Chinese people as administrators of humanity's memory. Memory as a gift from Lucifer. The re-ascent of the human being through meditation and concentration. The physical body as a temple; the soul's form as a worm. Stepping out of the body and seeing the

spiritual sun. Concerning instruments for seeing the aura and their injurious effect on the eyes.

FEBRUARY 23, 1912, STUTTGART..295
A distinguishing characteristic for distinguishing between the radiance of higher beings and the radiation of one's own forces (warmth and excitement of heart). Consequences of esoteric development: withdrawal of divine guidance; the transformation of the etheric body; the noticeable emergence of bad traits. Our duty to develop the forces placed within us. Concerning the way in which we fall asleep and awaken.

FEBRUARY 26, 1912, MUNICH..299
The problems connected the expansion of the esoteric movement; development of trust; the role of older members as advisors. Handling criticism: relate to the issue, not to the person. Consequences of the loosening of the etheric body caused by the exercises and meditations: seeing the body as a temple and the soul as an ugly worm; feeling the heaviness of the brain and the physical body. Concerning the four statements in Egyptian initiation.

MARCH 10, 1912, MANNHEIM...303
A connection with higher beings as the fruit of meditation. Usefulness of frugality in the soul and spiritual realm. Justification of egotism in the esoteric life, but not in the exoteric life. Concerning the handling of passive and active forces. The auxiliary exercises. Handling thoughts that storm into our mind.

MARCH 10, 1912, FRANKFURT...307
Dangers for esotericists; the significance of the auxiliary exercises; possible effects of the schooling upon karma.

MARCH 22, 1912, BERLIN...309
Exercise: Imagine a conversation between Moses and a student (smelting the golden calf, dissolving it in water, and drinking it). Four thought-feelings associated with this: previous worship of oneself; imprisonment by one's sympathies and antipathies; recognition of maya around us; destruction of every part of us that has resulted from previous incarnations. Use of this imagination.

APRIL 5, 1912, HELSINKI (HELSINGFORS).....................................316
Protective meditations for an esotericist: Aaron's staff and the Rose Cross. Concerning proper reading. The development of the sixteen-petalled lotus flower.

APRIL 14, 1912, HELSINKI (HELSINGFORS)..................................318
Visions that appear too quickly are atavistic. Effects of meditation: loosening of our thought life; need for an absolute love of truth; derailing of the feeling and will impulses: the effects of wrong attitudes even into the body. Earlier: results of these tendencies seen in insanity, rage, and death; the example of the four rabbis.

APRIL 24, 1912, BERLIN..321
The motherless human being (Adam) and the fatherless human being (Christ). The Isis cult. The work of the planetary father-forces and the cosmic mother-forces in the human being: forces of the father (filling with substance, "up-building" until the thirty-third year); forces of the mother ("down-building," awakening the soul and spiritual aspects). Feel oneself united with all esotericists.

MAY 9, 1912, COLOGNE..328
A healthy state of exhaustion as a possible help for meditation. The effects of alcohol and meat consumption. Changes in the esotericist: the intellect (concentration, judgment, memory); carriage of physical body; effects on the physical body. Example of powerful material for meditation; for example, I Timothy 3:16, "The mystery of God's path can be known..."

MAY 30, 1912, NORRKÖPING..334
In memory of Frau Danielsson. Distinguishing characteristics of an esoteric training that is proceeding correctly.

JUNE 7, 1912, OSLO (KRISTIANIA)..336
Excess of etheric forces in earlier times. Meditation as a means to get to the part of the etheric body that today is pushed back from the physical body. Meaning of auxiliary exercises. Meditation on the "unrevealed light"; producing inner emptiness.

JUNE 9, 1912, OSLO (KRISTIANIA)..342
The fundamental principles of the Theosophical Society: truthfulness; no blind faith from the student to the master. Sobriety. Consequences of improperly done exercises (megalomania, loss of reasoning capacity and memory). The example of the four rabbis. The question of publicly speaking about previous incarnations.

JUNE 11, 1912, OSLO (KRISTIANIA)..349
Dangers for an esotericist (self-complacency, untruthfulness, craving for sensation), and their overcoming. The example of the four rabbis.

SEPTEMBER 1, 1912, MUNICH..352
Consciousness soul getting the upper hand: faith in absolute truth; occult expression "Sadducee." Intellectual soul getting the upper hand: asserting the universal truth of personally recognized knowledge; occult expression "Pharisee." Sentient soul getting the upper hand: seeking the truth in inner immersion in one's self; occult expression "Essene." The Sadducee in us should serve the Pharisee and both should serve the Essene; overcoming all three by means of a proper feeling of shame. The how, where, and when of things is of great importance.

SEPTEMBER 20, 1912, BASEL..363
Experiences during the splitting of the personality; the appearance of the double; feeling of loneliness, feeling of gratitude; practice keeping silent.

SEPTEMBER 22, 1912, BASEL..383
The experience of "it thinks, feels, wills in me." The working of certain forces in the life of the soul. Fear creating a balance by opposing egotism; its transformation into awe and reverence in an esotericist. In the intellectual soul, cleverness and compassion; the danger of feeling oneself to be blessed. In the consciousness soul, conscience as the balance to oppose the dangers presented by the ability to exclude oneself, and by lack of conscience.

NOVEMBER 8, 1912, BERLIN..395
Three experiences of an esotericist as the result of meditation: *It thinks me* (exoterically: "In your thoughts the thoughts of the world are living"), connected with the feeling of devotion and religiosity. *It creates me* (exoterically: "In your will beings of the world are at work"), connected with the feeling of awe and reverence. *It weaves me* ("in your feeling weave the forces of the world"), combined with the feeling of gratitude. The Rosicrucian verse in connection these feelings. "You shall be as gods," spoken once by Lucifer, once by Christ.

NOVEMBER 19, 1912, HANOVER..403
The changes in the soul constitution of an esotericist. The serenity of soul after meditation. The experience of *It thinks me* (piety); *It creates me* (devotion); *It weaves me* (gratitude); this exercise in connection with the Rosicrucian verse.

NOVEMBER 28, 1912, MUNICH..407
The need to pay attention to the life of one's soul. The experience of *It thinks me, It creates me*, in connection with the feelings that in each case belong to the sentence: (piety, devotion, thankfulness.)

DECEMBER 16, 1912, BERN..410
Concerning the periodic appearance of certain faults that are always getting worse, and overcoming them. The three words given in relationship to the trinity: *It weaves me* (Father principle); submersion into the body mornings. *It creates me* (Son principle); I-consciousness after death. *It thinks me* (Holy Spirit); the awakening in the Holy Spirit. The threefold love: of the truth through the Father (against vanity); of life through the Son (through compassion); of creating through the Holy Spirit (against egotism). Truth—Spirit. Compassion—Son. Creative activity—Father. *It thinks me* (touched by an angel); *It weaves me* (Spirits of Movement); *It creates me* (spirits of will).

DECEMBER 17, 1912, ZURICH..416
It thinks me (touched by an angel); *It weaves me* (spirits of movement); *It creates me* (Thrones). Beholding one's own physical body; the Rosicrucian verse.

Editorial and Reference Notes   419
Rudolf Steiner's Collected Works   433
Significant Events in the Life of Rudolf Steiner   449
Index   463

INTRODUCTION

Christopher Bamford

"Steady drops hollow the stone."

"Spiritual life flows into us during meditation."

This, the second volume of the Esoteric Lessons, covering the years 1910 to 1912, follows the first volume, which covered the years 1904 to 1909. The origins of the Esoteric School (of the Theosophical Society), however, date back to 1884, to Madame Blavatsky, as described in the introduction to the first volume. It was she who led the Esoteric School until 1891, when Annie Besant assumed the leadership, at first with William Q. Judge, and leading it alone following his death in 1895. Thus, in 1902, when the German Section of the Theosophical Society was founded, with Rudolf Steiner as general secretary, one of the first things Steiner did was to apply to Annie Besant to join the Esoteric School. He did so because he knew its importance for the heart of what he sought to do. He knew that without the inner, esoteric work of meditation, theosophy would remain just another philosophy; that it would not inaugurate a new path of initiation, that is, lead to the foundation of a new Mystery School, which was what the spiritual world hoped for from humanity. Therefore, from the beginning of his work in theosophy, Steiner's aim, as he wrote to Hübbe-Schleiden, the former leader of the Society, was to "build upon the power that makes it possible for me to bring spiritual students onto the path of development." To do so was, in fact, as he confessed, what assuming the function of general secretary meant to him. From another perspective, as he wrote to Marie von Sivers: "Without a body of true Theosophists to improve the karma of the present by hard-working meditation, theosophical teachings would be expounded merely to half-deaf ears."

The history of Steiner's involvement with the Esoteric School and the foundational teachings he gave are documented in *From the History and Contents of the Esoteric School 1904-1914* (CW 264). We learn there that almost from the very founding of the German Section he was asked for esoteric instruction, but that it was not until visiting Anne Besant in London in May 1904 that he was officially named "arch warden" of the Esoteric School, and thereby officially "authorized" to teach.

Once authorized, he began to shape the Esoteric School in his own way. Conflating several examples, the rules he established for esoteric students were more or less as follows:

1. Every morning, rise at a fixed time and, preferably before eating, sit for a half-hour period of meditation.

    First, for instance, inner control, silence, peace; then, a sense of devotion to the divine in the universe, coupled with the inner understanding that one is united with the divine, to which end the following is held in the heart and allowed to penetrate one:

    > More radiant than the Sun,
    > Purer than the snow,
    > Finer than the ether,
    > Is the Self,
    > The Spirit in my heart.
    > This Self am I.
    > I am this Self.

    Concluding, one concentrates on a sentence such as, "Before the eyes can see, they must be incapable of tears."

    Finally, a mood of reverence toward what one holds as divine.

2. In the evening, for at least a quarter of an hour before retiring, one should meditate (inwardly repeat) a sentence given by Rudolf Steiner, and then conduct a "backward review" of the day.

3. At least half an hour daily should be devoted to the study of a suggested book.

4. Every two weeks, one should report what exercises have been practiced; and if they have not been practiced, state why not.
5. One should keep a daily record in a notebook of exercises practiced.
6. Alcohol is prohibited.
7. Abstention of animal food is not compulsory, but a vegetarian diet is recommended.

Generally speaking, the instruction for esoteric students that Steiner gave was of three kinds: 1. rules and exercises practiced by all students; 2. individual exercises and practices given to them personally by Rudolf Steiner; 3. esoteric lessons or talks. Within the Esoteric School itself, there were different grades or classes: Probationary Order of Hearers; the First Class; and after that, the Second Class (the opportunity to found the Third Class never presented itself). Members of all the classes would probably have attended the Esoteric Lessons contained here. Details of the Second Class are to be found in the volume entitled *Freemasonry and Ritual Work: The Misraim Service* (CW 266). The function of the lessons was to address intimate aspects of the esoteric path, while at the same time to direct students to the Masters of Wisdom and of the Harmony of Sensations and Feelings—the Mahatmas—who were the true leaders of the school.

Membership numbers remained small at first. At the time of the first General Meeting (October 1903), there were only 130 members. By 1904, however, when the Esoteric Section officially began with Rudolf Steiner as leader and teacher, membership had increased to 251—still a very small number. But by the end of 1909, when the previous volume concludes and this one begins, membership had reached over 1,500 in 44 branches. It continued to grow exponentially thereafter, up to the beginning of World War I, with the result that, not surprisingly, we find Rudolf Steiner expressing some frustration with its increasingly unwieldy size.

*

Before turning to the Esoteric Lessons of 1910-1912, and as a background to reading and studying them, it will perhaps be helpful first to recall the surrounding events and concerns, the contexts, in which they were held. Although Steiner's focus on the work at hand, namely meditation, is unerring, and there is little direct reference to these contexts, knowing something about them gives a sense of the lessons' urgency and purpose. At the same time, the very fact that the lessons remained "apart" and "uncontaminated" while, in a sense, the world was collapsing around them, is a lesson in itself.

As always, much else was going on, and Rudolf Steiner was engaged continually on many different fronts. Indeed, sometimes it is hard to imagine how he could have fitted the lessons in, and done so with such exemplary earnestness, dedication, and love. And yet, we would expect no less. In Steiner's view nothing was more important to theosophy/anthroposophy—not to mention the future of humanity and the spiritual world—than to build up "a core of meditators."

*

What made this focus especially pressing was the growing schism within the Theosophical Society—or more precisely between Rudolf Steiner's German Section and Annie Besant's leadership, headquartered in Adyar, India. This schism had begun to show itself as early as 1906/07 with the forced resignation for sexual misconduct of a leading Theosophist—the former Anglican clergyman, author, and clairvoyant, Charles Leadbeater (1854-1934). For Steiner, Leadbeater's "moral lapse" was a clear consequence of his *occult methods*, which from Steiner's point of view were "dangerous and apt to mislead." "Such methods," Steiner wrote to Besant, were "no longer appropriate to the current stage of Western humanity," because they required "the absolute authority of the guru—which is impossible in the West due to the general cultural situation." Westerners, Steiner felt, could be led to higher stages of inner development if the place of the guru was filled by intense, living, experiential reading of philosophy (especially the German idealists Fichte, Hegel, and Schelling) and by the esoteric Rosicrucian "consciousness" practices of meditative thinking.

The immediate upshot of the scandal was that Leadbeater resigned from the Theosophical Society. As to the question of what "methods"—"Eastern" or "Western"—were appropriate for humanity, following the international Munich Theosophical Congress of 1907 that clearly demonstrated the now explicitly Rosicrucian and, indeed, Christian basis of Steiner's teaching, Annie Besant was forced to acknowledge her incompetence with regard to Christianity and, apparently magnanimously, accept Steiner's primacy in this area. As she wrote:

> Dr. Steiner's occult training is very different from ours. He does not know the Eastern way, so cannot, of course, teach it. He teaches the Christian and Rosicrucian way, and this is very helpful to some, but is different from ours. I regard him as a very fine teacher along his own lines, and also a man of real knowledge. He and I work through friendship and harmony, but along different lines.

Thus, Steiner was given to go-ahead to separate his Esoteric Section of the Germany Society from the general Esoteric Section: to teach the Western way to Westerners. With Besant's blessing, two Esoteric Sections were thereby established: an Eastern School guided by Besant and a Western, essentially Rosicrucian, School to be established and guided by Rudolf Steiner.

Leadbeater's karmic work, however, was not yet done. Before long, he was re-admitted to the Theosophical Society and immediately began to foment the idea that the Second Coming, the reappearance of Christ in physical form, was imminent; and, in April 1909, not unsurprisingly, he found his sought-for "Teacher" on the beach at Adyar, India, in the form of a fourteen-year-old boy, Jiddu Krishnamurti (1895-1986). As a result, with Besant's blessing and *imprimatur*, and innocent of what was to be done in his name, Krishnamurti, now known as "Alcyone," became the principle focus of theosophical activity. The following month (May 1909), at the Budapest Congress, Besant spoke about the new "Teacher" to Steiner, offering him the role of John the Baptist. For Rudolf

Steiner, of course, this was only further and conclusive evidence of the widening split between Adyar and the German Section. For him, as for any Christian, a profound misunderstanding of the nature of the Christ lay behind the claims made on Krishnamurti's behalf. The Christ could not, and would not, incarnate physically a second time.

The response, as it were, from the spiritual world came in January 1910 (as these lessons begin), when Rudolf Steiner announced the "reappearance of Christ in the etheric world." For the first time, on January 12, in Stockholm, he spoke of this remarkable, world-significant phenomenon, which both manifested the continuing nature of the Mystery of Golgotha and revealed humanity's potential to evolve new faculties of consciousness as it emerged from the Kali Yuga and "crossed the threshold into the spiritual world." Curiously, Krishnamurti was being "initiated," more or less simultaneously, in Adyar. Later that month (on January 25), returned to Germany, Steiner spoke on the topic again in Karlsruhe and Strassburg. Further lectures on the topic followed in February, March, April, and May.

In Strassburg for instance, at the dedication of the Novalis Branch, after speaking of how Novalis united spiritual striving with a true sense of reality, and stressing the need for "inner truthfulness" in one's spiritual life, Steiner turned at the end of a brief evolutionary sketch to the present moment as an important *transitional* evolutionary moment:

> Today we are living in no unimportant time: we live in an important time. Certainly, people often say of their time, whatever it may be, that they live in a transitional time. Every period of human development has certainly been called "transitional," but not all such periods are of equal significance. Of our time, however, it may truly be said that it is a time of transition.
>
> To what extent is this the case? Allow me to point to the nature of another time of transition. For instance, it was a transitional time for human development when the forerunner of our Christ Jesus, John the Baptist, arose. When John the Baptist arose, he told the people what Christ Jesus then later repeated in the most

significant words: "Change your consciousness, for the kingdoms of heaven are near."

Steiner goes on to explain that the Mystery of Golgotha was a transitional time, because it marked the disappearance of the ancient higher capacities of perception and cognition. Thus, because of this, only with their physical eyes could human beings see that a God—Christ—had descended among them, into the flesh. Only through their senses could they grasp that for three years a God lived on earth in the physical body of Jesus and that the kingdoms of the heavens had come down to their "I."

Steiner then compares this epochal period with our own:

> We too live in a transitional time, a time of crisis. Around the year 1899, the Kali Yuga ended. Today, despite the fact that they do not know it, human beings are developing new characteristics. In the human soul, new qualities are developing naturally. The fact that so many people know nothing of this is no evidence against it. A hundred years after Christ Jesus, Tacitus [the Roman historian] could still write of an "unknown" sect of Christians... If human beings do not notice something, it is no evidence that a most important, most authoritative and incomparable event has not happened. More or less since 1899, capacities have been developing unnoticed in human beings—capacities that will emerge in the mid-thirties of the twentieth century, between 1933 and 1937. At that time, among a whole number of people, because the moment will be right, these new soul capacities will arise. Faculties of etheric clairvoyance will emerge. They will be there. Just as when Christ-Jesus was there, there were people whose "I"-consciousness was most highly developed, so too in our century there will be people who will see not just with their physical eyes. They will experience as a natural development what streams down from higher spiritual levels. Thus, out of their souls, soul-spiritual faculties will emerge that penetrate into etheric existence. And the joy of these people will be that they will understand this new world that they can see. One thing is true, and truly important, for our souls, namely, that

Christ Jesus said: "I am with you to the end of the world." He is here....

Spiritual science has the task—the utmost responsibility—to prepare human beings for this great moment. Christ will not appear in a fleshly body, because he was incarnated in the flesh only once. But he will be here! He will be here, returned, in such a form that those whose eyes are opened will be able to see him in the world that is visible only to clairvoyant eyes. Humanity will grow up toward him. That will be the return of Christ: a growing upward of human beings into the spheres where Christ is. But those who have not prepared for this great moment through spiritual science will stand there without understanding. This preparation must be undertaken seriously, for it is a great responsibility. Humanity must prepare itself, so that more will be seen than was seen before. Humanity must not lead this capacity into the darkness and allow it to wither. For it could also happen that the whole of the twentieth century could go by without bringing this goal to fulfilment. *We have the responsibility, the task, the obligation, through spiritual science, to prepare humanity for this great moment.* (Italics added)

The year 1910 begins with this great task for inner work. Therefore, although as mentioned, there is little explicitly said in these lessons of the need to prepare for Christ's reappearance in the etheric (since most members of the Esoteric School would have attended all or at least some the lectures on the subject) the esoteric work of spiritual science—the focus of the lessons for this volume, which, above all, is meditation and the inner purification and self-awareness that it requires—gains enormously in significance and purchase.

The lecture courses given throughout the year, likewise, seem at first glance to bear little relation to this great theme: *The Gospel of John in Relation to the other Gospels* (CW 116, January), *Macrocosm and Microcosm* (CW 119, March), *Manifestations of Karma* (CW 120, May), *The Mission of Folk Souls* (CW 121, June), *The Secrets of the Biblical Creation Story* (CW 122, August), *According to Matthew* (CW 123, September), and *Occult History* (CW 126, December/January 1911). Readers will have to intuit the connection for themselves, a task that will perhaps be easier to fulfill in relation to the new foreword to *Christianity as Mystical Fact* (CW 8), written in May, and to the first of the Mystery Dramas (CW 14), *The Portal of Initiation*, written in June and premiered in August.

Meanwhile, during this year (1910), the "Krishnamurti affair" hung in abeyance. Then, without warning, on January 11, 1911, George Arundale, principal of the Theosophical Central Hindu College, formed what he called "The Order of the Rising Star" to prepare for the imminent advent of the new Teacher and World Savior. To begin with, this seemed a local matter, limited to the College. A few months later, however, Annie Besant transformed "The Rising Star" into an international movement, changing its name to "The Order of the Star in the East." The implication was clear. Shortly, it would be announced that the new World Teacher, the Savior, had come.

For Rudolf Steiner, of course, this was patently false and contradicted the meaning of the Mystery of Golgotha. His response, accordingly, was a threefold deepening of his spiritual research and teaching. The Western tradition needed to be penetrated, understood, and revealed. The truth and reality of the Christ event in its fullness and actuality had to be established. And Anthroposophy—a thoroughly contemporary and free rendering of these—had to be deepened as a path of inner development, a spiritual science, and a way of life. Beginning to lay down the foundations, he deepened Christology with lecture cycles such as *The Spiritual Guidance of the Individual and Humanity* (CW 15, June) and *From Jesus to Christ* (CW 131, October). Individual lectures addressed separate issues, all of which spoke to the true meaning of Christ. There were lectures, for instance, on the life of Christ in relation to the first three years of the child (February and June), as well as various lectures on esoteric Christianity, discriminating the spiritual beings of the Buddha, Christian Rosenkreutz, the Bodhisattvas, Maitreya Buddha, Jeshu Ben Pandira, and Christ (March, September). At the same time, there was a renewed focus on the Western tradition with lectures on Goethe, Zoroaster, Galileo, and Giordano Bruno (January); Hermes/Thoth (February); and Greek mythology (August). In addition, Anthroposophy—as practice and reality—began to come into its own in such courses as *Occult Physiology* (CW 128, March), *The Soul's Probation* (CW 14, the second Mystery Drama, July), *Wonders of the World, Ordeals of the Soul, Revelations of the Spirit* (CW 129, August), *Inner Experiences of Evolution* (CW 132, December), *The World of the Senses and the World of the Spirit* (CW 134, December), and also in the paper he read in April to the Fourth International Philosophical Congress in Bologna on "The Psychological Foundations and Epistemological of Position of Theosophy."

Meanwhile, in the middle of the year, in June, the idea of the "Calendar of the Soul"—quintessential Anthroposophy—was born. It would appear the following Easter in *Kalender 1912/13*, likewise quintessential Anthroposophy, which would bear the symbolic motto "In the year 1879 after the birth of the I," and would begin the year with Easter, the festival commemorating the birth of the "I" through the resurrection of Jesus Christ on April 3, 33, of the Common Era. More esoterically, it would affirm the critical year of 1912 as thirty-three years—this, a repetition of the rhythm of Jesus' earthly life—after 1879, the year that Rudolf Steiner would come more and more to emphasize as the year when Archangel Michael, under whose aegis Anthroposophy is placed, celebrated his heavenly victory over the dragon and assumed the regency of the new, evolutionary time period.

On December 10, there was a general meeting of the German Section, in which there were now 2,318 members. Six new branches had been founded. There were numerous problems, but none was as decisive as the "Krishnamurti question." Adyar had appointed Dr. Hugo Vollrath, a member in questionable standing, to be the German representative of The Order of the Star in the East. Vollrath proclaimed Krishnamurti to be the Christ, and, in the process, attacked Rudolf Steiner. A heated debate ensued among the members as to what should be done. Finally, Steiner intervened, declaring that rather than "expelling" him, Dr. Vollrath should simply "no longer be regarded as a member." Steiner also emphasized that to engage in further argument with Mrs. Besant and her representatives would be useless—he could no longer "defend her"—and proposed that steps be taken to assure the threatened continuity and purity of the spiritual heritage out of which the German Section was working. On December 14, "those who were active on the basis of Rudolf Steiner's work" came together to create an association which, in its statues, had "nothing whatever to do with the Theosophical Society, either in form or content."

On a more personal level, in 1911, at the beginning of the year, Marie von Sivers fell seriously ill. It was a long illness. Rudolf Steiner supervised her care—through her recovery and subsequent convalescence—consequently giving him an insight into the whole situation of his co-workers, on whom he depended in so many ways: he began to understand in a new way the stress that his constant traveling had been placing upon others. As result, for the first time, he canceled a lecture course, and tried to cut back his activities. Changing his life in another way, on March 19, his wife, Anna Eunike Steiner, died.

Against this background, throughout the year 1912, "The Star in the East" was gaining in strength and membership as a movement, and opposition to Rudolf Steiner from Adyar increased. Accusations, harsh words, fantastic assertions (such as that Rudolf Steiner was a Jesuit!) began to circulate.

Steiner's program remained largely unchanged. The evolutionary meaning of the Christ event, at once singular and continuing, as well as the articulation of "Anthroposophy" as contemporary spiritual science, remained the center of his focus. We may note, above all, *Spiritual Beings in the Heavenly Bodies and in the Kingdoms of Nature* (CW 136, April), *The Spiritual Foundation of Morality* (CW 155, May), *The Human Being in the Light of Occultism, Theosophy, and Philosophy* (CW 137, June), *The Guardian of the Threshold* (CW 14, the third Mystery Drama, June), *Initiation, Eternity and the Passing Moment* (CW 138, August), *The Gospel of St. Mark* (CW 139, September), *The Esoteric Significance of the Bhagavad Gita and Its Relation to the Epistles of Paul* (CW 142/CW 146, December 1912-January 1913/May-June 1913.)

In September 1912, as if to demonstrate the fundamentally artistic nature of Western, and particularly Rosicrucian, esotericism, Rudolf created the new art of eurythmy in response to a request for a "new art of movement." At the same time, prescient of the coming Great War, Steiner turned increasingly to research both the meaning of Christ in the twentieth century and the theme of life between death and a new birth. Speaking of the latter, he remarked, harking back to the 1910 lectures on the reappearance of Christ in the etheric:

> Only now is it possible to see the deep moral significance that the suprasensory truths relevant to this realm exhibit. Besides all other conditions that make this possible...there is another, at least within our movement...This consists in the fact that if we work intimately and earnestly—really devoting ourselves to and studying this matter—we can enter into what is gained from the spiritual worlds. It may be said that for a number of years the relation of human beings on the physical plane to the spiritual world has changed from what it was, for example, during the whole of the nineteenth century. Until the last third of the nineteenth century, there was little access to the spiritual worlds. In proportion to the necessities of human evolution, very little flowed into human souls out of the spiritual worlds. But now we are living in an age in which a soul needs only to be receptive, needs only to surrender and to be prepared, for revelations from the spiritual worlds to pour into it. More and more individual souls are becoming receptive. These are souls for whom, because they are conscious of the mission of their age, the streaming-in of spiritual knowledge is a fact. (*Approaching the Mystery of Golgotha*, CW 152)

In a word: the year 1912 marked the preparation for the true founding of Anthroposophy and the Anthroposophical Society. Throughout the year, the association formed on December 4, 1911, continued to hold meetings. At these, there was much discussion of the importance of karma and reincarnation in the building of community. In August, Rudolf Steiner proposed that the new society should be called the "Anthroposophical Society." Finally, on December 8, the council of the German Section took the decision that one could no longer belong to the Order of the Star in the East and still be a member in good standing. Committed members of the Star in the East were asked to leave the Theosophical Society. If they did not, they were to be expelled. Additionally, Annie Besant's behavior was considered a betrayal of the fundamental theosophical principle "No knowledge higher than the Truth." Accordingly, on December 11, a telegram was sent, requesting her resignation. The die was cast. On December 28, without further celebration or formality, the "Anthroposophical Society" was founded in Cologne.

*

Very little is said explicitly about any of this in these Esoteric Lessons, but the imperative of Christ's reappearance in the etheric remains a constant presence:

> We are living now in a special time, an extremely important time. It is the time for preparing for Christ, who will become visible, will appear in the etheric realm. To be blessed by him, to see him in the etheric, we must prepare ourselves. Those who do not have the good fortune to come across theosophy now will not be able to experience this event.

Thus the task of the lessons is set: inner work, meditation.

Set apart from the "profane," everyday world, the lessons powerfully present us — even in the reading — a feeling of holy seriousness. As meditative readers—as esoteric students inwardly participating in the lessons through our hearts, minds, and will — we, too, can permeate ourselves with the deep peace, inner silence, and waiting that must have been experienced by the original participants. As they did, we can sense the possibility of inward intimacy with the spiritual worlds. Imaginatively at least, we can be there with them, and so to a small degree repeat their experience in our own way.

Thus we learn that to unfold in inner development we must lay aside the anxieties and egotistic concerns that events in the outer world stir up in us; and, for a "holy" period every day, we must enter into ourselves and sit in silent, attentive, dedicated, empty inner composure: uniting ourselves with the universal spirit, we must open ourselves to a different level of existence and being. Despite appearances, the fundamental reality is that we live and move and have our being in a spiritual world. From this point of view, all the rest is maya. Indeed, if we do not just read but "do" the lessons, we will find ourselves becoming increasingly at home in the processes of consciousness, and the struggles and often hidden (or secret) rewards of working inwardly through them to realize our own ongoing and intimate relationships with the beings and worlds with whom and in which we are unconsciously involved. Our relationship to the world changes. The veil of maya grows thinner.

The mood is set with the invocation of the spirit of the day. We may imagine the solemnity with which this was done and the palpable feeling of attentive dedication that filled the room—to be followed by a deep, reverent silence, out of which, after a while, Rudolf Steiner began to speak.

*

The theme in this volume is nearly always the path of meditation as it is practiced today. While in ancient times, those on a spiritual path often had to pass through life-and-death trials, our present human constitution and cultural situation makes such feats both impossible and unnecessary. We now have other "trials" or "practices," such as, for instance, in the first lesson (but recurring throughout the volume), "truthfulness, in the extreme, over against oneself."

Walking that path today demands a kind of transparent, direct, selfless self-honesty. This means an ever-deepening objective awareness of what takes place in our souls. Later, we will learn that much that occurs in our souls that is "negative" is the work or presence of other, frequently hostile, beings. Another trial, averred to in many lessons, is "patience." Patience is of the essence. (Rudolf Steiner advises using the same meditation for long periods of time, even throughout our lives.)

Though many students may feel they are getting nowhere in their practice, that is because they are still too attached to the kind of cause and effect results they expect in the physical world; esoteric work, however, occurs in another dimension. Without their knowing it, students are becoming "different people." For this, two things are necessary. First is faith; trust in the process is obviously a primary requirement. Second, we must make ourselves "worthy." As Steiner puts it in the first Lesson:

> The Lord's Prayer... is a meditation of great significance that any student can undertake daily. I know one of those whom we call the Masters of Wisdom and of the Harmony of Sensations and Feelings, who says: "I take the Lord's Prayer as a meditation only once a month. The rest of the time I attempt to make myself mature and worthy enough to be allowed to immerse myself in even just one of the sentences of this wonderful meditation." Thus, we must spiritually place ourselves in relation to a meditation: that we want to make ourselves worthy enough to be allowed to use it. *Theosophy is not just a theoretical study, but also a living praxis.* (Italics added)

And how are we to become worthy? In addition to inner truthfulness and patience (and, of course, humility, reverence, and gratitude), we learn we must work to overcome or transform the three deep-seated attitudes or soul dispositions that threaten our worthiness: doubt, superstition, and egotism. Throughout the volume, Rudolf Steiner will return to these under different names and suggest ways—meditation and life paths—by which students might overcome or transform them. However, it can be noted that, no matter how many different ways Steiner speaks about the path of inner work, in a sense, there is nothing to overcome/transform except our own egotism:

> On the physical plane we can do nothing, absolutely nothing, without egotism contributing to our actions. We should undertake to vow to ourselves to always bear in mind that all we do originates from egotistical motives.

> Our world of desires consists of nothing but egotism. And we can conquer this egotism only through deep humility.... Rather than killing the divine in us through egotism in our life of desires, we should allow Christ to live within us.

Every kind of egotism, every form of vanity must be eliminated in esotericists.

For us the essential factor is the battle against and the transformation of egotism.

As for how to overcome egotism, in different ways and most movingly, Rudolf Steiner turns again and again to the deeper meanings of Christ's teachings, and to the practice of the Rosicrucian meditation (*ex Deo nascimur, in Christo morimur, per Spiritum Sanctum reviviscimus*) and the Rose Cross meditation. For instance:

> Only what we do in the name of another, in the name of the one within us, whom we could call our God, does not proceed from egotism. In order to feel this god within us, we must permeate ourselves with the consciousness that we are a reflection of the archetype, according to which this god created us, and that only slowly and gradually can this reflection be transformed into the archetype. The archetype is our true self, our true "I" that was formed as seed in old Saturn, and this is what approaches us when we utter our Rosicrucian verse. The Rose Cross is the symbol through which the way is shown to us to ascend into the spiritual world. If it is seen as it is in the spiritual world, then the black of the cross is seen as white—the counterpart of the reflection—and the red roses are transformed into a shining green color.

The Masters of Wisdom give us many themes for our meditations. One of the most effective of these is the one concerning the Rose Cross.

We are to think of the black cross as the dying away of human passions, and see in the red roses a symbol of the purified human being who has shed the lower elements. If we transform the black cross into a white one in our meditation then this symbolizes for us the human being ascending spiritually. All egotism is then extinguished.

The student must say to him or herself again and again: I will not be able to be a participant in the spiritual world until I have learned to say to myself that I am full of egotism, and I cannot be anything else here in the physical world. However, the part of me that lives here in the physical world is only a picture, a form, a reflection of my archetype. This form, this picture is entirely permeated by egotism. And it is the karma of the world that permeates us in our course of evolution through incarnations. However, the karma of the world is God. God also lives in us. And when we advance to the point where we act for the good and noble, then it is *God in us* who drives us to it. And the God in us, who causes us to act for the good and noble, lives in our archetype. I myself am full of egotism—but I am foreordained to become a reflection of my divine archetype. This archetype rested in the bosom of God—it has descended to this physical form, and this form stands under the power of God who stands over my destiny, my karma, which is entirely permeated by egotism. I must never, never say that I am without egotism—for it is never true. Without egotism I could not even exist on the physical plane.

However, when I learn to look up to my God-given archetype, when I allow my thinking, feeling, and willing—all my soul-forces—entirely to die into this archetype, then I am allowed to hope to overcome the egotism in me and again approach my archetype.

"I am an egotist. I am not a Christian." These are two very fruitful sentences for meditation.

Thus, this volume is rich in practical suggestions and advice for those who meditate. There is very little "new" esoteric "information"—though some readers will be surprised and interested to see Steiner invoking Cornelius Agrippa's "four kinds of evil spirits, destructive in the elements"—the four demons Samael, Azazel, Azael, and Mehazael—when discussing ways of overcoming various characterological aspects of egotism.

Clearly, Steiner's aim for his inner circle of students was their inner development, and the consequent development of their faculties or capacities. Interestingly, too, though many students had been with him for a number of years, the teachings he gives here are not "advanced" or "esoteric," but go, as it were, back-to-basics, and build upon them. That is, they are useful for anyone, at any stage of practice. It is as if he realized that the critical times that were approaching (and already present in many ways) required a different kind of grounding—more psychological and ethical, it might be said—which he frames in terms of overcoming certain "character traits." Such basic work, he says, is much more important for esotericists than for others:

> Human traits are such that, when they remain in proper proportions, human beings can control them very well with their "I." However, if we allow one of them to become too intensive then the "I" can fall under the power of that trait. This is not so dangerous for people who are living only exoterically, as the spirit of the everyday will bring them back into balance. But it is different for esotericists. A character trait that acquires dominion over them can lead them into all kinds of dangers. Above all, something like this can come to expression already in their present life as an illness of the physical body.

Such characterological "imbalances"—symptomatic of egotism—are especially threatening in modern esoteric and spiritual work. This is because nowadays it often happens that in our inner work "we place ourselves outside the usual and customary framework of contemporary consciousness," thereby losing "the support that is given by conventions and traditions." Doing so, Steiner notes, "We become freer within ourselves. But just in this way our bad sides come more to the fore." Here, however, especially when we are under pressure, we can find support from an unexpected quarter, the New Testament:

> For every esoterically striving person, difficult, dreadful times will come; then it is good to have a support. We find this support in the New Testament. We find there advice for every situation, for

every case; a support for every weakness. We need only seek it. And if we do not find it, then the conviction of our own weakness that we cannot yet find the right passage should comfort us that it must certainly be in the New Testament.

Why the New Testament? Because it is addressed to the heart. In this sense, the heart lies at the center of these Lessons:

> An occult saying against all illusions states, "All paths into the spiritual world go through the heart." During meditation we can feel how from every point of our external physical body, lines go toward a centerpoint. This middle point is the heart. In their further course, these lines continue on in the opposite direction into the spiritual world. This is like a feeling of Christ within us.

This means, of course, that the root and fruit of the path, whatever our meditation, lies in and through selfless love:

> Let us consider for a moment what it means to love all beings; to bestow love without expectation of love in return, without recognition, without demand for reward—for our ideal should be that we love a human being because he or she is a human being! How far must we be in our development in order to be capable of such love! Can we educate ourselves to this selflessness, that we love all others as we love ourselves, by means of commandments and dogmas of the church or through the coercion of a moral law? Is it not much more fruitful for our soul if we bring this lofty virtue to blossom within us without any coercion whatsoever?
>
> In practicing this teaching of Christ, a Hindu, a Muslim, a Parsi, a Catholic, a Protestant, a Jew—indeed, even a heretic—could be a true Christian without even belonging to the Christian Church.
>
> And we also learn in our meditations that within them lies hidden the way that Christ showed us and that he himself is: "I am the way, the truth and the life."

In other words:

Love your neighbor as yourself; develop pure love of human beings. Those who love a human being because he or she is a human being—only those who do this—are in truth Christians, regardless of what creed or which religion they may belong to.

Only meditation that is permeated by Christ has value. There is an expression that has become trivial out in the world at large: the expression "universal love of humanity."

To live as a Christian means, above all, to accept with serenity whatever destiny may bring us, to never complain about the work of the gods, to accept with joy whatever they may send. It means that the sentence—"Look at the birds in the sky; they do not sow, they do not reap, they do not gather into barns, and yet they receive what they need"—becomes second nature in us. Accept with gratitude what is given to us.

*

All in all, this is an intimate volume. Rudolf Steiner is speaking not only as teacher but also as friend. When one considers the enormous tasks he is carrying—the public lectures and the seminal lectures to members; the creation of the Mystery Dramas and the Calendar of the Soul; and the gradual forging and revealing of free-standing anthroposophy, of what would become the Anthroposophical Society separate from theosophy, and the subtlety that this required; as well as all the while being aware of the depth of the spiritual crisis he is dealing with (not to mention the lies, libels, and hostility flowing from Adyar); the urgency of responding to the "Christ event of the twentieth century (Christ's reappearance in the etheric); and the impending disaster of the First World War—when one considers all this, one realizes what a pleasure it must have been for him to work intimately with a small group on essential things—*the essential thing that is meditation.*

Essential, intimate, serious: these are the hallmarks of this volume. *Essential,* because nothing can be achieved without it; *intimate,* because the role of "meditation teacher," which is that of "spiritual friend," is by its very nature the most intimate; and *serious*, because "the holy" requires no less. Anyone interested in inner work will be abundantly enriched.

PART I
NOTES OF THE ESOTERIC LESSONS
1910 – 1912

Written from Memory by the Participants

Meditation Verses Used Repeatedly in the Esoteric Lessons
from 1910 to 1912

Verses Directed to the Spirit of the Day

It has been reported that most lessons began with the invocation of the spirit of the day, yet this is not always recorded in the notes.

Meditations for Understanding the Time Nature of the Hierarchies

Friday Evening for Saturday: Saturn

Great all-encompassing spirit,
    You, who filled infinite space,
    when nothing of my bodily members
    was yet present.
You were.
    I lift up my soul to you.
I was in you.
    I was a part of your power.
You sent forth your powers,
    and in the first beginnings of the earth
    my body's original form was mirrored.
I myself was in
    the forces you sent out.
You were.
The archetype of my self gazed at you.
    It gazed on me myself,
    I who was a part of you.
You were.

Saturday Evening for Sunday: Sun

Great all-encompassing spirit,
    from your life many archetypes came forth,
    long ago when my life forces
    were not yet present.
You were.
    I lift up my soul to you.
I was in you.
    I was a part of your forces.
You united yourself
    with the earth's very beginning,
    with the life-sun,
    and gave me the power of life.
I myself was in your radiant forces of life.
You were.
My power of life radiated in your powers of life
    into space.
    My body began its becoming
    within time.
You were.

Sunday Evening for Monday: Moon

Great all-encompassing spirit,
    in your forms of life shone forth sensation,
    when my sensation
    was not yet present.
You were.
    I lift up my soul to you.
I was in you.
    I was a part of your sensations.
You united yourself
    with the earth's beginning,
    and in my body began
    the shining forth of my own sensation.
In your feelings
    I felt myself.
You were.
My feelings felt your being in themselves.
    My soul began to be within itself,
    because you were in me.
You were.

Monday Evening for Tuesday: Mars

Great all-encompassing spirit,
    knowledge lived in your sensations,
    when knowledge was not yet given to me.
You were.
    I lift up my soul to you.
I drew into my body.
    In my sensations I lived unto myself.
You were in the life-sun.
    In my sensation
    your being lived as my being.
The life of my soul
    was outside your life.
You were.
My soul felt its own being within itself.
    Longing arose in it.
    Longing for you,
    out of whom it came.
You were.

Tuesday Evening for Wednesday: Mercury

Great all-encompassing spirit,
    in the knowledge of your being is knowledge of the world,
    which is to come to me.
You are.
    I will unite my soul with you.
May the guide you appointed me,
    The guide who knows,
    enlighten my path.
    Feeling your guide
    I tread my path of life.
Your guide is in the life-sun.
    He lived in my longing.
    I will take up his being
    into mine.
You are.
May my strength take up the strength of my
    appointed guide into itself.
    Blissfulness enters me
    The blissfulness in which the soul
    finds the spirit.
You are.

Wednesday Evening for Thursday: Jupiter

Great all-encompassing spirit,
    in your light, life streams to the earth;
    my life is in your life.
You are.
    My soul works in your soul.
I go my way with your appointed guide.
    I live with him.
    His being is the forming image
    of my own being.
You are.
The being of the guide in my soul
    finds you, all encompassing spirit.
    Bliss is mine
    from your being's breath.
You are.

Thursday Evening for Friday

Great all-encompassing spirit,
in your life I live with the life of the earth.
In you I am.
You are.
I am in you.
The guide has brought me to you.
I live in you.
Your spirit is
the forming image of my own being.
You are.
Spirit has found the all encompassing spirit,
Blissfulness of God moves on
to creation of new worlds.
You are. I am. You are.

Every day after the preceding meditations:

These words, "Every day after the preceding meditations," which were lacking in the original, were given by Marie Steiner for the first printing of Aus den Inhalten der Esoterischen Schule, Vol. III, *Dornach 1951.*

> Great all-encompassing spirit,
>> may my "I" lift itself from below to above,
>> may it discern you in the all-encompassing.
> May the spirit of my being be illuminated
>> with the light of your messengers.
> May the soul of my being be enkindled
>> by the fiery flames of your servers.
> The will of my "I" take hold
>> of the power of your creating word.
> You are.
>> May your *light* stream into my spirit,
>> may your *life* warm my soul,
>> may your *being* permeate my willing,
>> so that I achieve understanding
>> for the shining of your light,
>> for the warmth-filled love of your life,
>> for the creative word of your being.
> You are.

Meditation
"In the spirit lay the germ of my body…"

The meditative verse with which the esoteric lessons were concluded from a certain point in time onward.

> In the spirit lay the seed of my body.
> And the spirit has incorporated into my body
> The eyes of sense,
> That through them I may see
> The light of bodies.
> And the spirit has imprinted into my body
> Thinking and sensation,
> And feeling and will,
> That through them I may perceive bodies
> And act upon them.
> In the spirit lay the seed of my body.
>
> In my body lies the seed of the spirit.
> And I will incorporate into my spirit
> Suprasensory eyes,
> That through them I may behold the light of spirits.
> And I will imprint into my spirit
> Wisdom and strength and love,
> So that the spirits may work through me,
> And I become the self-conscious instrument
> Of their deeds.
> In my body lies the seed of the spirit.

* * *

> In pure rays of light
> Shines the divinity of the world.
> In the pure love of all beings
> Rays the godliness of my soul.
> I rest in the divinity of the world;
> I will find myself
> In the divinity of the world.

Esoteric Lesson
KASSEL, FEBRUARY 6, 1910

Record A: From the collection of Elisabeth Vreede; Record B: Notes from Wilhelm Hübbe-Schleiden.

RECORD A

Sun, Earth — Meditation, Study

Many who enter an esoteric training are very disappointed, and say that they had imagined the exercises to be much more energetic and the effects of the exercises to be much more drastic. Those who say this to themselves should consider as soon as possible that they are caught in a great error, and they should make the greatest efforts to correct this error as soon as possible. It is not the exercises that are not energetic enough, but, rather, the human being. It is not the exercises that are ineffective, but the human being who is not making them effective. By living an esoteric life the student should become an entirely different person; he or she must add something new to the old.

In earlier times people were faced with the choice: esoteric training or death. People had to subject themselves to exercises and trials that if they were mature enough led them on the esoteric path; or they perished in these trials, physical death occurred. Students said to themselves; "If I cannot pass this test then I am not yet mature enough for an esoteric life, so continued life in a physical body has no value for me. It is better for me to go through physical death in order to prepare myself in devachan for a new incarnation that can then lead to an esoteric life."

Trials of this sort are no longer possible today; our entire constitution is no longer so organized. However, students should arrive at the point where they are indifferent to all physical events. The human being must become an entirely different person. Those who today already want to assert that they have overcome the physical (after doing exercises for a short period) are succumbing easily to a base illusion. Truly, students must work to overcome themselves. Truthfulness is the first virtue that must be acquired by those who wish to enter upon the esoteric path; truthfulness, in the extreme, over and against themselves.

Another essential word for those striving esoterically is patience. Consider the sun; imagine the spirit of the sun, how the spirit causes the sun to rise and set day after day, and has done this already for millions of years, and will continue doing this for unimaginably long periods of time to come, to lead the earth to its destiny. We should place ourselves in this patience; and then we will not think that an exercise is ineffective when it has not had an effect after three, four, or five years.

The Lord's Prayer, this wonderful rendering of the seven-fold lawfulness of the world, is a meditation of great significance that any student can undertake daily. I know one of those whom we call the Masters of Wisdom and Harmony of Feelings who says, "I take the Lord's prayer as a meditation only once a month. The rest of the time I attempt to make myself mature and worthy enough to be allowed to immerse myself in even just one of the sentences of this wonderful meditation." Thus, we must spiritually place ourselves in relation to a meditation: that we want to make ourselves worthy enough to be allowed to use it. Theosophy is not only a theoretical study, but also a living praxis.

We must feel the parables in nature. There is something spiritual behind everything physical. If we properly undertake our meditations, if we advance on the esoteric path, then we will soon reach the point where we feel something in us that corresponds to what we see in nature: sprouting and growing in spring and summer, and the melancholy of dying away in autumn. We will experience it in waking in the morning and in falling asleep in the evening. As we fall asleep in the evening, so too the plants in the autumn transition into what is night for them. Only the seeds remain. The capacities that were attained during the life of the summer are contained in them. These capacities awaken again in the spring to new activity, just as our strength and capacities from the previous evening awaken again in the morning. Again and again, we must fall asleep and then awaken; must use our abilities during the day and gather new forces during the night. Behind the physical plants there are lofty spiritual beings, who must advance to new activity again and again in the spring; and then, in the autumn, they are submerged in the night of the plants, when only the seed of the plant remains. But these beings are so advanced that they need to complete this alternation only once within a year, while the human being must go through this alternation of falling asleep and waking every twenty-four hours. It is simply no longer necessary so often for those lofty beings.

Feeling oneself unified with the universal spirit, with the spiritual, must not remain only a mere saying. We must truly feel, experience within ourselves, what lies hidden in the sequence of spring, summer, autumn; what lies hidden in nature's "springing to life" and "dying away."

Spiritual life flows into us during meditation. In order to be able to give a proper reception to this spiritual life, we must prepare ourselves in a suitable way. We do this through study. Just as the sun, which sends out its rays and power, would find only an empty space if the earth were not prepared and arranged to receive and use its power, so too, our meditations would not find soil to be fruitful. Our meditations would find an empty space if we did not prepare ourselves through study, if we did not make ourselves receptive for the spiritual life that flows into us through meditation. Thus we can see macrocosm and microcosm.

Students should give themselves to their meditations with total fervor, with complete devotion and concentration. They should completely and entirely suppress their thoughts of the everyday, and open themselves only to lofty spiritual forces. The meditator should think of every meditation as a sacrifice, as sacrificial incense that rises up to the gods. In this way, we contribute to progress and harmony, although lower, egotistical, selfish thoughts provide the ground for catastrophes. There is no human way to prevent these catastrophes—such as we have recently had, and such as are still to come—from becoming increasingly terrible; one can do whatever one wants, they will still occur.

In all that we do, in all our thoughts, we must bear the spiritual in mind; also in our feelings. We have descended from the spiritual; we will again ascend into the spiritual, enriched and perfected.

In the spirit lay the germ of my body...
In my body lies the seed of the spirit...

* * *

Record B

Sun, Earth, Meditation, Study

If spiritual exercises are not effective, then the cause is never in the exercises but always in the meditator. Those doing the exercises must immerse themselves in them with fervor, and as a result become entirely different persons.

In ancient times people were confronted with the choice: success or death!

Those who were not mature enough to pass the test could then hope for better success in the next life. That secured them passage through devachan.

Today, however, at least external life must become a matter of indifference to the student; he or she must become a different person.

In the first instance students must become truthful concerning themselves, then they must learn patience. Example: the patience with which the sun constantly shines on everyone and everything.

The Lord's Prayer as material for meditation

A master said: I take only one petition for meditation once a month; the rest of the time I try to make myself mature and worthy enough to understand this petition.

Theosophy is a living praxis. We must experience everything physical as a parable for the spirit, which is its foundation.

Thus we come to the point of sensing within us an alternation such as from spring to summer and fall: sprouting and growing in nature in the spring, and the melancholy dying away in the fall. Just as we fall asleep every evening, so do the plants in the fall; only the seeds remain, and in them the capacities acquired in the summer. In the spring these forces awaken again, just as ours do every morning.

There are lofty spiritual beings that stand behind the physical world. They are so far advanced that they need only once per year to perform this alternation that we go through every day.

Preparation for meditation through study in order to make the ground receptive.

Meditators should be devoted to the exercise with total concentration. They should set aside all everyday thoughts and open themselves only to the highest spiritual forces. They should understand meditation as a sacrifice. They should see it as the incense of offering, so to speak, which rises up to the gods.

Thus we should, too, of course, constantly keep the spiritual in mind in our lives and all our actions. In this way we contribute to the harmony of the great whole according to our best forces.

We originate in the spirit and we are spirit. This should be expressed in our whole being.

Esoteric Lesson
COLOGNE, FEBRUARY 27, 1910

Manuscript from Hulda Schouten-Deetz.

Doubt, Superstition, Illusions of the Personality

We must find our path in life through learning. We should not place ourselves in life with one-sided judgmental views. If we test everything that science, art, and the various worldviews offer us according to the state of today's science, then we will find on our way three threatening forces: doubt, superstition, and the illusion of personality. Do not avoid them; do your own research, for we are not allowed to close ourselves off from modern science, neither from its inventions nor from its research. It is even our duty to take notice of science, although we receive an entirely different teaching in our theosophical circles, which is laughed at and derided by modern science. Modern science, for its part, cannot assess our teachings because it knows only matter, and its research relates only to material and physical things of existence. However, in order to do justice to science, we should allow doubt concerning what is taught here to arise within us; we should not be afraid to doubt so that we can arrive at inner clarity in ourselves. In this way we struggle through to esoteric teachings out of our own consciousness.

And what does it mean to defeat superstition? The fetish that Africans see and worship in an idol, in a piece of wood, we call superstition. However, if they are not thinking of something spiritual that stands behind it, to that extent it is superstition. But we can just as well speak of superstition when we see how modern scholars build their fetishes in their hypotheses of atoms and molecules, which also remain as nothing but hypothetical matter if one does not admit to the spiritual standing behind it. However, we should not allow this kind of superstition to rise within us.

There is still a third thing that joins doubt and superstition. That is the illusion of personality. These three forces, which rise and sink within the human soul, want to rule the human being. If we have struggled through powerful doubt to knowledge of the truth, and through superstition to faith in the spirit that lies behind all matter, then we will also be able to overcome the illusions concerning our personality. However, this is often the most difficult. Even if we sometimes think we are inwardly free human beings and believe that we confront the facts of the world and other people without prejudice, nevertheless, this only too often mirrors the illusions of our personality.

One more thing must be brought to our attention. Do not carry our teaching into social gatherings of another kind; speak of our teachings only where you have come together for this purpose. Do not carry them forth to argue with outsiders, and speak just as little about them during your mealtimes, for on such occasions only light conversation should be conducted. It is best if you avoid society where only ordinary gossip of the day is exchanged. However, if you must engage in such gatherings because of your position in life, or if you are forced to do so for other reasons, then you should attend them in a spirit entirely different from before: not because you enjoy them, but, rather, you do this as a duty so that you do not offend anyone because of who you are. I do not say this in order to give a moralizing sermon, because I do not forbid anything at all; however, for this reason I have to say it to you.

Esoteric Lesson

MUNICH, MARCH 13, 1910

Manuscript from Mathilde Scholl.

In esotericism we must pay attention to something we call the spirit of the day. The creative divine beings have brought a different spirit to expression in each day; and the Masters of Wisdom and Harmony of Feelings have given us meditations with which we can approach these spirits on each different day.†

We want to begin today (Sunday) with the verse that the masters gave for it:

> *Great all-encompassing spirit,*
> *From your life many archetypes came forth…*

Today we want to discuss how easily an esotericist tends to forget even the simplest, introductory exoteric principles of theosophy. Such a principle is: "Everything perceptible to the senses is maya, is illusion." Every esotericist should use this as a constant meditation. Most, however, will think to themselves that they already understood this statement long ago. But very few consider how little they bring it into their lives, into their feelings; and few consider what they should include under this statement. For example, one might say: "Every morning I pray the Lord's Prayer and draw strengthening forces for the whole day from the spiritual contents of this wonderful prayer." Now a Master of Wisdom said that he prays the Lord's Prayer only once a month, while the rest of the time he prepares himself to pray it worthily. Thus, one could say that one also wanted to pray it only once in a month, for one must imitate a master.

But what would that be? That would be absolute arrogance. That would be an expression of the feeling that we could do the same as a master; that what he can draw from the spiritual content of the Lord's Prayer at his elevated position is also available to us. We often think that we have already eliminated a trait such as arrogance, but have only shifted it to another corner of our souls. For these traits are also maya; so too, the concepts we have made here on the physical plane of good and evil, just and unjust. When we spoke in the exoteric lessons of the influences from Luciferic beings, on the one hand, we formed the point of view that these influences are "bad," and that we must oppose them; on the other hand, we know that Lucifer brought us freedom. However, we absolutely must not carry our learned concepts of good and evil, just and unjust, over with us into the higher regions in which Lucifer and the good gods are engaged in what is expressed as a "battle"; indeed, as a battle that unfolds for the most part in human souls. There is an occult secret that certain human traits developed too quickly during earthly evolution. Lucifer is involved in this. How does this come about?

Lucifer comes from the old Moon stage of evolution, and brings the tempo of the moon to everything that falls under his influence. Since he influences our intellect and our reason, they have been developed far ahead in time. We will go through many incarnations with the most varied experiences; yet our intellect, our reason, will be the same as today. But what is the consequence of this premature development? It is that we cannot bring our intellect into harmony with the wisdom that we find given on the earth; and from this, error after error arises. I can give you a trivial example of this. After the first terrible eruption of Mount Pelee, the local scholars calculated that a longer pause would come next.† However, more eruptions came, worse than before, and lava and ash buried not only the proclamations of the scholars, but also the scholars themselves. This is an example of how our combinatorial intellect, instead of slowly permeating the wisdom of nature's powers, rushes ahead, and thereby finds itself on false paths.

Lucifer has his influence in play all over the earth. But we would be in error if we wanted to find an expression of this influence in earthquake catastrophes, in storms, weather, and hail. On the contrary, we are to seek his influence in everything that is blossoming quickly toward ripeness. And this acceleration must be held back, hindered by the good gods. Weather catastrophes are even often the expression of the good gods. They are the hindrances that the good gods must place against Lucifer in order to avoid an evolution that takes place too fast. And indeed, they are hindrances that also correspond to Moon-evolution in order to compensate for Lucifer's Moon tempo. What was proper during the Moon stage of evolution is now destructive in its effects.

And in the same way, the good gods must intervene to impede the development of an esotericist. What, then, is Lucifer's work in our esoteric life? It is his influence that causes us to take the maya of our everyday concepts from material life over into our meditations. However, so that we do not enter the spiritual world unprepared on this erroneous path, the good gods throw hindrances onto our path; hindrances such as all our bad character traits. They are arrogance, vanity, envy, anger, and ill-will, which break out when we approach ther spiritual world with our earthly attitudes and feelings. And until we have eliminated them ourselves, the spiritual world remains closed to us, because these worlds must be kept pure from everything that is maya.

When we reflect on this relationship of the good gods, of Christ, to the Luciferic beings, to Lucifer, then the meditative sentence "Everything around us is maya, is illusion" will appear to us in an entirely different light. We become aware how often we forget in everyday life that things and characteristics that we think are essential, are really only maya.

Esoteric Lesson

MUNICH, MARCH 15, 1910

Manuscript from Mathilde Scholl and Amalie Fugger-Gloett.

We want to begin today's esoteric lesson with a reading of the prayer to the spirit of the day. Exoteric churches direct their prayer to God in general. However, Theosophists know that every interval of time has its own regent, and so they turn in humility to the spiritual being who, under the name Mars, rules over today (Tuesday):

> *Great all-encompassing spirit.*
> *Knowledge lived in your sensations...*

Those who enter upon an esoteric training must be clear that they are thereby undertaking something very serious; that they must work on themselves with all seriousness in order one day to be capable of participating in esoteric work. In what way should an esotericist work on himself or herself? We know that the human being's etheric body is born only in the seventh year; until then, the etheric body surrounds the physical body like a mother-sheath. Now, until the fourteenth year, in which the astral body is born, the etheric body should be prepared in the right way for its later development. But all kinds of unfinished and undigested components are attached to it, partially from earlier incarnations, partially from the present one. Everything that lives in us as habit is developed in the etheric body from the seventh to the fourteenth year; and according to how we solidify our views into prejudices (educators can have a great influence here), according to this a person will be, for example, more or less able to take up theosophy. Those who acquire firmly defined opinions will find theosophy's teachings less accessible than those who remain open to everything new. The etheric body is fully developed between the seventh and fourteenth year. If children do not take in great role models; if they do not look up in reverence to an authority; then the etheric body during this age (seven to fourteen years) will not be soft and pliable. Such people then have a difficult time finding themselves in life. The etheric body is hardened, and it costs a great deal of effort to dissolve this hardening. The Moon forces, Luciferic forces, make use of this, and flow into it. Not without good reason did Christ say, "Watch and pray."

The astral body then develops from the fourteenth or fifteenth until the twenty-first or twenty-second years. The remnants that remain attached to this body are, by far, not as troublesome for the reception of the teachings of theosophy as the etheric obstacles, because the etheric body is a much denser mass than the astral body.

From the twenty-first year until the twenty-eighth year the self, the human "I," now develops. And the teachings of the Masters of Wisdom and Harmony are so designed to be appropriate for our time that they work primarily on the "I," are taken hold of by the "I." Earlier this was not the case. Then an esoteric teacher had to work not only on the "I," but also on the astral body. However, with the constitution of humanity today, with its much more individual inclinations, this would not be possible. If a teacher tried to intervene in an astral body today by attempting to direct the passions, drives, and desires, this would immediately call forth a revolution in these astral regions. For the human self, the "I," should be developed only in freedom in human beings of the present time. What people acquire in the "I" as knowledge through the teachings of theosophy, they must apply to ennoble their older, but less lofty, bodies.

Why can human beings understand all the teachings of theosophy through their thinking, through the "I"? We received the physical body on old Saturn. On old Sun the etheric body was newly added. Then the physical body was in the Sun state; the etheric body, however, was in the Saturn state; that is, the first state. On the old Moon, the newly added astral body was in the Saturn condition, the etheric body in the Sun condition, and only the physical body was in the Moon condition. On earth, the physical body is in the Earth state. The newly added, youngest part, the "I," however, is in the Saturn state. For this reason, the "I" understands everything that has happened since old Saturn times, for it is Saturn within us.

Esoteric Lesson

HAMBURG, MAY 16, 1910

Record A: Manuscript from Mathilde Scholl; Record B: Notes from Günther Wagner.

RECORD A

Among Theosophists one often hears that an esoteric development is associated with dangers. In response to this, it must be stressed that one should not let oneself be held back from treading the esoteric path because of a feeling of fear. Those who get instruction from a mystery school that has a right to exist, and who properly follow these instructions, will develop themselves in the right way. The main thing is to awaken the proper seriousness within, and to entirely permeate oneself with the knowledge one learns in the esoteric lessons.

It is always good for esotericists to say to themselves that they still have a long path ahead of them. One can already long ago have grasped something with the intellect and still not guide one's life according to that knowledge, by a long way. An example for this is found in the statement that should be well known to all theosophists, "Everything that surrounds us is maya." There are people for whom this principle is very obvious, who, however, never apply it to their lives, who allow pain and joy to affect them without saying, "If everything is maya, then the cause of my pain is also maya." But it is good that this is the case; for if people were to take this principle to heart, into their feelings, too soon, then perhaps they could not withstand the shock that they would thereby experience when they apply it to their pain. This requires great strength that must be slowly developed, before applying it to the great events of life. Indeed, we develop strength by practice in applying the truth of this principle to the small everyday occurrences that surround us in life. We know that everything that surrounds us shows itself to us in a way other than it really is. Let us take for example, a red object. By what means do we see the red color? By means of the light that falls upon it. If the object is in darkness, then we do not see it as red. But when light shines upon it, the red color arises through the fact that the object absorbs all the other colors called forth by the light. Only the red color is reflected back, which the object cannot use, does not want or like. It shows us precisely what, in its essence, it is *not*.

Can human beings manage to penetrate into this inner aspect? Can they come to know the true essence of things? They can do this only through meditative means. If we remain at visual perception, at the mental picture, then we also remain caught in maya. But we usually do something else. When we meet a color, say red, it then exerts an effect on our sensations, our feelings. We have a feeling of refreshment when are looking at the color red. A blue that is lightly mixed with violet will convey to us a mood of devoted reverence. We have these sensations within us, and we have them with respect to the feeling of the true. The objects that cause these feelings may be maya, may come into being and pass away, but the feelings themselves remain the same. We could go for a walk in the woods, hear a rustling, and be startled and scared by it because we imagine it to be caused by a snake, when actually a gust of air was the cause. Farther on, we might again hear a rustling, but this time it actually comes from a snake. Each time our fear is the same; it is true, even though the cause was an illusion the first time.

But how do we manage to get behind to the true essence of things through our feelings?

When we see the plants in the springtime sprouting, shooting forth and blossom, how are we to recognize the truth behind what they extend to us as maya? There is a moment in the life of plants when they show us something of their inner essence, and this moment occurs when they begin to die away. When does this moment occur? At fertilization. Until then the plant has expended all its energy to reject what it does not want; now it has received something from outside and its life is turned around, so to speak. It loses the power of defense and withdraws back into itself; the energy that it had applied outward, it now turns inward. Can we awaken a feeling in ourselves that is like this process in the soul life of the plant? When do we want to withdraw and turn within ourselves? When do we lose the power to defend ourselves toward the outside world? With the feeling of shame. When we awaken this feeling in us, without its being occasioned by an external event, and also observe a fertilized plant, then we become aware that exactly the same feeling lives in the plant; that it lives in the plant so intensely that it causes the plant's death. In the autumn, a feeling of enormous shame goes through the plant world. The red rose is a special example of this.

What color would we then choose for the feeling of dying away, of drawing back from the outside world and turning toward the spirit? Black; and therefore, we have the black cross, upon which red roses are blossoming. Black carbonized wood, in which everything external has died, is for us an expression of the fact that the spirit is revealed behind all death and dying. Goethe once spoke of the color that the earth will have when it is dying away at the end of the present cycle, and is passing over into a spiritual kingdom fructified by the spirit. It will have to "glow in flaming red."† And this statement originates in a deep knowledge. For how could the earth otherwise glow but with deep shame when it is ripe to be fertilized by the spirit?

If, in this way, we awaken within ourselves feelings that are caused by external things, then we will come closer to the truth behind external things. But we can also awaken pictures and feelings within ourselves without any external reason whatsoever; we can produce mental pictures and feelings all alone within us. Then we are together with a world within us that was not called forth by any external cause; and thus we can find our way to absolute truth.

This should happen in our meditation. When we look at the sun and meditate on its enlivening influence, we always have an external reason for the meditation. However, when we ourselves awaken a mental picture of light using the words, *In pure rays of light...* and so forth, and then imagine that it is the garment of God, then we have created something that is not bound to some external object. And when we awaken the feeling of love for all beings in the next lines, then we are permeating ourselves with this feeling; and it will become a powerful germinating force within us.

* * *

Record B

Well-known general principle: everything is maya, illusion. But it is very difficult to arrange one's life according to the meaning of this principle only.

And this is good; a soul would not be able to bear a sudden change.

Let us consider a red plant. The red that it appears to us is only an illusion. It would not appear that way in the dark; it is only the effect of sunlight. Indeed, the plant does not show us its true inner being. It rays back to us, not the colors that it absorbed, its actual characteristics; but what it does not want. Thus its color is indeed maya. However, a time does come when the plant shows something of its inner being: the time of bearing fruit, when it begins to weaken. Then it has only the power to work on itself, and no longer the power to hide its inner nature.

The feeling that then holds sway in it is shame; this is something real.

At the edge of the forest a rustling is heard. We believe that it is a snake and are alarmed. But it was only the wind. At the other end of the same forest there really is a snake. What is real in both instances is the feeling of fear.

We should learn to feel with the plant, which shows the feeling of shame when fading and dying. Then we will gradually learn the laws that stand behind the plant, and see that all color is only maya, illusion.

Goethe was right when he asked, "On the day of the last judgment when our earth will change its form of appearance, in what color will it radiate?" And he answered, "In fiery red." It is a feeling of shame, because it is beginning to pass away.

Esoteric Lesson
HAMBURG, MAY 19, 1910

Record A: Manuscript from Mathilde Scholl; Record B: Notes from the collection of Elisabeth Vreede.

RECORD A

Before we begin today's esoteric lesson, I want to direct a prayer to the spirit of Thursday. Esotericists should increasingly acquire a truer, higher modesty that leads them to turn, not to the highest divinity, but to consider that between this divinity, which we cannot even imagine with our highest human intellect, and all of us, the great hierarchies are present:

Great all-encompassing spirit.
In your light, life streams to the earth...

Today I again want to illuminate our meditations from another side. Esotericists, through their meditations, want to approach the spirit of Christ more intensely. They want to try to connect with him more intimately than they could through exoteric Christianity. The Christ-principle's entry into our earth evolution was so decisive, even for external history, that we calculate our time line according to it. At the time when Zoroaster beheld in the sun the approaching form of the spirit of the sun, he gathered disciples around him in order to make them into servants of the great Ahura Mazdao. And he prepared himself more and more to take this spirit of the sun into himself.

When the earth with all its beings looks up to the sun, then it must say that it cannot do what the sun can do: send forth light. The earth would be a dark, black body if the light of the sun did not permeate it, and if the earth could not reflect back this light. Now, since Christ became the planetary spirit for the earth through the event on Golgotha, he is in the forces that cause the green covering of the earth to shoot forth.

The Masters of Wisdom and Harmony of Feelings give us the great truths in symbols; and here, above all, it is the Rose Cross, which, mirrored in us, can awaken and strengthen the power of Christ in us. In the last esoteric lesson we saw that the red rose brings the feeling of shame to expression in the color red. Now we know that all colors stimulate their complementary color within us; thus red calls forth green (compare in *The Education of the Child*). Thus, the sight of the black cross awakens the white, radiant sunlight of the Christ in us, and through the red roses the power is stimulated that allows green life to shoot forth from the red roses. When we imagine the Rose Cross with this feeling and let it live in us in this way, we participate in part of the power of our earth, our earth-spirit, the Christ.

As esotericists we must constantly be trying to bring good thoughts to the things that appear to us as maya. We must be permeated by the feeling that in everything there sleeps a spark of this power, which will one day break forth in order to ray out over all that is evil. We should also bear within us complete trust that all that is good on the earth, all that is positive, will and must emerge victorious.

* * *

Record B

It is impossible for human beings to approach God directly; and therefore, it is better to try to approach the spirit of the day by reverently calling upon this spirit with appropriate expressions (the spirit of Jupiter is called upon).

The loftiest of all symbols is the cross. We can draw from it the entire history of the world, and even natural science could be constructed out of it. If we observe how colors have complementary colors, which are well noted by natural science, then we will also understand that the particular colors that are used for the Rose Cross exert a specific effect that we can experience in our soul as the complementary colors. It was already pointed out in the small pamphlet *The Education of the Child* how the color red has a calming effect within the soul. One would at the same time be able to see that the soul is immersed in green; it produces the complementary color. In the observation of the black cross with red roses, the black, which otherwise is darkness for us, becomes as white light. Thus one can understand that when meditating the black cross, light arises in our souls that can bring us to enlightenment. The red of the roses produces green as its reflection in the soul, and brings us to a very lofty feeling when we imagine the effects of Christ's power.

Zarathustra (or Zoroaster) saw how Christ (who for him was still connected to the sun), was to stream down to the earth. And as that happened the earth was fructified, filled with the spirit of Christ; and this spirit then became the spirit of the earth. The earth, which until then had been dark, was inwardly filled with light; and the effects of this light showed itself in the green that covered the earth. The living, sprouting green is the effect of the Christ-spirit in the earth. The earth is thereby permeated, so to speak; and it is literally true that we walk on the earth on the body of Christ. And the green is his etheric body.

Through the meditation of the Rose Cross we become illuminated within, and the effect of green will awaken in our souls the power of Christ, which also awakened in the earth by this same power. And when this power works in us, we will feel the greatest trust growing in us: that pure love must overcome all evil and that truth can be found. That is contained for us in the words:

In pure rays of light...

Esoteric Lesson
HAMBURG, MAY 25, 1910

Record A: Notes from the collection of Elisabeth Vreede; Record B: Manuscript from Mathilde Scholl. Record C: Manuscript from Alice Kinkel.

RECORD A

Great all-encompassing spirit,
In the knowledge of your being is knowledge of the world...

The last time we saw how the symbols that are given to us in our meditations can and should work upon us. Now, today, in order to enclose these three esoteric lessons in a circle, I want to speak about the erroneous paths upon which we can find ourselves as esotericists.

In ordinary exoteric life we have all kinds of terms for characteristic traits that we know as good or evil. These terms are often inadequate and one-sided for an esotericist, for every character trait has two sides, a good one and a bad one; and maintaining the proper balance must be one of an esotericist's chief tasks. Altogether esotericists must constantly guard themselves, be on the watch. Human traits are such that when they remain in proper proportions human beings can control them very well with their "I." However, if we allow one of them to become too intensive, then the "I" can fall under the power of that trait. This is not so dangerous for people who are living only exoterically, as the spirit of the everyday will bring them back into balance. But it is different for esotericists. A character trait that acquires dominion over them can lead them into all kinds of dangers. Above all, something like this can come to expression already in their present life as an illness of the physical body. I would like to clarify this with an example.

Who among us does not know irritation and a bad mood? All of us have certainly already been subject to them. But esotericists must now attempt to fight against them with the ordinary self, or "I." If they allow a bad mood to master them, something very specific happens.

They fall prey to the false spirits of heaviness. There really is a spirit or spirits of heaviness. In itself, the spirit of heaviness belongs to the primal powers (Spirits of Personality or *Archai*), and is the one who in the morning brings us back to our physical bodies when we awaken. That belongs to the field of work of the spirit of heaviness, and it is good and proper for us. Now among these spirits are those who go beyond their field of work and want to work in the realm of the Spirits of Form. These are the ones that overcome the etheric body of an esotericist who surrenders to irritation or a bad mood. They then change the etheric body so that the esotericist falls victim to hypochondria. In the physical realm, this is then expressed in illness of the digestive tract. This can also be said in exoteric lectures. We must remember that in our esoteric lessons we are receiving direct messages from the master, who intends these messages especially for esotericism.

Another character trait that an esotericist should constantly be on the watch for, should constantly be observant for, so that he or she does not succumb to it, is vanity and arrogance. We are often not aware how far we have already succumbed to it, and therefore must give this special attention. How many imagine that they would like to help others because they "love humanity." However, when one tells them that they can achieve this helpfulness only through unceasing, assiduous study, one notices that they really don't want to do this; they would like to take matters in hand and act immediately, without considering how much damage they could do with false help. This is, however, a very dangerous vanity, and all those "do-gooders" and confused dreamers have succumbed to it. They preach their worldview, for which they think they have a mission, with beautiful words and unclear sayings. Now what happens if esotericists do not suppress this vanity? They succumb to the spirit of light; and indeed again, not the normal good spirits that are recruited from the host of the spirits of wisdom, but rather the kind that work into the realm of the spirits of movement. The good spirits of light have the task of leading people into the spiritual world at night when they fall asleep. They are to direct the entrance of human beings into the spiritual world so that, although unconscious, they arrive there. If esotericists want to accelerate their development, and in so doing, do not learn what they of necessity must know about the spiritual world, the other spirits of light overpower them and influence the etheric body in such a way that the head is affected in the physical realm. Confusion, fanaticism, and finally, worst of all, insanity ensue.

Those who succumb to the spirit of heaviness injure only themselves, and we should try to help such people with all means possible; for we should love not only all of humanity, but every individual human being. However, those who succumb to the spirits of light can injure humanity, not only themselves, with their confused fanaticism. For this reason we should question ourselves again and again, asking whether the reasons we want to develop ourselves are really selfless. We should never tire of learning, for the more we learn, the more self-evident will our humility become.

We need have no fear if we feel the spirit of darkness in the following way: when awakening in the morning we feel exhausted, and our limbs feel so heavy that we can hardly move them. This is a passing stage, and is a sign that we have skipped over the false stage of hypochondria. And those who at certain times have the feeling that they can hardly hold themselves with their feet on the earth, that they must hover, they do not have to be worried either, for they have skipped over the stage of fanaticism, and this symptom is developmentally normal. The human soul is kept in balance by the spirit of heaviness and the spirit of light, and an esotericist should always be concerned not to disturb this balance.

Instruction concerning this balance is given to us from the Masters of Wisdom in the prayer that we speak at the conclusion of this lesson, a prayer that contains all the wisdom of the world that will be revealed to us more and more.

In the spirit lay the seed of my body...

RECORD B

First the spirit of the day is invoked: Mercury.

There are symptoms that appear in the esoteric life which have great significance for an esotericist. After the preceding lessons have had their effect on us, it is necessary still to receive these last in order to connect them to a whole.

In ordinary external life, the world itself corrects the mistakes we have brought with us through our inborn constitution; but in an esoteric life our character traits and predispositions have an entirely different significance. Indeed, this goes so far that the word that characterizes a certain trait no longer even expresses what is characteristic of this trait. We have been told that arrogance, vanity, and pride are dangerous. However, if we wanted to entirely eliminate these traits from ourselves with our striving for balance, then we would lose our feeling for self. The "I" would dissolve away, and we would become human beings without content. On the other hand, the character trait that could be called love works in a way just as dangerous. People who are always inclined to give only love and believe that they must help everyone, fall into the other extreme; there is danger that they are always concerned about themselves, and become wrapped up in their own "I." When characteristic traits appear, there are always two forces in play that work against one another.

If there were only love as the greatest thing in the world, then nothing at all would exist; an opposing force must always hold the balance. Thus today we will point out those forces or beings that work in us and call forth those peculiar states in us that every esotericist knows.

The first state is that of a bad mood, an irritation in the soul that rises apparently without any reason, which can find a reason in every petty problem, and can deteriorate into such vehemence that the entire nature of a person can appear changed. In this case, we are dealing with beings belonging to the hierarchy of primal powers (Archai), which are beneficial beings when they remain in their own realm; but when they step out of their own realm into that of the Spirits of Form, their work is destructive. They are called "spirits of heaviness," and they help us to come down to the earth in the morning when we awaken. This often gives us a feeling of heaviness, of lethargy upon awakening. But when we add a bad mood to this, then these spirits work upon us in a disadvantageous way and make everything heavy and dark for us. They then influence the physical body, and fill it with darkness so that one is as if tied to the earth. If the "I" does not oppose this, and does not suspect the dangers that threaten, then these spirits rule over the "I"; the human being becomes powerless and succumbs to hypochondria. Everyone knows how hard it is to heal hypochondria. This illness always points to an effect of an earlier incarnation as an esotericist, for it cannot arise in one incarnation. When the spirits of heaviness have thus overcome us, this shows itself in illnesses of the lower body and the organs of digestion.

Now we must also make the acquaintance of the spirits of light, which are also beneficial when they remain in their own realm. However, when they step outside their realm and move themselves into the realm of the spirits of movement, they bring trouble to human beings. This is the case, for example, when people imagine they must help humanity; but actually they have the desire to ascend higher without any effort, and they want to lose themselves in love. Then these spirits of light penetrate into these people and bring them to fanaticism, so that all their ideas are transformed into something untrue. Such people think that they are forces for the good and that they should improve the world. When people succumb to the power of these spirits, then the "I" is so filled with itself that it can no longer see the things outside of itself in proper perspective. Finally, such people succumb to a state where the body is influenced, and indeed the brain is destroyed. However, if they react against these forces and attempt to understand that it is all only fantasy that they believe they can help others, and so forth; and, rather, they attempt to redirect their forces away from this occupation with love, suppress within every desire for progress, and trust that the proper maturity will appear at the proper time, then these spirits work as beneficial powers, step by step bring them closer to the light. These are the spirits that help us at night when we fall asleep, that bring us to the light.

Thus we must constantly be on the lookout for these two forces, and when they show themselves in our feelings we should immediately be alert and direct our attention inward toward ourselves. If we have a bad mood, if we are irritated and have always wakefully battled it, then the moment will come when we feel that our body is "done in," that it pains us even into the marrow. This will be proof that we are victors. And if we are inclined to fanaticism as is here described, and we have courageously fought against it, then a feeling will come over us as though we no longer had any legs to stand on, as if the body were too light for the ground to hold it firmly. This is proof that we have won our battle with the spirits of light.

These are the consequences of exercises that have been properly carried out. And they should encourage us to go forward bravely, rather than becoming fearful and in a bad mood. When we gradually learn to understand how we are always surrounded on all sides by forces that influence us, then we learn to live through our days with full self-consciousness and establish a balance between all these influences working on us. Thus we also better understand the concluding words of our discussion, whose first half presented the spirit of heaviness:

Im Geiste lag der Keim meines Leibes... In the spirit lay the seed of my body... and in second half the spirit of light:

In meinen Leibe liegt des Geistes Keim... In my body lies the seed of the spirit...

* * *

Record C

The five-fold spirit, and where he works
and how he expresses himself.

1. the spirit of truth
2. the spirit of devotion
3. the spirit of a good attitude
4. the spirit of heaviness
5. the spirit of light

The kingdom of the primal powers is the kingdom of the spirit of heaviness. The primal powers or the Spirits of Personality work in the physical body. They are properly what hold the human being on the earth. The work of the spirit of heaviness, when they are working as do the spirits of form—that is, in the "I"—is improper. If the spirit of heaviness works there, then it happens that irritation, bad moods, hysteria, and hypochondria appear. The heaviness of the body is good. The spirits of wisdom work properly as spirits of light in the etheric body. They produce healthy judgment. It is wrong when they work as spirits of movement; then their work is revealed as confusion, fanaticism, as improper working even into the physical body.

The Rose Cross: Let us imagine a plant, the cross, and a red rose; it is the blush of a plant. In this case we need to imagine the cross as white, and the rose as green, that is, in its complementary color.

Esoteric Lesson

KRISTIANIA (OSLO), JUNE 16, 1910

Record A: Manuscript from Mathilde Scholl and Barbara Wolf; Record B: Notes from the collection of Elisabeth Vreede.

RECORD A

Exoterically regarded, theosophy is knowledge. What we learn in exoteric lectures, as esotericists we should take into our thinking, feeling, and willing, so that we can then let it flow out into our exoteric lives. This is esoteric work. And what happens through this work? How can we carry a simple theosophical truth directly into life? For example, there is the truth concerning falling asleep and waking up; that is, the truth that the physical and etheric bodies remain behind while the "I" and the astral body go into the spiritual world. In ancient times, human beings received prayers to say in the evening before falling asleep, and in the morning after waking. That was good, because they strengthened their souls with spiritual forces by preparing themselves before entering the spiritual realm. And after they had left the spiritual world, they permeated their souls once again with higher forces; they extracted soul forces out of the spiritual world, so to speak.

The three kingdoms below the human being—the mineral, plant, and animal kingdoms—are permeated by spiritual forces that are constantly renewed; so, too, the four elements fire, water, air, and earth. It is different with human beings. If they do not put themselves in touch with these spiritual forces, then they do not receive them. When they fall asleep without having prepared themselves, they do not receive an influx of spiritual forces in the spiritual world that they enter. Materialistic people, no matter how well educated, how scientific or prominent, when they enter the spiritual world unprepared, they stand far below the simplest primitive people, who through their prayer are already in touch with forces in the spiritual world. In our materialistic age, whose scientific accomplishments are so boundlessly amazing, human beings have more and more forgotten how to pray. They fall asleep and awaken with their everyday thoughts. But what are they doing in this way? For something is happening through this omission. Every time, they kill something of their spiritual life, of their spiritual forces on the physical plane.

Human beings are unconscious when they go into the spiritual world. If, for example, a man were to fall asleep around eleven o'clock, and wake up, unprepared, at twelve in the spiritual world, he would not recognize where he was. He would have the feeling that he was spread out over infinite space and had lost his center. Such a person would be in ecstasy, "out of himself," in the actual meaning of the word. This ecstasy was artificially induced in the Druid mysteries in ancient times, in order to cause the pupils to experience higher worlds consciously. However, so that the pupil did not lose himself, so that his "I" was not lost, twelve helpers had to stand at his side. These helpers poured the entire power of their pure "I's" into him at the moment when the ecstasy began. That much power was necessary in order to prevent this dissolution of self!

This Druid initiation was the *external* path (expanding into the cosmos), while the *inner* path was followed in the old Egyptian mysteries. There, those to be initiated had to seek a path through the lower astral world during three and a half days. That means that they had to climb into their own inner being. Twelve pure priests had to accompany the pupils so that they were not taken hold of and overcome by all the lower drives, desires, and passions that slumbered deep in their being; what otherwise only in the course of their incarnations would slowly be worked through (in ordinary evolution).

Unknown vices would have been awakened in them if the twelve priests had not protected them with their purity. Today, neither of these paths mentioned would be possible, because modern human beings would rebel against such an intervention into the "I," the self, and they would object to the patronizing treatment of their drives, desires, and passions.

The Rosicrucian school combines both paths, and at the same time allows human beings complete freedom. They themselves must, through the meditations given to them, acquire the power that was given to them earlier by helpers. Through this work on themselves, esotericists increase the spiritual forces that humanity needs. They battle against the desolation that will appear as a result of the terrible materialism because people have simply forgotten their connection with the spiritual world, forgotten how they can obtain forces from those worlds. When the time comes when human souls are becoming increasingly desolate and empty, then it will be the task of esotericists to let their spiritual forces work in a lively way. Under all blows of destiny, they will be able to maintain a cheerful balance in their souls, and thereby cause happiness to flow to the rest of humanity, and thereby relieve its soul pain. This soul pain will be felt by people as agony, as a consequence of the achievements of materialistic science. Today many ways have been found to anesthetize physical pain, to make it disappear. But in reality, the pain has not disappeared. We are also taught in exoteric science that no force disappears, and so the power of pain does not go away either, but, rather, it expresses itself in other ways. The pain returns again in later incarnations as soul agony. Thus, the human beings will have to go through intense psychological pain, and esotericists will then use spiritual forces that they bring down from the heights in order to relieve this agony. Every one of us has made a decision, even if unconsciously, when we entered upon the path of esotericism; a decision to intervene in a helping way in the suffering of humanity.

* * *

Record B

In earlier, less materialistic times, prayer was a customary activity before falling asleep and upon awakening. Humanity little suspects the injury it is causing itself by entirely laying aside this habit. Through prayer, people obtained strength from the spiritual world for daily life when they awakened. In the evening they took the strength that they had gathered in their daily lives with them into the spiritual world. Thus our exercises today are also intended so that our strength for the spirit may grow more quickly, and so that we learn to employ it consciously.

Esoteric Lesson

KRISTIANIA (OSLO, JUNE 18, 1910

Record A: Manuscript from Mathilde Scholl and Barbara Wolf; Record B: Notes from the collection of Elisabeth Vreede.

RECORD A

In the ancient Egyptian mystery schools, those being prepared for initiation intended that that incarnation was to be dedicated entirely to initiation, for it was a life or death procedure. They had to undergo trials that placed great demands on their courage, for example. They were shown things that could so stir up their fear that they fell over dead. If they lived through these trials, then they had arrived on the other shore and were newborn. They had descended to the god in their inner being; they had encountered the drives, desires, and passion in their own bodies, and had victoriously withstood the encounter. They could now say of themselves: *Ex Deo nascimur.* Now, one could ask about the evil that was encountered on the path to the inner god: does that also come from the gods? Here we must always say that it was originally something divine; that only we human beings made it into something evil.

The path of ecstasy was followed in the Druid mysteries. Those being initiated united themselves with the spirit that held sway everywhere in nature: *Per Spiritum Sanctum reviviscimus.*

In the Rosicrucian path the two paths are united; that is, from each was taken what is beneficial for us. The modern human being can no longer be initiated unconsciously. Since the advent of the Christ-principle, the human being must be present with his or her waking consciousness.

The meditations given to us by the Masters of Wisdom and Harmony of Feelings are all directed toward the Christ, even though his name might not appear in them. The words:

In pure rays of light...

are so arranged that, if one makes oneself deaf and blind toward the closest environment, one slowly lifts one's etheric body out of the physical. And in this way one is united with Christ's etheric aura, which is now the aura of our earth. If we were to lift ourselves out of our bodies without the content of our meditations, then the soul would be alone with itself. Now, however, it is permeated by Christ and experiences what Paul said: "Now it is not I who live, but Christ in me."

In pure love to all beings...

With these words we are reminded that everything soul-like is woven out of love. This meditation is a slow dying of the lower "I," the lower self. And in this dying and coming to life again in Christ, we have the connection between the two paths: *In Christo morimur*. It is a conscious expansion and living into the Christ-Spirit. For this reason we also have added the word *Sanctum* to the words *Per Spiritum*.

* * *

RECORD B

One of the greatest advantages achieved by esotericists is when they faithfully apply what the Masters of Wisdom and Harmony of Feelings have compiled in corresponding pictures or principles.

There followed as explanation of the meditation:

In pure rays of light...

It was described how one is gradually made free of the body and thus goes into the spiritual world. In the second part of the meditation, esotericists at the same time penetrate into their own inner souls. That which had to be experienced separately in the past should now take place simultaneously, since humanity is now further advanced. These meditations are based on that. When one has become so strong that one feels oneself transported into a spiritual world outside of one's body, then the next step is that one begins to perceive something in that world. However, since at the same time one is also penetrating into one's inner being, one also experiences the dangers of illusion all the more. At that moment we are in the grip of the forces of temptation, and we imagine pictures that we then take for realities. But precisely the most beautiful, the noblest visions are the deepest illusions. Only a long time after we have achieved the power to rise into the spiritual world is it possible for us to distinguish reality from illusion. Only the deepest seriousness with which we acquire theosophy makes this discernment possible. If we always carry in our souls, in our wakeful consciousness, the concepts given to us by theosophy, then we create the reality for the spiritual world. And if we achieve this, we will be able to recognize what we see. In the beginning we should defend ourselves against the visions—not allow them—and not, as usually happens, spin them out further and apply our fantasy to them. The moment will certainly come, if we wait in the proper frame of mind, when we will know whether we are dealing with something real or not.

Esoteric Lesson
KRISTIANIA (OSLO), JUNE 20, 1910

Record A: Manuscript from Mathilde Scholl and Barbara Wolf; Record B: Notes from the collection of Elisabeth Vreede.

RECORD A

Prayer to the spirit of Monday.

> *Great all-encompassing spirit,*
> *In your forms of life shone forth sensation...*

To support us in our meditations, there are helping thoughts that are given in all esoteric schools whose existence is justified. When you place these thoughts before you in the form of pictures and let them work on you, when you immerse yourself in them, then they are of unlimited value. It is not the same with these thoughts as it is with our ordinary, everyday thoughts; rather, when we occupy ourselves with these, they have germinating, awakening powers for us.

One such thought is the following. Just as we know our consciousness as both a waking and sleeping consciousness, so too we are imagining the consciousness of the surrounding spirits of the earth that work on us when we say the spirits of the earth sleep in the mineral kingdom, the plants are the waking thoughts and life of the spirits of the earth, and the animals are their dreams. If we immerse ourselves in these thoughts, and think about, for example, what our thoughts actually are (misty forms flitting about like whispers), and if we compare these (our thoughts) with those of the spirits of the earth, then we can feel the incredible distance between them. The thoughts of the spirits of the earth sprout forth from the earth as a carpet of green in endless variety. Their thoughts are thus creative forces in the physical world. These spirits once went through a human stage like ours, in the past evolution of the earth. Back then, they thought the same way we think now. They developed themselves higher and higher, and became creating beings. We can see in them what we should strive for.

We must always bear in mind that we are becoming different from other people. Our interests are changed; and one can often hear esotericists complain that they feel their interest in many things disappearing, things that they were interested in before, and that an inner desolation and emptiness overcomes them. However, this is an entirely normal state that quickly passes. And the emptiness of their souls will soon be filled with interests that will replace the others a hundred-, yes, a thousand-fold. Nevertheless, we should not give up our connection to other people, nor our interests that previously filled us. Above all, we should not expect of other people that they change their circle of interests. The difference between exoteric and esoteric individuals is this: that the exoteric people have their physical bodies firmly permeated by the other bodies; everything pushes forward toward the outer surface, so to speak. Ordinary people who are born into an ethnic group, into a family, thereby inherit certain concepts about good and evil, about honesty and other virtues that the creating gods in the course of evolution placed in them. Esotericists will gradually live out of their own knowledge according to these virtues. But, concerning these things, they are not allowed to place themselves beyond the concepts that live in the people, for they could slip into serious danger with respect to their development. In esotericists, the inner person is gradually separated from the external person. Their higher parts abandon their lower; and if they do not attend to the usual laws of humanity, concerning truthfulness, for example, they can slip into deceitfulness, which is naturally a hindrance for them in their development and can cause a great deal of damage. The strife and conflict among esotericists can be traced back to this.

We leave behind not only part of our etheric body and our sentient soul (we begin our esoteric work in the sentient soul), but also the physical body, and we experience all kinds of states in it—illness, too. We are now afflicted by states we have never know before. However, we need not consider them illness, and run immediately to a doctor. For of course an exoteric doctor naturally cannot give us anything for *these* conditions, and they will go away by themselves anyway. On the other hand, we should not think that every sickness that befalls us is caused by esoteric development, and that there is no doctor who can treat us. That is spiritual arrogance. One can continue for a long time to seek advice from a doctor for one's illnesses. Esotericists should always pay attention to their health in the right way.

One should not allow oneself to be prevented from developing spiritually because of laziness or cowardice, or because of the difficulties that one encounters, or through a loosening of the etheric body. This loosening is something that must occur if one wishes to penetrate into spiritual worlds. And if we struggle for this with earnest striving, then the Master of Wisdom and Harmony of Feelings will come to meet us with his strength, and his help will never fail.

If not in this life, then with absolute certainty we will achieve the goal of spiritual sight in the next lifetime.

* * *

RECORD B

[The basis for this formulation is that in the copy of these notes there is a text preceding, which contains word for word the discussion of June 18, 1910 (Record B).]

There are other aids that can lead one relatively quickly to a deeper insight into spiritual connections. They are the following three sentences:

> *In the mineral kingdom the gods sleep.*
> *In the plant kingdom they dream.*
> *In the animal kingdom they awaken and think.*

Taking first the animal kingdom, we must imagine that the spiritual beings in earlier times stood on our level and had confused thoughts at that time, as we do now. Meanwhile, they have advanced so far that their thoughts have become so regular and definite that they are able to spread out before us what we see as the world of animals. When we immerse ourselves in such thoughts, then the course taken by our developing thoughts will be strengthened and we will thereby come into a closer connection to the beings that have placed their thoughts into the earth, to those beings also that placed into the earth the force which in its wholeness is the power of Christ.

As esotericists, we experience great inner transformations, which in general are directed toward making the self an "I," free from the body, until we finally perceive our "I" as a higher or second "I" within us.

In comparison to exotericists, we develop, as esotericists, entirely different feelings and sensations in the astral body. Moral and ethical impulses now come from within, although earlier they came from specific, established norms, prescribed by religion or human laws, according to which we lived. Through this new way of experiencing, the connection between the "I" and the ordinary astral body is loosened and the feelings thereby become more independent, emerging more from within. This can have the consequence that people appear at first less moral than the ordinary, average person, while they are actually busy working their way out of conventional feelings and sensations.

The etheric body is also gradually loosened. Habits, prejudices, relationships are transformed; are set against what is forced upon us from outside by the spirit of our time and generally accepted ideas. What was accepted earlier as true, now appears deceitful to us, out of proportion, and one easily comes into conflict with the outer world. In this transition time it often happens that we ourselves become less truthful, that we can only see conditions as all wrong, and so forth.

Major changes also take place in the physical body; this could be called the loosening of the body, through which a feeling of illness can appear in all possible parts of the body. We then believe that our body is becoming sickly or more frail, and during this transition time it may also really appear so, but we will soon notice that we cannot cure these "illnesses" with medications as was previously possible.

The dangers of a loosening of the bodies lie in the disdain we can acquire for human beings and the conditions of the world, which would only lead us deeper into delusions. What we should do is apply a kind of averaging measure of ongoing inner reverence and awe, as we behold what human beings have accomplished precisely through the help of spiritual beings working from outside, as we understand the majesty of those spiritual effects on human beings who are not yet inwardly awake. Thus we can recognize the higher path of self-consciousness, and when we place ourselves between extremes we can be a help to human beings who are still less conscious.

Esoteric Lesson
MUNICH, AUGUST 24, 1910

Record from the collection of Elisabeth Vreede.

This lesson is merely preparatory for the lesson that will follow next Friday.

Lesson begins with invocation of the spirit of the day (Wednesday verse with extensive supplementary remarks). Those who begin an esoteric training must be clear about what they are doing. We are connected through karma to everything that we are and do as human beings. We are placed into the entirety of earth existence by divine beings who lead us. Everything that we think, feel, and will in terms of the greatest, loftiest beauty, the highest morality, is always connected to evolution in general. However, with this one decision, to want to enter upon an esoteric training, we take a step out of this evolution in general, which is guided by higher beings. We thereby start something entirely new. By means of this esoteric training, we develop from creatures who are being guided by divine spiritual beings, into independent partners with these creative beings.

On the earth the human being consists of these four elements: physical body, etheric body, astral body, and "I," which are kept in the harmony given to them by higher beings. When our decision to enter into an esoteric training is followed up with a deed, then we begin to work independently on the transformation of these individual bodies. Indeed, this happens through the exercises that are given to us. They gradually work upon the etheric body so that it is loosened from the solid constitution of the physical body. However, this influence is not exerted directly upon the etheric body, but rather upon the astral body, which is affected by our exercises. To begin with we work on the astral body by means of our regular, daily, or weekly periodically repeated exercises, and by pictures that we allow to work upon our souls.

In the verses of our meditations, every sound has its significance; every word, every sequence of sounds, every sequence of ideas. They work upon us through regular repetition accompanied by complete self-forgetfulness. When we awaken in the morning we sometimes have a quiet memory of the spiritual world, of the world from which strength flows to us through our exercises. And this quiet memory of that world, from which we have drawn strength and in which we were present at the source of strength, belongs among the most beautiful experiences of an esoteric student. If someone has taken leave of a dear person, it is possible that something of this person can flow into the esoteric student's memory of the spiritual world. And those who experience something like this should regard it as a special grace! After meditating for a time, we notice that we have changed. Many loveless actions that came from us earlier, we no longer commit. We acquire a much finer logic. We feel that we have become better. We are becoming better.

However, through the fact that we are placing ourselves outside the usual and customary framework of contemporary consciousness, we lose the support that is given by conventions and traditions. We become freer within ourselves. But just in this way, our bad side comes more to the fore; only now do we notice how bad we are. We really are much worse than we customarily think.

For every esoterically striving person, difficult, dreadful times will come; then it is good to have a support. We find this support in the New Testament. We find there advice for every situation, for every case, a support for every weakness; we need only seek it. And if we do not find it, then the conviction of our own weakness, that we cannot yet find the right passage, should comfort us that it must certainly be in the New Testament.

Illusions can easily appear along with beginning clairvoyance. We think we are seeing something before us externally, but it is something from within ourselves that is reflected there. It is even worse with sounds that we think we have heard. Beings that want to pull us down deceive meditators in this way. For those who are striving esoterically, it is necessary not only to undertake meditations and to pray (if "praying" is understood in the best sense), it is also necessary to watch, to be alert to bad influences that want to intervene when an independent transformation of bodies is undertaken. An esoteric saying against all illusions states, "All paths into the spiritual world go through the heart." During meditation we can feel how, from every point of the external physical body, lines go toward a center point. This middle point is the heart. In their further course, these lines continue in the opposite direction into the spiritual world. This is like a feeling of Christ within us. This kind of phenomenon is genuine.[†]

Every one of our bodily members is related to a sign of the zodiac; thus forces from the sign of Leo flow down into our heart. Forces from the sun also stream into our heart. So too, the spirits of fire work on our heart. All three are often used as symbols for the heart: Leo, the sun, and a flame. Like the heart, every member of the human being has a relationship to forces that stand outside us. We have come forth from, and are embedded in, the whole world.

When we allow this fact properly to live in our souls, then we are understanding this verse in the right way:

In the spirit lay the seed of my body…

Esoteric Lesson
MUNICH, AUGUST 26, 1910

Record A: From Paula Stryczek; Record B: Source of notes unknown; Record C: Manuscript from Barbara Wolf. Additional Record: Author unknown.

RECORD A

With the same intention as last time, we want also today to invoke the spirit of the day. When an esoteric lesson can be held on a Friday, it is to be regarded as special good fortune. The verse for Friday follows:

> *Great all-encompassing spirit,*
> *In your life I live with the earth's life...*

During the night, with the astral body and the "I," we are in divine ether-spheres from which we bring down strength for our physical life. For this reason, we should never have banal, everyday egotistical thoughts immediately upon awakening. We cut ourselves off, in this way, from the spiritual beings and forces in which we were immersed during sleep. Rather, before we engage in any task of daily life, before we engage in any thoughts of physical existence, we should devote ourselves to our meditations, during which we immerse ourselves in those regions of self-forgetfulness. All meditators should make it their holy obligation to undertake their meditation immediately upon awakening, or in any case, their first thought should be to think of higher beings with gratitude.

An even more sacred obligation, if there can be one, should be for all esoteric students to bear in mind with complete clarity that they do a great injustice, not only to themselves, not only to their fellow human beings, but also to higher spiritual beings, when they approach meditation with impure thoughts and feelings. They thereby pollute the spiritual spheres. The forces that have to be applied in order to remove this pollution are taken away from the progress of humanity.

We can carry out our exercises with good concentration and yet, in doing so, not be "holy" within. This carrying out of our meditations is only a matter of will, which, of course, should be consolidated and developed. However, in doing so, our entire inner life should be sanctified so that only lofty, holy content lives in our souls during meditation. Just as we should not go into meditation with impure feelings and thoughts, neither should we go into sleep at night with such thoughts. Also in this way, we bring impurity into the divine spheres when we take with us thoughts of arrogance, of vanity, and of pride. We should fall asleep with thoughts of reverence and gratitude for spiritual beings; for we could not live for a minute longer unless divine-spiritual beings maintained our physical and etheric bodies when the astral body and "I" are outside during sleep. We should fall asleep with reverence for great spiritual beings.

Esotericists differ from exotericists through this: that God lives in them consciously, that they really allow the power of God to become active within them. This does not happen through the ideas that they have of God. They can harm themselves precisely through these ideas when they later enter the spiritual world. For example, they want to find Christ there in the same form they think of him on earth, and they do not recognize him beyond that form. Yet he is different from even the highest idea that we can form of him.

Arrogance, pride, vanity—these are characteristics that especially an esotericist should above all set aside. Also, those esotericists who imagine that they have already set aside arrogance, pride, and so forth, must know that these traits are always present in a subtle way. The thought alone that one has already set aside these traits, that one has advanced far in one's development, contains a certain vanity that is much worse than the vanity of external life because it is strengthened and is related to higher spiritual things.†

We are living now in a special time, an extremely important time. It is the time for preparing for Christ, who will become visible, will appear in the etheric realm. To be blessed by him, to see him there, we must prepare ourselves. Those who do not have the good fortune to come across theosophy now, will not be able to experience this event.

We have come into being through higher spiritual forces, as we have heard throughout these days. We have descended from the divine womb. We have a divine origin. Thus, out of this knowledge we can place before our souls the Rosicrucian saying: *Ex Deo nascimur*—out of God we are born. But another statement should stand right next to it, one that makes us feel much smaller, so that we surrender and lose ourselves; we devote ourselves to Christ. And when this mood properly lives in our soul, then we can add *In Christo morimur* to *Ex Deo nascimur*. And as a further view of how we can consciously develop the spirit, the Holy Spirit within us, the Rosicrucian verse gives us the sentence that follows the first two sentences: *Per Spiritum Sanctum reviviscimus*—in the Holy Spirit we will live again, and again. And when we use this Rosicrucian verse as the fundamental mood of our meditations, then we will be taking it into ourselves with complete understanding and with a holy feeling. This is the verse that reads:

In the spirit lay the seed of my body...

* * *

RECORD B

An esotericist should learn to be awake and to pray; to be awake to all deleterious influences that want to intervene when an independent transformation of one's bodies is undertaken, and one prepares oneself to become an independent coworker with creative spirits. Here many powers and beings approach us that want to tear us away from this undertaking. We easily fall prey to illusions. An occult saying against all illusions: All paths to the spiritual world go through the heart. The heart is the center of spiritual movement. The brain is the center of intellectual movement. During meditation we can feel how, from every point of the outer physical body, forces are streaming toward a center. This is the heart. ☉ In their further course, these lines continue in the opposite direction, past the border of the skin and into the spiritual world. That is a feeling for Christ in us. At the same time, this is a sign that no illusion is present (also the gesture ♋).† From the constellation of the lion, ♌, forces flow toward the heart. Forces from the sun also stream toward the heart. The spirits of fire also work upon the heart. All three are often used as symbols for the heart. Lion, sun, flames. Prayer: we unite ourselves in the right way with our heart forces. Waking: esotericists should be clear that when they approach meditation with impure thoughts and feelings, they are doing a great injustice not only to themselves, not only to their fellow human beings, but also to lofty spiritual beings. They thereby pollute the spiritual spheres. And the forces that must be marshaled in order to remove this impurity are withdrawn from humanity's progress. One can perform one's meditation with relatively strong concentration, and yet, in doing so, be unholy within. This execution of meditation is ultimately a matter of will.

Of course, the will should be strengthened; but in doing so, the entire inner life must also be sanctified, so that only sacred and lofty content lives in our souls during meditation. And just as one should enter into meditation with pure thoughts and feelings, so should one also enter into sleep. Thoughts of arrogance and vanity pollute the spiritual world during sleep. We should fall asleep with thoughts of reverence and gratitude for spiritual beings. Esotericists differ from exotericists through this: that God lives in them consciously, that they really allow the power of God to become active within them—not the just ideas that they have about God. They can harm themselves precisely through these ideas when they later enter the spiritual world. For example, they want to find Christ there in the same form they thought of him on earth, and therefore they do not recognize the true Christ, for he is different from even the highest idea that we can form of him.

Arrogance, pride, vanity are characteristics that an esotericist should especially, above all, set aside. Even when one thinks that one has set them aside, these traits are still present, and in an even more subtle way. Even in the thought that one has already set aside these traits because one has already advanced so far, there lies a certain vanity, which is worse than the vanity of external life because it is strengthened by the fact that it is related to higher spiritual things. An esotericist must learn to be awake and to pray in the right sense.

* * *

RECORD C

Prayer to the spirit of Friday. This is especially effective.

> *Great all-encompassing spirit,*
> *In your life I live with the life of the earth...*

After awakening in the morning we should strive, as soon as possible, to immerse ourselves again in the spiritual world with our meditations. At night before going to sleep we should prepare ourselves for the fact that we are entering the spiritual world, but not with prayers having any kind of egotistical wishes, such as for a blessed end or anything like that.

We should bring nothing impure into the etheric world. Of course, through the intensity of our will we can penetrate into this world even when impure, but then our experience is totally worthless. It is a great advantage to enter into an esoteric life in this present time. This is more beneficial than in any other incarnation. In twenty years, many will experience the Christ event in the etheric; and for this reason we must strive with the greatest seriousness and with the greatest intensity to experience it purely, for many people experience only their own picture of Christ.

Additional Record

Bern, September 10, 1910. Under this date there is a record of an esoteric lesson in Bern the text of which is of such questionable quality that it is included here only for the sake of completeness:

"The essence of memory is this, that we can call up again through the power of our own 'I,' as a picture within, what we perceived through the instrument of the physical body, so that we do not need the physical body; but rather, out of the ocean of the etheric body, we create a picture of what we had previously perceived through the physical body. The picture that is newly awakened to an idea within us is formed from the ocean of the etheric. When we perceive with our external instruments, they are used up. Exhaustion sets in. In order to eliminate this exhaustion, human beings must experience the sleeping state in the night; when they are out there in the cosmos, they draw in divine-spiritual forces and behold how these forces work on the physical body to restore it. There humans work with the divine-spiritual beings who once created them. There they experience the *Ex Deo nascimur*. However, the etheric body is left without this restoration. In order to fill it with strength, we must do something else. We must ourselves create something within it. Just as the eye has been created through light and without light would not be an eye (but here we are talking about the physical body, upon which physical sunlight has worked), so there is a spiritual light that creates the spiritual eye. The spiritual eye is created from this power of light. We must allow this power to work upon us. It creates our spiritual organs, and this power of light also equips us with renewed forces for the etheric body. And we can receive these forces only when we carry out with our souls what lies in the words, *In Christo morimur*. Again and again, we must repeat this anew, conscious of the fact that only in steady and patient repetition, which corresponds to the principle of the etheric body, can we succeed in having the spiritual light experience. We die in Christ, whom we find in the depths of our bodily nature, just as we sleep into the cosmos at night. We unite ourselves with him. It is his strength that strengthens us in the etheric body. His power of light and warmth creates for us the organs with which we are permitted to experience and to perceive him. Here we experience *Per Spiritum Sanctum reviviscimus*."

Esoteric Lesson

BERLIN, NOVEMBER 4, 1910

Record A: Notes from Günther Wagner; Record B: Anonymous manuscript (Vreede collection); Record C: Manuscript from Camilla Wandrey; Record D: Notes from the collection of Elisabeth Vreede; Record E: Notes from Margareta Morgenstern; Record F: Manuscript from Alice Kinkel; Record G: Manuscript from Nelly Lichtenberg.

RECORD A

Learning to walk, to speak, and to understand.

All who have already heard an esoteric lesson know that what is said here is said not only from me; we want to ask for the aid of the spirit of the day. The verse for Friday follows.

When we observe life as it unfolds between birth and death, we must consider from an esoteric standpoint that it exists so that we can learn during this span of time; learn for our esoteric path. Now when we survey this physical life, we see that we bring the preconditions, the organs, needed for all that we are able to do in life; however, there are three exceptions. These three things we must first learn here in physical life. If an impression of color enters our eyes, then we are able to see it soon after birth; we do not first need to learn it. The ability is simply present; it is the same with hearing, and so forth. There are only three things we must learn: that is walking, speaking, and understanding; that is, forming concepts. In order to walk we must first of all, mainly, learn to stand. Before we can do that we simply fall over; we do not yet have a feeling for balance. We must first learn to feel our way into three-dimensional space. So too, we must learn to speak and to understand.

If we have learned to walk in the first year of life, then we can go on our way. If we have learned to understand, then we can give life to truth; we can bring life through the word. In our first three years of life we learn to walk, speak, and think. We find these three years of life symbolically in Christ's three years on earth. Everything that has come to us from Christ, we must find again as a foundation in the first three years of our life.

Everything esoteric students need for their esoteric life is given to them in the esoteric lessons. They receive answers to all their questions through what is given them in the meditative exercises; they must only listen properly, and apply everything properly. What is given to us as meditation must acquire life. Thus the verse:

In pure rays of light...

We should allow these lines not only to pass by in thoughts; they also should acquire life in us. We should give ourselves entirely to the content of the meditation, and forget everything that is around us in the physical world, our personal interests, and so forth. As a reward for the fact that we have given up our physical life, so to speak, that we have sacrificed it for the time of meditation, after the first two lines,

*in pure rays of light
shines the divinity of the world,*

a tone will sound forth within us, which will last as long as our karma prescribes. This is a tone that does not sound within us, but rather sounds forth to us from outside of us. Nothing more will be said about this here; one must experience and understand it oneself. And while this sound, this holy word, this unspeakable name sounds forth, the student should take a vow, which can already be taken beforehand; but it must be taken in this moment as well. The vow that the student says to him or herself is this: "Every other sound that reaches my ear, if it is not based in the physical world, every other sound aside from this holy word, I will consider to be a work of Ahriman."

This is a withdrawal, a turning away from what is around the student, which produces a feeling of cold within the student; a feeling of indifference and apathy takes hold of the student who feels him or herself to be left alone in an incredible frost. The student must bring love to this feeling of frost that is created by pure thought.

And when we have heard this sound, we receive with it the direction of "the East." The sound comes from the East. We can orient ourselves in the spirit; we no longer fall over like a child that has not yet learned how to stand and walk. We can now stand and walk in the spirit.

And if students allow the third and fourth lines to live within them,

In pure love to all beings
Rays the godliness of my soul

then they will feel warmth; radiant, living warmth. Only those experiences that come to them during this feeling of warmth have genuine value as truth; everything else is the work of Lucifer. And if the students have brought the last three lines,

I rest in the divinity of the world
I will find myself
In the divinity of the world

to life within them, then they will grasp the truth.

Thus students have achieved the way in the first two lines; the truth in the last three lines; and then life, spiritual life, flows to them from the middle two lines.

Tomorrow we will speak more about this.

There is something that students must develop within. Much is said concerning this in outer life, and yet it does not at all find expression; the depths of it are not even recognized or even suspected. Love of our fellow human beings is spoken of so much, and yet there is nothing corresponding to this feeling in what people think it is in outer life. Esoteric students should begin to say to themselves in all humility, I know nothing about love of humanity. We love people for various reasons, but none of those reasons are the right ones. We should love people because they are human beings. Christ gave us the right example for this.

In the spirit lay the seed of my body...

Record B

Let us summarize in a few words the life of human beings from birth to death, and review all that human beings must themselves develop during life, as well as what they bring with them already developed. There are three things that human beings do not bring with them when they enter the world, things that they must acquire in the course of their lives. Newborn human beings bring organs with them already finished: their eyes, for example, through which they perceive their surroundings, their ears, and so forth. However, the three things that they must develop themselves are walking, speaking, and thinking.

Why can we not yet walk when we are born? Because we cannot yet find our balance; we must first seek it and establish ourselves in a relationship to surrounding nature. Then for a long time we sway back and forth, seeking a footing that cannot be found so quickly. As soon as we have found it, we can stand and also find our way alone.

The second thing that we must acquire for ourselves is understanding, which leads to thinking, and through thinking, we come to the truth. The third is language, through which we send out into the world our thoughts and feelings, our inner life.

If we apply this picture, as a symbol, to the wonderfully beautiful words that Christ spoke to his disciples out of esoteric wisdom—"I am the way, the truth, and the life"—we will find that these words relate to the esoteric development of the human being.

When we begin our meditating it is the same for us as for a child, who must first learn to walk. We sway back and forth; we err to the right, then to the left with our thoughts, until we finally have found our "footing," the necessary serenity and collectedness that gives us balance, which is Christ himself. He wants to be our leader, and we should seek our foundation in him, we should find our inner balance through him so that we can walk in his path.

In ancient, pre-Christian times, students needed a guru who would helpfully stand by their side during meditation. Since Christ has walked on the earth, he has left his power behind in the atmosphere of the earth, so that we can fill ourselves with it when we open ourselves to it.

Furthermore, our meditation should become pure thinking, so the truth can become life through the words that we send forth to our fellow human beings.

Once we have found our way after a longer time of practice, without swaying to the right or the left we will come to an inner experience when we immerse ourselves in the first lines of our morning meditation:

In pure rays of light
Shines the divinity of the world.

We will feel this experience as something that cannot be expressed in words. A stream of warmth, a light from the East, will flow through us, and within us a tone will sound forth that allows us to feel that we are connected with the light of God.

When we ascend further in our development, a new experience again approaches us when we meditate the next two lines:

In the pure love of all beings
Rays the godliness of my soul.

Now we perceive a name out of the light and sound that comes to us from the East. We are not able to speak this name that thrills the soul and causes us to feel, "That is God's name"! At the same time a stream of indescribable cold will blow through us, combined with a feeling of abandonment and loneliness. This name will flood through our inner being, and we will know that He is this name. This experience will lead us to knowledge of the truth; and we will have arrived at a place where the spiritual world opens to us, where we can know whether what we see is truth or illusion. Everything we think we have heard in terms of sounds, knocking, or other phenomena from the physical world before this experience, none of that was the truth—we know that now. It was Ahriman or Lucifer doing tricks around us with their illusions. For this reason we should strictly turn away such experiences of sounds, and so forth, that come to us from the physical world.

For we know that we will not be able to experience true spiritual phenomena until we feel the warm stream that pours into our souls from the East, until we have lived through the freezing cold and the feeling of abandonment, until we have perceived the tone that causes the name of God to sound forth within us.

Let us once more consider the words:

In pure love of all beings
Rays the godliness of my soul.

The Christian Church chose this "practice of pure love" as its favorite saying. To be sure, this saying is used a lot by Christians; however, seldom are actions guided by it. Furthermore, it is also not easy when we consider all the consequences. Let us consider for a moment what it means to love all human beings: to bestow love without expectation of love in return, without recognition, without demand for reward—for our ideal should be that we love a human being because he or she is a human being! How far must we be in our development in order to be capable of such love! Can we educate ourselves to this selflessness that we love all others as we love ourselves by means of commandments and dogmas of the church or through the coercion of a moral law? Is it not much more fruitful for our souls if we bring this lofty virtue to blossom within us without any coercion whatsoever?

In practicing this teaching of Christ, a Hindu, a Muslim, a Parsi, a Catholic, a Protestant, a Jew—indeed, even a heretic—could be a true Christian without even belonging to the Christian Church.

And we also learn in our meditations that within them lies hidden the way that Christ showed us and that he himself is: "I am the way, the truth, and the life."

* * *

RECORD C

Esoteric students must learn to regard the course of their lives in the physical world in such a way that they *learn* during the span of time between birth and death; *learn* in order to find their esoteric path, so that they do not lose their connection with the world of their origin, the spiritual world. With the exception of three things that we must first learn here in our physical life, when we survey this physical life, we see that there is much we are able to do for which we have already brought the prerequisites, the organs. Soon after birth we are able to see, we do not need to learn that; and so it is with tasting, smelling, and hearing. These capacities are already present, even if we learn only later how to consciously make use of them. However, there are three things that we must learn after birth. They are walking, speaking, and understanding.

In the esoteric sense, learning to walk means being able to raise oneself upright through the power of the "I" that lives within and is increasingly strengthening itself. It means being able to maintain oneself upright in space with respect to the spiritual forces that permeate one; and learning to find one's way through them. Where to? Toward the [spiritual] East—which students learn of, at a certain step in their development.

When students have found this path, then in absolute quiet and loneliness over against the outer world, they must listen for what sounds toward them from the East. This is an experience that every student has sooner or later, according to when one's karma allows it. Students hear sounding forth from the East the "unspeakable word"; the name of God that "speaks itself." This sounds into the calm and loneliness of the student. And in the soul of the student this "word" becomes a power in the soul, which is enkindled to awaken in the student, in the depths of soul, something that is asleep. The creative powers of existence awaken in him or her.

The second step is: the student learns to speak. In the esoteric sense, speaking is a sounding forth of what was in the soul before as life, and now sounds outward. In the midst of these two experiences (hearing the name of God from without, from the spiritual East, and speaking within oneself), exactly in the middle, only in meditation, the student can receive revelations from the spiritual world.

This sounding into the soul (as a spiritual sound it is audible to physical ears, and according to a student's karma, it will remain a longer or shorter time); this holy word, this unspeakable name of God, cannot be said by the teacher. Every student must take hold of it and experience it for him- or herself. And while this sound is sounding forth, students must take a vow, which they could have taken earlier, but must take now. They must say to themselves: every other sound that reaches my ear (if it is spiritual; that is, not founded in the physical world), I will regard as a work of Ahriman. When students have had this experience, then descending into their own being, they can feel new life. Then they can know the truth of the spiritual world through their own experience. The real, the true path of an esoteric student proceeds only in this way. Everything else is deceiving illusions from Ahriman, which seek to reach students before they have perceived the spiritual sound, and deceiving illusions from Lucifer, which come before students have received the life rising in their souls.

But this spiritual sound that students perceive from the spiritual East of their souls, which enkindles a new light, the spiritual sunlight, within them, does not work as the external sunlight works when it enkindles light in the outer world and sends warmth streaming through it. The spiritual sound of the sun works in such a way that it creates an icy coldness in the soul of the students. They feel themselves to be lonely, as if entirely separate; hovering entirely alone in empty space that is filled only with thoughts. This must be so, and students must go through it. When they have struggled through this, then they will feel an entirely new inner warmth rising out of the depths of their souls. This is the warmth of Christ's love. And in the midst of cold streaming in from without, and warmth rising from within, there revelations from the spiritual world occur.

There the students find the truth. Only there alone. And they find it when they say to themselves, "Everything that I receive, I receive by going through the phases of development *spiritually*, just as I went through them physically in the first three years of my life as a child. Thus as a student, I must first learn to raise myself upright inwardly, spiritually, through the strength of my 'I.' Then I must learn to go to the East in my soul; then I must learn to speak (that means to form concepts), in order finally to find the truth." Only after Christ had been on the earth and the Mystery of Golgotha had taken place, only then could students of the spirit learn to follow such a path; only after Christ had set an example by living through these mysteries of soul evolution, which are expressed in the words, "I am the way, the truth, and the life."

Students must live through the stages of Christ's life by means of their own strength. This verse awakens life:

> *In pure rays of sunlight*
> *Shines the divinity of the world.*

We must learn to devote ourselves entirely to such meditative content in our souls. Then we will see how the content of this esoteric lesson is contained within it. However, if it is really to awaken life in our souls, we must forget everything that is present in physical life as our personal interest during the time of our devotion to our meditation. If we are inwardly entirely empty, entirely clear, entirely filled with a sacred mood, then the spiritual light that shines from without shines forth for us:

> *In pure rays of light*
> *Shines the divinity of the world.*

And now we allow the third and fourth lines to become active in us:

> *In pure love of all beings*
> *Rays the godliness of my soul.*

We will feel warmth—pure, radiant warmth. Only what comes to us during this feeling of warmth, in terms of experiences, really has value as truth. Everything else, perhaps a feeling of overwhelming floating in joy, is the work of Lucifer.

However, if we have brought these three lines,

> *I rest in the divinity of the world;*
> *I will find myself*
> *In the divinity of the world.*

fully into our conscious life; then indeed, we will certainly grasp the truth.

In this way we have achieved "the way" in the first two lines, and "the truth" in the last three lines. "Life" is opened for us in the middle two lines. And this, my dear sisters and brothers, is the most difficult to achieve. How much is spoken in outer life about human love. How little is done; for this is the most difficult of Christ's words to fulfill. Love your neighbor as yourself; develop pure love of human beings. Those who love a human being because he or she is a human being—only those who do this—are in truth Christians, regardless of what creed or which religion they may belong to.

Thus, in a genuine Rosicrucian training, we learn the path to enter the spiritual world under the guidance of Christ, looking toward him. We learn how to follow his earthly path independently in our esoteric training. Everything esoteric students need for their esoteric life is given to them in the esoteric lessons. They are given these lessons as an answer to all of their questions, whether expressed, or latent in their souls. They must only listen properly and properly apply everything so that it holds sway in their soul-awakening and maintaining life—and they will walk the path of esoteric training in such a way that their inner independence is completely untouched.

Such a Rosicrucian path is possible now, only since Christ has dwelt on earth. In earlier times, students had to take every step under the leadership and guidance of a guru. Looking toward Christ with a truly esoteric understanding of his words, as it was given to you today, we learn, without any interference in our independence, to find the path to the great universal guru—the Christ—while fully maintaining the independent self and while bearing in mind the guiding words: "I am the way, the truth, and the life."

Wisdom lives in the light (thought).
Wisdom shines in the light (feeling).
The Wisdom of the world shines in the light (will).

* * *

Record D

There are three essential powers that we must acquire after birth. They are walking, speaking, and understanding. Seen superficially, they are merely the natural result of our growth, but for an esotericist they have a very profound inner significance. In learning to walk we learn to find our balance within the three dimensions of the physical world; we are led to the truth through thinking; and speech gives life to the truth. Esoterically speaking, one could say learning to walk is learning to know "the way." Thinking is learning to know "the truth." Speaking is learning to know "life." In this regard, the first three years of life are the most important, for they correspond to what Christ spoke when he said, "I am the way, the truth, and the life."

If we want to understand the words of Christ, or even his parables, we must return to the first three years of the child. These years reflect the last three years of the life of Jesus of Nazareth, when Christ walked on the earth. We must return to our childhood in order to understand what Christ said.

In the meditation given to the student,

> *In pure rays of light*
> *Shines the divinity of the world...*

(which can be continued day after day for years before results are noticed), according to when our karma allows it, a moment will one day occur during which we are swimming in the light without distinguishing anything specific, entirely filled with serene calmness. Then a sound will be revealed to us in the space that we feel surrounds us on all sides, a sound that is unlike anything that can sound in the outer world. But this sound will fill the space and announce to us the unspeakable name of God. We will know then in that moment that we are hearing the unspeakable name, and with this experience something highly significant will happen. When we hear this sound, we will know that we have come into contact with something that we will feel spiritually as "the East."

When students have heard this sound, they vow to themselves that they will regard all other sounds and tones that they can experience, as impure compared to this sound. Every other tone or sound that we hear in meditation we must reject, and regard as an illusion what Ahriman wants to impose upon us as the truth. Also, the mysterious knocking that one can sometimes hear is made by Ahriman, and shows the effects that he tries to exert upon us. Those who pay any attention at all to such sounds or knocking, and do not exclusively hold on to the sound previously described, endanger their entire esoteric training. Something like this can hinder any progress for years.

While this sound is ringing within us, we feel ourselves surrounded by light that fills space. And in this light a second feeling arises within us, a feeling of icy cold. We feel ourselves totally alone in this cold light as if one existed all alone in that space.

When the meditator then immerses him or her self in the next lines of the meditation,

> *In pure love to all beings*
> *Rays the godliness of my soul,*

then the icy cold is transformed into a warmth that streams in from all sides, a warmth that is pure love from spiritual spheres, love that is the true life.

> *I rest in the divinity of the world.*
> *I will find myself*
> *In the divinity of the world.*

In these lines lies hidden the entire mystery of our unity with Christ.

In the course of the years we have looked at the Christ event ever more closely as a historical event in the course of humanity's evolution. Here, in this meditation we find Christ as our highest leader, our highest guru, who will lead us directly when we turn to him. In pre-Christian times, human beings needed a guru on the earthly plane. In order to advance they had to adhere strictly to the guru, to obey him. Since Christ has been on the earth, he has become the guru for all human beings. In an esoteric sense, everyone can be a Christian: a Hindu, a Muslim, a Catholic, a Protestant, a Jew, as well as a heretic, for it is "Christ in us" who can be found by all.

For the first time we become aware what love is, in this warmth streaming toward us. "Universal love of humanity" has become a trivial expression in recent time. People do not even suspect what it is, much less understand it.

If esotericists want to catch a reflection of this love, then they must feel themselves encompassed by this warmth, and at the same time say to themselves, "I know nothing yet of universal love of humanity; I must first begin to learn it."

* * *

Record E

For a student, nothing further is necessary than to understand what the exercises are all about. There are three things, above all, that are necessary when a human being enters the physical world. He or she must learn to walk, speak, and understand (think). We will take hold of our task here and be able to fulfill it, only if we pause to reflect on what Christ taught in the last three years of his life. He taught what was most important to him when he said, "I am the way, the truth, and the life."

The way is connected with walking; the truth is connected with learning to understand; and the life, with speaking. Thus, in the spiritual life on a higher level, we must learn to do what a child learns to do in the first three years: walk, speak, and understand.

When we learn to walk we are concerned with three directions in space. This is also the case in learning to walk spiritually, in which certain directions must also be balanced. In doing so, our starting point is complete rest, calmness of soul, that is necessary, above all. Meditation must also end in such calmness, whereby we vow to ourselves that only what sounds forth to us as tone as the meditation ends will be recognized as truth. On the other hand, every kind of knocking, or other sounds that we hear, must be considered illusion until it has become something harmonious. Only sounds from the spiritual world that come to us in serene calmness after meditation are what is designated as the "unspeakable name of God." When hearing this "word" after meditation, we realize what is meant by the two lines of the meditation,

> *In pure rays of light*
> *Shines the divinity of the world,*

pointing to the spiritual East, which is intended here. With this knowledge of God, something else appears in us, to which we must pay careful attention. In the following words,

> *In pure love of all beings*
> *Rays the godliness of my soul,*

a feeling of minor coldness and loneliness will appear in us. Space becomes empty to us, and thoughts also disappear, until later a feeling of inner warmth appears in us. As a consequence of this experience, a liberation from egotism then appears. However, between the two moments characterized, lie the revelations from the spiritual world that are revealed out of the meditations. As reward for our efforts, Christ can be seen for moments.

* * *

RECORD F

"I am the way, the truth, and the life." I am the way; with this is connected a human being's learning to walk; the truth, learning to think; and the life. A human being's learning to speak is connected with the life. Walking makes it possible for us to be oriented in space; thinking makes it possible for us to grasp the truth; and speaking gives us the inner warmth that belongs with the coldness of thought.

Spiritual sound comes from "the East," and brings vision. The unspeakable name of God is the revelation from the entire world. The first three years of life of a human being on the physical plane teach the human being to walk, to speak, and to think. The child's first three years of life and Christ's three years of teaching on earth have spiritual connections, but are understandable only by this way of comparison.

Do I know what the universal love of humanity is? No, I do not yet know anything about it. The universal love of humanity is loving a human being because he or she is a human being. It is Christ in the man or woman whom one loves—the Christ. He is always present!

Only the sound that floods space during meditation, during the influence of pure thought, is effective; but the sound must come to the student from the spiritual world. The student must not listen to anything else.

* * *

Record G

There are three important things that every human being must learn: walking, speaking, understanding, which means forming concepts.

> Through walking we learn the way;
> through understanding we learn to know the truth;
> through speaking the truth acquires life;

so we can translate this into the words of Christ Jesus, "I am the way, the truth, and the life." Every human being must change and "become like a child"; that means learning these three things that a child accomplishes in the first three years of life.

During meditation when we are filled with the content of the meditation, after we have previously ordered ourselves to be completely serene and calm, we will perceive a voice in the quiet, and we will know that it comes from "the East," from where all things spiritual come. It will seem to us as if we were set free with the content of the meditation and are floating in the room. We learn how to walk, so to speak, how to orient ourselves in space. All other voices that we think we have heard from the spiritual world lead us astray. They are whisperings from Ahriman.

Then there are moments during meditation when everything appears to us to be cold and austere; we feel ourselves to be completely alone, and that we can rely on ourselves alone. These moments must occur, for now with the words,

In pure love to all beings...,

we feel how warmth of soul is poured through the body.

Between these two (the spiritual light from the East at the beginning and the feeling of warmth of soul, the life, at the conclusion) is the only time that a revelation from the spiritual worlds, the truth, can flow into us.

Only meditation that is permeated by Christ has value. There is an expression that has become trivial out in the world at large, the expression "universal love of humanity." One could say that only those who admit that they know nothing about it are beginning to understand it in its rudiments.

There is only one who has taught it in the truest sense: Christ Jesus himself.

Esoteric Lesson

BERLIN, NOVEMBER 5, 1910

Record A: Notes from Günther Wagner; Record B: Notes from the collection of Elisabeth Vreede; Record C: Source of manuscript unknown. Record D: Manuscript from Nelly Lichtenberg; Record E: Notes from Margareta Morgenstern; Record F: Manuscript from Camilla Wandrey.

RECORD A

Noah's Ark

As always also today we want to ask the spirit of the day for help with our work — Saturday verse.

Yesterday already we said that students hear a spiritual sound, a sound from "the East." If students now want to say that they know how the spirit sounds, that they have now heard their first spiritual sound, then they would find themselves in a major fatal error. This tone that a student hears is much more the last word from the physical world. Every tone that could somehow come forth from a larynx incarnated in flesh is not from the spiritual world.

First of all, the spiritual world is completely colorless, without light, soundless, and so forth. Everything we see in terms of color is not spiritual, but rather comes from within us, and, indeed, presents us with characteristics that we do not yet have, that we have yet to achieve. For example, when we see a red color this means that we do not yet have love within us; that we have still to develop it. If we see violet, then that wants to say that we must acquire devoted piety.

When we hear tones like earthly sounds, this is nothing spiritual; but rather something that originates within us. If someone has a desire to eat a certain food, for example, if someone begins to eat in a vegetarian manner but inwardly he still has a longing for meat—even if he is not aware of it—then this craving sounds in tones, in discordant tones. All these tones and sounds are only occult squawking ravens.

If a figure from earlier times appears to a student, and he or she wants to interpret it immediately, that is all wrong. We must be able to wait with our interpretations. We should not interpret in the present moment, but only later. If such an image appears before the soul, then it will vanish as soon as we approach it with thoughts. However, if it is a genuine picture it will appear to us again later and remain still in its true shape, and we will know what it signifies. But we must be able to wait, to wait and keep silent. Even as we ourselves should not approach our experiences with our own thoughts, even less should we speak about them. We should regard and treat our entire spiritual life as something holy. With all these experiences of sounds, colors, and so forth, we must say to ourselves that they come not from the spirit, but rather from within us—from our own "I," which is inundated by waves from the sea of our desires and passions, just as Noah's ark was surrounded by waves of the sea. And we must live with the conviction that none of these experiences and phenomena are spiritual. And in saying this very clearly and relentlessly to ourselves we must surrender the "I"; surrender the desires of the "I" for experiences and let them fly away as Noah let a dove fly away from the ark, which then never came back.

Then later, another esoteric experience comes to the student. When we have understood that there is nothing, nothing at all spiritual in those experiences of sound and color—when we have recognized with inner strength that the spiritual world is entirely empty for us—then we recognize that those experiences nevertheless have significance for us. The colors come to warn and advise us; they tell us what we do not yet have, what we still have to achieve. From the sounds, we learn that they present us with bodily cravings. And when the pictures that we calmly allowed, tell us their significance, then the soul is enriched by such experiences. This is like the second dove set loose, which returned with the olive branch, the symbol of peace.

However, the soul is not left entirely alone to its own devices on this difficult path of the esotericist. There is something that it can hold on to. The Rose Cross is something like this. We should let it have an effect on us. We should understand that the black of the cross represents our bodily nature, which is hardened and withered;

that we must allow the lower self, which identifies with this bodily nature, to become just as dark and dead as the wood of the cross is dead. Then the higher self, the spiritual "I," will work in us, just as the black of the cross is transformed into bright, radiant rays of light. In the same way, the red of the roses will be transformed from the color of the love that works within into green, the color of the life that works outward.

When we experience symbols, those that make us happy, that we experience joyfully, are not genuine or originating from the spiritual world; rather, it is only those symbols with which we experience sorrow. And we must carry them around with us until we have grasped their meaning. The spirit must be born in suffering out of those symbols.

And there is something else that we must understand; that is this: we cannot even be non-egotistical. We are never non-egotistical—never, never, never! And when we imagine that we have now done something that is entirely selfless, that is an error. We cannot act selflessly at all. It is the karma of the world that causes us to act egotistically. World karma is God!

And if we ever get so far that we act nobly and for the good, that is God in us who is good. When we become less selfish, we will observe, for example, that we no longer feel fear or shock. If next to us a sudden sound occurs, we will no longer shrink back as before. God, who causes us to act nobly and for the good, is our archetype. Our archetype created us to be what we are. And we ourselves must again become an image of our archetype.

When we have properly understood all of this, then we will understand in the right way the genuine esoteric Rosicrucian saying:

Ex Deo nascimur.
In — — — morimur.
Per Spiritum Sanctum reviviscimus.

What has been left out here is unspeakable for an esotericist. When we begin to speak this one line, then our feeling must go to that which is unspeakable. And only when our feeling returns can we continue to speak. Those who experience this inwardly with the proper feeling will also understand the other esoteric verse properly:

In the spirit lay the seed of my body...

* * *

Record B

What was said yesterday concerning the unspeakable word, which is heard in meditation and indicates the direction toward the East, we should not think of as something representing a sound having anything in common with human speech. That which we hear as a vowel, as articulated sound within it, is simply what we ourselves have laid into it. Nothing of all that is seen or heard in the spiritual world; no sound, no color has anything in common with the things of this world. If we see a red color, then the red color is something that belongs to us; and indeed it represents what we ourselves are not yet. Red in the spiritual world signifies love. Therefore, when we see red, it signifies that we have not yet developed love.

While meditating, we are lifting ourselves more or less consciously into the spiritual world as though we were standing on a high mountain and the waves of our passions are pounding around us and toward us, just as Noah's ark floated on the flood. These are the passions that are revealed as sounds, as voices, at the beginning. As esotericists we are obligated at the beginning of our development to reject all tones (sounds), to regard them as the squawking of ravens.

We must begin by regarding everything we see or hear as wrong. So also when, for example, we see individuals whom we know as they were in their previous incarnations. All of this students should pay no attention to and should release in such a way that it does not return. What we see in this way, after a long time (for it can last quite a while before a change occurs), will dissolve and be transformed into something else. What is then newly formed is what is true! If a red color appears, we must understand this as coming forth from ourselves. Only when the red color is dissolved as if in a cloud, and then becomes another color, is the last color to be seen as significant. This is the dove that returns to the ark with an olive branch; this is a revelation from the spiritual world that has something to tell us. But this too, should be understood as a symbol that we should learn to decipher. Again, a long time can pass before one is in a position to do this. Even when a symbol is shown to us we should not stand still with it, but rather, much more, direct it away from us.

We should consider colors and symbols only when they have already previously appeared to us for a while, so that it is more likely that our personal interest in them has disappeared and we can perhaps find their true significance. We must get used to the idea that we are entirely permeated by self-seeking, and that we carry this with us into the spiritual world. We must have the courage and the strength to permeate ourselves with the certainty that on the physical plane we can do nothing, absolutely nothing, without egotism contributing to our actions. We should undertake to vow to ourselves to always bear in mind that all that we do originates from egotistical motives. This could perhaps discourage us; but if one manages to do it for oneself, one will notice that one makes certain progress. For example, fear and shock, which we feel when suddenly hearing a sound, will fall away.

Only what we do in the name of another, in the name of the one within us, whom we could call our God, does not proceed from egotism. In order to feel this god within us, we must permeate ourselves with the consciousness that we are a reflection of the archetype, according to which this god created us, and that only slowly and gradually can this reflection be transformed into the archetype. The archetype is our true self, our true "I" that was formed as seed in old Saturn, and this is what approaches us when we utter our Rosicrucian verse. The Rose Cross is the symbol through which the way is shown to us to ascend into the spiritual world. If it is seen as it is in the spiritual world, then the black of the cross is seen as white—the counterpart of the reflection—and the red roses are transformed into a shining green color.

The Rosicrucian verse is exoteric as long as one speaks it complete; it is esoteric when it is spoken this way: *Ex Deo nascimur. In* — —

— *morimur. Per Spiritum Sanctum reviviscimus.* One must feel for oneself what a great difference lives in the soul when doing so.†

Record C

We are easily prone to misunderstanding if we think that the sound that comes to us from the spiritual East and signifies the name of God proclaims itself in articulated sounds and tones such as we perceive in the physical world. It is an entirely different kind of sound, another kind of tone that has absolutely nothing in common, not even the least similarity to anything in the physical world. For this reason then, students must be incredibly careful, using their power of discernment, especially with their self-knowledge. It is a fact that when someone begins to perceive colors, forms, sounds, or even words from the spiritual world, these actually come from the spiritual world in the least number of cases. Mostly they come from the physical world; that is, they come from the individual him- or herself, often simply because the individual is inspired by a burning wish to experience something in the spiritual world. Then, phenomena, sounds, and so forth, appear from our own world. But in a certain way, these phenomena are nevertheless based on truth (and this must certainly be born in mind), inasmuch as they take part in our thoughts and in the character of a human being. What is expressed in colors and so forth, therefore, is not (as a rule) from the spiritual world; rather, it is often produced by some bodily malaise, or it could also be caused by the following. If we have become vegetarian, but have not yet lost the desire for eating meat, then this desire will torture us on the astral plane where we abide at night, and this malaise makes itself perceptible through sounds or words that we then think we are hearing as sounds from the spiritual world. This is what is known in esotericism as "squawking ravens."

Or let us assume that we see a red color (the red color signifies spiritual love); it is placed before our eyes spiritually because it is precisely the trait we are lacking. It is placed before our souls as a challenge. Many complain that they cannot hold on to the colors; but this is not necessary. The colors must disappear like a dove, and when they later return they will appear entirely different. The color red will be transformed before our eyes into green, blue, or yellow. That is the sign that it is based on a spiritual phenomenon and that we are at the stage where we are taught in symbols, and a view of the spiritual world is granted us.

At the beginning we will not understand the symbols; we must allow them to sink down into our memory, and gradually it will become clear to us in our meditations what is supposed to be taught to us and said to us by the symbol.

As students develop further, it is granted to them to read in the Akashic Chronicle. However, before they reach this stage they must have worked on themselves a great deal. Above all, they must recognize that all their actions on earth are based on self-seeking; that even in their ostensibly "selfless" deeds of love, self-seeking secretly lies hidden. As long as human beings live on earth they will not be able to entirely overcome self-seeking.

The Masters of Wisdom give us many things for our meditations. One of the most effective of these is the one concerning the Rose Cross.

We are to think of the black cross as the dying away of human passions, and see in the red roses a symbol of the purified human being who has shed the lower elements. If we transform the black cross into a white one in our meditation, then this symbolizes for us the human being ascending spiritually. All egotism is then extinguished. The red roses are meditatively transformed into green ones, and devotion to the divine awakens within us. The veil before our eyes is torn away, and we will see into the spiritual world consciously.

* * *

Record D

Referring to what was said the day before, the doctor said: We should not think that our visions, and so forth, are correct and of value, until we have heard the "unspeakable word," which is not a word in human sounds; it is altogether not a tone or vowel sound like any earthly tones or vowel sounds. Everything that might manifest to us like that would come from ourselves (Lucifer and Ahriman bring deception). And the sounds, for example, sounds of knocking and our interpretation of them, would have to be characterized with the expression "squawking of ravens"; and talking about those kinds of experiences would also be nothing more than the squawking of ravens. Only when we have perceived the "word" would we arrive at an understanding of what the expressions, "East, wise masters of the East," signify. If the objection were raised, "Yes, how do I know that I really have knowledge in colors, for example?" Then here the indicator would be that these pictures of color would have to change; so too, forms or shapes, which, if they do *not* change, signify nothing. If we have such pictures then we should keep quiet about them and try to correctly interpret them. That is like a dove that we send out and that never returns, so to speak. Neither should we become sad or impatient if, after we have once had a vision, none occur again for a long, long time. It is necessary to wait, to wait patiently. Example of an interpretation: if we see red, that does not mean love or that we have love; but rather, exactly that we do not have it, that we should acquire it. So too, with violet, where devoted piety is lacking. If we have found the correct interpretation, then it is like a dove that returns with an olive branch in its beak. The same is true with forms, symbols, and shapes. It is above all important for us to have in our consciousness the insight that we are egotistical, and never, never, never should we say: "I am doing this, or I feel this, entirely without egotism"; for egotism belongs to the karma of the world, and for the time being we cannot get free of it. But we should acquire the insight that this is the case, as a weapon against Ahriman.

Every human being is created from an archetype of him or herself, and is only a reflection of this archetype. All that we have been permitted to do in the world in terms of the good, the beautiful, and the noble, this we did not do ourselves but rather we must thank our archetype.

When we have developed this knowledge in ourselves, it is like a third dove that climbs higher but constantly returns to us, and in this way connects us with our archetype, which is contained in Christ. If this knowledge has fully come to life within us then we capitulate before Christ, and die in him. Exoterically we speak the words: *E. D. N.—I. C. M.—P.S.S.R.* Esoterically, they are not to be written down.

* * *

RECORD E

The word from the East we must take up in the right way. Above all we must be careful with inspiration, to distinguish between truth and deception. Everything that we hear from the spiritual world that is spoken with the character of something spoken by a larynx (that is, appears as a vowel sound), does not in truth originate from the spiritual world. There can be no characteristics of any earthly sound. For this reason the "word" from the spiritual world flows not as human language. Everything with a vowel sound character must disappear. As soon as something is present with the character of a vowel sound, one must say to oneself: this is a temptation to acknowledge voices other than those from the spiritual world and to follow them! — But the spirit never speaks to me with earthly sounds.

With time we will experience that the soul is changed by meditation; and what we experience because of this change can be shown to us with a certain sound. But neither should we consider this to be a true inspiration; it is nothing more than the occult squawking of ravens, of our wishes and desires reflecting the internal aspects of our physical body. This occult squawking of ravens is overcome when I send the ravens away.

Therefore, with the first messages that we receive, we must always say that is only our internal bodily nature that is so reflected. These deceptive images are indeed a danger; nevertheless, we should not allow ourselves to be discouraged because of them and say, "Now I have been at work for five years or more and still haven't experienced anything positive!" We must rather continue our attempts again and again, until we have arrived at a positive result.

Human beings clothe their experiences in the physical world in forms, colors, tones, and so forth. However, the spiritual world does not express itself in colors, forms, and sounds in the physical sense.

For this reason human beings must undergo an "inversion" of the self in order to be able to see in higher worlds; and they need inner strength for this. Indeed, we must learn to recognize that, to begin with, we ourselves create the colors and forms (imaginative pictures). We must confess this boldly, courageously. The voices we think we hear are usually only an expression of unpleasant moods in the body; this is much more the case with those who eat meat.

However, the solid faith must continue to exist in me that sooner or later colors and sounds will appear that are not merely the expression of an unpleasant sensation in my body, but really do originate in the spiritual world. The dove of our own spirit is no longer allowed to return to us, when it has once flown away!

We must learn to interpret the symbolic language that sounds to us from the spiritual world. Then the dove of our spirit no longer returns empty-handed, but rather with an olive branch. We must try to understand spiritual experiences in the language of pictures. The first symbols that appear to us should be a summons for us to acquire this capacity. If, for example, the color red, the color of love, appears to me, then I should say to myself in all humility: "You don't have it!" Violet is the color of devoted piety; it tells us that we should have patience, and we should be able to wait. One day when these colors are transformed into their complementary colors, then we can say to ourselves that we have taken a step forward and cleansed ourselves of egotism. The training guides the students and tells them what is important for recognizing symbolically the expression for the first impressions from the spiritual world. Only when we do everything in the name of God are we feeling rightly. Thus human beings must learn to regard themselves as an image, as an archetype of God. The threefold Rosicrucian verse tells us that.

* * *

Record F

Students should be as distrustful as possible of their esoteric experiences—above all, those characterized by a sound. Even when they want to believe that they are experiencing the sound of the unspeakable name of God, at a time when they have found the direction toward spiritual East; when they want to believe that it is spiritual truth when a sound comes to them that reminds them of a physical sound—they are deluded. For this "spiritual" sound that they hear is like a last residue from the physical world and at the same time like a first something from a higher plane, something that comes to one from the other side of the threshold in order to mediate a connection with higher worlds. Having the character of earthly sound signifies something from the physical plane. Vowel sounds sound forth only here, not there! Genuinely spiritual hearing is something entirely different, something that has nothing at all of a characteristically earthly sound. It does not come from a larynx incarnated in flesh.

Now when students are raised up in their "ark" on the "mountain," they feel themselves encircled by the "waves of the sea"; that is, their own sea, their own astrality, encircled by all that still lives in their drives, lusts, desires, and so forth. They look upon them; they surge around them like waves. They must see through them with understanding; they must know that what is sounding toward them there, or rather what appears to be sounding toward them from the spiritual world, is nothing more than the reflection of their own lusts and desires. To begin with, they experience a reflection of their own lower being. The reflection of their own thoughts is shown to them in colors and in light (Lucifer is at work in this), not their higher self. Sounds are reflections of something living in the physical body, as a craving that longs for satisfaction. For example, someone who lives as a vegetarian merely because of his or her decision rather than for spiritual reasons that rise up within, who perhaps still has a desire for meat and suppresses it, can experience how this desire sounds like a tone *apparently* from spiritual worlds. Here, for example, a student can see red, and must learn to say, this shows me that I lack something; I still do not have true love in myself. Red, the color of love, summons me to develop warm love for human beings. And if a floating light violet color appears, the student must say, this is merely a sign that I have to develop devoted piety. Or if an event or a personality appears that gives us instruction concerning previous incarnations, this tells us nothing about earlier incarnations, but rather that we are not yet mature enough to look into our earlier incarnations—that is, to look into the Akashic Chronicle. A higher development is required for this.

For this reason one must be as distrustful as possible. One is hearing, as is said in occultism, only the "squawking of ravens" from one's lower self, when one is on this mountain, surrounded by the waves of one's own astral sea. Then one gradually learns to distinguish. But one is still exposed to many deceptions.

Only when one has learned to say to oneself with complete resolve that all of this is nothing more than the product of one's lower self—not really true experiences of the spiritual world, which are nevertheless experienced at first, as they come toward the student—then one can gradually approach the truth, which can be achieved only by overcoming this phase of esoteric development. Then one sends the "ravens" away with complete resolve. Sending the ravens away means giving up one's everyday "I" that is bound to the world of the senses—and it must be so bound—giving up all one's desire for content that is connected with one's experiences. It means becoming entirely quiet, entirely empty, entirely without wishes within. If we have achieved this, then we understand that those experiences that still come to us from the physical world still have value; but the value is for us alone. Then, for example, colors tell us that they are advisors; warning us, telling us what we do not yet have, what we still have to achieve. And from the sounds, we recognize bodily desires. Then we calmly allow these experiences to work in our souls with their true significance.

Now through the inner calm and quiet in the souls, we have come far enough to send out the first dove. It does not return. And that is good. We wait. Then we send out the second. It returns with an "olive branch," the symbol of peace—this means having balance within oneself. What is this dove?

When the color-form is transformed so that its complementary color arises; when, for example, the color red "changes" and becomes violet, then this violet is really something coming to us from the spiritual world. This is the dove that brings a real message from the spiritual world. Students must experience something like a turning around of their own "I" before they can have this experience. And now students themselves must give form and shape to everything that comes to them from the spiritual world.

There is something that can give us a support on this difficult path, which is so full of self-denial: the Rose Cross we should carry in our souls!

A recognizing mark of what the spiritual world gives us is that everything that appears as a symbol is not immediately understood by students. They must allow these symbols to work on their souls for days, often for weeks, in silence filled with self-denial. They must do this with total peace and calm in their souls; without desires, without wishes. Then at a certain moment one turns around, so to speak, and suddenly understands what the symbol wanted to say to one. We let it work long enough in the soul as a force, and we are silent and wait. Patience—endurance—silence oneself! The esoteric equipment of a student should be this: that the student's soul lives in trust that it will be given what it needs; in the peaceful calm of the soul the confidence lives that the student will receive, at the right time, the right instruction from the teacher.

The student must say to him or herself again and again: I will not be able to be a participant in the spiritual world until I have learned to say to myself that I am full of egotism, and I cannot be anything else here in the physical world. However, the part of me that lives here in the physical world is only a picture, a form, a reflection of my archetype. This form, this picture, is entirely permeated by egotism. And it is the karma of the world that permeates us in our course of evolution through the incarnations. However, the karma of the world is God. God also lives in us. And when we advance to the point where we act for the good and noble, then it is *God in us* who drives us to it. And the God in us who causes us to act for the good and noble lives in our archetype. I myself am full of egotism—but I am foreordained to become a reflection of my divine archetype. This archetype rested in the bosom of God, and it has descended into this physical form; and this form stands under the power of God who stands over my destiny, my karma, which is entirely permeated by egotism. Never, never, must I say that I am without egotism, for it is never true. Without egotism I could not even exist on the physical plane.

However, when I learn to look up to my God-given archetype—when I allow my thinking, feeling, and willing, all my soul forces entirely to die into this archetype—then I am allowed to hope to overcome the egotism in myself, and again approach my archetype. We will also notice that in the same measure that we become less egotistical, we also become stronger physically. We will notice that we no longer feel fear or shock. We will no longer flinch in sudden fright. We will become powerful and strong in our whole human existence.

If we rightly understand the genuine, ancient esoteric Rosicrucian verse, then we say: *E. D. N.* Here the knowing essence of the human being goes to what is unspeakable, the creative word. Then the feeling returns and one can repeat. *I – – – M*. That is, we allow our egotism to "die into Christ" and resurrect to new forces of life through Christ's power of love. *In – – – morimur*: thus one speaks this mantra esoterically. And its meaning lights up for us: the God of my destiny releases me through this, that I die into Him. *In – – – morimur*.

Esoteric Lesson
KASSEL, DECEMBER 3 AND 4, 1910

Notes from Wilhelm Hübbe-Schleiden.

Esoteric lesson exercises are the technique of the spiritual life:

Maya = *Maha Aya; ya or ye* = being; *a* = negation; *Maha Aya*, thus: great not-being. We have become inhabitants of earth only through the influence of Lucifer and Ahriman, otherwise our "I's" would have remained in spiritual regions and guided our bodies on the surface of the earth from those regions.

Despite the fact that Lucifer and Ahriman battle against the direct workings of the divine spirit, they are intended by the spirit, because only through such resistance does the "I" arrive at a complete physical objectification.

If Ahriman did not exist, we would not see at all the green of the plants as such, but only the spiritual being represented by the plant. An individual plant is like a hair on the body of the earth, so to speak.

Our egotism arises only through Lucifer and Ahriman. However, it is necessary that these beings live in us and come to full expression, for only in this way can all life be completely physically formed. But we must become aware that all our actions have a selfish nuance. Our compassion drives us to help because we simply do not like feeling the suffering of others.

There is no point in the infinity of space that does not have force.

All human etheric brains of differ more than the leaves of a tree. The luminous points in a brain are like a photograph of the heavens full of stars.

The effects of *Atma, Buddhi* and *Manas* are formed in the human eye.

This symbol works on us in the night too. We should keep the chaotic impressions of the day away as much as possible.

We should also refrain from chatting, or speaking casually, about theosophy during our daily acts, such as while eating. It should be a sacred matter.

Esoteric Lesson

MUNICH, DECEMBER 11, 1910

Record A: Manuscript from Mathilde Scholl, Barbara Wolf, Amalie Fugger-Gloett; Record B: Manuscript from Alice Kinkel.

RECORD A

We have often spoken in our esoteric lessons about the paths that esotericists had to follow in the ancient mystery schools. At that time human beings in their soul and spiritual characteristics were turned inside out, so to speak, turned around relatively more quickly, by means of certain methods, because human souls and bodies back then were more robust than now. They had stronger souls, and because the soul is the architect of the physical body, the physical body was also stronger. This was at a time earlier than our historical research can reach. Humanity at that time was altogether less complicated, more unified. It came forth from the bosom of the Godhead; and its task is, after gradually losing its ancient clairvoyance, to raise itself again to divinity on its path through matter by taking up the Christ impulse, and filled with it, uniting again with God. Because of constantly increasing materialism, human beings have become gradually weaker in spirit, soul, and body. One can no longer subject the more delicate constitutions now to the kinds of trials imposed upon students in the ancient mystery schools. Back then work was done, in the first instance, to eliminate two traits that those to be initiated, in their instability, soon learned to know and set aside: egotism and fear. With our usual concepts of the physical plane we cannot judge at all what egotism really is.

Those to be initiated were put to sleep; then their souls were shown in the spiritual world what they had achieved up till then. The "I" was absorbed by the macrocosm, and they noticed that they were nothing. Of course, this standing before nothingness as before a dark abyss stirred up their feelings of fear, which they had to move beyond. They came forth from these trials either useless for external life because they fully understood the knowledge that everything transitory is futile, or they remained strong and resolved to use this incarnation as much as possible to evolve further and one day come to know the higher worlds. A modern person could not be handled in such a robust way. It is already a lot for people of today, when they say that the ground under their feet is swaying. The entire striving of modern people is to stand firmly. They do not wish to make a leap, but rather move forward at a slow pace. Esotericists, however, must make a leap over the abyss. They should allow the ground to slip away. For when they want to penetrate into the spiritual world, the concepts they have formed here on the physical plane will help them absolutely not at all. They are not allowed to take any of those concepts with them across the threshold. There is one thing alone they are allowed to keep: the ability to form concepts; a sense for truth and logic. The capacity for forming new concepts, and a sense for the new truths they will learn.

The Masters of Wisdom and Harmony of Feelings send us a comparison so that we can understand this matter. It is as though we were to see all the objects in our room in a mirror, and then were to go around behind the mirror in order to discover reality there. We would see that there is nothing behind the mirror. It is the same with our concepts in higher worlds. Here we must allow concepts about the higher worlds to flow into us from higher beings. These concepts must work on us so that we form such concepts for ourselves. When we have then acquired some for ourselves with earnest and honest work, then we must again step before the mirror, make a bold decision, and shatter it. Then a darkness, a gaping nothingness will again face us. But when we steadily endure this, then a light will appear for us in the darkness, and an entirely new world will be revealed.

Our esoteric work consists in this, that we gradually raise the astral body and etheric body into spiritual heights. In this way, however, the lower part of the two bodies remains behind in the physical body. Now the "I" plays a peculiar role between these two parts that have been torn apart. Because of the fact that we had been so anchored in the material world, the "I" is chained to the lower parts, and is their slave, so to speak. In this way, peculiar phenomena appear. The astral body, now left alone, might have some sort of vice, which we might have mastered easily earlier, when its better part was still connected with it. This astral body now finds such vices growing boundlessly, and the human being appears to him or herself as a totally dissolute person. If the "I" were united with the higher parts, then from there it could rule over the lower, and thereby over all drives, desires, and passions. Then the higher parts would also not be unconscious, as they are when the "I" is in the lower. Because of the fact that the higher part leaves, the lower bodies often become weak. Then the physical body also inclines toward illness. But this is a transitory condition. For when the higher parts have obtained enough strength from the higher worlds, they will again work upon the lower to harmonize and make them healthy. Esotericists must simply say, with such irregular phenomena in their lower bodies, I will stand firm; through thick and thin I will go my way to the spirit, whatever may come to meet me. If they remain anchored against their mistakes, then they will also master them. Art should be an aid in these battles. True art was given to us for this purpose. Any art that does not elevate us must perish—it cannot endure—it is not true art. When artists have recognized the mission of art; when art is permeated by theosophy; then it will become what it should be.

When the gods created human beings, they gave us weaknesses too, so that we could test our strength on them. For this reason we should be thankful also for our weaknesses, because fighting them makes us strong and free. But for that reason, we must never for a moment love them. We could never have thanked such gods as might have created us pure and perfect. For they would have made us weaklings at the same time. And we should say to ourselves, even if the world were full of devils, we nevertheless have our origin in God. *Ex Deo nascimur.* When we earnestly battle and strive without letting-up[†] to enter the spiritual world, then we will feel how the lower, the error-prone, part of us dies away: *In Christo morimur.* And then we will awaken in higher worlds consciously: *Per Spiritum Sanctum reviviscimus.* There is an exoteric version and an esoteric version of this verse. Used esoterically speaking, the most holy name can cause earthquakes, storms, and thunder, powerful events in nature, if the speaking happens unworthily. For our thoughts, even our hidden thoughts, have a destructive effect in the spiritual worlds if they are false. That is what is meant where it says in the Rosicrucian mysteries that the gods must often break worlds in order to repair the damage that we human beings have done. Therefore, the esoteric version of the verse is:

> *Ex Deo nascimur.*
> *In — — — morimur.*
> *Per Spiritum Sanctum reviviscimus.*

* * *

Record B

Manuscript from Alice Kinkel.

An esotericist must acquire entirely different concepts. As an example for this change in concepts, the masters have said we must see our task as a mirror that we have to break through. Esotericism must tear apart our entire being, and we must take the etheric body, astral body, and "I," and an extract of our physical body, above with us; everything that has been purified. The lower part of our being we leave behind below in all three bodies, which are then left to themselves. And if the physical body is not carefully watched, this separation of the higher from the lower brings about disease or weakness in the physical body; the body becomes especially susceptible to the diseases of the current age.

In the etheric body our memory is lost. In the astral body the passions are strengthened. This can be intensified to the point of dissolute behavior because of this split in the human being. Clear thoughts and feelings are realities in the spiritual world, and the expression is true that says, "The gods must break worlds…and so forth."

Consideration of the Rosicrucian verse exoterically and esoterically. Egotism in everyday life is something entirely different from egotism in the spiritual world. Physical life is simply not possible without egotism. An esotericist must acquire positivity and self-possessed composure.

Blasphemy of God is denial of the wisdom of the world; it is denial of all that encounters us. We should be grateful to the gods for our mistakes, because a stronger power is formed through overcoming mistakes.

Esoteric Lesson
HANOVER, DECEMBER 17 AND 18, 1910

Notes from Emilie Hübner.

i (English sound long "ee"): leads to the divine within
ei (English sound "a"): revelation of the divine
a (English sound "ah"): leading upward to the divine
o (English "oh"): enclosing the revealed form
oe (ö; umlaut): expresses the incomprehensible form, withdraws before, shy reverence
u (English sound "oo"): divine peace, rest
e (English sound "ae"): overcoming difficulties. Knowledge of the world (macrocosm); self knowledge (microcosm). This is a reflection of the archetype.

Esoteric Lesson

BERLIN, DECEMBER 20, 1910

Origin of Manuscript unknown (Vreede collection).

Esoteric lesson exercises are the technique of the spiritual life:

Ordinary human beings have their physical and etheric bodies bound closely together. When they use their physical bodies, whether in raising a hand or in thinking, they set the corresponding part of the etheric body in motion at the same time. This should become different for an esotericist; the connection should become looser.

Human beings have a backbone that is connected to the brain and the sense organs. When we meditate, we create in the etheric body a "front bone," which is the series of lotus flowers that lie behind the sternum. (The human being will no longer have a sternum in the seventh post-Atlantean age.)

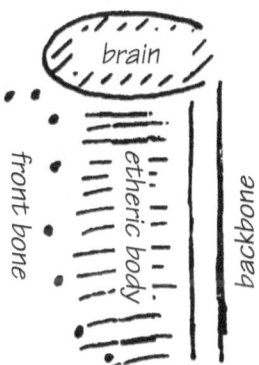

By means of the loosening of the physical and etheric bodies mentioned above, the human being now becomes able to heal his or her (own) wounds faster, and so forth. On the other hand, weaknesses of the physical body can appear that had remained hidden at first, because of the close connection between etheric and physical. Without any exaggeration, one should not pay particular attention to all these little pains and sufferings; it will all pass. In the transition time of this loosening, one can certainly feel unwell. Simply studying theosophy brings about this loosening already, although scientific development makes the connection between etheric and physical bodies even stronger.

Thus through meditation, the etheric body acquires the inclination to separate from the physical body. This can be strengthened by means of an appropriate diet. Through diet, it is the other way around: the physical body gets the tendency to expel the etheric body. This is an aid that brings about exactly what is wrong, unless it is supplemented with esoteric exercises. If that happens, then the physical body expels the etheric body, with the etheric body having developed sense organs. Then one is blind and sees only one's own fantasies.

As our sheaths undergo changes in this way, our connection with the macrocosm is also changed. This connection must be cultivated in the right way, otherwise harm results—not only in the human being, but in the entire universe. For example, if someone in an inappropriate society were to speak the holy, unspeakable name, something worse than earthquakes and volcanic outbreaks would be conjured up over the entire region. Therefore, there is an enormous difference in how the Rosicrucian verse is spoken, whether with a name that is merely a pseudonym for the highest spiritual being, or without this name. Only the last way of speaking the verse is an esoteric way.

Esoteric Lesson

STUTTGART, CHRISTMAS TO NEW YEAR'S EVE, 1910

Summary of two lessons; Notes from Günther Wagner.

Our esoteric feeling of responsibility must be increased; we must acquire theosophical conscientiousness. It is seldom to be found today outside in the world. Example: 1. A man who wanted to write a long book and also wanted to absorb something concerning theosophy, asked Dr. Steiner to tell him his opinion about it, because he had no time to concern himself with it.† 2. An American summarized the lectures he heard here by Dr. Steiner, as much as he understood them, and published them as a book in America.†

We must acquire theosophical tact and speak about the esoteric school, and so forth, only when it is appropriate. Never speak about esoteric matters while eating.

*

Our physical bodies have grown together very closely with our etheric bodies. A loosening is possible in two ways:

1. on exoteric paths with external exercises and vegetarian food;
2. on esoteric paths through training, meditations, and so forth.

The first works on the astral body; and the second works on the etheric, so that it is loosened. One could say that through meditation, concentration, and so forth, a frontal spinal cord of the lotus flowers is created as a counterpart to the physical spinal cord.

frontal cord with lotus flowers

brain
spinal cord

This is what is proper, so that no injury can occur to the physical body. If, on the other hand, only external means are used, then a loosening of the etheric body will occur without its being strengthened by meditation or the introduction of theosophical truths. The consequence must be illness of the physical body; or if the etheric body has also been loosened from the physical brain, then confusion, and so forth, will occur.

Esoteric Lesson
STUTTGART, DECEMBER 31, 1910

Manuscripts from Mathilde Scholl and Barbara Wolf.

Esotericists should bring clearly to their consciousness what they are actually doing with the exercises that have been given to us. We have often spoken about the fact that the striving of an esotericist is intended to loosen the etheric body, and altogether to loosen the four bodies with respect to each other. Now this can happen in two ways, an exoteric and an esoteric.

One can cause the physical body to expel the etheric body, to squeeze it out by sufficiently preparing the physical body through diet, breathing exercises, and so forth. Fundamentally speaking, our vegetarian way of life has the purpose only of supporting the physical body in this effort. This is an exoteric means of loosening the bodies. The esoteric means are our meditation exercises. And here it must be said that this is the main thing: that we must carry out our exercises with devotion and earnestness, that everything else should only be a support for this main thing. In our materialistic age there are many who in their materialistic longing would follow the most detailed dietary instructions and would do breathing exercises for hours if they could thereby achieve something. However, striving spiritually by means of meditations and concentration exercises is much less pleasant, and often only this reveals the spiritual lethargy present. But if we squeeze out the etheric body through physical influences alone, then the physical body would not be able to give the etheric body anything, and it would step out into the unknown empty-handed. Then certain mental states appear; for example, we would not be able to properly take hold of something with our thinking when we want to think our way through something. With the etheric brain we would be unable to make proper use of the physical brain, because we would not be properly incarnated in it. It would be as though we were swimming in water and wanted to grasp something that always slips away from us. Reasonable esotericists in such a condition would say to themselves that they must first of all create order here, through suitable will, concentration, and thought exercises. Also in normal development, some things will occur that we must say are a passing tribulation. The withdrawal of the etheric body has much the same significance for the physical body as the temporary loss of fluids has for a plant. It dries out. And the physical body also dries out, in part, although it is not visible physically; and where the physical body has a disposition toward illness, it will come forth. But when the physical body has been permeated by spiritual truths, it draws from them new strength, and this in turn brings health to the physical body. One can observe that even cuts in the physical body heal faster, and wounds altogether heal faster when we are permeated by spiritual truth; indeed, when we just allow theosophical modes of thought to work in us.

To begin with, we are working on the astral body with our meditations. This astral body is architect of the nervous system that proceeds to the spinal cord, or as one says today, proceeds from it.

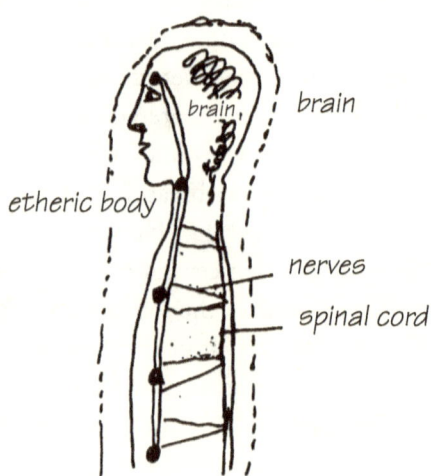

Now in the etheric body we are to achieve an imprint from the astral body that is developed as lotus flowers, which are connected to one another; and in this way create a "frontal cord," so to speak.

This "frontal cord" is, of course, present only in the etheric and astral realms, and can be formed only through meditation and concentration. For this reason, they are the most important part of our esoteric development. And the only thing that is directly injurious for an esotericist is the consumption of alcohol. In any case, alcohol must always be avoided. It is, of course, good for us to support the process with a vegetarian diet, because this lifting out of the etheric body is not at all easy today.

Many of our modern-day professions are directly set up to drive the etheric body firmly into the physical body. Thus it can often directly cause pain to clairvoyants when they see something like that. Also the food that is served today in our great hotels is entirely prepared so as to drive the etheric body firmly into the physical body.

Through esoteric work on ourselves, we should acquire a new way of thinking, feeling, and willing. When we have boldly taken the courage to walk the path of an esotericist, we must say to ourselves that we must "jump over an abyss." Once we have thought through a thought, we must pass it through our feeling, and permeate it entirely with our feeling so that we do not say something lightly, something that we have not actually grasped in its depths. A sentence that we can so often hear people say today, which is abused in its applications as few others, is "I am a Christian." Esotericists should be clear that "being a Christian" is a distant, distant ideal toward which they must constantly strive. To live as a Christian means, above all, to accept with serenity whatever destiny may bring us; to never complain about the work of the gods; to accept with joy whatever they may send. It means that the saying, "Look at the birds in the sky, they do not sow, they do not reap, they do not gather into barns, and yet they receive what they need," becomes second nature in us. Accept with gratitude what is given to us. Then we are living according to this verse. If we do not do this, then the verse becomes blasphemy in our mouths.

Altogether it should be clear to us that if we do not sufficiently prepare ourselves for the leap over the abyss into the spiritual world, we would perpetrate so much damage that the divine worlds would have to shatter in order to repair this damage. For what is ruined must be destroyed in order to be built anew.

We have emerged from the spirit. *Ex Deo nascimur.* And when we make the leap over the abyss, we express that with *In Christo morimur.* With firm confidence that we will live again on the other side in the Holy Spirit. *Per Spiritum Sanctum reviviscimus.* And because we should keep the name of the most holy being, who has always been connected with our earthly evolution, so holy that we do not speak it unworthily, there is an esoteric version of the Rosicrucian verse, in which the name is not spoken.

> *Ex Deo nascimur.*
> *In -- -- -- morimur.*
> *Per Spiritum Sanctum reviviscimus.*

Esoteric Lesson
STUTTGART, JANUARY 1, 1911

Record A: Manuscript from Marie Steiner; Record B: Manuscript from Camilla Wandrey; Record C: Manuscript from Nelly Lichtenberg.

RECORD A

Maha Aya – the great Not-Being

I

Existence

A

Ch forming oneself

Im becoming aware of oneself

The word works to educate and restore health. Morning and evenings as prayer for the benefit of children and the ill.

To battle against:

Ambition, vanity, arrogance — think on the teachings of theosophy.

Envy, jealousy — think on a beautiful work of art.

Chattiness, curiosity, anger, irritation — a quarter-hour of quiet daily.

* * *

RECORD B

A famous inscription, the Delphic *"E"* (this is the English vowel sound long "a" with the diphthong "ee" sound at the end dropped), stood above the gate to the temple at Delphi. It means "You are." (second person of the present indicative of the verb "to be"). Plutarch said that it was the greeting of the divinity on behalf of those who entered the temple.† The Delphic sound *E* signified the number five, or half of the zodiac; that is, the five ascending signs. The Delphic *E* is also the anchor of the Seleikids.† It was taken over by the Gnostics in order to signify the "Savior," and is often found among talismans and amulets of early Christians.

Maha Aya

A	Existence
I A	inwardly ensouled existence
AIA	non-existence; abolishes again
MAHA	Great, powerful
MAHA AIA	great non-existence, illusion
CH	diffusion
IN	inner reflection
IACHIN	creative word that calls the spiritual beings in the world. Works to heal, warm inwardly, gives strength.

RECORD C

Maha Aya

A	= existence
YA	=inwardly ensouled existence
Aya	=non-existence, abolishes it again
Maha	=great existence
Maha Aya	=contracted to: Maya, the great non-existence, illusion.

*

Ch   = Dispersion

In   = inner reflection

Iachin = creative word that calls spiritual beings in the world; works to warm inwardly.

Esoteric Lesson
STUTTGART, JANUARY 2, 1911

Notes from the collection of Fred Poeppig.

One must take the esoteric life seriously. For this reason an esoteric hour must always be something holy. One should never accept it as something routine. All were certainly not aware of the necessary earnestness when they were asked to join the esoteric circle. However, now they should become increasingly conscious of this necessity, and strive for a connection with the spiritual worlds so that they do not fall back into the everyday world.

We are to consider the exercises that have been given us as coming from the masters. Esotericists should attend to themselves and their feelings. Especially they should look at what concerns their self-knowledge. Most people (and we certainly belong among them) indulge in great illusions when it comes to themselves. We must attend especially to egotism. We often fool ourselves that we have done something selfless, or also we may feel jealousy and hatred toward someone to whom, as an esotericist, we must tell the "truth" and that we are not permitted to allow this or that from him. As soon as feelings like this arise in us, we should imagine that we are subject to great illusions whose deeper cause always arises from egotism. Feelings like this always express themselves with a feeling of warmth that flows through the etheric body (indeed, the part that we call the warmth ether), and then through the blood, and it works on the physical body. Feelings of this kind always have a deleterious effect on the human being and world evolution.

The hierarchies who are charged with guiding karmic connections then work in such a way that they employ certain beings that destroy certain constructive effects in us, and in this way these beings also work destructively in the soul and indirectly into the body. These are Luciferic beings who have been entrusted with this task. This then is their work upon us. Correct self-knowledge through insight into our own base nature will permeate us with a cold icy feeling in place of the feeling of warmth mentioned above, which satisfies us so. Everything that gives us satisfaction from our sensations and so forth, expresses itself as the feeling of warmth described above, as opposed to this feeling of cold that enters with true knowledge of the self.

These Luciferic beings who approach a pupil destructively in this way are revealed to a clairvoyant as certain multitude whose leader is Samael.[†] These beings, which are in no way similar to human beings, are always perceptible to the eye of the spirit. If we have a feeling of disgust upon waking, as is often the case especially with esoteric pupils, then such a feeling is almost always attributable to egotism, which often lies unrecognized deep in unconscious depths of soul.

Furthermore, we must direct our attention to everything connected with untruthfulness. Indeed, because of upbringing, we may never speak any blatant falsehood; nevertheless, we always have a tendency to want to appear better than we really fundamentally are. Or when it is a matter of life and death to admit the truth, we rather remain silent and conceal the truth. All of this also has an injurious effect on world evolution, and thereby works destructively on a human being. The effects of such untruthfulness work on the astral body, then on the etheric body, indeed upon the part we call the light ether. From here, such injurious influences affect the physical body, especially the nervous system. The Luciferic beings connected with this, whose leader is Azazel, are revealed to a clairvoyant as looking similar to a human being, usually as a head with the wings of a raven. Those who incline toward untruthfulness will usually be able to sense a choking, scratching feeling in their throat. They also often have the feeling as if they were being pinched with pliers and tortured by a thousand arms. Everyone who perceives him or herself with exactness will then notice how deeply he or she is still tangled in lies and dissembling.

Furthermore, it is important to become aware of a certain indifference and insensitivity to spiritual worlds and influences. Many esotericists listen to an esoteric lesson, yet what is presented finds no echo in them. They cannot lift themselves up spiritually out of their usual daily life to give themselves to spiritual thoughts. Others do so only out of curiosity. They have the intention to see something in the spiritual worlds, and then blindly start off meditating without wanting to devote themselves to a regular study because that is too much trouble. This has an injurious effect on the "I," and then from there into the astral body, then further on the etheric body, and indeed on the part we refer to as the chemical ether, and from chemical ether into the secretions and glands of the physical body.

There is a difference between the relationship that esotericists have with these Luciferic multitudes and the relationship non-esotericists have with them. For example, Azazel and his multitude constantly want to bring forth only good effects in non-esotericists, since they bring about only supplementary effects and are not injurious to health.

However, esoteric pupils are required constantly to be conscious of their complete responsibility for themselves and the world. For this reason, a dull esotericist will have a slight feeling of drowning when walking in the morning, indeed, the more he or she has surrendered him or herself to the usual life of the senses during the day.

Therefore, esotericists should constantly watch over themselves, and it will not hurt if they sometimes become melancholic brooders. Only in this way will they understand what is brought to us at the conclusion of every esoteric lesson by the masters:

> *In the spirit lay the seed of my body;*
> *In my body lies the seed of the spirit.*

Esoteric Lesson

BERLIN, JANUARY 17, 1911

Record A: Author of manuscript unknown; Record B: Notes from Günther Wagner; Record C: Manuscript from Camilla Wandrey. Additional Record: author unknown.

RECORD A

In our meditations we have given the techniques of our esoteric life. These consist in this, that we allow thoughts to work upon us and awaken sensations and feelings that are not taken from the physical plane.

All thoughts are of two kinds: those that are awakened in us by perception of the physical plane, and those such as are given to us by theosophy. Everything in the physical world is maya, including our physical body. How is it that this world is actually present? What do the planet, stones, and animals around us consist of? —Through the fact that higher beings formulated a thought millions and millions of years ago and then thought these thoughts again and again. These things follow the principle expressed in the old saying, "steady drops hollow the stone." — The same thoughts reinforce one another and finally create the physical object. The harder the stone is, the longer it is "thought" upon. Our physical body is also nothing other than the thought of many different higher beings.

When we think only the usual thoughts of the physical plane, they are not actually thoughts but rather mirror images, the illusion of a thought. For everything in the physical world has already been thought a long time ago. We are doing nothing more than repeating those thoughts, and improperly at that. For example, when someone hears a bell sounding, the tone from the bell isn't anything real, but rather the situation is as follows. What a bell is, was thought out millions of years ago. So too, what constitutes our brain was thought out millions of years ago. The interaction between tone and brain creates the sound that we hear. All physical thoughts are unfruitful and will have a destructive effect as time passes. They put the astral body into a certain vibration, but that was already planted in us by higher beings. Anyone who never thinks non-sensorily, never brings new forms into the astral body. What happens in the astral body works back upon the etheric body, but the etheric body is so constituted that it is designed to absorb new thoughts and forms. The old forms bring destruction into it, and from there also on the physical filaments of our nervous system. In sleep, all that must be built up again. The astral body is then inserted into the higher hierarchies for a time, and thereby gets strengthened again. The etheric body is separated from the astral body, and is thereby regenerated. Without sleep, the human being could not live very long.

But thoughts that are not derived from the senses have an effect that is fructifying and up-building. Because of those thoughts, the human being is counted in the ranks of the hierarchies. They build new forms, the lotus flowers, into the astral body. For this reason it is necessary to repeat a meditation hundreds of times.

The mental pictures that we make for ourselves from theosophical teachings (for thinking about something is also meditation) will not at first be entirely free of the world of the senses. For example, when it is said that old Saturn was a sphere of warmth, that the music of the spheres sounds forth in devachan; then this will at first be imagined in sensory images similar to the warmth in our blood, as a beautiful symphony, and the like. However, as the thought is constantly repeated, the sensory element that still adheres to it will fall away by itself, and then the suprasensory remains.

The most sense-free thoughts in the world are mathematical, but even when modern human beings think "triangle," they think it with color and a certain thickness, not abstractly enough. However, we come closer to suprasensory thoughts when we attend to relationships. Remembering a sound is still a memory of something sensory; remembering a melody is already something more, for it consists of a relationship between tones, which does not belong to the world of the senses. Or imagine a villain, and standing nearby, another villain (or even two good people standing near one another); and one villain is a greater villain than the other, or one good person is better than the other. Then in this relationship there lies something that is not in the physical, sensory world; something that leads us up into the spiritual world. When we think of or see a villain, then we are affected in an unpleasant way, but when we see two villains next to each other the worst villain will please us more than the less evil villain, because greatness always attracts. The effect of Shakespeare's various dramas is based on this fact, for example. For this reason it is so important for us to observe and study relationships in the external world, for this leads us away from the sensory world.

Another way to become free of the senses in our thinking consists in this: that we allow processes to unfold in reverse order, for example, saying the Lord's Prayer backward, or the reversed retrospective of our meditations.† We improve our memory only in this way. Memory has diminished enormously in the last four to five centuries, and that will be the case even much more in the future if people do not now take hold of the opportunities that are offered to improve it. The time for these opportunities is especially favorable now; later they will simply not exist. Then memory will become something other than simply waiting to see if the content wants to appear out of some dark corner. It will be a kind of probing toward the past, like sending out feelers that reach for the past as if it were something real. The present time is now especially favorable for this development, and for esoteric development.

So we see how the body is maya; thoughts come from beings, who are again themselves thoughts. *The thought thinks the thought.* This is a sentence for meditation of the highest significance. It is not the brain that thinks, not the etheric or astral body, but rather thought itself thinks thoughts. That is also what clearly emerges from our verse:

In the spirit lay the seed of my body...

RECORD B

Steady drops hollow a stone. The hierarchies have again and again periodically held firmly to the same thoughts; that is, they have perfected further the same thoughts, and in this way worked creatively. Thus our entire body and we ourselves were created through thought—actually nothing more than thoughts. Thinking about what already exists is never creative, but rather destructive for the nerves, and also for the etheric body, the actual organ for our advancing evolution. The disruptive effects of the astral body go into the etheric body during the day. The physical and the etheric body must be creatively restored in the night when they are freed from the astral body (thoughts). So too, the astral body is restored itself. Only when we think suprasensory content do we ourselves work creatively as a human hierarchy, and create lotus flowers through hundred- and thousand-fold repetition. Then we are also imprinting the etheric body as the hierarchies would. Although the meditative images are taken from the sensory world, they are stripped of the sensory content through constant deepening and repetition. Already the relationships between sensory things and between good and bad people, even the reversal of a time sequence during the evening retrospection, help toward sensory free thought.

Immersion in:

Thought thinks the thoughts.

We should use the present era for ascending upward; the times do not always offer such an opportunity.

* * *

RECORD C

The hierarchies have concentrated periodically on the same thoughts again and again (constant thoughts consolidate and strengthen what lives in wavering appearances). The hierarchies elaborate and perfect the same thoughts further and further. In this way they are creative. Thus the various bodies and the spiritual and soul substance that live in those bodies have been created by this thinking of the gods — actually, they are nothing more than the thoughts of the gods.

The thinking that we do with the help of the brain is not creative;

rather, it is destructive for the nerves, as well as for the etheric body, which is actually the organ for advancing evolution. During the day, it is injured by the destructive effects of the astral body. During the night, the physical and etheric bodies must be freed from this destructive influence of the astral body and restored again by creative thoughts. So, too, the astral body itself. Only when we feel ourselves to be the hierarchy of human beings—that is, when we think thoughts of the greater world—only then do we ourselves not have a destructive effect, but rather, creative. Through thousand-fold repetition of such lofty thoughts (with content as is given to us in meditation), do we create. To begin with, we create the lotus flowers. Then we also are imprinting the etheric body as the hierarchies would. The meditations contain images and words that are taken from the sensory world, to be sure; yet, through constant immersion and repetition that penetrate behind the words and images to the hidden essences, the words and images are stripped of their sensory elements. And when we penetrate far enough to rest in the essences that are hidden in the depths of the words and images, then by means of meditation we come into another world. Immersing oneself in the thought "Thought thinks thoughts" helps us achieve this. Knowledge is always addressed as light; wisdom addressed as a kind of fluid element, water (occult).

* * *

Supplement added by the German editor:

What is meant by this last sentence, "wisdom addressed as a kind of fluid element, water (occult)," is presented in greater detail in notes from a lecture on May 24, 1905 in Berlin (CW 323a):

If we want to acquire a real picture of four-dimensional space, we must carry out very specific exercises in imagination. First we form a very clear and deepened perception of water. Such a perception is difficult to arrive at. We must immerse ourselves very exactly in the nature of water; we must "climb into" water, so to speak. The second thing we must do is achieve a perception of the nature of light. Of course we know what light is, but only in the way that we receive it from outside. By means of meditation we can get an inner "counter image" of light, know where light comes from—and then for that reason bring forth light ourselves. Those people who allow pure concepts to work on their souls meditatively can do it; those who can think free of the senses. Then the whole surrounding world opens for them as flooding light. Then they must chemically combine (so to speak) the perception of water that they have formed, with that of light. This water entirely permeated by light is a body that alchemists called "mercury." Alchemical mercury, however, is not ordinary quicksilver. First we must awaken in ourselves the capacity to generate mercury from the idea of light. Mercury, the power of water permeated by light, is what we position ourselves to possess. That is one element of the astral world. The second thing arises when we create for ourselves a clear visual perception of the air, and then through a spiritual process we draw out of this perception the power of air—unite this power with feeling within ourselves. Then you enkindle thus the idea of "heat-fire"; then you get "fire-air." So one element is drawn out, the other is produced by you yourself. This air and fire the alchemists called "sulfur," luminous "fire-air." In truth you have in the watery element, the matter of which it was said, "and the spirit of God hovered over the waters.[†]

> Water is water and remains water.
> Water is water and remains water.
> From the Heaven of the Wise water rains down
> The Stone of the Wise weeps the water of tears
> But the world does not value water of this kind:
> Its fire burns in water
> And lives in water.
> Make water from fire
> Cook fire in water
> And you will have fiery water
> Like highly salted seawater
> Your child is living water—
> If body and soul are consumed in water,
> It becomes stinking, green, foul, blue like Heavenly Water.

Digest, calcinate, dissolve, and putrefy the water;
Seek the Philosopher's fourfold permanent water.
And if it is made well
Art becomes water.

Additional Record

There is another write-up whose author is unknown. However, the text is of such questionable quality that it is given here only for the sake of completeness:

The alchemical secret says to the human being: "Achieve for yourself the light-permeated power of water." This is a picture for the higher consciousness that is attained through initiation. Human beings learn to add to what they can learn from their senses externally about things; they learn to experience the inner being of things. And gradually they advance from the mere concept that one forms of a thing, to the essence that once creatively formed this thing, to the divine idea. And that then becomes true reality. Thus one grasps the difference between today's understanding and intellect and the creative powers in the world. Inner wisdom that has sunk into the darkness of the unconscious continues working in the human being in dreamless sleep. And the task of the esotericist is to lift up this inner wisdom into the sphere of consciousness. For this reason human beings have received the self, the "I." This is the I-consciousness, the I-am that every human being once was, before it was poured into the human being by that collective being that we have symbolized as water. Divine beings had it; human beings received it, after it was embodied. Here we have the difference between what we call in Christianity "the Holy Spirit" and "the Spirit itself." This is the Holy Spirit who is above with divine beings, before whom the embodiment took place; and Spirit itself who is embodied in individual human beings. The Holy Spirit is a unity and also is individualized in individual human beings. Separation, individualization always has something to do with egotism. Joining together, flowing together in love, uniting, all have their archetype in the Holy Spirit. E.D.N.

Wasser ist Wasser und bleibet Wasser
Vom Himmel der Weisen regnet Wasser
Der Weisen Stein weinet Thränen Wasser
Dennoch achtet die Welt nicht solch ein Wasser.
Ihr Feuer brennet im Wasser
Und lebet im Wasser.
Mach aus Feuer Wasser
Und koche das Feuer im Wasser.
So wird ein feurig Wasser
Wie ein scharf gesalzen Meer=Wasser.
Ist den Kindern ein lebendig Wasser.
 Vergeht auch Leib und Seel zu Wasser.
Wird stinkend, grün, faul, blau wie Himmel=Wasser
Digerir, calcinir, solvir und putrificir das Wasser;
Auf der Philosophen vielfach bleibend Wasser,
Und wenn es am besten gemacht ist, wird die
                    Kunst zu Wasser.

Esoteric Lesson
COLOGNE, JANUARY 31, 1911

Manuscript from Alice Kinkel.

The Essence of Meditation

Meditation has two sides:
1. A technical side
2. A side that is carried into life; that is, the way in which we think, feel, and act is changed by means of proper meditation.

Patience and conscientiousness are necessary when practicing meditation. What do we do when we meditate?

We imitate what divine-spiritual beings in the highest hierarchies did millions and millions of years ago; deeds that gave rise to our earth. Everything around us is condensed divine thought! Following the motif, "steady drops hollow out the stone," these spiritual beings were thinking rhythmically.

What they thought about often and in short rhythmic cycles became hard earthly substance; diamond, for example. Imagining things that do not exist in the physical world is creative work, not thoughts about what is already present.

"I am an egotist. I am not a Christian." These are two very fruitful sentences for meditation. We must get to know ourselves as monsters. An encounter with the Guardian of the Threshold is an awful experience for everyone. This must be said to an esotericist. Seeing beautiful things and forms is astral maya, is Lucifer.

Hearing the masters and similar things is etheric maya, is Ahriman. One must research what one sees and hears, then the true shape comes into view.

Esoteric Lesson
MUNICH, FEBRUARY 12, 1911

Manuscripts from Mathilda Scholl, Barbara Wolf, Amalie Fugger-Gloett.

It is important for modern human beings to become conscious of what they are doing when they enter upon an esoteric life, of the changes that are happening to them.

We have often heard there are two paths that lead us into the spiritual world: one in which we descend deep within ourselves, the other in which we strive outward into the macrocosm. The forces that we seek, that created us from outside, we also have within us. We seek them, not because we don't have them, but because we don't recognize them within us. In theosophy we learn of the two paths that should balance one another, for modern human beings are no longer suited to follow only one path. Both paths have their dangers, which we will discuss later, and both are difficult. The inner path we tread in our meditations, in our inspirations; the outer path we tread in imagination and through the thorough study of theosophical teachings about the evolution of the world. Not only is our intellect developed by this study, but our feelings are also influenced; and we will notice that we have become altogether new human beings after years of thoroughly studying these ideas. Theosophy has an effect on people whether or not they are receptive to it. Modern human beings fall into two categories: those who seek theosophy and find what they seek within it and those who have no idea what to do with it, who oppose it with animosity. Since 1879, a small group of people have grown mature enough to accept theosophical literature, but it is a small group only, while other modern people are still incapable of acquiring these teachings and consider them reveries or fantasies, or are even angered by them.

The etheric bodies of people who prove to be receptive for theosophical teachings are set gently vibrating when these teachings are allowed to work on them. On the other hand, those who completely surrender to the spirit of our age, who lose themselves in externalities, have etheric bodies that expand and thin out. If such people hear of theosophical spiritual teachings, then it is as if the wind were blowing through a narrow opening in their etheric bodies; this they experience as fear that appears externally as doubt. Such people notice only the doubt, which however is only an expression of fear and anxiety, both of which have moved into their etheric bodies as if into a space void of air. There they make themselves noticeable as doubt in our consciousness. To begin with, we cannot help such people who behave so dismissively toward theosophy. It is better if we leave them in peace without theosophy. However, whenever the opportunity presents itself, we should allow theosophical ideas to gently flow to them, following the principle, "steady drops hollow out the stone." For we have only 400 years left, approximately, to make this teaching available to all people in the form of theosophy. In order for everyone to have an opportunity, those people who have resisted the ideas of theosophy in their present incarnation will be incarnated again in the next 400 years. But then, too, a corresponding number of people must be present who can properly represent theosophy.

For a long time, before the event of Golgotha, human beings could tread only one path, the one leading inward. In ancient India and Egypt, people ascended into their inner being. Had they wanted to go into the microcosm they would have lost themselves within it; they would have stood before darkness, before the void. For human beings at that time were related to each other differently; their inner members were related to each other differently. This form of union with God extended into the Middle Ages because the human being changes only slowly. Mystics such as Meister Eckhart, Johannes Tauler, and Molinos teach us the inner path and describe it in detail.[†]

Molinos speaks of five steps of deepening immersion. He teaches how we must turn away from all that is external in order to arrive within. 1) We must turn away from everything creature-like that corresponds to our physical body; 2) From all life that corresponds to the forces in our etheric body; 3) From all the talents that correspond to our astral body; 4) From our "I" that coincides with our fourth part; and 5) That we must merge with God.

However, it gradually became necessary for us to tread both paths, the inner and outer simultaneously. For this reason, in the eleventh and twelfth centuries, the occult schools of the Rosicrucians appeared and taught both paths.

The writer of the Apocalypse first showed us the outer path. He showed us that we must be entirely separated from our personality in order to tread this path. In a humble way, he says that on the island of Patmos he was caught up by the spirit.† This has a very specific meaning. In order to tread this external path, that is, in order to find union with the divine in the macrocosm, it is necessary for us to choose a solid point from which we concentrate ourselves. So John, the theologian, calculated spiritually the position the stars would have on September 30, 395, and from this point he had his visions.†

On September 30 in 395, the sun was in the constellation of Virgo, the Virgin—that is, in front of the constellation—and the moon was below her. We expressed this picture in one of the seven seals.†

This time can also be calculated exoterically. Scholars have done this and concluded that the Apocalypse was written only around this time by John Chrysostom, who was alive at the time. But in reality, we are touching upon a great secret here; for the Apocalypse was, of course, written much earlier, and the writer had merely placed himself in the year 395.

Both paths, of course, harbor dangers that an esotericist must watch out for. Even esotericists who absorb theosophical teachings are attacked by many doubts, for this is according to nature; also it is better than if they were to thoughtlessly accept everything with blind faith. But they must, of course, overcome this doubt, and their strength will thereby grow.

A second danger, into which esotericists can fall on this external path, is instability. Everyone of us who has concerned ourself with the study of world evolution will have experienced how interests that we had previously, disappear; how we can no longer hold on to anything earthly. Here the danger that lies close at hand is not that we become conscious of the instability, but rather that it presents itself to us in the guise of a high ideal that we must strive toward, a mission that we must fulfill. If we see through this, however, and recognize it as camouflaged instability, then we are making great progress on the right path.

When descending into our inner life there are also two dangers that threaten us. Through immersion into our own souls we can attain a certain sensual pleasure, a feeling of comfortable ease in the divine, and thereby fall into a subtle egotism. This then leads us to turn away from everything surrounding us that ought to still interest us.

The second danger is that as we penetrate into the spiritual world through our inner soul life, we interpret what comes to meet us as a revelation of the spirit, when it may well be no more than our own feelings.

Mystics of the middle ages did not yet have the teachings of theosophy. We do not find them among those mystics. Their union with the divine is like a Neo-Buddhism. They do not yet need the external path.

The verse *Ex Deo nascimur, In Christo morimur*, is in mysticism also in the form: In Christ we live.

Esoteric Lesson
STRASSBURG, FEBRUARY 19, 1911

Manuscript from Alice Kinkel.

Suppose we asked the leaders of the present-day esoteric Rosicrucian stream why people today should devote themselves to an esoteric life; whether it might not be better for them to say to themselves, "If the will of the divine-spiritual world wants to allow me to enter higher worlds then it will do this by itself, and I will therefore wait." Then these leaders would answer, "You are forgetting that you as a human being on the earth are on a battlefield. Indeed, you are in the battle between the good spiritual forces against Lucifer and Ahriman. Both are striving to collect soldiers for their armies from the souls of human beings."

What does Lucifer want to make out of a human soul? From a one-sided point of view he has a high, noble goal.

We know that the previous incarnation of our earth was old Moon, a cosmos of wisdom; that it was entirely permeated by wisdom. But there one power that is now embodied on the earth was lacking: love. So, too, Lucifer is entirely permeated by wisdom; but he knows love not at all. He devoted himself entirely to wisdom; he became drunk with wisdom, so to speak, and for this reason he wants to fill all beings, all children of earth, with wisdom.

Therein the great temptation always lies for human beings. Lucifer, whose power lives in us, speaks to us approximately the following: "You want to see into all connections and relationships; you want to know everything. Everything will become clear to you if you take me entirely into yourself." He wants to give us wisdom without love, but this leads to self-seeking wisdom. Lucifer still believes that he can win human beings as soldiers for his army, and he works hard at achieving this.

Lucifer is present in all learning and knowing, in all perception. There is only one place where he cannot get to us, and that is when we are entirely immersed with devotion into our meditations, in wisdom—then we escape Lucifer.

And Ahriman, what does Ahriman want? He wants to give power to human beings. Ahriman is a spirit who fell away even earlier. At the time of old Sun, the archangels were human beings, but entirely different from us today. Thinking at that time was immediately translated into action. The human beings of that time were mighty beings. Thought immediately became reality. Wisdom had not yet achieved the level of old Moon, but there was power. Power alone, without wisdom, leads to black magic, to darkening.

We conquer Ahriman through the attitude that we want to devote ourselves to the world-spirit; through the desire to be the instrument of the world-spirit alone and allow only the world-spirit to work in us. If we do our meditation with this attitude, then we can conquer Ahriman.

We conquer Lucifer by filling the "I" entirely with this meditative content: Lucifer can enter my astral body only, not my "I."

The Christ-Impulse is love.

Love without wisdom would be very bad. An example of this would be the mother who loved her daughter like an idol, and therefore could not refuse her anything. Because of this wrong-headed upbringing, the daughter became a famous mixer of poisons at the beginning of the nineteenth century. This same daughter's individuality is incarnated again as a black magician. She was incarnated again so quickly because such beings are "spit out" of the spiritual world, so to speak.

Lucifer is redeemed by Christ.

Human beings who take Lucifer into themselves on future Jupiter will become mighty beings, but they will experience burning of their "I" in wisdom without love.

On future Venus it will then be a case of black magic, a condition that will be like spiritual drowning. In order for pure love to shine on Venus, it is necessary for human beings already now to have a will toward esotericism.

Esoteric Lesson

HANOVER, MARCH 5, 1911

Record A: Notes from Paula Stryczek; Record B: Manuscript from Nelly Lichtenberg; Record C: Manuscript from Alice Kinkel.

RECORD A   Drowning — Burning

Daily verse: Sunday

Two verses are given to pupils in the Rosicrucian schools to support them in the meditations. They are: Beware of drowning in your esoteric striving. Beware of burning in the fire of your own "I."

Protect yourself in your esoteric striving from drowning
Protect yourself from burning up from the fire of your own "I."

There are two ways to strive toward the spirit, an inner way and an outer.

Everything around us is like a veil, like a covering over the spirit, which we must penetrate in order to get to the spiritual world lying behind it. But in which direction? This covering surrounds us on all sides: above, below, in front of us, behind us, to the right and left of us.

And within also, all that we experience as joy and pain is like a veil, like a mist that conceals the spiritual world within us. And this is the same spiritual world that we find when we penetrate through the external covering.

So that humanity can develop further and grow into the spiritual world, from time to time there always appear those who are more advanced than is normally permitted by the current stage of humanity's evolution. These people have messages for us concerning the conditions of human development that extend far into the future. Such advanced beings must exist in order to lead humanity into the future. John, who wrote the Apocalypse, was one such person. Wanting to write down a revelation of the future, he said to himself: If I write this book out of my present environment, out of all that surrounds me, it will be influenced by the self that lives in my body—by the "I" that was created out of, is bound by, and is connected with all that surrounds me and with all that is in me. I must free myself of all of this. He had to place himself on something like a rock that would serve him as a solid foundation, upon which he would not waver, and would not be influenced by anything surrounding him or within himself that might cause him to falter. And he transported himself to the evening of September 30, 395, on the island of Patmos at sundown, when the sun had already disappeared below the horizon but its effects could still be felt, and as the stars and the moon appeared. And the constellation of Virgo, the virgin, was present above the western horizon, illuminated by the glow of the descending sun. And below it, at the virgin's feet, was the moon. This picture is represented again in one of the seals: the virgin with the radiant sun and the moon at her feet. Thus all of these seals were brought forth out of deep mystical relationships.

John broke through the covering that surrounds us in the direction of the constellation Virgo. There are twelve star constellations. Seven of them are good—those represented on the seals. The other five are more or less dangerous.

Just as John chose this particular point in time and space in order to free himself completely from himself and from all things temporal, so too, Rosicrucian pupils must find solid ground in themselves. And the best way for this to happen is for us to allow theosophical teachings to work upon us.

The astral body, and thereby the etheric body, becomes expanded by listening to theosophical ideas. This is the effect upon everyone who hears something about theosophy. But the effect upon those who are inclined toward theosophy is different from the effect upon those who are not so inclined. The former feel the expansion of their etheric bodies, and fill them with theosophical teaching, by accepting this teaching. The others feel an emptiness in their etheric bodies because they do not accept these ideas, which would have filled the expansion. Then doubt and skepticism arise because of this emptiness. However, the former feel themselves being poured into the universe, and they must be careful to not let themselves go too far. For then they would have a feeling of hollowness, of not being at home in these widths of space, much like a fish that is removed from water and yet cannot live in the air because it has not yet adapted its organs to this changed element. If a theosophist devotes him or herself to the teachings of theosophy and he or she continues expanding, then he or she becomes lost in this unknown, unfamiliar element. One must be careful not to drown here. And this is certainly possible, that one can study theosophy earnestly, take it in, and penetrate it.

It is possible for one to take hold of theosophy with one's feeling, not only in thinking and willing, but also to completely permeate it with one's feeling. One can do this only with great earnestness. One must acquire a solid foundation in oneself—like John when he wanted to write the Apocalypse, and set himself on the island of Patmos in the evening of September 30, 395, at the time of sunset. Astronomically, this position of the stars (Sun, Virgo, Moon) on that evening can be checked, and has been. Now materialistic scholarship has concluded from this that the Apocalypse was written at that time. And then we hear that scientific scholarship has ascertained this. In this way, scientific scholarship has ascertained this fact!

On the inner path, one finds all the joys and sorrows, pains and bliss that live in us. But all of this is nothing more than what lives in our lower, transitory self. This whole world of desires surrounds us like a misty fog that hides the spiritual world. We must break through it to reach the spiritual world. There are forces that approach the esoteric pupils to make the fog denser. Unless we fight against it, this fog gets thicker. We must burn off this fog in order that we not burn up in the fire of our own desires. If we do not overcome this fog, if we do not set ourselves against this ever-thickening fog caused by Luciferic and Ahrimanic powers, then we are prisoners, as it is called in occultism. As a matter of fact, there are people in the present time who enter existence with great gifts and quickly attain a certain stage, but they are then completely enveloped by the adversarial powers, in just such a fog, and are unable to escape. This is called occult imprisonment.

Our world of desires consists of nothing but egotism. And we can conquer this egotism only through deep humility. What is the thought that can lead us to overcome egotism? It is the thought that we already discussed yesterday in the exoteric lecture; the thought that we have killed the Christ.† We are murderers; yes, that is what we are. We can transform this fact, but only by allowing the Pauline saying "Not I, but Christ in me" to become a truth in us, to live in us. Rather than killing the divine in us through egotism in our life of desires, we should allow Christ to live within us. With awe-filled earnestness we should approach this easy and yet so very difficult task.

We have arisen out of the divine. This is expressed in the Rosicrucian verse: *Ex Deo nascimur*. We should take upon ourselves all suffering, willingly and patiently with the thought that we have killed Christ; we should devote ourselves to him completely, we should die in him: *In Christo morimur*. Then we will be born again through the Holy Spirit; we will awake again: *Per Spiritum Sanctum reviviscimus*.

This verse sounds different when expressed exoterically rather than esoterically. But the difference is found only in one word that is left out. In leaving out this word, when we refrain from speaking this word out of awe-filled reverence for the one whom this word expresses, then our feelings go to him whose name is not spoken out of deep reverence.

Exoteric:

Ex Deo nascimur.
In Christo morimur.
Per Spiritum Sanctum reviviscimus.

Esoteric:

Ex Deo nascimur.
In — — — morimur.
Per Spiritum Sanctum reviviscimus.

In these lines is presented again, how the human being has arisen out of the spirit; how the human being was originally contained in the spirit:

In the spirit lay the seed of my body ...
In my body lies the seed of the spirit ...

* * *

Record B

Two meditations are given to the disciple in Rosicrucian schooling to support the meditations. These are:

In your esoteric striving guard yourself against drowning.

And secondly,

Protect yourself from burning up in the fire of your own ego.

There are two paths for those who are striving esoterically, the one outward and the one inward. Something lies before our eyes like a veil, like a covering, that we must penetrate in order to get to the spiritual world lying behind it. This veil lies not just in one direction, but all around us—above, below, left, right—the veil must be penetrated in every direction. And the same veil is found on the path inward.

All that we experience in terms of joy and suffering is like a fog around us that covers the spiritual world, the same spiritual world that we find when we penetrate the outer covering. So that humanity can advance toward the spiritual, there are from time to time, people who are further developed than current human development would otherwise allow. They have messages to deliver concerning times that reach far into the future of human evolution. One such person was John, the writer of the Apocalypse. However, before he wrote this revelation concerning future human conditions he said to himself: Before I can do this I must manage to escape my present surroundings entirely, these surroundings in which I am influenced by my own self, which is connected and bound to all that surrounds me. I must get free of all of this. He had to place himself as if on a rock that would serve him as a solid foundation, upon which he would not waiver, upon which he could not be influenced by anything of that which surged in him and around him. So he transferred himself to the evening of September 30, 395, at sundown on the island of Patmos. When the sun had nearly disappeared from the horizon, as the moon and the stars emerged, the constellation of Virgo, the virgin, stood in the western sky with the radiant sun, and below at her feet was the moon. This picture of the virgin with the radiant sun, the moon at her feet, is given again in the seal. Thus all the seals are derived from deeply mystical connections.

Thus John penetrated the outer covering in this direction, in the direction of the constellation Virgo. However, there are twelve directions, toward the twelve constellations—seven of them are good; five are more or less dangerous. Just as John chose this specific place in time and space in order to free himself from himself and from everything temporal that surrounded him, so too, the Rosicrucian pupil must find in him or herself a firm foothold, must find solid ground.

All who hear theosophical teachings sense an effect upon their astral body, and through this their etheric body: an expansion of the etheric body occurs. That is the case with everyone. But the effects vary. Those who feels themselves drawn to theosophical teachings will have their expanded etheric body filled with the content of this teaching. Those who are repelled by theosophical teachings also feel an expansion of their etheric bodies. However, because they cannot accept the ideas, emptiness arises; and through this emptiness, doubt and skepticism.

Those who are permeated by theosophical teachings can sometimes become poured too far out into the universe because of their expanded etheric body. Then they have a feeling of hollowness, of not feeling at home in these widths of space, like a fish that comes onto land out of the water and cannot live there because its organs are not adapted to this environment. One is lost in this unknown place to which one is unaccustomed. One must guard against drowning. And one protects oneself from this by taking up theosophy with great earnestness; by taking hold of it with feeling, not only with thinking but by being entirely permeated by it. One must acquire a firm foothold in oneself as John did when he wanted to write the Apocalypse.

He placed himself in the evening of September 30, 395, on the island of Patmos. This can also be checked astronomically, this arrangement of the stars (Sun, Virgo, Moon), and it has been checked. And from this, materialistic scholarship has concluded that the Apocalypse was written at that time. And then we are told that scholarship has verified this. Thus scholarship has proven this!

On the path inward we find all the joys and suffering, pain and bliss that live in us. Yet all this belongs only to our lower, perishable self. This whole world of desires surrounds us like a fog that covers the spiritual for us; it prevents us from seeing and noticing the spiritual. We must break through it to reach the spiritual. There are powers that approach the esoteric pupil and make this fog thicker and thicker. This fog becomes increasingly dense around us; we must burn it off if it is not to burn us, if we are not to burn up in the fire of our own desires. If we do not overcome it, then we are imprisoned by Ahriman and Lucifer in this fog. Thus, as a matter of fact, there are people who enter life with great talents and very quickly achieve a certain level, but are then are entirely enveloped by the adversarial powers. This is called being "held in occult imprisonment." Our world of desires is entirely made up of egotism. And we can overcome this egotism only through deep humility. What is the thought that can lead us to overcome this egotism? It is the thought that we discussed yesterday in the exoteric lecture; the thought that we have killed the Christ. We are murderers—yes, that is what we are. And all of this we can compensate for only by allowing the Pauline saying to live in us, to become truth in us: "Not I, but Christ in me."

We do not want to kill the divine in us through egotism in our life of desires, but rather allow Christ to live in us. With painful seriousness we must attempt to carry out this easy, yet difficult, task. We have arisen out of the divine. This is expressed in the Rosicrucian verse: *E.D.N.* We should accept all suffering willingly, with the thought that we have killed Christ. We should devote ourselves to him completely; we should die in him: *I.C.M.* Then we should be born again through the Holy Spirit, awaken again: *P.S.S.R.* This verse sounds different when spoken esoterically than when spoken exoterically, but the difference lies in just one word that is omitted. When we do not speak this word, out of awe-filled reverence for the one whom this word expresses, then our feelings go to him whose name, out of deep reverence, is not spoken.

In this is presented again, how the human being arises out of the spiritual world, how he is originally contained in the spirit, as the Masters of Wisdom and Harmony of Feelings say in the verse: *In the spirit lay the seed of my body...*

* * *

Record C

The two paths that lead us into the spiritual world:

The first path is going out into the macrocosm. The experience that a person has thereby is like drowning in fear; this is especially strong for someone who has not been properly prepared.

The second way leads down into one's own soul. This is the descent into the microcosm. It is like a burning in shame.

Esoteric Lesson
MANNHEIM, MARCH 10, 1911

Manuscript from Alice Kinkel.

The first fruit of our meditation is this: that we get a feeling for our striving to unite with the beings of the higher hierarchies, and this should express itself as a feeling of being taken up into higher worlds, of having arrived at the place where we stood at the very beginning of existence; this is how we should experience it. This feeling of being taken into the spiritual world should become warm and alive. Those who would enter the spiritual world must say to themselves that everything, everything must change for esotericists; their concepts, feelings, and knowledge must change. Take the egotism of human beings: it is Luciferic beings who have given us memory. And while we practice thriftiness in the physical life, we are terrible spendthrifts with the powers of our soul and spirit. However, we must become thrifty with these wasted forces, and transform them into powers of vision. In order to do this, we need to practice self-knowledge. From morning to evening, we scatter and waste our feelings and sensations too selfishly. Therefore, we must first go through egotism with our spiritual-soul forces. There is a danger here for an esotericist: the danger that egotism will be strengthened, therefore all genuine esotericism must be accompanied by a moral and intellectual purification of the human being.

We must be clear that as esotericists, we are required to do the impossible, and that we must strive for the impossible. All striving is precisely this, a striving for the impossible; and it is also impossible to be non-egotistical.

We must attempt to have the proper feeling for all striving for inner development. Greed for knowledge and advancement is not appropriate, but rather, a serious feeling for the duty to develop. This is what we should have, because the divine spirit has put powers in us and then developed them without our involvement, but also placed active forces within us that we ourselves must develop through deeds.

It is the greatest sin to oppose the divine spirit, and not develop these forces that the Godhead placed in us for the salvation of human evolution. These forces in us are so strong that they will lead us up into the spiritual world, if only after a long period of time. For this reason an esotericist should say: "I will wait, for I know that the powers in me lead me upward one day into the spiritual world." These forces can do this if we are devoted in the right way to the spiritual world.

The auxiliary exercises create the character traits necessary for us on the physical plane. They are control of thinking, self-chosen actions, imperturbable composure, and so forth. Gradually we will develop a chamber in our hearts, in our souls, in which we can keep our most holy soul content, where we are esotericists; while at the same time we are in external life. Battle with ourselves and with the world is, of course, inevitable; we must become fighters if we are to become esotericists.

The many complaints of those who meditate that thoughts storm them and disturb them are to be answered this way: these thoughts are beings that flutter about us, that increasingly attack us. And one can only say: be happy that this is happening, this means success in meditation; it shows you that thought is a spiritual power. Courage, fearlessness, and faith are the character traits that esotericists need on their path.

Esoteric Lesson
BERLIN, MARCH 15, 1911

Record A: Anonymous Manuscript (Vreede Collection); Record B: Manuscript from Nelly Lichtenberg; Notes from Paula Stryczek with addenda from Günther Wagner.

RECORD A

As was explained the last time [January 17, 1911] our meditations should stand under the motto: "Steady drops hollow the stone." The study of theosophical works serves as an effective preparation for the exercises. It is better to have read one work twenty-five times than to have read five books five times each; and anyone who has read a book two or three times must not imagine that he or she has read it at all. If on a specific day of the year we have experienced something specific while meditating, then on the same day a year later, if we have really studied in the meantime, we will be able to experience much more. It is good to retain the same meditation through long periods of time. This is much better than constantly changing one's meditation.

Not only should we enrich our thoughts through study, we should also develop certain feelings. We can find a starting point for understanding very deep things in simple sensations. For example, we should at some time or another become aware of what it feels like to take hold of something, say, an object of some kind, versus what it feels like to be taken hold of, for example, by the hand. Here we can feel a clear difference, if, for example, we imagine the feeling that is stirred in us when we take hold of a snail or when a snail crawls over our hand without our knowing it. If we develop well these different feelings, then we can form a concept of the difference between the subsensory world and the suprasensory world.

The whole physical world, with our feelings of this kind, is maya or illusion. We can picture this world as a field or a plane; above it is a suprasensory world, under it is a subsensory world. The suprasensory world is such that it can be brought together with the feeling of being taken hold of; the subsensory world, on the other hand, can be associated with the feeling of taking hold of something.

In Rosicrucian teachings, the subsensory world was always called the elemental world; this is the world of the elements: fire, air, water, and earth.

One penetrates to the element of earth by meditating on triangles, squares, pentagons; altogether on geometric figures. This should be done by writing these figures with the fingers of one hand on the palm of the other hand. Then one should drop every thought of the hands and writing, and imagine the feeling of the figure being written onto one's hand as if floating freely in space. One should immerse oneself in this feeling. In this way, one gradually takes hold of the earth element.

The element of water is grasped by imagining a fixed, material point and another mobile point that moves in a circle around the first point. Then one should write this on one's hand and proceed as with the first figure. One should think of the second point as one that rotates continuously.

For the air element one thinks of two fixed points that want to fly apart from each other into infinite distances after they first describe a kind of semicircle around each other. If we work with this figure exactly as with the preceding figures, then we grasp the air element. Then we do not merely feel the air flowing past us and caressing us, we rather take hold of it.

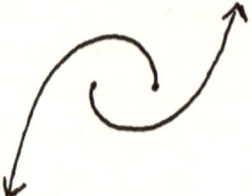

For the element of fire, we think of a closed figure such as a loop or a lemniscate (a figure eight on its side). One should especially feel that there is an intersecting point where the curve touches itself.

One should do these exercises constantly for an extended period of time. They are not easy. One must first acquire a certain skill in feeling the sensations in space without using one's hand; and secondly, in holding the figures firmly in mind. But then these exercises lead to perception of the elemental world; one learns how to take hold of the elemental world.

However, there is a rule, without exception, that these exercises simultaneously make one egotistical. For this reason, one must never do them without at the same time developing an all-encompassing feeling of compassion for everything that causes joy and pain to develop in the human soul.

When we ascend into the suprasensory world, we are actually taken hold of by higher beings who use us as instruments, just as we use our eyes, ears, and so forth. The danger that accompanies this experience is that one loses oneself, in the negative sense of the term. That is why it is necessary, at the same time, to develop courage and fearlessness. Then we can calmly allow ourselves to be taken hold of by spiritual beings in the spiritual world, so that we feel: now an angel is inspiring us, now an archangel, and so forth. Imaginations lead us into the subsensory world; inspirations lead us into the suprasensory world.

We see how these two directions, above and below, are united in the Rosicrucian path. It is necessary for us, as clairvoyants, to learn to strictly distinguish between the elemental world and suprasensory beings, between two aspects of what appears as a unity here in the physical world. Anyone who would see the two together—in one picture, the being and its elemental expression—such a person would be making a fundamental mistake, and confuse everything. In the beginning it is not easy to separate the two regions, because the astral vision and the devachanic vision both exist. But one gradually learns, when looking upward at a being, to immediately descend in order to find the elemental expression of this being; just as when looking at an object, one can immediately look down into a body of water to see its reflection.

The Saturn condition of the earth could not be described if one could not, on the one hand, raise oneself to beings such as the spirits of will or the spirits of personality; and on the other hand, penetrate to the spirits of fire. So too, for the Sun stage of the earth, one must recognize and know the spirits of wisdom, and the archangels and the element of air. In the description found in *An Outline of Esoteric Science* both are given together: how the thrones send out the heat of Saturn, and so forth. However, it is necessary in observing this, to experience this as a duality.

One must prepare oneself to see and hear things in the spiritual world that one has never seen or heard here below. Those who expect to find on the other side only what they already know will never be able to penetrate into the spiritual world. This is what is expressed in the second sentence of our Rosicrucian verse: *In — — — morimur.* Only when death in Christ occurs in us, can we again be reawakened by the Holy Spirit. This is again expressed in more detail in what is, to a certain extent, a commentary to our two-part verse; that is what is given to us by the masters:

In my body lies the seed of the spirit...

* * *

Record B

We have already seen the last time that we should not long for new exercises. Rather, it is just when we steadfastly, faithfully do the same exercises daily (example: "Steady drops hollow the stone.") that they affect us in a fruitful way. Feelings will settle in us that lead us up into the spiritual world.

It is very much the same with reading theosophical books. Theosophists must not think they really know a book if they have read it only three times. That is as good as never having read it. And instead of reading five books five times, we should read one book twenty-five times. We will then certainly notice the results; unconsciously they flow into our meditations and create mile-markers in our path into spiritual heights.

Everything around us, the entire world of physical, sensory perceptions, we must imagine more or less as a large wide field (a surface). The suprasensory is spread out above it; the subsensory is spread out below it. (Imagine the sensory world, and the ordinary world of thoughts bound to the brain [maya] as a surface, a field; above it the suprasensory world [hierarchies, and so forth]; below it the subsensory world, from which comes the uppermost sphere of the elemental world. How do the two differ?

We are confronted by the subsensory in this way, as if we lay hold of it; by the suprasensory world, as if we were taken hold of by it. For example, imagine taking hold of a snail or letting it crawl over your hand, that is the difference. If we imagine these two sensations often enough, we will certainly find the difference between suprasensory and the subsensory worlds.

If we want to get to know the subsensory or elemental world, we should imagine geometric figures (triangle, square) and meditate upon them. Indeed, we should do it in the following way:

First we draw a triangle in one hand with the other hand; then we carry this activity over into free-floating space, as if it no longer had anything to do with us. But we are to call forth the same feeling in ourselves as before, when we drew the figure onto the hand.

If we want to understand the watery element in the elemental world, we must think of a point around which another point is constantly circling. Again one first draws it on one's hand and then carries it over into the air, but in such a way that one imagines the movement as well as the sensation that is thereby brought about.

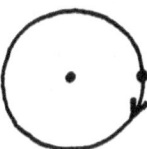

If we want to live into the part of the elemental world that creates the air, then we must imagine two points that at first circle around one another in a half circle, but then fly apart and are lost in space.

Finally, to live into fire we must imagine a point that is moving and touches itself again and again.

Both of these last two symbols must also be first drawn in the hand and then carried over into freely floating air.

When we meditate on these symbols in the indicated way, we will certainly notice how we live into the elements, how we will recognize which beings live in them. At the same time we will feel how we are constantly becoming more egotistical. These exercises can benefit us only if we simultaneously develop a sense of universal compassion, which allows us to experience every cry or sound of complaint, every moan of pain in our surroundings, as if they were originating in our own tortured hearts.

And just as the danger of egotism is great when we settle into the subsensory world, so the danger of losing ourselves to the world is not any less dangerous when we settle into the suprasensory world. It is factually true that we are possessed by higher beings; they move into us, take possession of us, in order to work through us. Now it is incumbent upon us to preserve our "I," our own self; not to lose it. Courage, steadfastness, and fearlessness help us to do this. It is entirely useless for us to fear the possibility of any particular accident ahead of time. On the contrary, one should carry one's karma with courage and fearlessness; it is of no help to be afraid of it. From the beginning, we must imagine that we will find something in the spiritual world that is different from the physical world. Spiritual beings present there come to meet us. If we enter that world expecting to find the spiritual beings in their element, then we will easily be misled. It is true that by means of such exercises we come to understand the earlier conditions of the earth, and also learn how to set ourselves into them. But such experiences only stimulate us in such at way that the intuition awakens the imagination. If we, for example, imagine the thrones and the spirits of personality at work on old Saturn, and at the same time the element of fire, then we will be misled by our picture of old Saturn. We will understand this condition only if we are able to picture both of them (the spiritual beings and the element) entirely separated. Fire must be pictured as something entirely separated, as a mirror image. The same is true for the sun and the moon. The spiritual beings, whether angels or archangels, work from above downward. They want to enter into human beings, take hold of them in order to work on the earth. We should open ourselves to them, but without surrendering our sense of self.

(Working one's way into the spiritual world is connected with a feeling of being grasped by the hierarchies, which want to work through us; working our way into the subsensory world is connected with the feeling of grasping something. The two feelings must be kept separate. For example, while we are meditating into the Saturn condition of the earth, if the Thrones and the Spirits of Personality appear together with the element of fire, this is wrong and misleading. One must feel clearly the two as separated. Rise up to the hierarchy, dip down into the elemental world, and then back up again.)

Esoteric Lesson
PRAGUE, MARCH 29, 1911

Record A: Anonymous manuscript from the Vreede collection; Record B: Manuscript from Alice Kinkel; Record C: Notes from Günther Wagner.

In one manuscript, these words follow the Rosicrucian verse: "We close our gathering with the prayer of the day. The stones are silent; I have laid the eternal creative word into them." Compare this to CW 265 *Freemasonry and Ritual Work,* where we find this verse in a somewhat expanded form in Rudolf Steiner's handwriting in a facsimile reproduction. In a lecture from October 13, 1906, Rudolf Steiner speaks of an old Rosicrucian verse: "I have laid the eternal creative word into the Stone." (*The Christian Mystery*, CW 97).

RECORD A

If we wish to follow the path of esoteric development, we will be given certain verses from an esoteric training, in which lies the power to develop our higher, spiritual organs, if we apply the verses and meditations in the right way. Wisdom and the harmony of feelings were given. (Mantra: Daily verse Wednesday for Thursday)

When we wish to immerse ourselves in the first lines of our morning exercise:

In pure rays of light,
Shines the divinity of the world —

we should understand that we will gain nothing for our elevation into the spiritual world if we let only the literal meaning of these words work on us. We should realize that we cannot see the divinity in the physical rays of the sun. Rather, we must look for this divinity in its high spirituality behind the rays of the sun. The sun's rays are only the outer garment for the divine. We should not take any picture from the outer world for our meditations, but rather, such a picture should be created out of the spirit.

To begin with we must eliminate anything in our consciousness that reminds us of our outer surroundings. We must be able to forget everything, large and small, that stirs us in our daily lives. All outer impressions should be silent within.

If we have prepared ourselves in this way, then we are immersing ourselves with our thoughts and feelings in the right way in these verses. After we have done these meditations for a longer or shorter time, then we must attempt to empty our soul of these thoughts also. In this way our souls arrive at a condition of calm and quiet; and when the intellect has been brought to silence, the higher members of the human being are lifted out of the physical body and enter into the spiritual world.

However, this does not mean that the pupil has attained everything. For if we are not in the proper soul condition, having prepared ourselves for a long period of time by working on our weaknesses; that is, if we enter the spiritual world without the proper humility in our souls, and without correct knowledge of our bad character traits, the spiritual world will appear to us in a false light. It will appear to us in a false light to the same extent the outside world would appear falsely to someone who, after wearing red colored glasses around the house, forgot to take them off when going outside. Everything outside would appear would appear in a red light; that is, entirely differently from the way it looks in reality. Just as wrongly would esotericists judge the things in the suprasensory world, if they were to see them through the colored lenses of their personality. Esotericists would see the angels, for example, which stand one level above the human, not as radiant beings of light as one should see them in reality, rather, these angels would appear before them as horrible animal forms or other grotesque things. If they should meet on the astral plane the beings that stand at the stage between the angels and humans (that are Luciferic or Ahrimanic beings), these beings could appear to them as shining, radiant angels, as dissembling, alluring figures, and, yes, even in the form of the Masters of Wisdom—in order to mislead the occultists because they are still ruled too much by their arrogance and their own personalities. Esotericists should guard themselves against this, and be concerned to lay aside their pride. If we want to tread an esoteric path, we can prepare ourselves only with the greatest humility in our hearts and through limitless reverence for the divine.

There are other verses that can also lead us to the development of higher organs, and to imagination, inspiration, and intuition. But these exercises can also be done wrongly, or be misunderstood so that we are led down a false path. For example, if we were to meditate with a certain egotistical self-awareness, "Yes, a part of the Godhead itself lies in me!" In this way we cultivate arrogance within us, and we achieve nothing more than strengthening our personality. We would all too soon forget that a part of the Godhead can be found in every animal, in every plant, indeed, in every one of God's creatures. However, to be able to enter into the spiritual world, we must leave behind precisely everything in us that is personality in the physical world. Above all, we must acquire a subtle feeling for the truth. If esotericists lack this feeling, they will soon perceive in themselves that they must bear the consequences. Esotericists are not allowed to be satisfied with the excuse that they thought they were telling the truth. Esotericists will never succeed with this excuse, for they are responsible for every one of their words; the consequences of untruth will fall upon them, even if they thought they had spoken the truth. In our everyday life, it is often difficult to stay with the truth; things often have a nuance that leads into an untruth. How often one hears, "I thought it was the truth." It is not easy to tread the path that leads into the higher worlds.

A good method that we can all use in order to come to greater clarity concerning our personality is to look often at certain portions of our life at least once per year, perhaps on our birthday. Then we should ask ourselves what we have to show for good and bad deeds in the course of this stretch of life? If we examine ourselves very earnestly, we shall find in most cases that our good deeds do not arise from our personality, but rather that we allowed them to happen out of an inner impulse.

This inner impulse is our guardian angel, who drives us to our good deeds. On the other hand, we must not rely entirely upon our angel, thinking at every opportunity that our guardian angel will give us an impulse soon enough; for this would be completely wrong.

Our guardian angel would soon leave us—that is, in a certain sense, leave us.

If we continue this exercise for a number of years, we will experience that nothing contributes more to our discovery of character failings and their improvement than this taking stock of our accounts. Thus, we gradually prepare ourselves to tread the esoteric path in a fruitful way. We do this by constantly freeing ourselves more and more from our personality; in a certain sense by emptying ourselves so that the Christ principle can enter us as Paul indicated with the words "Not I, but Christ in me." This being filled by the Christ principle frees our personality of egotism and leads to a vision of the highest. The name "Christ" is actually not the name of the principle that should be expressed, for the divine power that one names with this name is not to be spoken aloud. For this reason the Masters of Wisdom and Harmony of Feelings did not speak this name during their hours of consecration when they spoke these words:

Ex Deo nascimur.
In — — — morimur.
Per Spiritum Sanctum reviviscimus.

* * *

RECORD B

Prayer to the spirit of the day (Wednesday for Thursday)

When we find ourselves in an event such as the one that is to be held here today, we begin with a verse in order for us to be inspired in the proper way. We address the spirit of the day. These verses are mantras and possess great power.

This evening we stand before an especially beneficial day for an esoteric lesson, the evening before Thursday, the day of Jupiter. We call not only to the great Spirit of the Sun that stands behind Thursday, but also to the spirit that is best able to inspire us in a corresponding way.

You all have certain exercises in order to fulfill your meditation in the right way, and this is actually the technical part of the esoteric life. These exercises are to be repeated with energy and endurance day after day. The intention is to fill the soul with such a content that can gradually lead up into the spiritual world.

To begin with this content is to fill the soul in a conceptual form, with complete exclusion of all other thoughts and pictures of the physical world; all cares and worries. It should live in the soul for as long as possible, as vividly and pictorially as possible.

For many, because of their karma, this filling of the soul with this meditative thought content must remain as the only correct kind of meditation.

Along the path that we undertake when we devote ourselves to esotericism, we will see how weak we are. We will see how weak we are when we step out into the great macrocosm; and how egotistical we are when we attempt to enter into our own inner soul life. It would be wrong for us to want to say, "Indeed, God is in me, the divine seed is in me; therefore, I do not need to look out into the world." No, the Logos is everywhere, in stone and in plant, in animal and in human beings. It reveals itself out there in everything! The Sun is its garment.

And when we observe human beings: Are these sheaths that surround them like a cloak? No, they are what we are to work with; not a cloak that would have nothing to do with us. And when a hammer is broken; only after other things have been done to it, can it be again used for work.

Every kind of egotism, every form of vanity must be eliminated in esotericists.

We have been given two tasks: first, to fill ourselves with the content of the meditations, to permeate our soul completely. Second, we are then to empty our souls completely of the content of the meditation. The soul does not then remain empty, but rather the spiritual world streams in. The pupil knows this moment when all subjectivity is completely overcome. But only then is it the true spiritual world; for otherwise, one becomes a deceived deceiver. It may appear to such people that the master appears, but in reality it could be that an evil being has taken on the mask of the master.

Truthfulness is an unconditionally necessary requirement in esotericism. One is not allowed only to believe that something is true, rather one must first research, and only then is one allowed to say something.

We should take one day per year for a retrospective on the previous year, perhaps on the birthday, and we should review all the events of the year in an exact way. In doing so, we will discover that we have done more good in the year than we thought. But this examination will also show us that it was not ourselves, but our good angel who did the good things; and that it was we who did everything that was botched.

* * *

RECORD C

In pure rays of light...

For example, for a longer period of time think yourself into a spiritual Sun, from which divinity shines into the world; forget yourself completely; then let the words fall away too. Then with time the spiritual world will be revealed.

Do not meditate on, "In me is a divine self." Then one does not remain humble. If we lack humility, angels easily appear caricatured—in an animal or similar form—and Luciferic spirits appear as forms of light. Even if an pupil stands at a stage such that he or she is consciously in the presence of the masters, but does not remain humble—perhaps even brags to others about the experience—then it is easily possible for evil spirits or an evil occultist to use the appearance of a master, and then lie or seduce the pupil.

Without humility, even when researching Atlantean conditions, for example, errors easily arise; so that perhaps something spiritual, say the etheric parts of a human being, are not seen.

An unconditional striving for truth is also necessary; even speaking an erroneous statement in good faith has severe karmic consequences.

When surrendering one's personality in meditation, it is easy for everything to flutter away. Against this happening one should hold firmly to Paul's words, "Not I, but Christ in me." The Christ-principle holds everything together.

From time to time, for example on one's birthday, it is good to look back on the past. One will gradually get the feeling that the good deeds were not done by oneself, but rather by something within one; one's guardian angel. On the other hand, one also gets the impression that one has botched much by oneself. Therefore, we should look up to our guardian angel.

Esoteric Lesson

BERLIN, JUNE 12, 1911

Record A: Manuscript from Nelly Lichtenberg. Notes from Günther Wagner; Record B: Manuscript from Louise Clason.

RECORD A

My dear sisters and brothers! We must be very clear that there is a great difference between outer, exoteric knowing, and the knowing that theosophy provides. When we allow an outer perception to work on us, pictures and concepts are formed in us. In this way, we get to know the thing that we are perceiving. We know something about it. Are matters the same with theosophical knowledge? Here too, when we are told about the four members of the human being, or something concerning the planetary conditions of the earth, or the Akashic Chronicle, we form concepts, pictures in our mind, concerning these things. But there is something else involved. While exoteric knowledge does not enrich us, leaving nothing behind that goes beyond death, things are different with all esoteric knowing. It flows into us, into the astral body, where it creates certain new members; new threads are woven into the astral body and remain attached to our being. We know that the astral body surrounds the human being in the shape of an egg. Since an "I" is at work in it, therefore it radiates out.

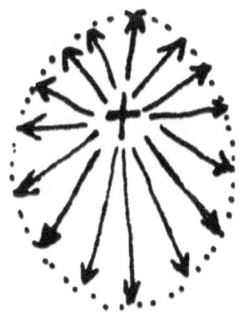

New threads, new knowledge is woven into this astral body, so that we can call it the "body of knowledge" or "cognition-body." This body of knowledge will become ever denser and stronger, and eventually will be spirit-self. The advancing planetary evolution of the earth is possible only by means of our developing this body. On Jupiter this body of knowledge will already be as dense as the astral body; on Venus as dense as the etheric body; and finally, on Vulcan it will have become about as physical as our blood.†

Now, how can this theosophical knowledge become so fruitful that the body of knowledge is formed in the astral body? Let us clarify this with an example.

We are surrounded by physical, material air. We breathe it in. In this way we live. This is described in the Bible with the words, "God breathed living breath into the human being, and he became a living soul." But what we exhale, carbonic acid, cannot sustain life; it is lethal air. Death began because we were released from the womb of the gods. Human beings ate from the Tree of Life; that is, with Lucifer's help they achieved independence and freedom. For this reason they were driven out of paradise; that is, they were no longer "human beings of air," as in Lemurian times. They became "water-beings," and then "human beings of earth." As long as we are on the earth, Lucifer will have power over us. But this is what is tragic about this being: Lucifer's power does not extend above and beyond the earth. All pain and suffering arise through Lucifer, and are connected with this tragedy.

On Jupiter there will also no longer be any exoteric knowledge. Had human beings remained in paradise, they would have continued to eat from the Tree of Life. Lucifer's influence removed the Tree of Life; and in so doing, also the possibility of humanity's sinking even deeper than they already had after eating from the Tree of Knowledge. But now the Tree of Life is transformed into the symbol that, indeed, did at first signify death; but it holds a life within that is all the greater—a life that we can attain when we make the cross with the red roses our own.

Just as the earth is enveloped by the air that we breathe, so there is also in this air a spiritual substance that wants to flow into human beings. It is up to us whether we exhale this spiritual substance as deadly air, or whether we connect it with our theosophical knowledge, and weave the fruit into our astral bodies. And this is important not only for ourselves alone, but for the entire cosmos. If we breathe in this spiritual substance without making it fruitful in us, then we are taking something from the cosmos but giving nothing in return, and thus we hinder evolution. It depends upon us whether the Earth condition can be followed by the Jupiter condition by means of our increasing these spiritual forces surrounding the earth.

When we look at old Saturn we know that our physical body first arose there in seed form, so to speak. It came about through the thoughts of the gods. These thoughts were then condensed into what we are today. But already on old Saturn it was counted upon that human beings would continue the work of the gods. And we do this when we allow the spiritual substance of our surroundings to flow into us in order to create, out of this substance, our body of knowledge.

That is the purpose of the Mystery of Golgotha; to give human beings this opportunity. What is it then that we are taking into ourselves with this substance? It is Christ himself. Before the Mystery of Golgotha this was not the case. Then people could certainly say: *Ex Deo nascimur*. Those to be initiated in those times were prepared so that they could go back to what had been handed down by the ancient gods. But we know that with the Mystery of Golgotha the spiritual aura of the earth changed, because Christ became the spirit of the earth. He poured his very substance into the earth's aura, and since then is contained within it. And again the time has come, when this substance of Christ, which was poured out, has again been concentrated, so that it can be taken up by human beings. *In Christo morimur* means nothing more than immersing ourselves in this spiritual substance. And thus we are taking in Christ with this substance so that we can say, "Not I, but Christ in me."

But there is one thing that we must not forget: where there is much light there is also much shadow. Many errors will insinuate themselves along with the new wisdom that is given to our time. Then it is our holy duty to test everything that we hear with our healthy common sense. This has always been stressed in all Rosicrucian esotericism. However, we should always be tolerant with those who fall into error. We must always say to ourselves that if what we have is really the truth, then it will exist through itself. But if it is error, then my passionate striving for the truth will achieve for me the certainty that in my next incarnation I will find the truth.

In the spirit lay the seed of my body...

* * *

Record B

Knowledge on the physical plane, such as science, art, even spiritual knowledge through a medium, is Luciferic knowledge that is doomed for death, just as exhaled air is dead. Theosophical knowledge, on the other hand, is something with substance that creates the body of knowledge, the future spirit-self on Jupiter.

Just as air surrounds us, so also does a spiritual region that is the light of Christ since the event of Golgotha. It has now been so condensed that we can absorb it. We must absorb it with our body of knowledge, so that it is not killed, but rather works in us in a living way. There is a Rosicrucian verse that says, "Man is immortal because he wants to be." The body of knowledge is what is immortal; what we can take with us beyond death. Rosicrucian esotericism has formulated every word so that these words educate the power of logical thinking, human reason. Thus everything that is presented to us as the results of research from the spiritual world must be understood and tested. Blind faith must not hold sway in human beings; blind faith in authority kills logical thinking and the spiritual in us.

Lucifer is a tragic figure. He knows that his power over humanity is at an end with the earth. All the pain and suffering in the world is Luciferic. Earlier, human beings were in the atmosphere around the earth; only through Lucifer did they fall into the watery element, and then into the earth element. This is the foundation for the picture of the *fall into sin*. Without Lucifer, human beings would have instinctively woven their other three members into the body of knowledge. The plan of freedom has been added as a second plan to Earth evolution. The gods rested on the Sabbath; this is to be taken literally, because now human beings must themselves continue the work on their higher members. They themselves must build up the body of knowledge through theosophical thoughts and knowledge, just as on old Saturn the gods created our physical bodies with their thoughts and mental pictures. Clairvoyance in our time is the appearance of spiritual forms in the consciousness of human beings. We create these forms by taking the light of Christ into our body of knowledge. Human beings were not allowed to eat from the Tree of Knowledge in paradise because they would then have had to remain with their knowledge on earth in Lucifer's kingdom. Now, since the Tree of Knowledge has become the "tree of the cross"—of dead wood—from which new life—the roses—arises, now they should eat from the Tree of Life and drink the juice of the rose. *In Christo morimur* means to rise up in meditation into the spiritual atmosphere surrounding the earth. Christ needed to come to the earth only once, because humanity since then has progressed and will be able to see him in a different way in the future.

Esoteric Lesson

MUNICH, AUGUST 23, 1911

Record A: Notes from Günther Wagner; Record B: Notes from the collection of Fred Poeppig; Record C: Manuscript from Mathilde Scholl and Barbara Wolf; Record D: Anonymous manuscript from the Vreede collection; Record E: Manuscript from Alice Kinkel; Record F: Manuscript from Louise Clason.

Artur Rösel (Wiemar) wrote in his diary about this hour: "Morning 11 o'clock was the first esoteric lesson that I experienced. Dr. Steiner held it in the Princess Hall; all the listeners were members of the Esoteric School, to which I now also belonged. A festive quiet held sway in the room until Dr. Steiner stepped forward with an earnest expression and spoke the prayer, and then spoke about the proper way to meditate. He closed with a festive prayer that was almost sung. A deep quiet hung over the entire room until Dr. Steiner gave the sign for leaving. He spoke at the behest of the Masters of Wisdom and Harmony of Feelings."

The form of human rays of force ... compare with the lecture of August 20, 1911, in CW 129, *Wonders of the World, Trials of the Soul and Revelations of the Spirit.*

RECORD A

Dear sisters and brothers! As you know it is our duty, at the beginning of every esoteric lesson, to call upon the ruling spirit of the day, who is involved with directing the earth in world evolution. [Verse for Wednesday.]

Today we want to say some things in general; next Saturday we will be more specific. Today we want to look at something that can be characterized as the only true and proper beginning of clairvoyance.

The primary focus in all esotericism, in all inner development, is to create absolute calm; inner peace and quiet, and to maintain it after the actual meditation. After we have meditated on the verses or have done other things the Masters of Wisdom and Harmony of Feelings have given us for our training, we should abide for a while still in absolute quiet.

Nothing of our everyday life, no memory of it, not even a feeling for our body should penetrate here. We must feel ourselves to be without a body, as if empty; we should also drop all thoughts of our own existence, only the fact of our own existence should be admitted. And in doing this we should not fall asleep, not fall into a dream or sleeping condition.

Then the condition can enter in which clairvoyance can begin. What then appears before our inner eye comes from the spiritual world. There are signs that indicate whether the pictures appearing here are pure spirit or deceptive images.

What would happen if the etheric body were to leave the physical body, even for a moment? The physical body would contract, shrivel and become wrinkled; it has the tendency to contract into the smallest space possible and ultimately dissolve into nothing. The tendency of the etheric body is to expand into the widths of space; it feels itself connected with all the forces out in space. It fills the physical body and spreads it out to the size that it has.

Because of the physical body's tendency to shrivel up, we get wrinkles in old age. The physical body shrinks together because the etheric body no longer works in it the way it did in our youth.

Something similar occurs with the etheric body in our meditations. The etheric body spreads out in space and feels itself to be within everything. The same thing is also the case at the first moment of death when the etheric body leaves the physical body; this can last for days.

It is a blissful feeling when the etheric body feels itself as if dissolved in space. And if the astral body were not present, then the etheric body would remain that way until the next birth. But the astral body draws the etheric body together again through its desires, drives, and passions, and in this way the human being enters into kamaloca.

Now in meditation we should strive toward the having the feeling that the inner human being is illuminated through and through; and after years of effort this can be achieved. We ourselves become light; we become sources of light that illuminate objects in the spiritual world that approach us. The things that appear to us in moments of deepest soul-calm are not the same as those that appear to us in outer, physical life; those we see from the outside, for example, when we see the sun rising over the horizon. But rather—to stay with the picture of a sunrise—we would feel ourselves within the sun that rises above the horizon of our clairvoyant consciousness. We would feel ourselves there spread out within space.

However, deceptive pictures arise before us if we bring personal feelings of sympathy and antipathy (especially antipathy) or an inappropriate bias for individual people, and so forth, into our meditations. Those who lie and are disingenuous in everyday life carry the lies within their etheric bodies, and with them into space. The deceitfulness is reflected by the forms that the pupil sees there, just as a mirror reflects our face, or an echo, our voice. Seductive forms and visions, beautiful forms of angels, then appear there, caused by the deceitfulness that streamed out with the etheric body. These forms are increasingly attached to us because of the kinship of these forms with our own deceitfulness. In the end, we are simply unable to distinguish between truth and lies.

Now many people may think that there must be means by which we can protect ourselves from these deceptive visions. But just as true as it is that I am standing here and speaking, representing the esotericism behind which the Masters of Wisdom and Harmony of Feelings stand, just as true is it that there is no means to banish these deceptive pictures all at once in order to prevent their appearance. Only gradually through very patient, very gradual, steady work by oneself, on oneself, to overcome deceitfulness and untruthfulness, is it possible gradually to work in the direction that those deceitful visions no longer appear. This will happen when the lies are no longer mirrored because they are no longer present.

Those who are too ambitious, those who have a false ambition to enter into esoteric training, those who feel an intemperate longing to experience all the truths of the spiritual world—they create thereby error within themselves. They become susceptible to all kinds of chatter and gossip out in the world. They are happy to be occupied with the everyday destinies of people, and eagerly listen to all kinds of sensational explanations and events. They can no longer distinguish between what is true and what is not true.

Thus, excessive ambition and error are connected. We must battle within ourselves against excessive ambition and unhealthy desire for the highest truths, against lies and dishonesty—each one of us within ourselves. We must lift ourselves to the highest morality in our daily lives if we wish to arrive at correct clairvoyance that can proceed from properly carried through meditations. And for them to be properly carried through, we must not allow ourselves to carry feelings and thoughts from daily life into our meditations; otherwise we would pollute the etheric substance that should radiate out into space.

The longer and more intensively the meditations are carried out, the more intensely they work on us; yet we must be careful here. Those who notice that they do not feel well, who feel dizzy or something similar, should not extend the time very much; and they must seriously consider what they are doing wrong.

One's sense of well being should be the same after meditation as it was before meditation. We should reflect on our esoteric life often, very often. We should recognize our faults; we should be very clear about how corrupt we are. But this knowledge of our baseness should not depress us. Again, that would be crass egotism, for our depression would only prove that we thought we were better than we are in reality. Actually we have precisely the faults that we ourselves acquired in our earlier life, and thus they became part of our karma. We must clearly survey our faults and then go to work to eliminate them.

We must learn to think objectively; those who say that they already think objectively are often found to be suffering from a great error because this assumption is itself only subjective. It is an illusion.

Ambition leads to error, to superstition, which we must not fall prey to. We should approach everything that we encounter, whatever it may be, with a wakeful, open mind, with clear thinking and sharp logic. We should not have absolute confidence in something that may well appear to us at first as true; we should investigate it critically and not give ourselves over to something randomly. We should act this way in our esoteric life also; there is no demand for faith in any authority.

My brothers and sisters, this is what the Masters of Wisdom and Harmony of Feelings would say to you: that you should maintain your clarity of thought and apply it to what I am here justified in representing, to what is given out of clairvoyant consciousness, and to me also. You should approach what is given and represented here with healthy common sense, with reason and unprejudiced, sufficiently expanded thinking. You should not have absolute confidence in this or that, but rather judge for yourselves.

This esoteric lesson, like all esoteric lessons, should be sacred to us. So once again we want to summarize all of what this lesson has brought us in this sacred verse:

In the spirit lay the seed of my body...
In my body lies the seed of the spirit...

* * *

Record B

Discipline of the Will and Inner Enlightenment

We know it is our duty, at the beginning of every esoteric lesson, to call upon the spirit that is the representative of the day, to the extent that it is involved in the leadership of the earth in world evolution. (Verse for Wednesday is spoken.)

What can help us further along in life should pass before our souls in this esoteric lesson. To begin with, we want to observe what one should consider as the only true and first beginning of clairvoyance. As we already know, from the moment of spiritual insight, a feeling enters us as if we were expanding and dissolving into the universe. This comes from the expansion of the etheric body, an event that occurs to some extent in every meditation, and takes place completely after death. When the etheric body is completely or partially loosened and separated (from the physical body) it is expanded and pushes far out into space. This experience is accompanied by a feeling of blessedness, and the human being would as a matter of fact be able to abide in this feeling during the life between death and new birth, if only the astral body were not present. The astral body's forces, which are still connected with all the drives, desires, and passions, permeate and pull the etheric body together. Because of this, we at first enter kamaloca. On the other hand, if the etheric body were not present in our physical life, then the physical body would pull together and shrivel up because it has this tendency to shrivel, even down to the smallest space, in order ultimately to dissolve into nothing. This happens through aging when our forces diminish and we get wrinkles.

In every meditation we should then strive for the feeling that we are inwardly filled with light; and after years of effort this can be achieved. We ourselves become light, become sources of light that illuminate the objects that approach us in the spiritual world. What appear to us then in the calmest moments in the depths of our soul are no longer similar to the appearances in the physical world. We do not see things from outside, such as when we see the rising sun in the morning. Rather, staying with the example of the sun, we then feel ourselves in the sun that rises on the horizon of our clairvoyant consciousness; we feel ourselves distributed and spread out in space.

However, illusory pictures can also arise, especially when we have feelings of sympathy and antipathy in an unfounded way for individual people, which we then take with us into the mediation. For example, the deceitfulness of those who in ordinary life are dishonest and lie streams into space with their etheric bodies and is then reflected from the forms they behold, just as a mirror reflects back our image. Thus deceptive forms in the shape of beautiful angels can arise, which are caused by the deceitfulness that streams outward with the etheric body. All beings are attracted that are related to the feelings of the esoteric student; and they suffocate the student even more in his or her weaknesses and vices. All around us in space are many beings both good and evi, and we call to these divine forces and powers through our esoteric training.

Now many people may think that means must exist to protect oneself from these kinds of deceitful visions. But as truly as I stand here and speak and represent the esotericism behind which the Masters of Wisdom and Harmony of Feelings stand; just as truly is there no means to banish these deceptive pictures once and for all in order to prevent their appearance. Only gradually through steady work on oneself is it possible to work in the direction that these deceitful visions no longer appear. Only by working on ourselves through an inward training of the will, so that the lies are simply no longer present in us, can we stop the illusions. Then they will not be reflected back through the etheric body.

Those who enter into an esoteric training with too much ambition—for example, if they want to discover, if possible, all the truths of the spiritual world—and those who feel such an intemperate longing, thereby create error within themselves. They become susceptible to all kinds of chatter and gossip out in the world. They happily occupy themselves with the everyday destinies of people, and eagerly listen to all kinds of sensational discussions and stories. They can no longer distinguish between what is true and what is not true. Thus are connected ambition and error. Each one of us must battle excessive ambition and unhealthy desire for the highest truths within ourselves. We must lift ourselves to the highest morality in our daily lives if we wish to arrive at correct clairvoyance, which can only proceed from properly executed meditations on the foundation of a moral life strictly followed. But in order to meditate in the proper fashion, all thoughts of everyday life must be excluded. However, if we nevertheless bring those kinds of thoughts and feelings along into our meditations, we contaminate our etheric substance. The longer and more intensively the meditations are carried out, the stronger is their effect upon us. However, one must be careful here. Anyone who notices that he or she does not feel well; who feels dizzy, or anything similar, should not extend the meditation too long. One must give serious thought to the question, "What have I done wrong?" After meditating, one's state of health must be the same as it was before meditating.[†] Yes, we should think often, very often about our meditative life. We should recognize our mistakes and become very clear how evil we still are. But this knowledge of our baseness should not depress us, because these character weaknesses that we have prepared for ourselves through previous earth lives remain in our karma. We should survey our faults very clearly and then set about eradicating them.

In doing so we must learn to think objectively, just as we would observe a stranger's thinking. We acquire this precisely through the study of spiritual science. Those who say after a short period of time "I do not think subjectively but in an entirely objective way" are very mistaken; for this assumption is itself still completely subjective. It is nothing more than vanity, since to begin with we cannot think objectively at all.

Let us think about this one more time: all ambition, all untruthfulness with regard to ourselves will lead inexorably to error, to superstition. We must not fall prey to this. We should approach everything that might come to us—whatever it may be, wherever it may come from—and, above all, we should approach ourselves with a wakeful, open mind, with clear thinking and sharp logic.

This means we must not swear by something, even if it at first appears true, if we have not yet critically researched it ourselves; it means never blindly accepting the truth of anything. So here too, in the esoteric life, faith in authority is not required. And this, my dear sisters and brothers, is what the Masters of Wisdom and Harmony of Feelings want to have said to you: that you should maintain and use your full powers of reasoning when receiving these truths from them, which I am here entitled to represent to you out of clairvoyant consciousness. You should use your full powers of reasoning even over and against me. What is presented here should be approached only with healthy common sense, without prejudice, and with sufficiently expanded reasonable thinking. You should not swear upon this or that, but rather form your own judgments. This esoteric lesson, like all esoteric lessons, should be sacred to us. So once again we want to summarize all of what this lesson has brought us in this verse:

In the spirit lay the seed of my body...

Record C

The most important for our development, the most significant moments in our esoteric life, are those that occur after our meditation, when we allow complete calm to enter into our souls in order for the content of our meditation to work upon it. We should strive to extend these periods of time increasingly over time. For by means of this "lifting ourselves out" of the circle of our everyday thoughts and feelings, by means of this emptying of our souls, we put ourselves into contact with another world. Out of this, world pictures come to meet us—pictures concerning which we must admit that they are new to us, that there is nothing in our life in the physical world with which we can otherwise compare them. Whether they are correct or not, this they will tell us themselves.

What are we actually doing when we produce this calm in our soul? We are doing the same thing that certain beings do with us macrocosmically at the moment of our death. We have often said that the four members of our being are firmly woven together. Mainly the physical and etheric bodies stand in a special relationship to one another. What would happen if we separated the etheric body from the physical body? The forces in the physical body have the tendency to draw it together more and more. If separated from the etheric, the physical body would become increasingly smaller, would shrink together into a ball, and ultimately disappear into itself. On the other hand, the etheric body has the tendency to spread out more and more. In this way it gives the physical body its form. Outside the physical body it spreads itself out into the cosmos, and this "self-expansion" is connected with a feeling of blissful blessedness. After death, this expansion is limited ultimately only by the astral body. What is present in the astral body in terms of drives, desires, and passions, draws the etheric body together again, and thereby brings about kamaloca.

During our moments of meditation, which should be sacred to us, we independently induce this state; we loosen the etheric body from out of the physical body. Of course, this is not perceptible to our physical senses; nevertheless, we lift it up into spiritual worlds. In such moments, we should forget our physical bodies as much as possible. We should not feel it; we should forget that we are alive. Of course, not to the extent that we fall asleep (that would be wrong and injurious) but rather, in full consciousness of our life, we nevertheless should pay no attention to it. Thus, we should allow nothing from our daily life or feelings into our souls, especially nothing of our sympathies or antipathies, which are so often unjustified. For what would we do with them? Through the fact that we pour the etheric substance of our souls into the etheric world, we come into contact with other hierarchies from which good and evil beings live in this world. And the substances that we pour into this etheric world attract other substances that are similar to them. When we carry our character defects along with us into this world, then they flow toward the other etheric forces and are mirrored back to us by them—but not in their true form. Rather, they are mirrored in figures that are often seductive, that dazzle us, and dim and confuse our judgment. As an unclean room attracts flies, so too an etheric body permeated by faults attracts in that world beings inclined to deceive. If deceitful or excessively ambitious people carry these character flaws along into their meditation, then it can happen that they may increasingly prefer to give themselves over to deception, that they learn to love lying and deception.[†]

For this reason an esotericist should pay twice as much attention to his or her faults. With courage and modesty, we should say to ourselves that we are bad human beings and that we will endeavor to set aside our faults. However, we must not be depressed over this and allow ourselves to be beaten down by the consciousness of this fact, for that would be egotism. We must say karma is the reason why we are the way we are. We must not wish to be otherwise through divine grace, which we have not earned. Rather, we should strive to become otherwise through our own knowledge. This is not easy, but in this way we come to the right path. In the beginning of our esoteric work, we should not expand this "lifting out" of the etheric body to the extent that it disturbs our physical sense of well being. Upon return, we should find our physical body to be the same as when we left it. And if we experience dizziness or anything similar that we were not experiencing before, then we should shorten our meditations.

Nowhere in genuine esoteric schools is it required that students become dependent upon a teacher; on the contrary, esotericists should test what is said to them; they should permeate what is told to them with their intelligence, compare it with what was told them in the past, and seek to supplement it. Faith in authority is never required in schools that stand under the guidance of the Masters of Wisdom and Harmony of Feelings. Great caution is called for whenever such faith is required, wherever such a pledge is demanded. Students should strive and test what they are told independently; their knowledge will guide them. There is no magical formula to give them that will remove the faults and weaknesses that reveal to them a world of deception instead of the true spiritual world. Only through slow work and honest self examination can a student gradually become a different person; a person who can bear to look at his or her true being with all its weaknesses, and not lose courage and inner composure while seeing the truth. Students must take the transformation of their being in hand with great strength. Students must not be filled with a feeble longing for truth and knowledge, but rather a healthy longing for the truth, in which lies the power to behold one's faults.

If, immediately after awakening in the morning, one attempts to dip back into the spiritual world from which one has just come by emptying one's soul and immersing oneself in meditation, then in this way one can achieve again the connection and the memory of one's nightly experiences in the spiritual world.[†]

* * *

Record D

In this hour we are to be given teachings that we have sometimes already received; that is, concerning the way we are to behave when practicing our meditative exercises. Complete tranquility of soul should rule in our minds before and, especially, afterward. We must attempt to keep external impressions away from us; in our soul all must be quiet that would surge forward from our inner life of feeling, and also all that would storm in upon our thoughts. Only then, only in such a mood of soul can the veil be torn that allows us to see into the spiritual world, which then spreads out before us in a wealth of images or pictures. But the most important thing that students must know when they see these pictures before them is that what they are seeing does not always express what it appears to express. Although what is revealed to the eye is a reality, too often, it consists of deceptive and seductive forms that we have awoken and woven out of our own souls.

Such forms appear before us especially when, as esotericists, we still have an inclination toward untruthfulness, toward lies, if we are only dishonest; but especially when we are filled with ambition and arrogance, for then we unconsciously send these feelings into our meditations. These personal feelings are woven into the forms that appear before us. And then the condition of our own souls ray forth back to us in the etheric pictures of the suprasensory world. However, if students purify their minds and souls, and then approach their meditations with humility, they will recognize soon enough what they are to consider the truth.

There is yet another way a human being can get insight into the suprasensory world. It happens when we have achieved the stage where we can step out of the physical body. This comes about by loosening the etheric body from the physical body. When we see someone standing in front of us, we usually think that we see only the physical person. But this is not so. For if we were seeing only the physical body then something entirely different would appear to us.

We know that the human being consists of a physical body, etheric body, astral body, and "I." If we were to subtract the physical body away from the etheric or life body, then the physical body would shrink, shrivel up, and finally disappear entirely. This is because the physical body has the tendency to shrink together, whereas the etheric body holds the opposite tendency; that is, it strives to expand itself. In the moment of physical death the etheric body expands itself out into the cosmos. For those who have died, who have gone through the door of death, there is a feeling of the greatest blessedness, of the greatest sense of comfort, as they are expanded into the widths of space. However, because they still carry a desire for the material world from the previous life they are drawn back into the earthly, and then the kamaloca time begins.

In a way similar to the one just described, those people who have achieved a certain stage of esoteric development can lift the etheric body out of the physical body. However, we should not exaggerate our exercises, especially at the beginning of our development. They should not claim too much time. Above all, we must guard ourselves so that they do not make us sleepy, or even fall asleep. For then it could happen that more or less evil beings overpower us. In all that we undertake for our higher development, we must always maintain full consciousness.

Today there are many esoteric streams that constantly acquire increasing influence over humanity, especially when they are recommended by a kind of authority. Whatever may approach human beings, in whatever way, they should never blindly believe, even if something is spoken by an "authority." Always and in every case, we ourselves should test what we hear. We should always use our reason. We should also approach everything that we have learned in the course of the years with our own thinking, with our own logic, and ask whether we can reconcile it with our own understanding or whether we must dismiss it as illogical.

* * *

Record E

The same thing happens to a human being in meditation as happens in death. Only gradually can we recognize the enormity and power of what we undertake in meditation; can we recognize that we breach the deep, powerful mystery of death when we devote ourselves in the right way to meditation.

The physical body has in itself the tendency toward contraction. If we were to think away the etheric body, then the physical body would shrink together more and more, down to the smallest space, and then disappear into itself. The etheric body maintains the physical body the way we see it. In old age, wrinkles are the result of the diminishing forces of the life-body.

We were reminded of the importance of being awake and remaining awake.

* * *

Record F

The physical body has the tendency to shrink together; the etheric body has the tendency to expand out into the cosmos. In meditation the physical body is made passive, just as after death; our higher members are extended into the spiritual world that surrounds us, and is filled with good and evil beings. If we take our desires and passions, sympathies and antipathies, vanity, ambition, and so forth, with us into our meditations, then we attract evil powers. (The moments after meditation are especially important—the quiet time.) Spiritual Mercury is everywhere filled with good and evil spiritual powers, except there where a human being sends his or her forces out. There the spiritual world is pushed back.

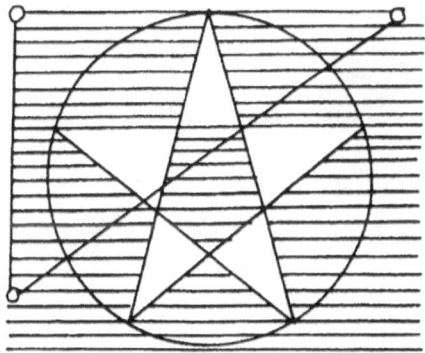

The empty areas in the drawing above show the form of the outward streaming forces of the human being. The higher hierarchies work into it. The spirits of form, movement, and wisdom; the thrones, cherubim, and seraphim; and the evil powers work from the periphery as far as the circle. The archai work within the circle as far as the pentagram along the human streams of force; the archangels work within the pentagram as far as the pentagon; angels permeate entirely the human being. The human etheric body is capable of being expanded out to the stars without becoming fragmented. The astral body can also be expanded out to spiritual beings, whether good or evil, but it becomes more passive and leaves behind part of itself. The "I" must now achieve the power to hold together these parts by means of lines of force that it can achieve through the study of spiritual and esoteric science. Everything must be grasped with the intellect; there must be no blind faith in authority, which undermines the intellect. The present time is filled with the possibility of falling victim to errors; one must use one's common sense and reason against this danger. We must maintain peace with those who are following false paths, but we must also use our good judgment.

Esoteric Lesson
MUNICH, AUGUST 26, 1911

Record A: Notes from Günther Wagner; Record B: Notes from Günther Wagner; Record C: Notes from the collection of Elisabeth Vreede.

The following entry was found in Artur Roesel's diary: "I must also mention that Dr. Steiner this morning held the second esoteric lesson in the esoteric school. At the conclusion he appealed to the members not to allow themselves to be influenced by any kind of authority at the upcoming Congress in Genoa; not to accept anything that they could not test themselves.

RECORD A

My dear sisters and brothers! It is our duty to call on the spirit of the day, of whom we may hope, must hope, will help us with our esoteric striving. Verse for Saturday:
Great all-encompassing spirit,
In your life I live with the earth's life…

Further:

Great all encompassing spirit,
My "I" is raised from below to above,
May it sense you in the all-encompassing…

In the last esoteric lesson [August 23], we saw that when we are meditating the etheric body is poured out into space. This spiritual space is filled with all possible kinds of beings, good and bad, with which we are connected, with which our etheric body becomes connected. Different spirits work into history at different times; furthermore, the same beings are not active in all places at the same time.

Those in Asia have Europe to the west. In Europe, they have Asia to the east. The realms of other beings limit their individual spiritual space at various places. But in the spiritual space where a human being dwells, there is always an empty spot, so to speak (as if spared from other spiritual beings), that the human being fills out him- or herself. Here the streams that work through the human being hold sway.

If we wanted to draw how these beings, the good and the bad, work in space and are kept away from the space occupied by the human being, then the following occult sign would result:

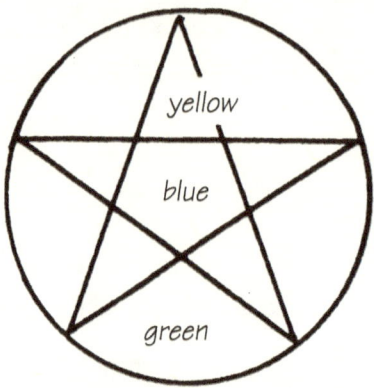

In the present time it is mainly the spirits of form who work here. However, they cannot work into human beings. Into this space the three lower hierarchies work: angels, archangels, and spirits of personality. Only the angels can work throughout the entire space of this five-pointed star.

If we want to bring to mind how far the archangels can work, then we must divide up this pentagon (blue) that we already considered in an exoteric public lecture.† They do not enter into this pentagon—only as far as the five triangles (yellow).

If we want to show how far the spirits of personality can work into this diagram, we must draw a circle around the five-pointed star. If we stretch out our arms and think of a circle going all around from head to fingertips to the tips of the toes, then the spirits of personality can go only into the parts that are bounded by the head, stretched out arms, and the particular arc of the circle, and so forth (green).

The spirits of form can no longer get to the human being. They reach the circle described above, and are pushed back by the forces that are at work in the fourfold being of the human being. Now when the etheric body is expanded during meditation, it is in all of these beings and facts that are outside the circle, out to the stars. It is "poured out," without interruption, without a gap, over everything. If one followed it with clairvoyant vision one would not see it ever end; it is simply present everywhere.

Now if the student still has character traits such as mendacity, dishonesty, untruthfulness, ambition, and so forth, such as were discussed last time, then these qualities accompany the etheric body into the spiritual space. And if there is an evil being here or there, then the evil in us feels related and attracted to it.

Now the astral body goes with the etheric body into spiritual space. The intellectual, the thinking part of the astral body expands out of the upper tip of the star; the feeling part expands right and left out through the middle tips; and the willing part downward out of the two lower tips of the star.

However, the astral body does not remain as unbroken as the etheric body during this expansion. Individual shreds of it can become separated, which we then can see and follow in space. If we have a connection to an evil being that dwells there in space, then part of the astral body because of its wish-nature becomes attached to, and connects with, this being. This part of our astrality is separated from our astral body. The astral body is broken into fragments, in many individual fragments. Thus we have in the most varied places, parts of our astral body widely scattered in space, which appear to us as individual beings during meditation. But we do not know that they actually belong to us, so they lead us into error and deception. However, between these individual fragments of our astral body there are threads; they are connected to each other and to the pentagram. This connection is produced by means of the human "I."

Before the Mystery of Golgotha, human beings had to have been extremely evil to have lost mastery over these scattered astral fragments. Other beings worked with them in their souls, just for this purpose. Now, after the Mystery of Golgotha, human beings are destined to take over this mastery themselves, working out of their own "I." Even quite advanced esotericists can err by not properly recognizing these connections. In order to prevent this, esotericists must dedicate themselves to a study full of devotion. By studying to acquire knowledge of all that is in spiritual space—of the entire evolution of Saturn, Sun, Moon, and Earth development, and of the beings and hierarchies that have worked in those stages of evolution to create the human being—by such a study the "I" can control the connections between all the individual parts of its astral body. In this way, we can protect against error and deception.

Esotericists should not study merely for themselves, out of curiosity, or anything like that; rather, they should make the most devoted study into their duty for the sake of human and Earth evolution. And when, through intensive study, we have come to understand our own being, when we thereby know how and by what means we have come into existence, we acquire a holy feeling for it all. This feeling we then express in the sentence, "We are born out of God: *Ex Deo nascimur.*"

We should permeate ourselves with this feeling, deeply, ardently, and we should make the etheric currents (which have been already discussed in an exoteric lecture on the etherization of the blood) stream upward from the heart to the brain, surrounding the brain with light and activating the pineal gland; we should make these currents luminous like flames in which all personal concerns fall away. We must entirely lose ourselves in the feeling that we want to sacrifice ourselves completely for world evolution like the spirit beings did; like Christ sacrificed himself. Then we can learn to express this feeling in the sentence, "We die in Christ; *In Christo morimur.*"

Then the certainty lights up in us that we ascend to the spirit; that we resurrect in the spirit. *Per Spiritum Sanctum reviviscimus.*

Ex Deo nascimur. In Christo morimur. Per Spiritum Sanctum reviviscimus. This is the exoteric verse of the Rosicrucians.

When esotericists say this verse, they pause at that which expresses what we characterize as the word "Christ." This is sacred to them. They do not even want to go that far with the word; they do not speak the word but allow the feeling to speak. Then, when genuine Rosicrucians, in their deepest meditations, speak the verse, it sounds like this:

Ex Deo nascimur. In Christo morimur.
Per Spiritum Sanctum reviviscimus.

*

Then there was a longer discussion concerning the upcoming Congress in Genoa. We should strive to reflect and evaluate for ourselves what we hear in terms of esotericism; what the Masters of Wisdom and Harmony of Feelings give; what Dr. Steiner himself represents. We may well not be able to discover occult truths ourselves, for example about the two Jesus children, but we can and should reflect upon them.

It would be wrong to present a specific person who is alive today as the incarnation of a specific being, whether or not it is based on truth. It is one of the most important occult laws that such pronouncements concerning living personalities are not to be made in public. It is something different to present such ideas in an esoteric lesson where one can sense and feel how such a statement is working and how it is taken up by individuals.

Today is an age in which people easily fall into error. Such a pronouncement would cause the thinking of individuals to suffer inhibitions. Because of this people would regress in their capacity to think.

People must be seriously warned about such pronouncements, which are made for the purpose of propaganda. And one must seriously decline any possible involvement in such propagandizing; of course, however, one should do so with complete personal tolerance and with a feeling of peace toward the personalities who are committing this error.

We must succeed with true knowledge, and then we learn, know, and feel that we come forth from the spirit.

In the spirit lay the seed of my body...
In my body lies the seed of the spirit...

Record B

Only the three lower hierarchies work directly upon the human being. The angels work into the human being up to the crosshatched pentagram, which represents symbolically the human being, specifically the etheric body. [See p. 176]

The archangels work only into the five points of the star that are not cross-hatched and the spirits of personality only up to the pentagram, that is, in the rest of the parts within the circle (for example, with arms outstretched, in the space between the top of the head and the finger tips left and right, and between these finger tips and spread legs, that is, the tips of the toes). Higher hierarchies exert their influence only up to the circle. This is the case with all human beings.

Now, esotericists extend their etheric bodies out beyond the pentagram as far as the planets. They remain, however, connected as coherent wholes, and meet there good and evil beings. It is different with the astral body that expands with the etheric body. If the astral body finds there is a being or something that is attracted to the astral body's wish-nature, then a portion of the person's astrality becomes attached to it and is separated from the main part of the astral body. In this way the astral body can be separated into many pieces.

The tendency arises for the intellectual part, the thinking part, of the astral body, to expand out of the top point; the feeling part to expand right and left out of the middle two points; the willing part to expand below out of the two lower points.

This "partitioning" of the astral body gives rise to the danger that we lose the feeling of coherence: the "I" cannot hold together, rather, we feel the "I" in the various separated parts. The esotericist's greatest task is to hold together the threads connecting the various parts. This task is accomplished with healthy common sense, that is, through calm, logical thinking with a thorough study of the general and specific teachings of theosophy and through rationally thinking of and testing the teachings. Only in this way do we make the teachings entirely our own and strengthen the "I." Not accepting anything on authority. Doing so would take away the "I" to the point that it would no longer have control over itself. Such an effect would result, for example, from imparting to unprepared people the knowledge of the earlier incarnations of certain individuals now alive; publicly known individuals. (This deleterious effect would hold entirely independently of the truth of these assertions.) This would happen because the listeners could not feel the truth or comprehend the connections, the probability, or the meaning of these reincarnations. Such announcements would have to be accepted on authority. For this reason, people must be warned of the seriousness of participating in such announcements that are undertaken for the purpose of propaganda in the public arena.

We must combine this serious rejection of any possible invitation to participate in such propaganda with personal tolerance and friendliness toward those who are making this mistake.

* * *

Record C

When we take our esoteric development in hand we will get a feeling that there are spiritual streams that want to gain influence over us, either in a good or an evil sense. Where does this come from?

If we look back at the world's earliest evolution, we know that from the very beginning, spiritual beings have worked on us; higher beings have worked upon us from the outside. But there are also those who have worked on the inner evolution of our earth. Now what happens when one begins esoteric development, and in meditation is immersed in the first verse?

In pure rays of light
Shines the divinity of the world –

What happens then to the etheric body? In the previous lesson we heard that the human physical body has the tendency to shrink when a human being gets old, because the etheric body is gradually drawn out of the physical body. We heard too, that the etheric body holds the opposite tendency; it wants to expand itself out to the macrocosm, up to the stars. Such a self-expansion occurs to a greater or lesser degree in meditation; and even with a mere peripheral study of spiritual science. As long as it is connected with the physical body, the etheric body remains limited by the form of the physical body. Since we know that the entire macrocosm is filled with spiritual beings—with beings of the highest hierarchies as well as with many other good and evil beings—we can imagine that the human being is completely embedded in them. But the space that the human being takes up is excluded from them.

It is not always the same beings that work into human beings; they are different depending upon country, climate, or the characteristics of nature. We can picture what has just been said by means of this drawing.

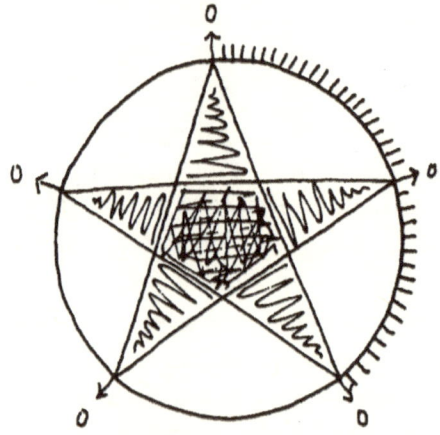

In the pentagram we see the streams of force that are at the foundation of the entire human being, and that have created the human being. We must think of the outer surrounding area as filled with beings that penetrate to the human being. The middle pentagon determines the magnitude of the forces of the physical body; and especially into this area the hierarchy of those beings that we call the angels or *angeloi* work. The etheric body is expressed in the five points of the star; and into this area the archangels work who exert their influence upon human beings. The area limited by the circle signifies the astral body, and into this area the *archai*, primal beginnings, or spirits of personality work. Other hierarchies impinge from outside; the spirits of form, of movement, of wisdom and of the will, all the way up to the cherubim and seraphim.

We are constantly sending thoughts out of the astral body up to the brain. We know that through the cooperation of the three bodies, a spiritualized stream of our thoughts goes forth and streams into the space around us. This stream is then taken up or attracted by beings that are attracted or repelled, according to the kind of thoughts we have. We must think of it this way: a part of our astral body is repelled, so to speak, and then in the space around us it is connected with this or that being that is in our spiritual environment and is sympathetic to it. This can happen in every direction of space, toward the most varied beings.

If then, students do not allow themselves to be guided by their healthy common sense, and become connected with such beings that are to be found in astral space, then they will come to a certain inner absentmindedness.

This can also happen if students accept on blind faith what they have not researched themselves, or if they do not take the time to grasp esoteric studies with their reasoning understanding. They will then easily lose themselves; if they do not want to apply their healthy common sense when seeing in the spiritual world, they will constantly observe wrongly and come to wrong conclusions.

Let us now look back to a specific point in world evolution, to old Sun. In the middle of old Sun sublime spiritual beings left it because the finer substances of their being could no longer be united with the sun's constituent particles, which had already become denser—these particles could even be called "solid" for the conditions of that time, but they were nevertheless still etheric substances. One such sublime being separated from those that left, remained behind on old Sun, and permeated the substance of the sun with a fine spiritual power. In the ancient mysteries this power was already spoken of; it was known as the power of Christ. It is the same power that was sacrificed again in later earthly evolution, and remained behind on the earth when our sun withdrew from it to become a fixed star. For a while it remained with the earth, then it went over to the moon and mirrored from there the power of the sun onto the earth.

This being of Sun-power was Yahweh-Christ; the same being who revealed himself to Moses, and announced to Moses that He would one day dwell with us in the flesh.

Since the Baptism in the Jordan and the event of Golgotha, this Christ-power has united with human beings and with the earth. He enters even today into those human beings who want to take their higher development in hand. Esoteric students who expand their etheric bodies through meditation into the widths of space connect their etheric bodies in their emanation with this fine Christ-substance. They no longer feel the "I"; and the Pauline expression "Not I, Christ in me" becomes a reality.

Human beings should develop this spiritual seed within themselves, so that after they have brought the spiritual seed to the highest perfection they can once again return to the spirit from which they once came. Then one will know the kind of reverence with which Rosicrucian students spoke the holy prayer:

In the spirit lay the seed of my body...
In my body lies the seed of the spirit...

RECORD D

There are spiritual beings present in the entire cosmos; they fill it; and hence they permeate and surround human beings as well. Nevertheless, we can distinguish between what belongs directly to human beings and what is a part of our spiritual environment. This spiritual environment varies according to where the human being is located. These spiritual surroundings are different in Europe than in Asia: in Asia, Europe is to the west; in Europe, Asia is to the east— that alone determines a difference.

The beings of the third, or the lowest, hierarchy work into human beings more or less directly. The spirits of form up to the cherubim and seraphim work in the environment into human beings. This can be represented in a picture:

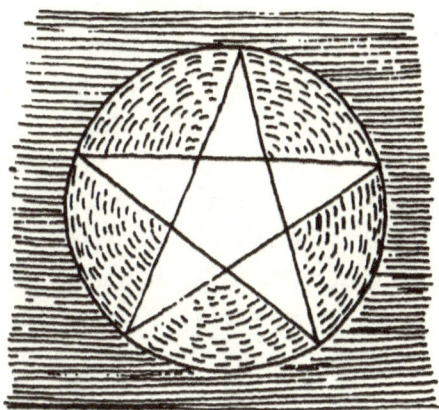

If we represent human beings and the forces that work in them as a white surface, then we have a five pointed star, the pentagram. Angels penetrate into human beings the most, into their physical bodies; that is represented by the innermost pentagon. Archangels cannot penetrate there; rather, they remain with the five outer triangles that surround the pentagon. The archai work into those parts that are not directly within the pentagram; they work into those parts indicated by what lies between the pentagram and the circumscribing circle.

In the lecture cycle *Wonders of the World, Trials of the Soul, Revelations of the Spirit*, we have already seen that the inner pentagram represents the physical body, the five triangles represent the etheric body, the space between these triangles and the circle belongs to the astral body, and the circle itself must be seen as the ego itself. If we imagine a circle drawn from the head to the extended arms, these are the parts that are brought about by the archai. Outside this circle, the higher hierarchies are at work, beginning with the spirits of form.

We know that the physical body has the tendency to draw itself together, to shrink, while the etheric body has the tendency to expand itself. In meditation and even with continuous, serious study of theosophy, such an expansion in space more or less takes place, and can be extended out to the stars and the sun without the connection with the physical body being broken. With the astral body it is the reverse: it can lose the connection and partially be split off from itself. This can be the case if students firmly cling to certain things in space that are sympathetic to them; or when they are attracted by astral beings, whether good or evil. If, for example, an evil being is to be found in our surroundings, ☊ , then the etheric body, if it feels itself drawn toward this being because of character traits at work in the soul, will expand itself out that far and surround the being. However, with the astral body, such an expansion can cause a part to separate and then surround the being. In this way, the astral body can split up to encompass several beings in its surrounding. In this way, it leaves part of its essence behind, but between the scattered, separated parts a connection remains. In this way, a splitting of consciousness also takes place, because consciousness is connected with the astral body. We then no longer feel ourselves as a unified, self-contained personality, but rather as if split into several personalities. This experience is indicated by the passage in the Gospel when the demons who possessed a sick man were asked the question, "What is your name?" and they responded by saying, "Legion."†

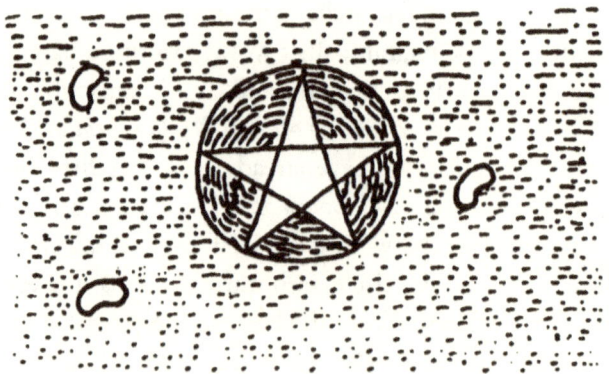

Therefore, those who are driven by a strong desire for esoteric development, unless they strengthen their "I" at the same time, are in danger of having the astral body fragmented in this way. Then they are no longer capable of recognizing which being has taken over a part of the astral body, whether good or evil. Only serious study, above all, of what is given in *An Outline of Esoteric Science*, the lecture cycles, and so forth, can make the "I," the self, so strong that it can unite the individual parts again—whether among each other, or directly with one's own being. Those who have sufficiently devoted themselves through such study are not as easily deceived with respect to the nature of a spiritual being that is directly before them. The possibilities for error are otherwise very great, and were never as great as right now. One of the worst things one can do is to point out publicly this or that human being as the reincarnation of a specific personality; for this is something that cannot be proven, and it leads to the destruction of the intellect, which precisely now should be in a process of development.

Esoteric Lesson

KARLSRUHE, OCTOBER 10, 1911

Record A Notes from the collection of Elisabeth Vreede; Record B Manuscript from Mathilde Scholl and Barbara Wolf; Record C Notes from Günther Wagner.

RECORD A

Before we can begin with the esoteric lesson I am obligated to say something. Because of a brochure handed to me by one of the members of our inner circle, who is motivated by a good impulse, I am moved to say something. As all of you know, every pupil of esotericism receives meditations according to his or her disposition and capacities. These exercises are designed in their structure and sequence of words out of deeper underlying reasons to bring about exactly what pupils needs for their spiritual development. And it is of the greatest significance how the words are sequenced; indeed, even which word is employed and where it stands, so that what is intended can be achieved. Many of you have received as a morning verse the following words:

In pure rays of light
Shines the divinity of the world.
In pure love to all beings
Rays the divinity of my soul.
I rest in the divinity of the world.
I will find myself
In the divinity of the world.

Now I have received here a brochure[†], in which the following is to be found:

"I see in the pure rays of the light
The divinity of the world;
In the love to all beings

Rays the divinity of my soul.
I live in the divinity
And find myself again
In the divinity of the world."

It is difficult to ascertain how the writer of this brochure came to this formulation, for it belongs exclusively to our esoteric school. It could be that one of our pupils had the lack of caution to share it with an outsider. We could also imagine another case (a case that actually happened several years ago), the case in which someone was meditating over these lines in a hotel or pension, and in the next room there was someone who clairvoyantly caught these thoughts. In the first mentioned case, we should (actually we should always) feel the greatest compassion with respect to such things. As esotericists, we know that such things bring their own punishment, even when nothing malicious is intended. This must happen because every word of the meditation has been placed in its position in the most careful way, and if it is taken out of its context then the effect that results will be the opposite. By means of this arbitrary change in the sequence of words, indeed, through the use of this positive little word "I," one has created the opposite effect. In the original verse everything flows, sustained in an objective way so that everything should work through the imaginative picture. Our meditations should always proceed from our inner moral impulses. The external world, and especially our personal "I" should be entirely excluded. We should take hold of the divinity of the world with complete objectivity in our thoughts, just as it flows through and permeates the world with its divine light. In doing so, our "I" should not intrude itself; for then the effects would be transformed into the opposite. Entirely different spiritual effects would then have to appear—that is, Luciferic effects.

The moral impulse that with all humility suppresses the "I" and that should be completely devoted to the divine spirit of the world in which one reposes does not emerge in the line "I see in the pure rays of light."

Also in the last lines

"I live in the divinity
And find myself again
In the divinity of the world."

the egotistical principle protrudes markedly, for something entirely different is experienced in the words "I rest."

We see in this how extraordinarily precise and careful we must be, so that we apply the words of our meditations absolutely correctly; also in our thoughts.

Now we will go to some pictures that we can use for our esoteric training because they have a very powerful effect. We know that the path to higher worlds passes through Imagination to begin with; then comes the path of Inspiration; then that of Intuition. The pictures that are now to be given strengthen the organs that lead to imaginative vision.

In our theosophical teachings we have often heard that the world is maya; that we ourselves are maya. If modern science also now begins to explain the world in this way, then it should certainly not be an empty phrase for us.

When we observe a rose, it shows us its upright blossom with the stem pointed downward. Nevertheless, what we think we are perceiving is not a true picture. Modern science teaches us that what we see comes about through a crossing of the rays of light, so that in our eyes an upside down picture of the rose arises, while we are perceiving the outer picture of the rose with the blossom above. That is the reflection of the real light-appearance in us. From this we see that what appears to us out there in the external world is maya; and, indeed, a reversed maya, in which that which is below appears above. Thus it is with everything around us; the whole world, the surface of which we believe we are perceiving, and ourselves with it—in the real view, everything is on its head. If we want to perceive the true form of the world, then we must not seek the reflections, but rather the realities behind them before they are reflected in the outer world. Everything, absolutely everything is turned around from how we see it. What appears to be above is below; what appears to be behind us, is in front of us; what appears to be left, is right. In short, we must be able and willing to recognize this, so that we can become free of maya. If, for example, we hear sounds and think that they are coming from the right, then in reality they are coming from the left. If we see objects standing in front of us, then in reality there are forces that pressing on us from behind. It is the same with the stars in the sky. We see the sky before us when we look up; in reality it is reflected back to our eyes by forces that are located behind us.

If we want to arrive at the truth of the world, we must ascend from the spirits of form to the spirits of movement so that they can help us to see what is placed before us as a reflection by the spirits of form, as a reversal of reality. As an exercise in doing this, the following drawing can serve as a symbol. When we see a rose with the blossom above, we move it in our thoughts downward, and thereby perform a movement that can symbolize for us the forces of the spirits of movement.

There is, however, one thing in human beings that is no mere appearance of the senses, that is not maya. This is the Word that sounds forth from human beings, the living Word, the Logos. The Word does not come to us from outside of us; it is something living in us, it is our actual, true being. It streams forth from our soul life, we are it ourselves with all our feelings that we allow to flow forth between our lips outward into the world. And if we think this through deeply, how the Word is the Logos; how everything that is spoken in the world, is spoken out of this source, then we will feel deeply our responsibility for our words. More about this in the next lesson.

Only what people have spoken in their words will carry over into the next planetary condition and survive the earth. What we hear coming from the left actually comes, as stated, from the right; but the sounds that we speak are the only thing that is not otherwise than it appears to be. It sounds forth from our inner life, and it actually comes from our inner life. Divine beings, the Logos, speak to us from these sounds.

* * *

Record B

Before we go to the esoteric lesson it is necessary to stress something. Many of those present here have received a meditation for acquiring certain occult forces and for strengthening the soul. Such meditations can be given only in harmony with the Masters of Wisdom and Harmony of Feelings. Not everyone has this verse, because such things are not necessarily equally appropriate for everyone. Such verses should, of course, be kept strictly secret. It is not allowed to pass them on, because doing so would bring as a result heavy karmic consequences.[†]

Now a brochure has been brought to me by someone (whose impulse to bring it to me was correct) in which the formulation:

In pure rays of light
Shines the divinity of the world… and so forth.

can be read in a somewhat altered form. Now we do not want to judge this in a strict way, but rather practice gentleness and mercy. Already giving someone the verse correctly written would create bad consequences. Now the verse could have arisen in such a way that the individual involved incurs no guilt. Let us assume that an individual who has a certain clairvoyance lives in a room next to someone who is meditating this verse properly, and simply reads the lines from their thoughts. This can certainly happen. The individual meditating would naturally incur no guilt.

Now in a verse like this, every word is essential and meaningfully placed by the Masters of Wisdom and Harmony of Feelings. In the sentence that begins this verse, it is stressed that the soul should objectively permeate into this spiritual world-content, and not with that which is permeated by the lower forces of the "I." In the altered form, exactly the opposite is stressed. The soul that is filled with the "I" permeates into the spiritual world. We read there:

In pure rays of light
I recognize the Divinity of the world

In the correct formulation it continues so that the soul gives itself passively, while we read in this version:

I live in the divinity of the world

in which the word "live" points to something active. This difference is found also in the concluding sentence. In the correct formulation we find:

I will find my self
In the divinity of the world

while in this altered version we read:

I find myself
In the divinity of the world

Exactly the opposite is expressed in the altered form. It will still be early enough to speak of this and these consequences when the time comes to read the true verse in its correct formulation.

We have already heard exoterically that there are three ways to penetrate into the spiritual world: through Imagination, Inspiration, and Intuition. In connection with our meditations, certain imaginations have been given to us that should help us to achieve our goal and to strengthen our souls. Now to these we can add pictures that give us certain powers. Let us return to a saying that we have often heard, and have certainly recognized as truth, but which we nevertheless do not always call to mind often enough—that is the saying "The whole world around us is maya." Strictly speaking, what does this mean? With our senses we perceive the external world. Let us consider a rose standing in front of us. It says to us, "I am here; you perceive me with your senses; you must picture me." But is this process really correct in this form? Do we really see the rose the way it really is? Even modern science can help us here.

We know that the visual nerves cross behind the eye. There they call forth an inverted picture of the object, which when projected outward, shows the object as we see it outside us. The real image of the rose arises in us upside-down: the blossom below, the root above. If the external world is maya, then it is a mirror image of its true form. It is as if we imagined a mirrored reflection of a landscape in still water. We see everything around us in a mirror image. We must think of everything around us as inverted: human beings and their entire surroundings. Thus the rose that stands before me I must think of as behind me, with the roots above and the blossom below. When we think we are hearing with the right ear, it is maya. The force is coming to us from the left, and we become aware of it in the right ear. What appears to lie in front of us is only maya—only a mirror reflection of what lies behind us—and is revealed through us, and thus conjures the things in front of us. Just as the true image of things arises from within outward, so it must be the case with true morals. For true morality must have its source in inner conviction, not in external prompting.

We must think of everything as reversed. The starry sky that spreads before my view, I must think of as behind me. We must go further: where darkness rules there is mighty spiritual light; where physical light does not appear to the eye, there is spiritual light. Connected with this is what was said earlier, that when we begin to see clairvoyantly it easily happens that we first see the light of our own etheric bodies in our own shadows.

Thus, when we observe the world, not in its mirror images of external maya, but rather attempt to see it in its true form, we are doing something very specific. We are setting everything in motion; and we set ourselves in relation to the spiritual hierarchies that stand above the spirits of form, which are the spirits of movement.

Everything that we see around us is, as we see it, maya—everything that we see, hear, feel, and so forth. There is only one thing that is given to us by the wisdom of the world that is really real: the Word, the Logos. Air is also not real. We have one thing that does not penetrate to us from outside and appear to us as maya; rather, it streams forth from within us, revealing our inner being: speech, the Word. And so this gift from the gods should be sacred to us, and we should not misuse it. Nothing should sound forth from us, other than the content of our souls in all uprightness. For we find the fact in the Akashic Chronicle that everything will dissolve and pass away, and only what people have spoken remains as something eternal, giving form to the next planetary formation of the earth. In the beginning was the Word, and the power of the Word is divine!

We must gradually acquire the power to observe the world the way it is without losing the self in doing so.

* * *

Record C

Esoteric exercises must be practiced exactly and with the words as they were given. These exercises have been taken out of the spiritual world and must be carried out exactly as they are prescribed.

As soon as one brings an "I" into these exercises, which are intended to create a very specific mood, great cosmic (karmic) effects are thereby called forth for the one involved. This is connected to both; that is, the first four lines of the verse:

In pure rays of light
Shines the divinity of the world
In pure love to all beings
Rays the divinity of my soul.

This verse was published in a brochure; but not entirely correctly, with "I" in the sentences. Dr. Steiner referred to these verses.

The same holds true for passing meditations on to others; especially so when they are reproduced in printer's ink and become the general property of the masses.

There are three steps to knowledge of higher worlds.

1. Imaginative knowledge
2. Inspired knowledge
3. Intuitive knowledge

When we start at the first step, it is very valuable for the soul if we awaken in our souls imaginative pictures that must come forth from inner morality. Several such pictures would be the following:

Imagine light; spiritualize the image in your mind until you can imagine colorful, flowing light as the substance of the world.

Feel warmth that can be intensively felt as love that shines though the world and can be felt as the love of God.

Also, something that can be especially valuable: think of the essence of things, and, in so doing, feel that everything that we can see with our senses is illusion, is maya.

For example, that which is above, imagine below, and vice versa; for example, flowers, people, and the starry sky. Whatever happens on the left, feel on the right. See in front of us that which takes place behind us, as an intersection of forces and as a mirroring of what is behind us.

Also think of light as darkness, reversed in the same way. For example, a clairvoyant can see the spirit, which a human being has as inner power of illumination, in his or her shadow.

The spirits of form have ensouled and permeated with their being everything that lives and weaves—that has taken on a form—and everything that we perceive with our senses.

However, because everything that exists in the world of the senses is a reflection of the spirit, we must turn to the spirits of movement and, with them, carry out a "turning around" to the actual beings and origin of things. In this way a deep, inner reverence will also be wakened in us.

The only real thing in our sense world is the Word. The Logos stands behind the Word, the archetypal sounds. The Word of the original language is the archetype of God's creative speech.

Every word spoken sends forth the soul substance from which it originates. What lives in our souls is impressed upon the Word just as we speak it. The Word of the original language is the soul-content that creates worlds. The languages of the world, these many various differences and divisions, are caused by Luciferic spirits.

In the spirit lay the seed of my body ...
In my body lies the seed of the spirit ...

Esoteric Lesson
KARLSRUHE, OCTOBER 14, 1911

Record A: Notes from the collection of Elisabeth Vreede; Record B: Manuscript from Mathilde Scholl and Barbara Wolf; Record C: Notes from Günther Wagner; Record D: Anonymous notes; Record E: Manuscript from Louise Clason; Record F: Notes from the collection of Fred Poeppig; Record G: Manuscript from Alice Kinkel.

RECORD A

Last time we discussed how everything that is in the outer world is maya, and that everything must be imagined in reverse. And we stressed that esotericists should learn to live in such a consciousness that they observe everything around them in this way. If they look at a flower, then they imagine it inverted. If they hear a sound coming from the right, they think that the sound is coming from the left. They can go further, and in many other cases think the same. There where it is dark they should say to themselves that it is actually bright; where there is light, there is actually darkness. If we anchor these feelings of reversal of the maya that surrounds us, if all our thinking is oriented in this way, then we will observe a great transformation within us, which leads us to truth. However, if we want to understand all of this with mere reflection, then we are led to great dangers. Esotericists know, of course, that all symbols and all esoteric teachings can harbor a certain danger if they are wrongly understood and applied. But then, too, as esotericists we are not small children.

Those who have attempted what was described here the last time will have gotten a feeling as if the ground had been pulled out from under them. And if one attempts to understand these things with reason, then it is as if two mirrors were set up facing each other, so that an endlessly repeating reflection appears. The danger consists in this: that human reason begins to dance with this endless repetition as in a whirling vortex. Healthy common sense says then: here my reason must remain stationary! Only an unhealthy soul life allows itself to be pulled into the whirling dance.

We can go even further with this inverting, and involve the human being. Imagine a human face with a lighter or darker coloring, with lighter or darker hair. Now we imagine the light face to be dark, the dark hair to be light, and so forth. Furthermore, we should think of the places where the face has hollows, as pushing outward; and where it is puffed out, as having hollows. At the same time transform the skin color. Where it is colored rosy, think of it as dark green; there where it is pale, as bright green.† If we could feel this, we would be in a position to know this person according to his inner being. The dark green color for example, would show us that we are dealing with a man who stands firmly in a life that works in the three lower kingdoms of nature. If the color appears bright green, then he would be more inclined toward the spiritual. And where we see blue, the highest spiritual traits would be displayed. However, if we were first to imagine the color and then carry it over in thought onto the face as it stands before us, then we would come to the worst false paths.

We must also imagine that something that looks ugly is, in reality, beautiful. That is the reason why Christ on the cross, especially in the old paintings, was not presented as "beautiful," but often as ugly and distorted.

Those who are always busy talking about their difficulties, about their physical pain, and who daily give an account of all the sufferings, both the large and the small, that they must endure, would be weak esotericists. Those who would advance must develop the strength within not to always want to cure their suffering through all kinds of medications and cures; rather, they must understand that all of this belongs to an esoteric development in which the entire being of a person is subject to a transformation. For example, it would be an instance of a thoroughly ill soul life if a man were to walk through a meadow, see an autumn crocus, and then think that it wanted to swallow him. However, it can happen to esotericists even if they are not sick that one may feel that one is about to be grabbed from behind by a higher being and be "absorbed."

Among ordinary people there are those who are afraid of open windows when they are on an upper floor of a tall building because the desire arises to throw themselves out the window. Or there is also the fear of open spaces, agoraphobia, when someone is afraid to cross an open space. This fear ceases if the person feels someone next to him. Official medicine provides causes for all these phenomena, but the true reason is that such people have a deficit of justified solitude. Solitude is something that everyone needs to a certain extent; it is not mere egotism. Those who always want to help others will one day feel that they cannot help any longer until they have obtained the strength from solitude. Those who always want to speak will one day sense that they are speaking only empty words unless they allow spiritual forces to come to them in solitude. We need solitude for prayer and meditation; communal prayer can only bring us to a certain experience out of a group soul. Those who think that it is egotistical to go into solitude simply have the need to be with other people, not in order to help them but only because they do not want to be alone. Even the selfless "desire to help" can in reality arise out of egotism, if someone simply wants to socialize with others. Thus, for example, "mesmerizing," which is ostensibly used to ameliorate the suffering of others, can come from the need to feel pleasure oneself through stroking someone else's body. Although love and egotism are opposite poles, it is nevertheless true that in certain borderline cases these two come very close, and it is difficult to distinguish one from another.

We are surrounded by the three lower kingdoms of nature. Although it would be evidence of an unhealthy soul life for someone to fear being devoured by the beings of the mineral kingdom or the plant kingdom, it can certainly happen to esotericists that through their meditations they feel they are being swallowed up by higher beings. Just as we have the three kingdoms of nature below us, so do we have above us the three spiritual hierarchies; and it is these beings (and also those that have more to do with the inner evolution of humanity) that influence us, and cause the feeling described above. However, at the same time, we are given strength through our I-consciousness so that we are not entirely absorbed by higher beings; so that we do not become a will-less tool. It is rather the case that a higher development leads precisely to our being able to make our feeling and sensing independent; otherwise we would lose our self-consciousness entirely. We should develop ourselves up to the higher hierarchies consciously.

Those who have grasped the great truths concerning the world and the human being through the study of theosophy in such a way that they are permeated and ensouled by these truths; such people learn to feel themselves among spiritual beings in such a way that their independent existence cannot be endangered. Then, no matter what may happen to us, we learn to say from out of our inner life: this comes from God. We learn to say in suffering, God is sending us this suffering as a loving reminder of our past mistakes; and when happy we will say, this is grace that God is sending us. And it leads us to gratitude, not to arrogance. Then we learn to see the work of divine powers in all that happens; then we will gradually feel that we have found the proper relationship to the cosmos.

RECORD B

We heard the last time how effective it is for our soul, to allow the imagination to work on us that the outer world is maya, that only the inverse picture brings us the truth. We can go even further with this imagination. If we look at a person's face, then we could imagine its inverse. Everywhere there is a raised surface, imagine a depression; think dark hair to be light; light hair to be dark, and so forth. Also the color of the face we could think in reverse; but not just imagining a dark color instead of a light color; rather, we could imagine the individual spots of color in their complementary colors; for example, a red spot as green. If we live into this process properly, then the colors will announce to us something of the traits of the person. A bright green, thought of as a complementary color, would signify that the person cannot get free of all that is connected with their bodily nature. A dark green signifies a striving toward the spirit; blue signifies an especially strong striving for the spirit. These colors then become as if transparent for us. These are the colors of the etheric body. This all works only if we inwardly feel it.

By observing in this way, we will gradually come to recognize the true qualities and traits of people, much more than in any other way. Our intellect can at most reach the point of saying the external world is a maya; in its inverse image I see it in its true form. Here at this point, the intellect must remain stationary, otherwise it lands in confusion and loses the ground beneath its feet. Our thoughts are mirror images of the outer world. Think of a mirror and of an object reflected in it. If we place another mirror across from the first mirror we get reflections of reflections on into the blurry distance. This would happen to us if, instead of simply contemplating occult facts, we wanted to brood over them and draw conclusions in order to find new facts. That would have to lead us to a certain kind of confusion. We must, rather, experience these things with our feeling.

Just the way a human being stands between the etheric image and his or her physical maya-image, gives us a proper image of the human being. If a person in the physical body appears ugly, the middle image already reveals this, and vice versa. There was a certain stream in art that pointed to this. There are pictures of Christ that show the figure of Christ as not at all beautiful.

It is good for the soul to have the possibility, the necessity, to experience solitude. The soul needs solitude from time to time, and it is good for it to stand alone. Those who devote themselves to prayer and meditation feel the need for solitude for this purpose. The need to be with other people often arises from egotistical feelings. We think we would like to help. There are certain borderline areas where egotism and love can hardly be separated from one another. We would like to do something for other people, and fundamentally we are doing it only because it gives us satisfaction. A "mesmerizer" may think he or she is especially able to help someone with a stroke of the hand, and in reality it happens only because the stroke causes a certain pleasant feeling.

Now someone might wrongly object that it is still egotism when we enjoy solitude. That is not correctly thought through, and would not be selflessly thought in the proper sense of the word. For I acquire strength from solitude; from this "egotism," I get the strength for deeds of love. The need for solitude is a blessing for the soul. It can be a feeling that brings happiness to the soul. But a feeling can also arise that says: I stand here alone and can depend upon myself alone, all other people are distant from me and are alien to me and none of them can understand me. Such a feeling can fill the soul with pain, but it must be able to lift itself above and out of that feeling.

It would certainly be a very sick soul indeed who would walk through a meadow, see an autumn crocus in blossom, and say, "I am afraid of this crocus; it could devour me." As stated, a soul that could speak in that way would definitely be disposed toward illness. And yet similar feelings could arise in an esotericist, and we must certainly be prepared for something like this. An esotericist can reach the point of saying, "I feel myself devoted to spiritual worlds; they are taking possession of me; it is as if I am begin absorbed by higher beings." And in such a soul, resentment can arise with respect to the gods. Just as there are three kingdoms below us: the animal, plant, and mineral kingdoms, so too, we have above us the three lowest kingdoms of the higher hierarchies: angels, archangels and archai. And at a certain moment a soul can feel as if angels were taking possession of it, and it resists.

What are we really doing when we devote ourselves to the facts of esoteric research that are brought to us in theosophy? What is it that we are taking into ourselves? It is nothing more than the thoughts of the Godhead that existed from the beginning, and according to which all things have come about; the archetypes of all that has come into existence. Now if we could do nothing other than take up the thoughts of the Godhead with our minds, we would have nothing more than mere "after-thoughts." With our minds we would think the truths, but they would leave us cold. That would be like the feeling that we would have if we stood atop a high icy mountain, which no warmth from the world could reach. Thus it would happen to our souls if we would take up the esoteric facts, which are the thoughts of God, in a way that is merely intellectual. In the past, in Lemurian times, when people took up these things, they thereby devoted themselves entirely to the gods, and the warmth of the spiritual world permeated them; they felt themselves intimately connected to the spiritual world. In the course of ages, the intellectual grasping of these truths became increasingly unemotional, and feeling always colder and colder. At the time of the Mystery of Golgotha, the soul was already dripping with ice. But in the instant the Christ left the Christ-bearer on the cross and gave himself to the world, then with his holy fire he radiated glowing warmth into the coldness of the spirit and transformed thereby the spirit into the Holy Spirit.

And now we confront the esoteric facts differently again. We take them up not only with our minds; we also enliven them with our feeling. We permeate and "soak" our most intimate feelings with esoteric facts; we allow what we have experienced to flow into all that we do. To the extent to which we do this, we have something of the Holy Spirit within us. Then, if we have a bodily sense of well-being, we say, "For this I thank the divine spirit in me." And if a thought again arises within me, a thought that I have had in the past, then I say to myself, "Not I; rather, it is the divine spirit within me, who causes this thought to light up again within my soul. I no longer feel that the spiritual world simply takes possession of me, but rather that I have united myself with the divine spirit. And then we will feel the warmth of the divine spirit that permeates us.

Record B

We heard the last time how effective it is for our soul to allow the imagination to work on us that the outer world is maya, that only the inverse picture brings us the truth. We can go even further with this imagination. If we look at a person's face, then we could imagine its inverse. Everywhere there is a raised surface, imagine a depression; think dark hair to be light and light hair to be dark, and so forth. Also the color of the face we could think in reverse, but not just imagining a dark color instead of a light color; rather, we could imagine the individual spots of color in their complementary colors; for example, a red spot as green. If we live into this process properly, then the colors will announce to us something of the traits of the person. A bright green, thought of as a complementary color, would signify that the person cannot get free of all that is connected with the bodily nature. A dark green signifies a striving toward the spirit; blue signifies an especially strong striving for the spirit. These colors then become as if transparent to us. These are the colors of the etheric body. This all works only if we inwardly feel it.

By observing in this way, we will gradually come to recognize the true qualities and traits of people, much more than in any other way. Our intellect can at most reach the point of saying the external world is a maya; in its inverse image I see it in its true form. Here at this point, the intellect must remain stationary; otherwise it lands in confusion and looses the ground beneath its feet. Our thoughts are mirror images of the outer world. Think of a mirror and of an object reflected in it. If we place another mirror across from the first mirror we get reflections of reflections on into the blurry distance. This would happen to us if, instead of simply contemplating esoteric facts, we wanted to brood over them and draw conclusions in order to find new facts. That would have to lead us to a certain kind of confusion. We must, rather, experience these things with our feeling.

Just the way a human being stands between the etheric image and his or her physical maya-image, gives us a proper image of the human being. If a person in the physical body appears ugly, the middle image already reverses this, and vice versa. There was a certain stream in art that pointed to this. There are pictures of Christ that show the figure of Christ not at all as beautiful.

It is good for the soul to have the possibility, the necessity, to experience solitude. The soul needs solitude from time to time, and it is good for it to stand alone. Those who devote themselves to prayer and meditation feel the need for solitude for this purpose. The need to be with other people often arises from egotistical feelings. We think we would like to help. There are certain borderline areas where egotism and love can hardly be separated from one another. We would like to do something for other people, and fundamentally we are doing it only because it gives us satisfaction. A "mesmerizer" may think he or she is especially able to help someone with a stroke of the hand, and in reality it happens only because the stroke causes a certain pleasant feeling.

Now someone might wrongly object that it is still egotism when we enjoy solitude. That is not correctly thought through, and would not be selflessly thought, in the proper sense of the word. For I acquire strength from solitude; from this "egotism" I get the strength for deeds of love. The need for solitude is a blessing for the soul. It can be a feeling for the soul that brings happiness. But a feeling can also arise that says: I stand here alone and can depend upon myself alone, all other people are distant from me and are alien to me, and none of them can understand me. Such a feeling can fill the soul with pain, but it must be able to lift itself above and out of that feeling.

It would certainly be a very sick soul indeed who would walk through a meadow, see an autumn crocus in blossom, and say, "I am afraid of this crocus; it could devour me." As stated, a soul that could speak in that way would definitely be disposed toward illness. And yet similar feelings could arise in an esotericist, and we must certainly be prepared for something like this. An esotericist can reach the point of saying, "I feel myself devoted to spiritual worlds; but they are taking possession of me; it is as if I am begin absorbed by higher beings." And in such a soul, resentment can arise with respect to the gods. Just as there are three kingdoms below us: the animal, plant, and mineral kingdoms, so too, we have above us the three lowest kingdoms of the higher hierarchies: angels, archangels and archai. And at a certain moment a soul can feel as if angels were taking possession of it, and it resists.

What are we really doing when we devote ourselves to the facts of esoteric research that are brought to us in theosophy? What is it that we are taking into ourselves? It is the thoughts of the Godhead that existed from the beginning and according to which all things have come about, the archetypes of all that has come into existence. Now if we could do nothing other than take up the thoughts of the Godhead with our minds, we would have nothing more than mere "after-thoughts." With our minds we would think the truths, but they would leave us cold. That would be like the feeling that we would have if we stood atop a high, icy mountain, which no warmth from the world could reach. Thus it would happen to our souls if we would take up the esoteric facts, which are the thoughts of God, in a way that is merely intellectual. In the past, in Lemurian times, when people took up these things, they thereby devoted themselves entirely to the gods, and the warmth of the spiritual world permeated them, and they felt themselves intimately connected to the spiritual world. In the course of ages, the intellectual grasping of these truths became increasingly unemotional, and feeling always colder and colder. At the time of the Mystery of Golgotha, the soul was already dripping with ice. But in the instant the

Christ left the Christ-bearer on the cross and gave himself to the world, then with his holy fire he radiated glowing warmth into the cold of the spirit, and transformed thereby the spirit into the Holy Spirit.

And now we confront the esoteric facts differently again. We take them up not only with our minds; rather, we also enliven them with our feeling. We permeate and "soak" our most intimate feelings with esoteric facts; we allow what we have experienced flow into all that we do. To the extent to which we do this, we have something of the Holy Spirit within us. Then, if we have a bodily sense of well-being, we say, "For this I thank the divine spirit in me." And if a thought again arises within me, a thought that I have had in the past, then I say to myself, "Not I; rather, it is the divine spirit within me, who causes this thought to light up again within my soul. I no longer feel that the spiritual world simply takes possession of me, but rather that I have united myself with the divine spirit." And then we will feel the warmth of the divine spirit that permeates us.

RECORD C

In the previous hour we discussed a mighty meditation that was placed before our souls; some of you may even have attempted to see what presents itself to you in the sense world as maya. We can carry this meditation even further by attempting to perceive and feel the face and hair color, also the color of the eyes and any redness in the cheeks, of any person who stands in front of us in their complementary color. And the surfaces that appear as raised or as depressions would be seen as inverted. For example, if a person had cheeks that appeared more red, then they would have to be felt as bright green; and it is a sign that this person still stands very much in (external) life. If, with a lighter reddish coloring in the face, we feel a dark green coloring, and if a bluish color shimmers over it, then a clairvoyant would be able to determine the degree of spirituality on this more or less intensive coloring. This is the beginning of being able to see a person's aura.

All these things can only be sensed and felt. The connecting link[†] between the etheric and the physical bodies is constantly the opposite of the outer, visible human being. If someone appears ugly, then the connecting link appears beautiful. In many art movements today we can see that this spiritual aspect (unconscious to the artist) is expressed in works of art; for example, in the many paintings of the crucifixion with ugly features distorted by pain.

If we understand maya and illusion with our intellect and want to think through these exercises involving inverting, or reversing, then the mind, if it has developed healthy thinking, can accompany the exercise only to the fact of the reversal or inversion; otherwise, it would only become a constantly repeated and frustrating reflection of one's own thoughts, which could then degenerate into pathology.

We must attempt to stand firmly with esoteric development. We must patiently bear all pain, suffering, states of fear, and so forth. It is not a good sign for esotericists when they complain and take all possible cures. We must be clear that a change in the body takes place, and can call forth just such conditions. We can also be sought out by every possible nervous condition, such as we observe in neurasthenics: agoraphobia, wanting to jump down from heights. Then one must bear in mind that this is all maya, and, above all, that this kind of mental state signifies a strengthening of difficulties that appear later. We should be ruled by the thought that the more we have to suffer and overcome, the more we are favorites of the gods, .

Loneliness of the soul, not being understood by others: these come to meet us as the first difficulties of soul. Loneliness or solitude brings us the highest fruits of the soul. Praying and meditating in solitude brings us the strongest spiritual streams and strengthens our own individuality.

Praying in a mass of people is only group-blessedness.†

Solitude affects people differently according to their degree of development. It brings despair to one person, joy to another person. The drive for social interaction is sometimes excused with the claim that one wants to help other people and likes to be able to do so. Love and egotism go hand in hand. Talking too much leads to banality. As an esotericist one must even fight for justified solitude.

Before us we have the mineral, plant, and animal kingdoms. Behind us stand the lower hierarchies, angels, archangels, and spirits of personality. The feeling often fills us that an angel is entering into us and taking possession of us. All that we experience in terms of suffering and joy is a gift from the gods, that is the Holy Spirit who works in us. If people had within them all the thoughts of theosophy that have now been given to the world, then they would have the thoughts of the gods. However, these thoughts would only release pure thinking within us and produce the frosty, icy-coldness of wisdom.

However, just as the first feelings of life stir in an egg, so too, we should produce warmth within us; love that streams through us and ensouls these thoughts of the gods is possible only through the Christ-event. From the age of Lemuria until the Christ, there was even an ebbing, but now through Christ there should be a rising up again. Now it is possible to connect wisdom and love.

We should meditate these feelings and thoughts of the gods as proceeding from the Father; we should then warm these feelings and offer them to Christ, and then be born anew. The spirit that is in us, through the Holy Spirit, meditated in the right Rosicrucian way, gives us certainty and independence that we *should also have faced with the higher hierarchies.*

Addendum: We should not merely believe in karma theoretically. It is very difficult to feel it really as a consequence of the past in the case of difficult life experiences. However, the esoteric exercises help us with this; for example, dispassionateness or poise. We should not only stand above joy or sorrow, but also in every fiber of our hearts we should be entirely devoted to the great justice of the world. ("Lord, your will be done.")

During the retrospective review of the day, it is very good if points occur to us that escaped our notice entirely during the day.

Another good imagination is to picture a plant as it appears green, but actually knowing that is maya, or illusion. One should imagine it with the leaves having a violet-red coloring, the stem blue, and so forth. Also one should imagine the placement as reversed. Then if one is feeling properly, one will feel oneself to be the plant, will grow into it, and grow with it into the spiritual heights. The same thing is given in the book *How to Know Higher Worlds*.

All imaginations will appear to us in the right way if we imagine the world within ourselves as maya. It is very good to carry out this exercise with animals...

We must be thankful to the beings that hinder our progress, that work against our karma, for if we were to remain as impure as we are as disposed to be in our karma then we would be tossed into the abyss…

* * *

Record D

We can go even further with these efforts if we stand in front of human beings and attempt to view even their external appearance as illusion and maya. So, for example, we would attempt to sense and feel their face coloring, their hair, eyes, and cheek coloring in the complementary colors. So also we would imagine all the elevated portions of their faces (that is, nose) or the depressions as reversed. In this way we come to the negative form: what as hollow space is left out of the physical body and constitutes the spiritual part. (Compare this with the chapter in *Theosophy* titled "Spiritland.") This is also the beginning of living into the aura of the human being. All of these experiences can only be felt and sensed. If we approach this with the intellect, we can carry out this kind of exercise only up to the reversal, the "turning-inside-out," or we experience only a constant reflection of our own thoughts thrown back at us without penetrating into the spiritual world. If someone has, for example, very red cheeks, then these will have to be experienced in their complementary color, bright green, a sign that that person still stands very strongly in a vegetative life. For clairvoyant perception, a lighter shade of red presents a bluish shimmer over a somewhat darker green tone. Thus clairvoyants can recognize the degree of spirituality of the person standing in front of them.

The connecting link[†] between the etheric and physical bodies is constantly the counterimage of the externally visible human being. Externally if a human being appears to us as beautiful, then the connecting link is ugly, and vice versa. We can see this often in many art movements of the present time, even if it is expressed unconsciously. For example, this is seen in some crucifixion paintings with the unattractive, pain-distorted features.

If we want to place ourselves in the right way with our consciousness in the sense world without being delivered over to its purely external maya and getting stuck there, then we must be clear about the following. Before us stand the kingdoms of the minerals, the plants, and the animals. Behind us stand the kingdoms of the hierarchies that border on humanity: the angels, archangels, and the spirits of personality. We can often have the feeling, especially when we are doing the above-mentioned exercises, that we are being absorbed by the hierarchies standing behind us; also the feeling will often appear as if an angel were entering us.

In order properly to encounter this feeling of being absorbed, we must learn to regard everything that we experience as joy or sorrow as a gift from the gods—as brought to us by the spirit of the Father, as brought about within us by the spirit of the Father. In this way, we develop the inner serenity and poise that we need as inner strength and solidity, in contrast to the higher hierarchies. One can say that if we were to take up into ourselves all those thoughts that are given today in theosophy, these would be the thoughts of the higher hierarchies, the gods; nevertheless, thinking in us, these would produce an icy-coldness. For this reason we must connect these thoughts of the gods with warmth that awakens love in us. Even if this is possible only in a very weak way within us, nevertheless it is the same as with the first feelings of life in a plant seed. Only since the Christ event has it become possible to connect wisdom with love.

In this way we can feel and meditate the thoughts of the gods as proceeding from the Father, and we can warm this feeling in view of the sacrifice of Christ through whom the spiritual substance was taken up within us; we can be born again in the world-thoughts of the Holy Spirit, who is permeated by love. This lies in the threefold Rosicrucian verse:

> *Ex Deo nascimur.*
> *In Christo morimur.*
> *Per Spiritum Sanctum reviviscimus.*

This, practiced in the proper way, gives us the certainty and the independence that we need facing the higher hierarchies.

> *In the spirit lay the seed of my body...*
> *In my body lies the seed of the spirit...*

Record E

The last time a mighty imagination was placed before the soul. If this imagination works correctly, we will say that we should take up such esoteric facts with feeling, with a feeling-sensation; not with the intellect, which leads reflections on into infinity and makes the soul, the spirit, confused. But we are to imagine not only that in front and behind, above and below, are light and darkness, but also the human being who stands facing us, and imagine this in such a way that the parts of the face that spring forward, recede, and the coloring appears in its complementary color. For example, red appears as green. In this way we are to push forward toward the spiritual world: bright green, still stuck on the bodily nature; where green becomes darker into blue, there a tendency toward the spiritual. Thus we are to slowly penetrate forward to vision of the etheric body. That which lies between the etheric body and the imagined opposite image: beauty as ugliness, ugliness as beauty, just as many painters have presented the spiritual as distortion in portrayals of Jesus on the cross.

With esotericists, the external sheath will not immediately find the change that goes on in the inner human being. Physical complaints, but don't pay attention to them. Fight against them in order to strengthen the soul. Agoraphobia and dizziness are caused when we do not get enough justified solitude. Solitude is necessary for an esotericist. Common meditations and prayers create a groupsoul quality. The soul should become strong in itself. On the path of esotericism there will be feelings of aloneness and of others not being present. This can cause either pain or joy. If we have all theosophical knowledge within us, then the thoughts of the gods are at work within us. How the four-fold human being evolved, or the evolution of the planets, existed in the thoughts of the gods before the human being was created. During the time of Lemuria these thoughts were living in human beings with the fire of the gods. But the thoughts became ever colder up to the event of Golgotha; then Christ came, and now the thoughts of the gods should be ensouled again through divine fire.

Just as there are three kingdoms of nature behind us, so also, behind us we have the three hierarchies of angels, archangels, and archai. Just as a person with a sick inner life has fear of being devoured by a flower, there is a moment of fear in esoteric development when one feels that one is as if lifted up from behind, as if absorbed. Against this we can say with every pain, with every joy, "The Holy Spirit is causing this in me." In this way you acquire solidity and self-preservation when ascending into the spiritual world. We proceed out of the kingdom of the ideas of the spirits: of the gods of the Father, through the fire of Christ, of the son, into the kingdom of the Holy Spirit.

RECORD F

Overcoming inner states of fear

What is above all important in esoteric development is that we try to endure patiently all pain, suffering, and fearful states through inwardly standing firm. This is the first, big condition. It is not a good sign for esotericists if they complain, and apply every different kind of cure for their suffering. Rather we should be clear that a change is taking place in ourselves, which simply causes such conditions of fear and pain. Also, all kinds of nervous conditions can be observed: for example, agoraphobia. All of these things can happen to us. To oppose this, it is necessary to arrive at a clear consciousness that everything is maya, illusion, and that these conditions and similar phenomena in reality signify a strengthening for later difficulties in inner development that will have to be overcome.

In all of this, the thought should guide us that we are favorites of the gods, the more we have to overcome and to suffer! This gives us the proper strengthening and solidity that we need on our path.

One of the first soul difficulties that comes to meet us is, above all, loneliness or the solitude of the soul; a not-being-present for others. But it is precisely solitude that brings us the highest and strongest spiritual streams and solidifies our individuality. On the other hand, prayer in a Mass always brings a group-soul quality.[†]

Solitude has different effects, depending on the degree of development of the individual person; one person is brought to despair; another is brought to inner joy. The drive toward social contact to escape solitude is often excused by saying that one wants to help others. Nevertheless, excessive talking does not have a beneficial effect on us; it causes brutality.[†] In this connection, love and egotism go hand in hand when we lose ourselves too much in sociability "in order to help others."

Nevertheless, one must learn to fight for justified solitude. This is often seen as egotism today. Still, an esotericist must be egotistical in certain cases, otherwise one would never achieve the level where one can be used as an instrument for humanity. Only a path through the trials just characterized leads us to the heights where we can find the spirit, and then later serve it as a selfless servant.

Record G

All that we see is maya. In truth, we must say to ourselves, everything is the opposite of that which we see.
That which is in front of us is in truth behind us, and
What is behind is in front;
Right is left,
Left is right;
Above is below,
Below is above;
High is deep and
Deepening is raising, and so forth.
It is necessary for an esotericist to say this about all that is experienced.

Esoteric Lesson
BERLIN, OCTOBER 27, 1911

Record A: Manuscript from Camilla Wandrey; Record B: Anonymous manuscript from Vreede collection; Record C: Notes from Günther Wagner; Record D: Manuscript from Louise Clason; Record E: Anonymous notes.

RECORD A

Great seriousness should hold sway in the esoteric life. An esoteric lesson should be something sacred—something that is entrusted to us—and we should never receive it as something familiar. We were certainly not all conscious of the necessary earnestness when we asked to be accepted into the circle of the esoteric school. Now we should increasingly recall this earnestness, and strive for the connection with the spiritual worlds that we can reach through an esoteric training, and not fall back into everyday life. All the exercises that have been given to us are to be considered as proceeding from the Masters of Wisdom and Harmony of Feelings.

In the esoteric life one must be alert to egotism. We often convince ourselves that we are doing something selfless, or we feel hate or envy against someone, which does not even come to consciousness. We think that, as an esotericist, we must tell a person the truth, or that we just cannot bear this or that from him or her. As soon as such feelings appear, we should remember that we are subject to great delusions, and that their origin always lies in egotism. Feelings of this sort are always expressed in a feeling of warmth that permeates the etheric body; indeed, the part of the etheric body that we call the warmth ether. This warmth reaches the physical body and works through the blood. We must be clear about the fact that these kinds of feelings always have a destructive effect on world evolution. The hierarchies, whose task is to guide karmic connections, then work in such a way that they employ beings of a Luciferic sort, who destroy these effects in us by working in a destructive way within the physical body.

When we acquire proper self-knowledge, genuine insight into our own base nature, then a thoroughly ice-cold feeling passes through us, while that which lives in us in terms of impulses toward gratification is expressed in a feeling of warmth—just the opposite of self-knowledge. Samael is the chief instigator of the Luciferic beings that work in this cold, bringing self-knowledge to people. They are perceptible in the most varied forms, usually similar to human beings—perceptible to the clairvoyant.

People are often much more untruthful and dishonorable than they themselves know. Many say, "I really no longer have untruthfulness in me, I have set that entirely aside." But this untruthfulness is often so subtle that it usually does not come to our consciousness at all. For example, imagine the following. We read an announcement in the newspaper about a theosophical lecture in another city and decide to go there. We are convinced that we are traveling only for this purpose; it does not rise up into our consciousness that precisely in this city a good friend of ours lives, whom we would be very happy to see again, or that a pleasurable event is taking place that we would gladly participate in. We believe that we want to travel there only on account of the lecture; whereas, in reality, there are other reasons for us to take this trip. We have, of course, been brought up not to tell any crass untruths. However, we have perhaps not yet overcome the tendency to appear better than we are or, in the light of strict self-examination, if it is a matter of life and death, to admit the truth and yet, nevertheless, to be silent about it, to veil it and put a cloak over it. All of this has a deleterious effect on the evolution of the world. The effect of such lies goes first to the astral body, then to the etheric body, indeed to the part of the etheric body that we call the "light ether." Then these effects go further into the physical body, and work upon our nervous system.

All these dishonesties bring us to the attention of Azazel. He and his beings, whose leader he is, are revealed to a clairvoyant as similar to a human being, usually as a head with the wings of a raven. With egotism, jealousy, and hate, when we awaken we have a feeling of disgust, of loathing, that can be accounted for as the working of our double. Those who are still inclined to dishonesty feel a choking, scratching feeling in their throats when awakening. They feel as though they were being pinched by claws, tortured by a thousand arms. Azazel is doing this with his swarm. And when we feel his effects in the way indicated, we should be stimulated to reflect upon how deeply we are still entangled in lies and deception.

Another stumbling block is indifference and obtuseness with respect to the spiritual world. Many students listen to an esoteric lesson, but what has been given them finds no echo. They are unable to free themselves from everyday life. They are unable to raise themselves to the spirit or surrender themselves to spiritual thoughts. Others are merely curious to see or hear something from the spiritual world. They simply throw themselves into meditation without dedicating themselves to a regular study of the subject because that would not be easy for them. This works directly upon the "I" and from there upon the astral body and then upon the etheric body, and, to be sure, upon that part we call the chemical ether. From there it works into the physical body in all its glands and fluid secretions. This is the effect of Azazel. With people who are not esotericists, Azazel and his swarm constantly foster only beneficial effects because they work into such people, not in a way deleterious for one's health, but rather in a supplementary way, so to speak. With esotericists the effects go deeper, and they are required to constantly be aware of their complete responsibility for themselves and for the world. When awakening, a lackluster esotericist will have a feeling of drowning, as in a flood. It will be all the stronger the more the esotericist surrenders to the life of the senses.

Esotericists should constantly watch themselves. It is alright for them to sometimes brood on themselves. Only in this way will they realize what is brought to us at the conclusion of every esoteric lesson by the Masters of Wisdom and Harmony of Feelings:

In the spirit lay the seed of my body...
In my body lies the seed of the spirit...

RECORD B

Only with great earnestness should an esoteric life be taken up. All too often it is curiosity that drives people to esotericism. They would indeed like to develop themselves, but are unwilling to study beforehand the esoteric material that has been given to them. For example, we often speak of "conscious falling asleep and waking." What happens when we consciously awaken? Then we are submerged into what we really are: what our karma has made out of our various sheaths. In order for us to be to be able to submerge consciously, we must constantly practice self-knowledge. We can deceive ourselves all too easily concerning our motives for this or that deed. As soon as our reasoning leads us to conclude that we have selfless motives for a deed, we should be on the watch and consider well that it is most probable that in reality the reverse is true. We could be filled with envy for another person, or we might think that we must do something to oppose another person, and the motives for doing so are entirely different than we imagine; indeed, in by far the most cases the motives lie somewhere other than where we supposed.

If we feel anger or envy, this feeling can grant us a certain satisfaction, but thereby we injure not only ourselves but also the entire world. Such a feeling immediately influences the etheric body; indeed, the part of the etheric body that belongs to the warmth ether. Also the satisfaction that follows a truly (not imagined) selfless deed affects the warmth ether of the etheric body, but then works back upon the entire world in a beneficial fashion. When a human being surrenders to selfishness in general, those beings of the higher hierarchies who are responsible for seeing to it that nothing improper enters into world evolution send certain other beings that belong to the Luciferic swarms into the etheric body, so that the consequences of selfishness are destroyed. Thus these beings must constantly be at work in the evolution of humanity to work against these deleterious effects of egotism upon the warmth ether, and from there upon the physical body and upon the blood. Their leader is known by the Kabbalistic name of Samael.

If, as esotericists, we want to escape these effects, we must hold clearly before our eyes this exercise: if we are ever confronted by someone who makes us very angry, then we should take the feeling of warmth that otherwise fills us with the satisfaction of anger, set it aside, and cause it to pass over into a feeling of freezing cold.

Another tendency that adheres to human beings is the inclination toward falsehood. Even if this tendency is held in check by education, nevertheless we are dealing with the fact that people have the possibility of being untruthful in certain circumstances, even if one does not often speak a lie. A lie has an immediate effect upon the astral body, and from there upon the etheric body, specifically upon the light ether, and then finally upon the physical body in the nervous system. These consequences too are destroyed by divine-spiritual beings who are under the leadership of Azazel. These have the following effect upon human beings (in particular upon esotericists). Upon awakening, we have the feeling as if a horrible monster had crawled into our throats and wanted to strangle us. This experience does not need to come to all esotericists, but some must go through it; not all are spared it.

The external form of these beings as a clairvoyant sees them is not what is especially important. They can show themselves in the most varied forms, but they have especially developed the human form; although Samael, for example, is a being that belongs to the salamanders. Especially Azazel has developed the human form well, with wings instead of arms. However, for an esotericist it is important to know that Azazel shows himself as a being who wants to penetrate into his throat and strangle him.

Human beings can also be so constituted that they are actually insensitive with respect to the spiritual world of the mind. This can even occur with esotericists who would like quickly to penetrate into the spiritual world, but do not study what has been prescribed for them to understand. This also has deleterious consequences that would appear in the world unless they are destroyed by spiritual beings under the leadership of higher hierarchies. For example, in Austria all teachers, young and old, once had to be tested anew because of new requirements that were established by law for the acquisition of a teacher's license. An instructional inspector, who did not want to make things too difficult for the old teachers, decided to test them only on the contents of the books they had been using for instruction all those years. And behold, it became evident that the majority of these teachers did not even know what was contained in the textbooks they themselves used. That is how insensitive they had become with respect to the spiritual-mental world.

Those spirits that are under the leadership of Azazel are actually a blessing for esotericists who have this tendency, because Azazel does not need to destroy anything for them; rather, he must bring something to them. Azazel is unbelievably busy with his swarm in the world. They work upon the chemical ether in the etheric body, and thus upon the fluids in the blood that are transformed by mental apathy. Azazel has the effect upon esotericists such that they feel they are drowning upon awakening. One does not feel properly adjusted to the physical world and one would preferably immediately fall back asleep. One often imagines Luciferic beings as exclusively evil, but they do bring about much good in the world.

* * *

Record C

We must take the esoteric life seriously. An esoteric lesson must be something holy to us; we should never experience it as "the usual."

None of us were conscious of the necessary seriousness when we asked to join the esoteric school. Now we should place this before our souls again and again, and strive for a connection to the spiritual world in order not to fall back again into everyday life.

The exercises that are given to us are to be seen as proceeding from the masters. Esotericists should pay attention to themselves and their feelings, especially to everything having to do with self-knowledge. Most people—and we certainly also belong to this group—deceive themselves greatly with respect to matters that concern them.

1. One must especially attend to egotism. We often tell ourselves that we are doing something selflessly, or perhaps we feel hate or envy toward someone, of which we have not yet become conscious; and we believe that as esotericists we must tell that person the truth, or perhaps there is something that we cannot stand about the

person. As soon as such feelings appear we should remember that we are subject to great delusions, whose causes always lie in egotism.

Feelings such as this always express themselves with a feeling of warmth that permeates the etheric body, indeed, the part of the etheric body we call the warmth ether, and it works all the way down into the physical body through the blood. Feelings such as this always have a destructive effect upon the evolution of the world. The hierarchies whose job it is to guide karmic connections then work in such a way that they engage Luciferic beings to destroy these effects in us, and then work destructively on the etheric body and indirectly work destructively upon the physical body. Correct self-knowledge, insight into our own baseness, induces a cold-as-ice feeling to flow through us. Everything in us that lives as emotion, driving us to gratification, is expressed in the feeling of warmth indicated above, which is just the opposite of the effects of self-knowledge.

These beings, whose leader is called Samael, with his large swarm, are revealed to a clairvoyant in various forms, usually appearing similar to human beings; they are almost always perceptible, frequently for clairvoyants.

When awakening, a feeling of disgust and loathing can always be traced back to egotism. Those who incline to dishonesty experience a choking, scratching feeling in the throat, as if they were being tortured by a thousand arms. All those who observe themselves will then notice how entangled they are in lies and dissimulation.

2. Untruthfulness. Through our education we are raised not to speak any gross untruths. But we have the inclination to appear perhaps better than we are, when push comes to shove, instead of admitting the truth we say nothing or obscure it. All this has a deleterious effect upon the worlds unfolding. Such untruths have an effect upon our astral body, then upon the etheric body, indeed, upon the part we call the light ether, then further upon the physical body and our nervous system.

The beings whose leader is Azazel are also revealed to a clairvoyant as appearing similar to human beings, usually as a head with the wings of a raven.

3. Third is indifference and insensitivity toward the spiritual

worlds. Many of us listen to an esoteric lesson, but then there is no response to what has been given. They are unable to raise themselves in spirit in ordinary daily life and to think spiritual thoughts. Others are merely curious to see and hear something from the spiritual world, and throw themselves into meditation without devoting themselves to systematic study because that is too inconvenient for them. With esotericists this works upon the "I"; from there upon the astral body, then further upon the etheric body, indeed, upon that part we call the chemical ether, and from there upon the physical body in all its fluids and glands. Azazel with his swarm wants only to further good effects in non-esotericists, since those effects are not destructive to a non-esotericist, but work in a supplementary way, so to speak. Esotericists are required to be fully conscious at all times of their responsibility for themselves and for the world.

When awakening, insensitive esotericists will have a feeling of drowning (flood); the stronger, the more they surrenders themselves to ordinary, everyday sense impressions.

Esotericists should constantly watch themselves; there is no harm in esotericists occasionally brooding over themselves; only in this way will esotericists realize what is brought to us at the end of every esoteric lesson from the Masters of Wisdom:

In the spirit lay the seed of my body…

* * *

Record D

We cannot take the esoteric life seriously enough. Exercises are given to us for our advancement, but the enemies that are opposed to this advancement are our old everyday habits of life; the gratification of egotistical wishes works destructively for the entire further evolution of humanity, while the satisfaction of selfless deeds helps to foster this evolution. So too, all impulsive emotions, passions; the propensity for untruthfulness, for lies and spiritual insensitivity; these all work destructively, hindering evolution. The gratifications of egotism, of emotional impulses and passions sit directly in the etheric body, in the warmth ether; and work from there into the blood, warming it. Only proper self-knowledge that leads to disgust at oneself can work to cool it down. Self-knowledge is always a battle.

In order to eliminate this damage, swarms are sent out by the good spiritual powers to destroy these effects; swarms, under Samael (who belongs to the fire salamanders, but appears to a clairvoyant in human form with wings instead of arms). Habits of untruthfulness sit in the light ether, also a part of the etheric body; and they work by means of the astral body into the nervous system. Azazel is placed against these effects; we must fight with him when we have a feeling of being strangled upon wakening, as if one had to swallow an ugly animal. This is a certain sign that this propensity for lying is present in one. The third enemy is spiritual indifference, no interest in spiritual facts; this one sits in the chemical ether, works from the "I" out into the astral body, even into fluids. Azazel is present to eliminate these destructive effects. The presence of this spiritual insensitivity brings about a feeling of drowning; a feeling of not being able to find oneself upon awakening. An esotericist should fight with these three powers. The worst for an esotericist is being satisfied with oneself; then there is no further advancement on the esoteric path.

* * *

RECORD E

We have already seen how esotericists through proper meditations and concentration exercises must manage to develop themselves consciously through the world of illusions to spiritual reality. On this path those beings that are allowed by the wise powers as Luciferic swarms are helpful, so that esotericists can achieve their goal through trials. From this point of view these are good Luciferic beings, whose leader is Samael. Now there are still more such beings; and here we have to begin with, to observe Azazel with this swarm. Human beings usually possess more dishonesty and untruthfulness than they themselves know. I see that there are many who say, "I really don't have any more dishonesty in me; I have set that aside!" But this dishonesty is so subtle that we are usually not even conscious of it, since we often ascribe entirely false motives to our actions, although in reality we are actually motivated by entirely different grounds. All of this dishonesty brings us to Azazel's attention with his swarm. When we feel as if we were being pinched by pliers and tortured by a thousand arms, then we should reflect upon how deeply we are still entangled in dishonesty and lies.

A third being that approaches an esotericist is Azazel. This one, too, can call forth a feeling of being pinched, and also a strangling, scratching feeling in the throat. And again we need to be clear about the bad character traits that we still must set aside; for example, all our insensitive indifference toward world events. An esotericist should not feel indifference toward what happens in the world. Most people are so indifferent because they are entangled in egotism, so that they are entirely indifferent toward everything that happens around them. This is where the apathy of the masses with respect to spiritual beings comes from.

Esoteric Lesson

BERLIN, OCTOBER 30, 1911

Record A: Notes from Rudolf Meyer; Record B: Anonymous Manuscript from Vreede collection; Record C: Manuscript from Camilla Wandrey; Record D: Manuscript from Louise Clason.

RECORD A

When we immerse ourselves in our own inner nature we find many beings there. This may, at first, seem strange, but the farther we come, the more we learn to see into the spiritual world; the more we will see that a number of spiritual beings are at work in us, often to compensate for the destruction we human beings in our foolishness perpetrate.

Let us ask ourselves: where does illness come from? We know that every illness has a spiritual cause in addition to the physical cause. This spiritual cause can be found in immorality, passions, or other misdeeds in this life, though usually in the previous incarnation. The victory over every illness sets forces free; however, this does not mean that we should draw out an illness for as long as possible in order to advance as quickly as possible. Rather, everyone should do as much as possible to become healthy as soon as possible. However, if we have been ill for three weeks, or for three months, we should regard this as karma, and bear it with patience and equanimity.

But there is a second reason why an illness is something beneficial. Ever since Lemurian times, through Atlantis up till the Mystery of Golgotha, humanity has sunk deeper and deeper into matter. And because we follow our instincts and passions, we have had to sink deeper and deeper, constantly brought further away from the aims that God has set for us.

It is illness that diverts this impulse downward, so to speak, and gives us again an upward direction. Contemporary academic scholarship condemns theosophical teachings as daydreams, but one need only to take a book in hand such as John's Gospel, or any theosophical book, and one will see how enlivening, how refreshing its effects are, while a materialistic or monistic book dries up and withers the soul. And because this purely materialistic thinking only consumes forces, the consequences will appear in the next existence. Such people will be afflicted by a kind of feeble-mindedness. Their brains will be an entirely spongy, watery mass; they will want to think but won't be able to think. This feeble-mindedness is a blessing that protects these people from sinking down into matter irredeemably. This is so because the existence of feeble-mindedness protects the brain from materialistic thinking; then the eternal self can work on the essential core of a person's being, two times consecutively in devachan, and influence it so that it again strives upward.

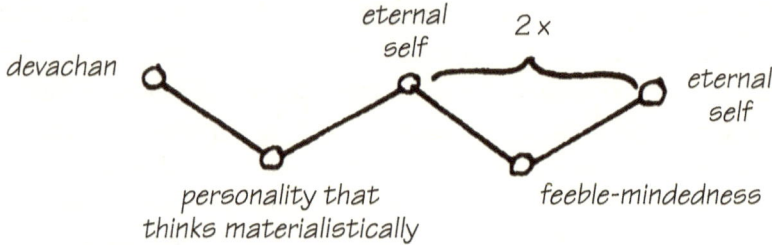

All of you have already experienced or still will experience that in meditation one feels detached or uncoupled; the etheric body is expanded and one feels oneself carried out into distant borders of the world, and then suddenly one feels oneself again firmly bound to this world: one cannot detach from it; one sits as if in a vise. This is actually quite good. It is our karma from earlier incarnation that holds us so firmly. If, as a consequence of our meditations, we would immediately ascend into the spiritual world without having carried out our karma, the consequence would be a steep fall. The leader of the swarms that tie us firmly to the earth is Mehazael. We come to know him when we ascend within ourselves; so, too, with Samael, Azazel, and Azael. We will then realize that our inner being really is a field of action for demons. "And their number is Legion!"† as we read in the Bible. On our esoteric path, we should learn these names so that we come to understand and gradually outgrow them. Through his work Azael compensates for what arises in us through insensitivity to the spiritual world. When we acquire complete dispassionateness and serenity, then we take over the work of Azael. But this is what dispassionateness means: not jubilating in joy, not complaining in pain, but rather, recognizing the reality of karma working in everything. We should not believe in the idea of karma only theoretically; rather, we should feel that karma is at work in everything that we meet. In the stages of Christian initiation, this is called the Scourging; that is, self-composed, we calmly confront all the pain and suffering of life, which hits us like the lashes of a whip, knowing that they are karmically determined. This is genuine serenity, composure.

We know that the physical world is only a mirror image of the astral world, in such a way that everything appears inverted or turned around. An infinitely important meditation useful for making the saying "The world is only maya" effective is the following. Everything that we have around us is actually inverted. What we see from above to below is actually from below to above. Plants have their roots above and blossoms below. The starry world above us and in front of us is actually the result of spiritual beings that in reality are at work behind us. The sound that the left ear receives actually comes from the right. We must live into these facts, also with the complementary colors. We should imagine that the red spots on someone's face are actually green; or what protrudes we should imagine as inverted inward. With a plant we should imagine green as reddish-lilac; the brown root as dark blue. We should permeate these exercises with reverence and devotion. Altogether this is the feeling in which we may hope to approach the divinity of the world; God remains only an abstraction through mere thinking. We must permeate our thinking with devotion, reverence, and humility, then we can hope to penetrate into the spiritual world.

* * *

Record B

It can, of course, happen to anyone that they become ill sometime. Although we should look for the appropriate medicine, an esotericist should ask where the cause of the illness lies. It will be found that there is always a spiritual-soul reason for the illness; either a moral or some other kind of wrong from this incarnation, but usually from a previous earth-life. But why do human beings become ill anyway? Because in every human being there are instincts that draw one down and that can be transformed through illness into ascending instincts.

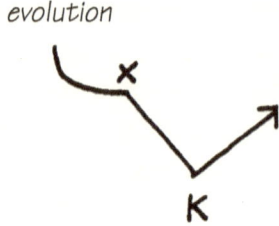

If we represent by means of this curve the evolution of the human being, then x represents an impulse downward brought about by a wrong action at a certain moment. A human being would follow this impulse, and be completely lost to those worlds that are the goal of human existence, if the creator of humanity had not at a certain moment allowed illness (K) to appear, which can transform this impulse into an upward-striving impulse. There are many such impulses leading the human being upward. But this is not otherwise possible if we consider that our entire evolution from Lemurian time until the event of Golgotha was nothing other than descending, and that only since that time has the possibility come to lead human beings upward again. And the time that has passed since Golgotha is, of course, very short compared to the long period of time that lies before it. Also there are downward-leading impulses in humanity that are still to be revealed in the future. A striking example of this is the entire field of materialistic academic scholarship. This makes human beings insensitive to spiritual worlds; and the materialists that are now seen as authorities will be born in the next incarnation with brains that will be like mush, so that they cannot serve as instruments for thinking. But this will happen only so that the downward direction can be turned around into an upward direction. Such human beings will then experience two successive periods in the spiritual world (devachan) without undergoing an earthly life between them that could transform the ascending impulses acquired during the first devachan into descending impulses.

It is clear to esotericists that our feelings, thoughts, and all that we find when we descend into our own inner being, is not we ourselves but other beings that are present within our being. (Concerning these, the Gospel says: "Our name is Legion.") In the moment when we descend into our inner realm, we find these beings on all sides striving outward; beings such as those we heard about the last time: Samael, Azazel, Azael.

But it can also happen that esotericists say to themselves, "As I am able to strive, I am too weak even in order to properly carry out my meditations; other thoughts always intervene." This originates in those downward-leading impulses that constitute our karma. Even if they do not lead to illness, they are what create a wall around us, like a mountain burdening us, that prevents us from soon entering the spiritual world.

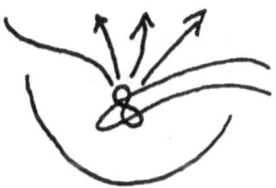

People could, for example, according to the energy invested in their meditations, enter into the spiritual world in a few days, but their karma prevents it for many years; indeed, for good reason. Otherwise they would bring along all their faults and weaknesses. However, those who constantly meditate with diligence and devotion, ideally on one and the same object (constant change in meditations is a sign of weakness), will assuredly eventually have a certain experience. Those who have not yet had it will definitely one day later have it; that is, a certain feeling of blessedness, of detachment from the body as if carried through space on wings. And when one returns, it feels like one is in a prison, like being chained to a single spot when one is again enclosed within the limits of the body. This feeling also originates in a swarm of spirits, whose leader's name, in the same nomenclature used previously, is Mehazael.

These four classes of beings are what we find within us. Their outer appearance, the way they appear to clairvoyant vision, is not very important; it is more important how we feel them. These are the beings that saints and ascetics are referring to when they speak of their temptations and visions. And when they describe the feeling of being attacked with glowing pinchers then they are referring to Mehazael. In esotericism we are working, in a certain sense, against these beings. Those who, for example, are really permeated by the idea of karma, and do not merely think it theoretically, arrive at a certain equanimity with respect to joy and suffering, and all that can occur to them. In this way we work against Azael, who is to remove the consequences of human insensitivity toward the spiritual world. Those who have attained such equanimity are very observant of their surroundings. Apathy, such as that demonstrated by the teacher already described, cannot occur with such an imperturbable person. This apathy is extraordinarily widespread in the present time. For example, students who diligently take notes at a lecture usually do so only because they can do so mechanically and are not required to think at the same time; for this reason, immediately afterwards, they have no idea what they have written down. Those who have passed through Christian initiation and have gotten as far as the appearance of the Scourging are also working against Azael.

The world is maya; these words should acquire content and significance for us. Even those in science have discovered this, here and there. In the coming years they will discover still more esoteric principles, but they don't realize it. Johannes Müller, who lived at the beginning of the nineteenth century, has already discovered that the world actually shows itself to us in its reflection. If we see the sun in front of us, then we know there is a spiritual sun behind us that calls forth the illusory picture of the physical sun before us. If we see the stars above us, then below us are the beings that project through us the image of the starry heavens. The red color of a face is, in reality, bright green; where there is light, there is darkness; and so forth. If we see a flower, then we should think of it inverted: the dark roots above are colored blue (?) [question mark in the German], the green leaves reddish-violet. The retina is not in the eye, as the materialist thinks. The outstanding physiologist Johannes Müller, who is highly respected by materialists and yet far surpasses them, taught that the retina is outside; the entire world around us is the retina, and the one in the human eye is only a reflection of the same. The entire human being is out there, spread out in space.

These are effective imaginations if we carry them out properly and do not attempt to capture them with the intellect.

* * *

Record C

When human beings descend into their inner being, they find not only themselves but also entire swarms of beings that are enclosed within them—beings whom human beings should overcome and liberate. If we have a serious illness, or otherwise a difficult destiny through life, we should be clear that this is a karmic consequence, usually from previous incarnations. These arise from immorality or other human weaknesses, which then in this incarnation serve to give us new impulses for advancement by overcoming them. Human beings have the tendency to fall into the abyss because of the various mistakes they have made in previous incarnations. Through illness, they get a new impulse that protects them from sliding down into the abyss; that gives them an impetus to lift themselves up toward the spiritual powers. Nevertheless, we must do all that is possible for a reasonable person to do, in order to get rid of the illness.

People who are materialists in this life will in their next life be feeble-minded. They will have a brain that is too soft, because in this life they have given too little nourishment to their souls. Were the feeble-mindedness not to occur, these people would be irredeemably lost, because a healthy brain would simply lead them further in the earlier direction. Esotericists often experience moments of great blessedness because their etheric bodies are completely spread out in the spiritual world. Afterward, when they return, they feel enslaved, shackled. They feel themselves as if chained to the physical body. Countless swarms of beings bring this about, swarms that are named after their leader Mehazael. Esotericists will always know when they are experiencing this depressing feeling of being enchained that Mehazael's swarms are working against them and want to pull them down. Often they will feel as if they are being pinched and tortured by glowing hot pinchers. In Christian initiation this is called the Scourging.

We must not think of the human being as if the human being were a "bundle" of instincts, passions, and strong emotions. Rather, it is the case that we have within us entire swarms of beings. This is mentioned in the Gospel. For human beings who encounter these four swarms, the swarms of Samael, Azazel, Azael, and Mehazael, it doesn't matter whether they see them clairvoyantly or not. The only thing that is important is how human beings feel when encountering them. We can learn from this that our entire personality is maya, illusion, and that we can find our sustaining support only in what belongs to the spiritual world, in our individuality, in our higher self.

Record D

The last time we heard that when we descend into ourselves, we encounter beings that are not character traits in us, but are real bundles of beings that are enclosed by our sheaths. Those were Samael, Azazel, Azael, and additionally now Mehazael. We encounter these after blessed moments in meditation, after we have been carried out into other worlds, and we return to our own being, within which an enormous sum of mistakes, lies, and immorality have piled up through many incarnations. For these, karmic compensation must be provided. With these karmic consequences we bring an impulse downward; through illness and the blows of destiny this impulse is blunted and turned upward. Mehazael works on this karmic balancing. When we return from meditation we feel him as if we were being squeezed in a vice. On the Christian path this corresponds to the Scourging. Whether we advance along the esoteric path more quickly or slowly depends upon our karma; we feel resistance within us that prevents us from meditating in the correct way. Here it is good for us to be lenient with ourselves. We must be so egotistical and unbelievably arrogant to think that we are such highly developed beings that we can enter into the spiritual world in three weeks or three months. We should not merely have abstract thoughts about the external world, but rather develop living forces. The world is maya, a mirrored image of spiritual actions that work through us from behind.

Esoteric Lesson
MUNICH, NOVEMBER 19, 1911

Manuscript from Mathilde Scholl and Barbara Wolf.

Today we want to make clear about how one in esoteric life should answer questions that are brought to one. For example, if the question is posed, "What is the heart?" The answer, "It is the cause of the blood's circulation in the human organism," is an answer an esotericist should never give. An esotericist should never give something physical as the cause of anything. Everything physical, all of our organs, indeed, the entire human being, are only symbols for something spiritual—for what the higher hierarchies have created.

The spirits of movement have already worked on our blood circulation on old Sun. The spirits of form then descended and stamped a form and a sign on all that had been created. Thus the heart is only a sign for work the higher hierarchies have done in us.

All that surrounds us is maya. And the good gods have created this world of maya for us, like a blossom from the world of truthfulness, so to speak, so that human beings can be developed—so the "I" (self) can be enkindled and permeate this world—in order to get back to the world of the truth. In our present condition, we absolutely need this world of maya. The words of Goethe are to be understood in this way: "For why else, in the end, is this beautiful world, this canopy of stars here, if not to form and teach the human being?" This is the apparently naïve expression of the fact that the world as we perceive it with our physical senses really exists only for us in this form. For in reality, seen from the word of truthfulness, everything appears differently, with the spiritual causes behind.

The world of maya does not exist for the lower kingdoms of nature, from the mineral and plant kingdoms, to the cold-blooded animals. It exists beginning only with the warm-blooded animals. However, because these animals do not have an "I," a self, that could be enkindled within them, they make the impression on a clairvoyant that they have been brought into an evolutionary condition that is not fit for them; and this has the effect of a bad mood. Especially the apes, the animals most similar to human beings, create a feeling of grotesqueness.

Now esotericists want to struggle out of the world of maya through their meditations; this is an intention of which we should become increasingly conscious. Esotericists seek to connect themselves with the world of truthfulness. They can do this only with the meditations from the spiritual world, which are given by those beings who support the work of the higher hierarchies, the Masters of Wisdom and Harmony of Feelings. And they have given us, for example, a concentration exercise that enables us to work with them on evolution.

If esotericists concentrate their thoughts on the heart; that is, on the place within which they feel their own hearts, they will notice that their thoughts do not remain with the object of concentration, the heart; but rather, that their thoughts pour forth, ray out from that place. It often requires hours and many attempts before they feel this. Then they will see something like a shining star arising, whose center is a figure—a form—an archetype for which the heart is the sign. And the lines and rays of the star will begin to sound forth; and the sounds will be formed into words, into the primal words that created the heart out of the world of truthfulness—and the words found in translation in the words of the prayer to the spirit of Sunday:

Great all-encompassing spirit,
From your life many archetypes came forth

The rays shooting out from the star are always the words: *You were...* —while the lines between the rays are the other words.

Thus esotericists, through proper earnest practice, arrive at such an experience. Their meditations, when done intensely enough (many do not do that!), allow them to penetrate into the world of truthfulness. Then, in that world, they can feel very good and happy, or they can feel rejected, depending upon what they bring with them. Rejection causes them to feel pain and to suffer because of the nature of things. For in this world the good gods can only allow what belongs there; all else will be rejected. Esotericists often have character traits that they themselves do not bring into clear consciousness, which however, work back on them, and which are then brought to the esotericists through certain symptoms.

If esotericists do their meditations diligently and properly, and it happens to them that, for example, they awaken in the middle of the night with a feeling of hot fever, they can oppose it by creating a chill from the soul. Then they clearly feel that they are not alone; that through their esoteric striving they have awakened a "doppelganger," a double. What does the double want? And who is it? The good gods have assigned certain Luciferic beings to exclude from their world the human character traits that do not belong there. One such being is Samael, who jumps into action if an esotericist has not overcome a certain untruthfulness (from which we all suffer). So often, it sits in our unconscious so deeply that without more wakefulness we have no suspicion of it. For example, a woman can decide that she will travel to a theosophical gathering in a city, because such a gathering is informative and good for her. In reality, however, she has entirely different purposes in that city, intending perhaps to meet there some other person, but does not even admit this actual reason to herself. This is perhaps a crass example, but it serves to illustrate many. Here Samael must intervene with his activity. And we notice him through the heat of fever that befalls us at night as long as we are afflicted by this error.

Another error difficult to recognize is the following. We often think that enthusiasm is driving us into the spiritual worlds, whereas we would only like to wallow in the pleasure of the feeling that is enkindled in us when we concern ourselves with such matters. If we do our exercises properly, and want to penetrate into the spiritual world, we can experience that we get a feeling like a nightmare, as if we were being strangled around the throat. And here too, it is again a Luciferic being who causes it: Azazel. He prevents us from entering the spiritual world until we have set this fault aside.

If we carry out our daily tasks in a lazy, inattentive, and careless fashion, then one day, perhaps upon awakening, we will have a feeling of drowning, as if the air were cut off from us and we were dissolving away. He who causes this is called Azael. The attention that we should pay to the world surrounding us is of far greater importance than many think. It is a great help in penetrating into the spiritual worlds if we carry out our exercises with true joy. For with every event, every encounter, we should think of the spiritual causes behind them. What we leave undone, spiritual beings must do on our behalf, for the work must be done. Just how inattentively we often do our work, I will illustrate for you with this example. In a school, new regulations for instruction were to be introduced, and all teachers were subject to an examination. The very humane school inspector thought to himself that he would not test the old teachers now, who had finished teachers' college so long ago, on subjects taught there. They wouldn't remember any longer what was taught there; instead, he would test them on what they teach every day. And the result was that many of these teachers did not know what they had taught their students more than twenty times. So little had they been present while teaching. Similar to these teachers, we often are not present with our thoughts while thinking. And the one whose job it is to compensate for this is called, in the language of occultism, Azael.

These three points are straightforward examples of misconduct. Additionally, as a fourth, we have a character trait that we must also set aside, this is "getting out of the way of karma" instead of courageously approaching it. If we penetrate into the world of truthfulness with this attitude, mornings on awakening we will have a feeling of being bound, as if we were returning to a prison; and additionally, will experience pain over the entire body. This is caused by Mehazael.

Esotericists must of course also bear the consequences of their errors, of their misconduct. But these are expressed in esotericists differently than in others, for example, in bodily illness. And it does not occur to them how they could have attracted something like this. Esotericists should gradually acquire the ability to "call everything into consciousness," and esoteric schools can help them to do this. What we can perceive of this with our senses is, of course, only a tiny fragment, a weak, external sign. Just as everything physical, even sensations we perceive, are only symbols for the realities, so too, the esoteric school as it appears on the physical plane, is only a symbol for what it is in the spiritual world. When such a school is formed, it is usually the case that a human being is spiritually deepened and, for example, has the experience described (from the heart) through concentration. The experience is shaped in this individual into a formula, which he or she then gives further to a number of students, through which they are again set in touch with spiritual truthfulness. This is also expressed in the concluding prayer; what as the creative power is active in the spirit.†

Esoteric Lesson

BERLIN, DECEMBER 16, 1911

Record A: Manuscript notes from Therese Walther; Record B: hand notes from Louise Clason; Record C: hand notes from Alice Kinkel; Record D: Stenography from Franz Seiler.

RECORD A

In our meditations we will soon notice that something opposes us, as a hindering force. We must thoroughly acquaint ourselves with this force and recognize that it is related to the destructive power of the entire earth. The earth is in the grip of a destructive process. Orthodox science, too, recognizes the destructive process, and the new forms on the surface of the earth as the product of the destructive forces. Since the middle of Atlantean times (and already prepared even earlier), these destructive forces have been increasing through what the human being has created as karma. It is karma that strengthens the destructive forces of the earth, which the earth has already created. Uncompensated karma is what strengthens the destructive forces of the earth; and the earth has already become a physical corpse that would have had to fall into separateness, entirely out of the evolutionary plan for the earth, had it not been for a strong intervening power-force. Everything involved with Earth evolution is permeated by these destructive powers, which are the Luciferic beings that remained behind on the old Moon. There was one who out of his cosmic wisdom recognized this and remained even further behind during Moon evolution (actually, already on the Sun, but we are speaking now of the Moon) in order to bring something virginal to Earth evolution, something that has not been taken hold of by the powers of destruction. Until the middle of Atlantean times, up-building forces were at work. The human being saw them working behind maya. Through their uncompensated karma, human beings increasingly strengthened the load of destructive powers so that, by the time of the Mystery of Golgotha on April 3, 33 A.D., the balance beam of the scales was horizontal, and then the Mystery of Golgotha was placed in the other balance pan. Christ united with the earth so that every human being can find him in the depths of his or her soul. Human beings had to drown in the maya that surrounded them, then Christ united himself with the evolution of the earth so that the human being can find him again behind the maya.

We know why this maya was woven by the gods: so that human beings would not have to live in a world chained to the glory of the world of truthfulness, but rather they could turn to it in freedom. We know what our conditions of waking and sleeping are. In ancient times, human beings in the moment of waking saw the divine beings through the veil of maya. By the time of the Mystery of Golgotha, however, all they could still see were the demons. Then the gate closed entirely, and the human being had to drown in maya. In ancient times the cloak (the power) of Elijah had to be given to Elias so that he could separate the Jordan River, to cross it without danger; the predecessor of Christ [John] immersed the people in the Jordan. The human being had to go through the water, but a substance was given with which to make a bridge in order to cross it, instead of drowning in it. Christ gives himself as this material.

Now it is possible for us to see a hindrance to our freedom in the fact that we must attach ourselves to this victorious power of Christ. But Christ leaves us so free with respect to the acceptance of his being that he does not allow himself to be found with anything earthly, not even with the intellect or reason, because these exert a compelling force on human beings, for intellect and reason are permeated by the forces of Lucifer. Before these interfered, Christ stayed behind, and therefore is discovered by human beings in the mystical ground of their being. Previous religions were an expression of their contemporary state of science. Christianity is burdened by the fact that nothing connects it with external science. Today it is discoverable only in inner experience, but in times to come it will go beyond everything externally knowable. It has often been pointed out that the revelation of Christ will occur in times soon to come.

Surrounded by maya wherever we look, something truthful sounds forth from within us: the strong longing that lives in every human soul, for we are born out of God. And we will not drown in further maya, because we die in Christ. The separateness that kills, ends in the selfhood of God. And we will rise up whole, powerful, and free; we will resurrect out of the Holy Spirit. There is so much contained in these words, to which you should open yourselves in meditation; you have many more decades of work with this content than the rest of this incarnation encompasses. Take these facts into your souls; exclude the swell of maya, and they will become living forces within you.

RECORD B

When we place the content of our meditation in the center of our consciousness, we feel forces intruding that create a hindrance, so that we are unable to entirely devote ourselves to our meditation. When we clearly recognize these forces that we encounter in our souls, we see that they are destructive. They are the same destructive forces that are at work in the earth, and they brought it about that our earth was destined for a decline and fall that would have cut it off from the cosmos. These destructive forces began in the middle of Atlantis, and by the time of the Mystery of Golgotha had reached the point that they just balanced out the up-building forces; indeed, this was the case on April 3, year 33 of the Common Era (or 14 Nisan of the contemporary era). The Christ brought a new power to the earth and humanity, which worked against these destructive forces. In order to be able to bring this power, the Christ being had to remain behind in the earlier age of the Moon evolution, when the earth showed a condition still virginal; this was even before the Luciferic beings remained behind to work against evolution. We must connect ourselves with this power of Christ, which slumbers in every soul; it frees us from the destructive forces that our karma has implanted in us in the course of our incarnations, forces in which we would drown as if in a deep river. We must pass through this river of existence. Before the event of Golgotha, it was the ancient gods of other religions who offered human souls a wagon or ship in order to get across; now to build a bridge across we must take hold of the power that Christ offers us. Elias experienced it when Elijah left him his cloak in order to cross. Now things are different. When ancient peoples observed external maya upon awakening, they found the spiritual world by looking through it; we do not find the divine anywhere in external maya. It is a corpse, yet in our souls a longing then arises, and this is the divine in us that shows us the path into the spiritual world. Not outwardly, as Zarathustra still could, do we find Christ. In ancient times, religion and science were still united, but the intellect today cannot find Christ. Until now Christ could be found only through faith; only new soul forces can restore the union again.

* * *

RECORD C

Esotericism tells us that April 3, in the year 33, was the Friday on which the Mystery of Golgotha took place. We can notice within ourselves, if we earnestly immerse ourselves in our meditations, that opposing forces appear from all sides out of our souls; they surround us and gradually become a very unusual opposing image. What are these forces?

They are the karma that we have created ourselves in the course of time. We will learn to know that these forces in us are related, closely related, to cosmic forces in the universe; that these are the same forces in us, in human beings, that are the destructive forces of the planets outside of us. And if these were the only forces at work, then the Earth as planet would fall out of the entire evolution of the world and become desolate.

As much as we manage to connect ourselves with forces coming from the other side, with the forces of Christ, to that extent we create within ourselves and for the earth, forces of ascent. Christ is united with the earth since the Mystery of Golgotha. However, this mystery was prepared for a long time before (actually it should have happened in the middle of Atlantean times).

Now if we decide, with the help of Christ, but in freedom, to enter the path, then we will recognize that we are serving humanity and ourselves. As a picture for this path it is said that one has the experience of water, and one should cross over on a bridge to be used for this purpose.

It is the guardian of karma who appears in the picture of water, the karma created by our own selves, which we are to walk over; we will soon recognize that it is intimately connected with all of humanity, and that we are to improve it. If we do this, then it benefits all of humanity.

The human being must learn to rise up into the cosmos.

* * *

Record D

1. Concerning the two forces that are [at work] in humanity. One part, which [is] destined for decline and fall; the other part, which can still be raised up to life.
2. Concerning the forces that have come into our life-forces, and have ruined them.
3. Concerning the decline and fall that threaten these beings and forces.
4. Concerning the Baptism in the Jordan, the total immersion.
5. Concerning the life that can find a place in us through the submersion of the human being.
6. Concerning the human being raised up again out of the state of being swallowed by the forces that are devoted to death.
7. The forces of a destructive kind are in the human being and have the upper hand.
8. How the forces of life were implanted into these destructive forces. The entry of Christ, who had saved up forces from the time on the Sun.
9. Concerning the expulsion of the earth, of matter, that had to be expelled from the system of life as unfruitful.
10. What does it mean that the human being had to be imprinted by Christ?

11. Concerning the overcoming of death; the transformation of matter into spirit.
12. How evil is enclosed in the human body and works there destructively.
13. How the human being is chained to evil, but the bridge is built from Christ over the river, the Jordan, in order to escape from the same.
14. Concerning the baptism of Christ and the disciples. How, through complete immersion in the water, the disciples were brought to a state of fright and amazement, in order to work into the body.
15. How the entire cosmos works into Christ, …he is one with the Father and thereby again creates a relationship to what is alive.
16. The connection of this living substance that works into Christ with the earth, was made possible through the death of Christ Jesus.
17. This occurred on April 3, on 14 Nisan. In this moment, the life of the cosmos united again with the earth.

Esoteric Lesson
HANOVER, DECEMBER 31, 1911

Record A: Notes from the collection of Elisabeth Vreede; Record B: Manuscript from Mathilde Scholl and Camila Wandrey; Record C: Notes from Günther Wagner.

RECORD A

To begin with, today we want to ask what result we have attained through our exoteric study of theosophy. The answer will be (at least theoretically) that we have become conscious of the fact that the entire world, and we ourselves, at least our physical bodies, are maya, illusion. We assume this, at least theoretically, and it remains for us more or less a hypothesis. However, when we begin with an esoteric training, this mere hypothesis should increasingly become the truth. It should penetrate deeply into our consciousness that we actually have no firm ground at all in which we can root ourselves; that we are merely living on the surface of reflecting waves of foam of the ocean of life; that we never dip into the true sea of reality; that we are constantly a plaything of deception. And everyone who wants to walk the path of the esotericist must arrive at this insight. And a certain experience will come to most on this path: a feeling of despair, of abandonment, of fear. This is a fear such as one knows if one stands on the edge of a mountain and becomes aware of a deep abyss below. Despair, abandonment will surround the esotericist, because every fall that one believed one experienced previously in life will become as maya, as an illusion. God will appear to have been torn away, because one sees all of creation as something false, an illusion; indeed, this insight can bring a person to atheism.

Why must we walk this path? Why must we look deeply into the world of illusion with full consciousness? Why, we ask ourselves, have the gods placed us in this unreal world? They could have presented us directly with true reality, instead of this trifling play on the waves of life's surfaces!

Later we will understand that it is wise and good that the world is maya, illusion. If everything were true reality, we ourselves would no longer seek after truth, after perfection. We would be unable to develop any abilities; and since there would be nothing that is not right, there could be no vice. We could not develop any virtues in ourselves; we could not develop ourselves freely at all. Because we would always be living in the working and wielding of God, we would never have the opportunity to seek true knowledge out of ourselves, out of our own freedom. We would not have the opportunity to immerse ourselves in the depths of reality. We would cease to seek God. "Seeking God" has a deep Biblical significance that can only be understood esoterically. At the end of the sixth day of creation we read in Genesis, "And God rested on the seventh day." God was active during Saturn, Sun, and Moon stages of evolution; He rested on the seventh day, after the world had been created, then God was nowhere to be found even to the horizon of our Earth evolution. Then He was invisible, and this has a deep significance.

The truly divine lies hidden behind the visible creation; this is a great truth that as esotericists we must seek behind the appearances presented to us by our senses. And because the world is illusion, it gives us an opportunity to develop the "I" or self through all false appearances, so that we ourselves can find reality; find God himself. And what is the path that esoteric training shows us? What are the means that it gives us, so that we can come to knowledge of higher worlds more quickly than the man or woman on the street? It gives us certain exercises: concentration and meditation exercises through which inner soul forces can be awakened within us when we practice them, forces that would otherwise remain asleep for a long time still. Here I would like expressly to stress that students should not set out on this path because of mere trust in a teacher, or perhaps out of blind veneration, for that would be entirely the opposite of what is intended. They should use their own minds and judgment in all that they do; they should not let others do their thinking for them. Rather, they should test everything, including what concerns their meditations. When they are immersed in their meditations, they should not believe in any suggestive power in them, for that would be an entirely false assumption. These meditations cannot work through suggestion because they are composed in such a way that everyone through one's own efforts can arrive at Imagination, toward which the meditations are only pointing.

Consider the meditation that is known to most of you:

In pure rays of light…

What here could work in a suggestive way, when the content actually does not even point to something physically real? For everyone knows while saying it that God or the divine is not to be found in the rays of (external) light. The exercise gives us a symbol only as a stimulus for us to form an imaginative picture out of ourselves, while we attempt to immerse ourselves with our souls in the soul of the divine. We should always allow only our own thoughts to speak, and not act blindly based on faith in a teacher. It is better, when in doubt, to persist until we attain to knowledge of the truth through our own work. One day we will get that far.

And what is that other unavoidable experience that the human being must go through inwardly? It is unavoidable because it is the consequence of faithfully following esoteric exercise. It is a splitting of the personality that appears here. We will gradually feel as if something is accompanying us, something that is thinking and listening with us, and even, if we are not inwardly very strong, speaking with us. This is a second "I" that comes forward; a double or *doppelganger*, which we have set outside of ourselves. The more seriously we are on the esoteric path, the more we set outside of ourselves our "old human being"; that is, like a snake, we toss away one skin after the other. These skins (speaking for comparison) become a second body, a double that never leaves us. In ancient Egypt, a human being who had set the double outside of him or herself was called a "*Kha*-human being." A double is chained to *Kha*-human beings to remind them constantly of how their former life was, or how it still is. This is not always a pleasant feeling. But the awareness that this double is always accompanying them reminds them of their faults, so that they may improve themselves. They should constantly feel this presence, otherwise it would become dangerous; because of all their high ideals and intentions, they would forget what their inner life and their faults actually are. Despite their striving, under certain circumstances, it could even become life-threatening for high initiates if they should forget this double for even a moment. They could actually lose the physical body through death, more or less in the same way as someone who while deeply immersed in a difficult problem might forget to pay attention to his or her body, and as a consequence of this inattention, were to be run over. The stronger the double appears, the better it is for our development, otherwise we would succumb to great illusions concerning ourselves. For we are not able to see and recognize our own progress in our development, only our teacher can do this. Let us remember the passage in the creation story where the Elohim, after they created the human being together, ascended to the sun. Only there for the first time, could they judge their work, which we find expressed in the words, "And they beheld their work and they saw that it was good." They had attained their perfection, and for this reason they could judge their work.

* * *

Record B

From the teachings of exoteric theosophy we receive, for practical life, the knowledge that the external world is only maya, illusion, behind which is hidden the spiritual world as the world of reality. The external world, with all that happens in it, appears to esotericists increasingly like the play of waves on the surface of an ocean. They feel that they want to get to true reality, to what produces these swells and waves of external events, and thus they must descend to the place where the forces are that underlie these external happenings. They must descend into the depths, to the bottom of the ocean in the soul. Esotericists must come to a true experience of this knowledge. It must not remain mere theory. But the path to this experience is long and difficult. If we know that everything surrounding us is the world of maya, that we live in this world of maya and the world of reality is closed to us, then how are we to find solid ground? How are we supposed to arrive at true reality? True esotericists stand there with this question. It is as if the ground beneath their feet had been torn away from them; as if they stood before an abyss; as if they hung like a black point above this abyss. The greatest courage, the greatest fearlessness is needed here in order not to sink into this abyss that opens up there in front of one. Everything appears dark and impenetrable; indeed, one even begins to doubt the existence of God in this world of illusion. This is a difficult time in the evolution of the soul. But it is necessary that one go through this experience.

Let us ask ourselves once more why a human being must go through this. Why did the world of true reality have to be veiled from us? Why must we live in this world of maya without being able to enter the world that lies behind this maya?

The gods have led human beings through the ages of Saturn, Sun, and Moon. Then, the human being was still only a spiritual being. The gods created for us the sheaths in which this spiritual being "human being" should live as an I-being. But we would never have come to our selfhood if things had continued in the same way. Therefore we read at the beginning of the Bible that the gods created for six days, and rested on the seventh day. Six days of creation: Saturn-day, Sun-day, and Moon-day; and their repetition at the start of Earth evolution, the Polarean, Hyperborean, and the Lemurian epochs. They worked on creating the human being. Now on the seventh day they rested; that is the age after the Lemurian age; the age of Earth, our time, so that the human being can arrive at a free, independent development of the "I," the human self. But for this to happen it is necessary that, for a while, we not be allowed to see the world of the gods, the world of reality. And we must be thankful to those who created this world of illusion for us, whether gods or devils; those who to begin with, cover the true world, the world of reality, the creative world of the spirit. For we could not live in the world of reality with the present-day "I," or self; that is, with the self that is experienced in our personality.

With this self we would perish; we would be destroyed in anxiety, fear, and terror in this world of reality. When we leave this world of illusion—that is, when we fall asleep—this self, which expresses itself as personality, drops into unconsciousness because we are not able at first to endure consciously the forces and effects of the higher worlds, which we enter upon falling asleep. Our personal self or "I" is conscious only when it is immersed in the world of illusion. It must pass through this world in order to become strong and powerful; in order to consciously enter the world of reality with this acquired strength.

Through meditation and concentration we gradually reach the point where we recognize that what we call our self in ordinary life also belongs to the world of illusion, and we can move from the consciousness of this self into becoming conscious of another self, which stands behind the ordinary self. With this other self we can then enter into the world of reality. The contents of meditations are always given in such a way that the soul is filled with pictures and ideas that are taken from the spiritual world.

Let us consider, for example, a very simple meditation, which is relatively well known to all of you:

In pure rays of light…
Shines the divinity of the world…

When in meditation we immerse ourselves in these words, then we come to the point where we experience something like a spiritual sun in which the divinity of the world is shining, and we experience the pure rays of light as a garment, as a revelation of God shining outward, as the glory of this God. However, to really experience this vividly it is necessary completely to forget oneself, that is, one's ordinary consciousness of self. One must also forget the words that are actually also something originating in the physical world. Then, the spiritual world is gradually revealed through the power of this meditative material as a world of light. One sees, in actual experience, this spiritual world of light. In the further continuation of this meditative verse one should also not think that the further words, "I rest in the divinity of the world," apply to one's ordinary self or "I." It is not this everyday self that experiences itself in the spiritual world, but rather the spiritual self that we are to find just through the power of this verse. For this reason the content is such that it leads us out of the world of illusion. For when we go out into the physical world, we really cannot tell from anything there that light is the garment of God, and that we must seek behind this light—in this light—the being of the divinity itself. Such thoughts are not taken out of the physical world. They come from the spiritual world, and through them something can come to life in our souls that is related to the spiritual world, something that can lead our souls into the spiritual world.

If students again and again allow such meditative content to work on their souls, an event occurs that we are to consider as the actual beginning of an esoteric training; as the beginning that at the same time signifies great progress. This experience is that we suddenly perceive something like a second figure next to us; we perceive a kind of *doppelganger*—a double—next to us, that we have set outside of ourselves, so to speak. But at first, the presence of this double torments us; it is discomforting. This is the appearance of the "division of the personality" (compare with *How to Know Higher Worlds*). Here the higher, spiritual human being is separated from the lower. From then on this double is with us; we always feel its closeness. Indeed, it can even come to the point where we hear it speaking. And we must know that the more discomforting we feel its presence to be, the faster and more thoroughly we advance. It must be fundamentally discomforting and problematic, for it shows us again and again everything that binds us to the world of illusion through our physical being—the world of illusion whose chains we are trying to escape. Through this double we thoroughly learn to know all that we must set outside of ourselves. It shows this to us anew, again and again. All of our dishonesty, lovelessness, egotism, and all the other bad traits in us; all this comes to meet us when we experience the double. And the fact that we still carry these character traits around with us, that we have not been able to shake them, brings about the feeling of discomfort brought to us by our double. As long as we still had these bad character traits within us, in our unconscious, in the ocean depths of our souls, they did not come to our consciousness with their full strength. However, as we develop spiritually and look admonishingly at these characteristics in our soul, then they torment us through their presence, so that we can no longer tolerate them. Therefore it is very good when this feeling of tormenting discomfort afflicts us, for in this way we can get rid of this double.

Now the being who brings about the experience just described for the advancement of an esotericist is a Luciferic being, who is "commanded" to do so for this purpose. This is Samael, aided by his swarm. Esotericists must regard his work as absolutely beneficial for their progress, so that they come to know all the character traits and vices that hinder them in their development. They should be strongly stimulated to liberate themselves from these shortcomings. Samael is the being that makes us aware of the presence of our double.

* * *

Record C

Exoteric theosophy leads us to put into practice the knowledge that the external world is only maya, only illusion, behind which the spiritual world, the world of reality, is hidden. The external world appears like the play of waves on the surface of the ocean; if we want to get to reality then we must descend to the bottom of the ocean.

Esotericists, however, must get to the point where they experience this knowledge within themselves, and the path to this point is long and difficult. If we know that everything is maya, that the world of reality is veiled to us, then how are we to find solid ground? How do we get to this reality?

Something comes to meet true esotericists that causes them to feel that the ground under their feet has been torn away, as if they stood before an abyss, and the greatest courage, the greatest fearlessness is necessary so that they do not sink into the abyss that opens here for them. When esotericists reflect deeply and earnestly, they also come to doubt the divine in this world of illusion. This is a difficult moment, but it is necessary that one go through it.

Now we ask ourselves why the world of reality must be veiled from us. The gods have guided us through Saturn, Sun, and Moon stages of evolution as spiritual beings, but we would not have arrived at our selfhood if things had continued in the same way. For this reason, we read at the beginning of the Bible that the gods created for six days, and rested on the seventh day. They created through Saturn, Sun, and Moon stages, and are resting now in our stage, so that the human being can come to an independent development of selfhood. However, for this to happen, it is necessary that we not be able to see the world of reality. We must be thankful to those who created for us the world of illusion, whether the gods or the devil, for we could not live in the world of reality with our present-day "I," or self; we would perish. The "I" sinks into unconsciousness when we go out of the world of illusion because we cannot consciously endure the powers of the higher worlds into which we enter. Also the "I" had to be immersed in this world of illusion and pass through it in order to become strong and powerful, so that we can consciously enter the world of reality.

Through meditation and concentration, we gradually manage to become conscious of the self. The contents of meditations are always given in such a way that the soul is filled with pictures that are not taken from the physical world only.

Let us take for example the very simple meditation that is relatively well known to all of you.

In pure rays of light
Shines the divinity of the world...

When we go out into the physical world, there is nothing present there that tells us that light is the garment of the divinity. Such thoughts are not taken from the physical world; they come from the spiritual world, and for this reason something can come to life in our soul that leads our souls into the spiritual world.

Now I want to mention something during today's esoteric lesson that we should see as a first beginning of our progress in our esoteric schooling. This is the experience of suddenly perceiving another form next to our own form: a kind of *doppelganger*, a double that we have set outside of ourselves, so to speak, whose presence torments and discomforts us. This is the splitting of our personality, the separation of the higher human being from the lower. This double is constantly around us; we feel its closeness, and it can even reach the point where we hear it speaking. The more unpleasant we find its closeness, the more quickly we stride forward. This must be the case so that we set outside ourselves all our dishonesty, egotism, and other bad character traits. These bad characteristics that we still carry around with us, that we are not yet able to shake from us, cause this feeling of discomfort and unease. As long as we have them within us, we are unaware of their full strength. When the spiritual human being grows and develops, then they disturb and torment through their presence, which this spiritual human being can no longer endure. For this reason it is very beneficial when this feeling of discomfort shows up very strongly, for this is the fastest way we get rid of the double.

The being who brings about this event for the sake of an esotericist's progress is a Luciferic being who has been assigned to this task. It is Samael, aided by his swarm. And esotericists must regard this work as something absolutely beneficial for their progress, so that they become aware of all those character traits and vices that hinder them in their development. Then they can strive to liberate themselves from them.

Esoteric Lesson

HANOVER, JANUARY 1, 1912

Record A: Notes from the collection of Elisabeth Vreede; Record B: Notes from Günther Wagner.

RECORD A

In our previous esoteric lesson we had come to the point where through our training we set outside of ourselves what we call the *doppelganger*, or double. Truly it is not a pleasant feeling when we see objectively all that which until now we have harbored within, which now follows us close at our heels, step for step, as a companion. We heard that it is Samael, one of the Luciferic beings, with his swarm, who brings the double out of us. From this we see that Luciferic beings also do good things, and not always evil. If we always carried our faults unconsciously within us, we could never become aware of the destructive, ruinous force that they unfold in the body, as well as in the substance of the cosmos. Until Samael has brought forth our faults from within us, until we see them placed before us objectively as our double, God graciously keeps hidden from us the ruinous, destructive power of all our emotions (such as jealousy, hate, and envy); altogether, all the passions that we send forth into the world around us. A clairvoyant can see how these passions destroy and tear down something in the body, and also in the substance of the cosmos, whereas the good activates constructive forces. Thus Samael is fundamentally a blessing for development. He shows us our inner being all the more accurately, the more seriously we take our training in hand. Then we see ourselves objectively with our faults, of which until now, we have been unaware. Now we will become increasingly disgusted by them, and they will spur us on to improve ourselves.

Esoteric students will now increasingly have a second experience, which they become aware of through the feeling that they cannot get any air, as if they were suffocating. This feeling arises because the students gradually begin to pay close attention to the subtle events that occur in their souls; in particular, attention to the untruths and lies that exist in every human being, at least the possibility for them. We do not mean here the coarse lies and hypocrisies that afflict our lower natures, but the finer nuances that we do not notice because of our superficiality; those we often don't even acknowledge. An example of this follows. Let us assume a man discovers that a theosophical lecture is to be held. He thinks this is something good; he will travel there. But at the same time, he thinks that he will meet this or that person there, with whom he would like to be together. Nevertheless, he convinces himself that this is not the main reason, and imagines that he is traveling there because of the lecture. Such things happen daily; we lie to ourselves and do not notice it, or do not want to notice it. But it is precisely these untruths, which we have not noticed until now that will reach our consciousness in numerous cases, so that we believe that we are suffocating on them.

Another example will show us how much we live only on the surface in all our actions. [There follows the example of the teachers who were to be tested a second time, and who did not know what was to be found in the textbooks that they used on a daily basis.] And this superficiality spreads out over our entire soul life, so that we do not even recognize the untruths that we tell ourselves.

At the beginning of our exercises we may perhaps not notice any progress; from all sides thoughts about everyday concerns will stream toward us. It will take a long time before we notice any success from our exercises, and it will also be a long time until a second being, called Azazel, can with his influence begin to bring us to deeper knowledge, that is, to make us aware of our superficiality. Both Samael and Azazel must reveal to us something from within ourselves, but a third being, Azael, must also bring something to us. He must bring us a longing for the higher, spiritual life. The next example shows us what is intended. A scientist who is filled with the desire for knowledge, and who would like to acquire more and more knowledge, suddenly finds himself at the limits of his knowledge and cannot push on further with his intellect. In most cases he will say that his intellect—or human intellect altogether—is no longer sufficient, and he will resign himself to this. Others however, who feel their souls to be a bit more alive, will seek further and will be led to theosophy or spiritual science. There they will feel they can research further, even beyond the limits that materialistic science placed before them. However, as soon as they follow the esoteric path, they will feel themselves confronted by an unpleasant situation; they will have a feeling, a sensation, that could be expressed as the feeling of being drowned. You see, as we penetrate ever deeper into esotericism, the limits extend farther and farther until we come to a point where everything moves away from us, where we stand at an abyss. We no longer feel a foothold anywhere; everything disappears beneath our feet. Only by courageously pushing onward on the path we have begun, will the knowledge dawn on us that maya must first fall away before we can recognize the spiritual world, which is the truth. Azael brings us this knowledge; he preserves the human being from spiritually drowning (apathy).

Now there is a fourth being, Mehazael. He makes us aware of and awakens in us a feeling for the fact that we are bound to space and time. The best way to clarify this is to call to mind a condition that many of us have already gone through in life. That is when we awaken in the morning and feel ourselves burdened by the duties and cares that the new day brings with it. Many will know this feeling, which is accompanied at the same time by the desire to shake loose the chains that have bound us to these burdens, which are so much heavier to carry because of our knowledge that we are powerless against them, that we must bow to them. Here Mehazael shows us our karma.

However, as soon as we begin on the esoteric path we will be able to carry these burdens more easily. Mehazael shows them to us so that we do not uselessly balk at them, for doing so would only worsen our karma instead of shaking it loose from us. Thus these four Luciferic beings are in the end a blessing for us.

We have seen that every time we do not control our passions—when we let our anger and hate run wild—we are destroying something within ourselves; we are transforming it into earthly dust in ourselves as well as in the cosmic substance into which our feelings, sensations, and thoughts are constantly flowing. In doing so, we not only harm ourselves, but also create karma for the world around us. Until now in the esoteric lessons we have studied karma only theoretically. Now we will see how much deeper and more complicated is the working of karma.

In order for us to become completely aware of the work of these four beings in us, we must energetically continue our meditations. We should meditate not only on the meditations and esoteric verses that have been given to us, as for example, the meditation on the Rose Cross, we should also attempt to meditate on feeling and sensations, which is much more difficult. For example, let us meditate on sympathy: let us immerse ourselves completely in this feeling, and warmth will flow through us; the meditation on antipathy will activate a cold feeling in us. If we, for example, first meditate on the Rose Cross and then on a strong will impulse—meditate on a good deed—then we will see inner light, together with a stream of warmth. All our meditations do not at first meet with success; with one it may go more slowly, with another more quickly, according to our karma and our evolution. Some will achieve success after fifty times and others will need an entire lifetime, but we should wait with patience and courageously move forward. Where did the sun get its power to shine every morning in the same place, so that its light rays forth?

The life of an esotericist should become entirely different than it was before. Esotericists actually lead two lives: one that is gradually crumbling apart, dying out, and the other that gives them light from the spirit from which they came. In the ancient mysteries, the wise masters expressed the course of human life (that is, the death of the old human being through the spirit of Christ) in these words: *Ex Deo nascimur*. (And because the name of Christ was too sacred to them to speak it forth) *In ---- morimur. Per Spiritum Sanctum reviviscimus.*

* * *

Record B

Yesterday in our esoteric lesson we saw how, through proper meditation and concentration, esotericists must manage consciously to develop themselves through the world of illusion, up to the reality of the spiritual world. And good Luciferic beings, whose leader is Samael, help along the way.

Now there are, however, more such beings; and here, we are first to consider Azazel with his swarm. Human beings usually possess more dishonesty and disingenuity than they realize. I see many now who will say, "I no longer have any dishonesty in me; I have set that aside completely." But this dishonesty is so refined that we usually do not become aware of it at all. This becomes clear from the following example [going to a theosophical lecture with other motives]. All this dishonesty brings us to the attention of Azazel and his swarms; and when we feel that we are being pinched with a vice, tormented by a thousand arms, then we should reflect upon how deeply we are still entangled with lies and dishonesty.

A third being who approaches an esotericist is Azael. He too can call forth an oppressive feeling, a pressure similar to nightmares; and also a choking, scratching feeling in the throat. Again we should clarify to ourselves any bad character traits we still have to set aside, even indifference toward world events. An esotericist should not be indifferent with respect to what is going on in the world. Most people are so entangled in egotism that they are indifferent to everything happening around them. For this reason the masses are indifferent to theosophy.

Furthermore, some esotericists feel disgust upon awakening for the situation in which their karma has placed them! They feel as if they are chained to the ground with iron chains. Mehazael with his swarms cause this. Esotericists must pay attention to all these occurrences, so that they can become aware of the faults that still live in them, and strive to gradually overcome them.

Esoteric Lesson
BERLIN, JANUARY 6, 1912

Manuscript from Louise Clason.

By advancing further on the esoteric path through meditation and concentration, we come to know our own *doppelganger*, or double, to which we are chained. We experience within ourselves a feeling of isolation or solitude with respect to the world; indeed, with respect to our loves. This feeling gives us strength, and we should cultivate it. Yet another feeling we should practice is the feeling of gratitude toward spiritual beings in the meditation:

In pure rays of light
Shines the divinity of the world…

The third thing is maintaining silence concerning the meditations given to us, and concerning everything esoteric. Refraining from speaking awakens powers; chattering weakens the etheric body, altogether it is a weakness of the etheric body.

Esoteric Lesson

BERLIN, JANUARY 7, 1912

Record A: Notes from Günther Wagner; Record B: Manuscript from Camilla Wandrey; Record C: Manuscript from Rudolf Meyer.

RECORD A

Invocation of the spirit of the day (Sunday).

In the last lesson we discussed how human beings carry a being around with them, the double; how they are connected to the double; and how the Luciferic spirit Samael brings about this division in human beings and makes us aware of it. Through the cravings and passions in which we indulged in the past, and which are attached to the double, it can happen that this double wants us to lose control, so that we go wild with rage or some other passion. This does not usually amount to much in the average person. However, this should never happen to esotericists because they should watch themselves much more closely; the feeling and instinctive life of esotericists become entirely different.

One should not think that esotericists should become loveless and indifferent. Especially love should become much deeper, and be raised to a higher level; an esotericist should become more willing to sacrifice and more selfless.

An esoteric training that teaches the death of love and of compassion is entirely on a false path. Especially through the change in our feeling life, we acquire a more sublime feelng for the beauty of the world, and also for art.

Neither should we mourn emotional losses nor say, "I cannot resist myself"; but rather, in such despairing moments, we should say again and again, "Patience—be strong!" This is also true when we think we have not advanced, just because we haven't had any experiences in higher worlds.

Our aim in esoteric training should be isolation or solitude for the soul. This must remain the fundamental attitude or mood of the soul;

it should not be disturbed by anything, even by our dearest people. The gates of the spiritual world open for us through solitude. This is a precondition for the pure spiritual life. However, this does not mean that we intentionally seek isolation and thereby escape the duties we have in the world; rather, we are to allow this feeling of solitude and isolation to awaken in the soul. Furthermore, we should not silence it with foolish thoughts, and so forth.

Another important requirement is that we not change our meditations very often. The best is to carry out an exercise through an entire lifetime, but properly, indeed, so that new impulses are constantly awakened in us because we immerse ourselves ever more deeply into the meditation. For example, in this meditation:

In pure rays of light
Shines the divinity of the world...

we should not only imagine rays of light radiating outward, which symbolize the divine, but also the forces and power of the divine that take possession of our inner life, and then feel within ourselves gratitude so perfect that it should be carried out into the cosmos; we should swim in the feeling of thankfulness and feel ourselves unified with the divine. Often we can hold onto this feeling for no more than a few seconds, but with continued practice we can do it for much longer.

Often we are called back to reality again by a ringing tone. But this exercise leaves in us a feeling of commonality; a feeling that we exist within God (with humanity), a feeling entirely opposite to the feeling of isolation.

Talkativeness does a great deal of damage. What a student reveals of his or her esoteric exercises is lost to that student. We should be clear about this. It always signifies a weakening of the etheric body; people with weak etheric bodies are always talkative. Therefore, it is demanded of us that we enclose our inner life and keep it secret. At most, we can enrich our esoteric life in small circles of friends who are on the same spiritual step by discussing esoteric communications and truths. But there is a precondition: the proper mood must be present in all those present. The forces and the strength that allow us to advance grow through our refraining from speaking.

In the spirit lay the seed of my body...

RECORD B

It can happen that the double (using the desires and passions that we instinctively indulged in the past and that are now attached to the double) wants us to lose control so that we lose ourselves, whether through rage, hate and lovelessness, envy, or other explosive passions. This does not usually amount to much in the average person. However, it should not happen to esotericists that they follow such explosive passions. They must watch over themselves much more closely. The feeling and instinctive life of esotericists must become very different from that of the average person. Nothing should happen with an esotericist merely out of instincts; without having it in hand, so to speak. It should gradually become impossible for one's double to cause one to lose control through what the double wants. Esotericists must become the master of the double. (The servant must not be greater than the Lord.)† The impulses that reigned over them previously are now reigned over by the esotericists from their higher I-consciousness.

Now we must not think that these people thereby become loveless and indifferent with respect to the world around them. Especially the ability to love—true love—is raised to a higher stage when the student arrives at this step. It loses the egotistical character that love always has in the average person. It becomes more willing to sacrifice, more selfless. (Rosicrucian Mystery, scenes 9 and 10: After "O man, experience yourself," thus [after Johannes] had acquired consciousness of his higher self, Theodosius, the bearer of cosmic world love, approaches Johannes who says, "I will reveal your being in my deeds. They should bring healing salvation through you.")† An esoteric school that teaches students to kill love and compassion is entirely on a false path. We are not dealing with mortification here, but with a transformation in full consciousness. Esotericists must penetrate with their clear consciousness all that is involuntary or instinctive in their souls. It must be an entirely conscious decision whether a person decides to love or not in any particular situation. It is precisely through transforming our feeling life in this way out of our higher I-consciousness that we acquire a more sublime feeling for the beauty that weaves through the world. This is the beauty that originates in the love that stands behind the world, and which makes true art possible. On this step esoteric students learn to stop complaining about the poverty of their soul life, about that which can appear as psychological loss. And when the double threatens to become strong, students are allowed even less to say, "I cannot oppose myself." Even in moments of despair, they must always say, "Patience! Be strong!" The same is true when we believe that we have had no experiences in the spiritual world, and therefore are making no progress.

What is to be achieved in esoteric training is this: that the soul becomes inwardly entirely self-sustaining. (Johannes in scene 9: "I feel the being of the world in me"; "I rest in myself"; "I have the first confidence of a human being. I have achieved certainty of being.")† This can be achieved only through solitude of the soul. This must remain the basic mood of the soul, even in the presence of our most beloved people. The gates of the spiritual world open only through the lonely solitude of the soul. Only in this way is the condition present for a pure spiritual life. But, although this loneliness of the soul is a condition of the soul, students should not intentionally seek external solitude or withdraw themselves from the responsibilities that they have in the world. This is not what is intended. One should allow the feeling of aloneness to grow in the soul as a force, and not force oneself to be quiet because of some foolish thoughts. Everything depends upon strength from the solitude of being entirely dependent upon oneself only.

A very important demand placed upon esoteric students is this: do not wish to change your meditations so often. It is best to keep a meditation for one's whole life, but to carry it out properly. This brings it about that new impulses are awakened in us through them because we gradually draw up onto ourselves the forces that are contained in them in order to make them into forces in our soul. For example, in the meditation,

In pure rays of light
Shines the divinity of the world…

Here we should not only imagine the rays of light streaming outward—the rays that symbolize divine forces which take hold of our inner life—and then feel within ourselves the most perfect gratitude, which then is carried out into the cosmos, we should also feel ourselves swimming in and at one with God. Often we can hold this feeling only for seconds, but with continued exercise the feeling will last much longer. This exercise leaves behind in the soul a feeling of commonality; of being at one with God—in God—and with humanity. This creates a tremendously strong force in the soul that is a complete contradiction to the feeling of loneliness.

Much damage is done through talkativeness. Students should constantly remember that the results of their esoteric exercises, if revealed through talking about them, is lost to the student. We should be very clear about this. It always signifies a weakening of the etheric body. For this reason it is a demand put on us that we close off our inner life as a secret. At most we should enrich our esoteric life in small circles of friends who are at the same spiritual stage by discussing esoteric communications and truths. There is a basic precondition: there must be the proper mood in all those present; we must know that the forces of strength that bring us forward lie in silence.

* * *

Record C

There are three feelings that an esotericist should develop in particular:

1. Feeling of solitude. In ordinary life it is usual for us to experience a longing for the people we like. Developing a feeling of solitude does not mean becoming insensitive or indifferent toward the

external world. However, we should also be able to distance ourselves from what we like; from what we are dependent on. We should remain in our solitude and become very fond of this solitude.

2. Over and against this, we should develop a second feeling. There are people who think that they are advancing quite rapidly when they change their meditations very frequently. Exactly the opposite is the case. For most people it is the most advantageous to stay with the same exercises, assuming of course that the meditations speak to them with increasing depth and intensity.

For example, in the meditation, *In pure rays...* it is not sufficient simply to imagine the light in which the Godhead works, but rather one must at the same time develop a feeling of gratitude, the warmth of thankfulness; an enthusiasm must fill us. It must seem to us that we are swimming in a sea of gratitude. Just as we earlier concentrated on ourselves and developed a feeling of lonely solitude, now we should pour ourselves into the universe and feel ourselves connected with all human beings.

3. And then there is a third feeling that we must acquire in our esoteric life: the feeling for remaining silent at the right moment in time. This does not mean that we display a secretive attitude; we can of course speak about our exercises with other esotericists; however, there is, among other traits that hinder development, the one called talkativeness. All esotericists should break the habit of entrusting just anyone and everyone with a new experience just as soon as they have had it. Such talk destroys precisely the forces that have grown in one's etheric body. Tension arises in those who, as soon as they experience something new, cannot keep it to themselves; this tension is dissipated only when they have gotten rid of it by passing it on to other people. Tension arises in esotericists too.

The more we keep the secrets entrusted to us, the more forces we thereby collect in the etheric body. We are not alienated from all that is beautiful, good, and true; on the contrary we get a more refined understanding for art.

Esoteric Lesson

BERLIN, JANUARY 10, 1912

Record A: Manuscript from Barbara Wolf; Record B: Manuscript from Alice Kinkel.

RECORD A

Through our esoteric exercises we want to concentrate completely upon a thought and afterward allow an emptiness to enter us, and then wait to see what flows to us as a result of our meditation. What we achieve depends upon the strength of the perseverance we then employ. One might think that by changing meditations one would advance faster than one would by staying for a long time with the same meditation; but the deepest esotericists have always asserted that they have advanced the most by doing the same exercises with great patience and perseverance for years.

It can happen that we have an opportunity only once in our lifetime to meet with someone who gives us a spiritual exercise, and that we never see this person again on this earth. However, if karma is favorable and if the exercise is done properly, it can be sufficient for a lifetime and be fruitful until one finds the teacher in the spiritual world.

Esotericists will notice that when they expend energy on their inner development, certain flawed traits that they had earlier emerge more sharply. Among these traits belongs, for example, an exaggerated criticism of other people. All human beings criticize. Esotericists however, should be aware of where this desire to lash out at others originates. Through spiritual exercises we strengthen our feeling for the self (sense of the "I"), our egohood, and this criticism represents our desire to assert ourselves over others, a need to separate ourselves. Esotericists lose interest in many external things to which they paid much attention in the past. This goes so far that many esotericists have the feeling that they can no longer see as well as they did in the past. Most also complain of the loss of their good memory. From the last esoteric lessons we have learned that this lack of attention for the world surrounding us is a fault. It can happen that we do not carry out our meditations intensively enough to fill the inner emptiness with spiritual content, the emptiness that we can no longer fill with our earlier interests. In this way we would get a stressed feeling, a driving restlessness, the need to fill our inner emptiness with something from outside. Then we fall all too easily into the temptation to criticize what is outside of us. In a way this criticism is understandable and justified because after we first closed ourselves off from the outer world and then again exit out of ourselves we would like to assert ourselves over and against the world. Egotism lies in this, however, and it must be suppressed, just as the desire to criticize must be suppressed. When we achieve this, the forces that we would otherwise have wasted are turned inward and fructify our soul life. The need to separate oneself from the world is entirely justified for esotericists, for they can make progress only in solitude. For most people the feeling of lonely solitude is unbearable. An esotericist, however, should gradually acquire the ability to endure loneliness. In this way the esoteric life is greatly furthered. People who have a longing to go outward into society dissipate their forces in this desire. It is as if this longing were thrown from them in all directions out into the space around them. They should rather see to it that these forces are gathered within; bend them inward, so to speak. They will thereby have achieved much.

 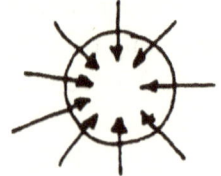

There is another, apparently opposite attitude, esotericists must also develop. It is opposite to the first only in the sense that the right side of a pendulum swing is the opposite of the left side. One results from the other, and yet they are exactly opposite to each other. Thus it is necessary for esotericists to bring two character traits, or attitudes, into balance with one another like pendulum swings. First of all is the ability to endure lonely solitude—that is, strengthening the sense of self, of ego—and secondly, complete devotion up to the limits of self-surrender, of self-forgetting, in order to fulfill the demands of duty that come to us from outside.

When we have reached the point where our hearts thirst after solitude in the midst of our environment, where the world surrounding us actually pains us and we suffer from it; and yet nevertheless, we bring to the surrounding world our fully devoted love, then we have the union of the two apparently contradictory attitudes.

A third character trait that we should practice is the habit of remaining silent about our esoteric experiences. With undeveloped human beings the need to keep a secret feels to them like they are about to burst, and the opportunity to really speak out is a great relief for them. Esotericists, however, should reflect on the fact that this power that threatens to shatter us would become a strength if we could just save it up it within ourselves. Therefore, we read: "Learn to keep silent and power will come to you." This is the power to rule in our own souls. An esoteric researcher can perceive clearly the change, the influx of forces that enters the soul of a person who must suppress the vocal expression of a secret for any reason. A woman, for example, may have something in her soul that she would like to share with a friend. While hurrying to him, she meets another acquaintance at the door, who is also coming to visit him. But she cannot, nor does she want to, share it with the acquaintance. Then, it is too late to go to the friend; and, therefore, she must suppress the secret. An esotericist can see that a power has developed in the woman to whom this has happened; a power that was not present before and that also would not have developed if she had been able to fulfill her wish and actually told her secret. For an esotericist the saying does not hold, "Those whose hearts are full, words flow from their mouth."

For those who are not esotericists it can sometimes be good and appropriate for them to express their opinions, but not for esotericists. By outwardly sharing their innermost thoughts and feelings they discharge forces into the world that would have been necessary for their souls. Every time we are in a position to keep quiet about our thoughts and feelings, especially those related to our esoteric experiences and difficulties, we acquire a power in our souls that cannot be lost to us. However, concerning things of general human interest, concerning what can be useful to people, about this we should speak, and not just not about our own internal concerns.

Where does this need to impart come from anyway? We seldom have the need to go to other people because we love them disinterestedly. Usually we go to them because they have qualities that are important to us, that give us something. We should also drop the wish to be carried by the hands of other people. On the contrary, we should be grateful to those who treat us badly, because they give us an opportunity to exercise our strength to patiently endure. Then we should nevertheless try to feel love toward them. We will then soon enough notice that it is the right thing to do.

Something else that an esotericist should stop doing, is complaining. What do we complain about? Usually about the fact that when we begin our meditations, thoughts storm in toward us from all sides. But we should be thankful for this, and regard it as progress that we are noticing what a reality the world of thought actually is, that it can assert itself so powerfully. We only need to apply our strength against it, for in this way our powers increase. We should listen to these thoughts to find out how they do it; we should see them as paragons, showing how we can concentrate. We should use them as examples and tell ourselves that we should immerse ourselves in our meditations with the same intensity, then we will attract spiritual forces that can support us. It would be a very easy meditation if angels or any other spiritual beings would come and sweep away the undesired thoughts before we started.

If esotericists have overcome all these traits, and also learned to practice silence in proper measure, then they will arrive at something that mystics have always called "the gate of death." It is called this because through their silence and through mastery of their character traits they have come so far that they find themselves in the same condition as a human being who stands before death, in whom all interest has turned away from the external world. They have turned within, or toward the divine spiritual world. That is what is intended in the second part of our Rosicrucian verse: *In Christo morimur*. We die in Christ by transforming ourselves completely and turning again to the spiritual world. *Ex Deo nascimur*. We are born out of God and must incarnate in the physical world. It is our task to develop ourselves forward so that we can say: *In Christo morimur*. We turn away from all that is physical and raise ourselves to the spiritual, which has always been called the Holy Spirit, and are then born anew in him. *Per Spiritum Sanctum reviviscimus*. And the verse that the Masters of Wisdom and Harmony of Feelings have given us is like an interpretation of this.

In the Spirit lay the seed of my body...

* * *

RECORD B

Esotericists must get used to enduring certain feelings and doing certain things; and leave other things undone, things that those who are not esotericists do not have to be concerned about. Among them:

1. The feeling of lonely solitude. Esotericists must learn to endure this; they must become sufficient unto themselves and be able to live with what rises up in their own souls without feeling unhappy in this loneliness. What will appear first is that one will see everything entirely differently. Interests will change completely.
2. The second is devotion, which an esotericist must develop.
3. The third is maintaining silence in the face of the desire to engage in casual conversation.

Through these three things an esotericist experiences the truth: "I have arrived at the gate of death!"

Many students complain about the flood of thoughts into the soul during meditation. We should be thankful that we can have the realization that thoughts are realities that are stronger than we are. We should not complain, but rather rejoice when thoughts show themselves in this way; they reveal themselves as forces of soul. Through remaining silent, we develop certain forces in the soul.

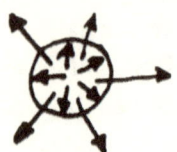

Criticizing and expressing that criticism presupposes a very specific quality in the soul: that in our ego, our selfhood, we want to assert that we are ahead of others in some way.

If we are able to store up many such soul experiences without talking about them, then we will come to a very specific point in our development known to every esotericist, and characterized in all mystical writings as "having arrived at the gate of death."

Devotion, how is it practiced? We can thirst after solitude and yet in every moment be prepared to devote ourselves to others in love, for the sake of other people and their endearing traits.

People usually seek out others because of egotism. They get something from the others. The others have qualities that please them. They seek the presence of others not for the sake of the others, but for their own sake.

Devotion to an inner experience must be so powerful that we forget ourselves completely, give ourselves to what rises up in the soul, so that we can objectively see the power.

At first the egotism of esotericists becomes greater. They strive for separation, alienation from other people. When we feel the longing for people rising within us, then we must tell ourselves that through this longing, useless forces are dissipated into the world, forces that we can make good use of within.

It is the same with talkativeness; forces are consumed uselessly. We should remain silent about the things that interest us within, the things that interest us subjectively. The power that would otherwise be used up is then turned inward and gives an esotericist great strength.

On the one hand we must make the ego, the integral self stronger; on the other hand, we must forget ourselves.

Esotericists should move their meditations into the center of their consciousness with the will, not by using the memory, and so forth.

Esoteric Lesson
ZURICH, JANUARY 16, 1912

Anonymous notes from a notebook of Günther Schubert.

When human beings behave in ways that are not in keeping with world evolution, they disturb the order of the world. These disturbances must be compensated for by certain beings.

When a human being is "out of himself" or "out of herself" then a certain kind of Luciferic being must compensate for this disturbance. The being is called Samael. People feel themselves as if they were two; it seems to them as if a second person were walking alongside them. This second person occasionally says things that one would have said years before, but now in the present time, these things seem foreign. People have a vision of a form similar to a human figure.

When human beings lie or are dishonest with themselves (for example, a man who thinks he has come to Zurich only for lectures, but in reality, he has come because he wanted to visit a certain person, who also has also come), then the spirit Azazel must compensate for this disturbance in world evolution.

If human beings do not engage in the world around them—are not interested and pay no attention to the things around them—then the spirit Azael must compensate for this disturbance. The effect that human beings feel because of this inattention expresses itself in a feeling of drowning, drowning in a spiritual ocean upon awakening or falling asleep. They have a vision of a form similar to a lion.

If human beings have no faith in karma, if they do not surrender themselves to their karma, if they do not accept with devotion and courage something they encounter that is horrible and burdensome, if they do not accept it as right and despite the pain courageously take it upon themselves, then the spirit Ahazel (Mehazael) must bring this disturbance back into harmony with the world order. Human beings feel as if they were bound to the earth, as if chained to the earth, and in vision they see a form similar to a bull.

Even if our lives are an indecipherable confused maya, nevertheless, we must not forget that we are born out of a divine ground of existence.

Esoteric Lesson
BERLIN, JANUARY 26, 1912

Record A: Notes from the collection of Elisabeth Vreede; Record B: Manuscript from Rudolf Meyer; Record C: Notes from Günther Wagner; Record D: Manuscript from Camilla Wandrey; Record E: Manuscript from Vrauke Titringh.

RECORD A

Esoteric development must be different at different times in history; otherwise the sequence of incarnations would have no meaning. But certain things remain the same through all ages. For example, we find that Egyptian esotericists speak of:

- Arrival at the threshold of death
- Passage through the underworld
- The experience of the four elements
- Seeing the sun at midnight
- An encounter with spiritual beings that are immediately present.[†]

What is intended with this cannot be fully explained now, but a few simple things will be said. One of the feelings that the esoteric life can bring us is that waking life seems to us as if it were actually a sleeping life. This is not a mood that we could live with constantly; but then it should never be our intent to extend and spread over our entire life any esoteric moods that we might experience in certain moments. If we did that we would become unable to meet our responsibilities in the external world. From time to time, all esotericists should experience a longing to penetrate through to what stands behind the kingdoms of nature they see around them, a longing to experience the true reality toward which we strive and in relation to which all ordinary sense impressions have no more value than those in sleep. Those who would like to live constantly with such esoteric moods would have to withdraw into a kind of monastic life. However, that is not the kind of esotericism that Rosicrucians strive for.

Those who would like to withdraw in this way in order to prepare themselves through several incarnations must also be aware that they are acquiring certain privileges with respect to their fellow human beings, and that if everyone wanted to live the same way human evolution would be made impossible.

Our exercises are designed to bring us into the spiritual world; however, because of our inattentiveness, we often do not notice the progress that we are making with them. So we can have the feeling that we are making very poor use of the forces that have been poured into our thinking, feeling, and willing. But it would be impossible for us to live in such thinking, feeling, and willing; it would shatter and destroy us. The feeling that one gets when having an experience that is overwhelming was called by the ancients "coming to the threshold of death." For one then feels, "What I am now experiencing I can master neither with my thinking, nor with my feeling, nor with my will; now I am feeling what it means to be dead." No doubt the majority of you has already been through this experience. That one does not know this is the result of a lack of attention. During meditation one will have often had the feeling that one was "away" for awhile, and then coming to oneself, think, "I have been sleeping." If one makes the effort to pursue what was experienced in such moments, one would sense that one had just had the greatest experiences that one had ever gone through.

Another experience is this: it does not necessarily have to come after the first. One can get the impression that this second experience was experienced first, because one slept through the first. One arrives at the feeling that one is stuck in one's body; that one carries it around with oneself. Just as one can distinguish between the weight one carries around in one's arms from the weight of the muscle of the arms themselves, so too, one learns to experience one's arms themselves as a foreign weight that one carries. Then one can have the feeling that one sits bound and tied in a lower world—not bodily, but all the more in one's soul. This is the "walking in the lower world." In our meditations we feel ourselves to be entirely "paralyzed," and afterward we have the feeling as if lukewarm water were being poured all over us inwardly.

One can also have the feeling that the evil thoughts we have are not only thoughts, but something real. When we have harbored bad thoughts concerning someone, then we see this like an arrow shot into that person, injuring the soul more than a physical arrow shot into the body. As soon as we realize what we are doing, we notice how the arrow flies back to us and burns us like fire, as if we were in the "flames of the underworld." This is the "going through the elements." It does not have to be seen as a vision; we can feel it in ourselves as if we had burns all over the body, so to speak.

When we feel this way, we are sending forces out of the etheric body; however, they can reach only as far as the borders of the aura. There they meet the cosmic forces that are at work everywhere at the periphery; these cosmic forces turn around our etheric forces and direct them toward certain centers where they cause suprasensory organs to appear. Thus it is the same as with our physical organs; they too, were formed from undifferentiated organs by the light. We could not see as long as the light was working on the eyes, that became possible only when they were finished. So, too, we can use our higher organs only after they have been created in the way described.

 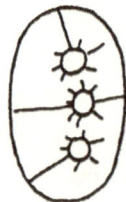

Record B

All esotericism, all esoteric striving, is subject to change, to progress; this means that the form is changed, but the essence of esotericism remains the same at all times. If that were not the case, the teaching concerning repeated earth lives would have no meaning; that is, we are led again and again to the earth, so that we can have experiences and our souls become more mature. The form in which human beings are introduced into higher worlds today, had to become entirely different from the past. Contemporary human beings, with their differentiated soul life, would be hard-pressed to endure what was demanded of esoteric pupils in the ancient Egyptian mysteries. They underwent a preparation in the course of a few weeks under the eyes of a priest. Violent means were employed, for example, to stir up their compassion to the highest level; to test their fearlessness. They were fully aware that their lives were at stake. It is different with people today. Indeed, they still stand under the guidance of a teacher, but they are lifted into higher worlds through the power of the meditations given to them; through their own work on their souls.

If asked about the stages of development, an Egyptian esotericist would have answered with the following summary:

1. Passage through the gates of death
2. Descent into the underworld
3. Passage through the elements
4. Beholding the sun at midnight
5. And thereby recognizing spiritual powers

It is very difficult to describe these individual steps. They are based on soul experiences that everyone must go through. But it is not said that the sequence must always be the same. It can happen that the first step is missed, so that the second moves into the first position. Everything that happens in the soul is very fine, very subtle. We must accustom ourselves to pay attention to these intimate moods of the soul.

1. When we listen to what is happening in our soul, something soon shows itself as if the soul were wrapped up in itself, asleep to the external world. It will say to itself: all of you beautiful meadows, all of you beautiful valleys, I have no longing for you. There is longing in me for what lies behind you! A mood such as this is like sleep, like dying. One cannot think, one cannot feel, as before. One cannot lift one's little finger; the will is also dead.

All one's limbs become heavy and useless. The soul finds itself outside the body. It is as if the material world is falling away. One feels abandoned by God.

Of course, this feeling must only be allowed to be passing. Otherwise we would become completely useless for our professional life. In today's world, our esoteric life is arranged in such a way that it is compatible with every profession. Precisely because we have lived in such moods, we should be fresh and flexible for our external life. Those who would want to live entirely for their own development would have to withdraw as a monk and claim in advance this particular privilege for themselves for many earth lives to come.

This feeling of being wrapped up in oneself over and against the external world, esotericists have at all times called "going through the portal of death." It is really like an anticipation of the feeling of dying.

2. The second feeling, that of descending into the underworld, appears in such a way that a feeling of shame arises in us concerning our own unworthiness; that we have not made full use of abilities present in our soul, the use of which we would actually be capable. The feeling that we get is as if the body were something apart that we must carry with us, and that occasionally weighs us down like lead. For example, we have this feeling in our arms. We have the feeling as if the body were something alien to us. Then all at once we feel ourselves illuminated, as if drenched with lukewarm water.[†]

3. And then a third feeling: we become clear about the fact that our thoughts are realities. Earlier we might well have had a thought, then a second followed, and we believed that the second extinguished the first. Now, with an evil thought we will feel as if a deadly arrow had been shot at the object of our thought. However, this arrow comes back and is directed at our own soul, and then burns in our soul. Then this burning spot remains through our entire lifetime. Sooner or later, through our karma we must put it right. Esotericists begin to see imaginatively; they see the fire that is enkindled by their evil thoughts. It will often

seem to them as if the entire body were burning with flames blazing up. Esotericists of all ages have called this: going through the elements. Analogously, there are experiences that correspond to fire on the other steps of the elemental world.

Many complain, "I am making no progress; I do not seem to be advancing." The teacher often sees that esoteric students are unnecessarily struggling with this perception. It is only a lack of attention that they bring to the most intimate stirrings in their soul. We should live completely in our meditations, identify with the contents of the meditation, and banish everything else, every thought of the external world; and then live for a few minutes in the aftereffects. Centers of force are created that work within the astral body, but only up to the circumference of the aura. There they meet with the forces streaming into us out of the astral world that create and form the organs of the astral body, the lotus flowers. These lotus flowers bring it about that the configuration of the astral body is changed when the purified astral body works into the etheric body and makes it independent from the physical body. They also make the etheric body capable of further stages of development, which lead to beholding the sun at midnight and acquaintance with the great spiritual world of the cosmos. This then is immense blessedness.

* * *

Record C

We would very much like to extend the mood of meditation to include all of life. But this does not work because we would then be useless for everyday, physical life. Those who assume this privilege for themselves and dedicate their present lives entirely to meditation—that is, lead a cloistered, monk's life—will all the more in their next lifetime, despite perhaps strengthened spiritual forces, be assigned an active life. Many complain that they are making no progress; they notice nothing in themselves that would indicate progress. The teacher often sees that esoteric students worry unnecessarily. But the problem is merely a question of how much attention the student brings to the subtle stirrings of soul. Nevertheless, this attention is absolutely necessary for progress..

At all times people have carried out esoteric exercises; in earlier times it was done within the mysteries. Also, in the ancient records of the Rosicrucians, we find a form provided for the experiences that people who want to develop themselves should be having. Very specific experiences are mentioned there, as are to be found in all such records, especially in the Egyptian mysteries.

1. At the threshold of death; that is, of the other side
2. A descent into the underworld
3. Passage through the elements

We must also go through all these feelings, but they do not have to happen in this specific sequence. In earlier times, these feelings and their corresponding exercises were pursued much more intensely. Today a human being could no longer bear them, because modern soul-life has become more differentiated.

The first experience: crossing the threshold of death. This makes itself perceptible to all mystics in the following way. A person for a moment briefly loses consciousness. Limbs become heavy and useless. The soul finds itself outside the body. We feel ourselves abandoned by God and humanity; the material world falls away during this moment when we see ourselves in our own world as if buried, and feel a strong longing for the other, true world. We are unable to do anything with the will, neither with feeling or thinking. We must feel this powerfully, but not get stuck too strongly in this feeling, because the physical world is our school, where we are to go through our physical and spiritual evolution. The feeling of actually dying can go on for moments. The main thing is to notice what is happening to us.

The second feeling, that of descending into the underworld, appears in such a way that a feeling of shame arises in us that we ourselves are unworthy, that we have not made enough use of the soul abilities given to us or done what we could have been capable of. The feeling we get is that the body is something apart from us, something that we must carry with us, which is occasionally as heavy as lead—our arms, for example. We get a feeling that something foreign to us has entered our body. And then we feel at times as if water were being poured over us.

The third feeling is the passage through the elements. We experience the reality of thoughts, and know that they are things. If we send negative thoughts toward someone, we usually comfort ourselves by saying they are really only thoughts. In reality this is, however, worse than shooting someone with a deadly arrow on the physical plane. In imaginative pictures we then experience how these "thought-arrows" fly back at us and touch our soul like a flame, "branding" us, which we must make good in our karma.

On the other steps of the elemental world there are corresponding experiences.

We should live completely in the exercises that are given to us. Afterward we should abide for a few moments in the aftereffects of meditation, realizing in doing so that we are living in these aftereffects. Through all these experiences force-centers are formed, which work within the astral body, but only to the extent of the aura. There they meet up with forces that stream into us from the spiritual world from outside. In this way the organs of the astral body, the lotus flowers, are formed. They bring it about that the purified astral body works into the etheric body, whose configuration is changed, and the etheric body is made independent from the physical body. Thereby a person becomes capable of further steps, beholding the sun at midnight and further getting to know the great spiritual world of the cosmos. This then is enormous blessedness.

* * *

Record D

Threshold of Death
Descent into the Underworld
Passage through the elements

Often we would like to extend the mood of meditation to encompass our entire lives. But this will not work because we would then become useless for physical life. Those who would assume the privilege of dedicating their present life entirely to meditation, that is, to leading a kind of cloistered or monastic life, would then be all the more placed in the task of being active in a practical life, perhaps with strengthened spiritual forces.

People have carried out esoteric exercises through the ages; in earlier times, in the mysteries. For those who wanted to develop their soul capacities, we find described in the ancient records of the Rosicrucians the forms of experience that the human soul must pass through. And they always spoke of very specific experiences. This is also the case for the ancient Egyptians, and altogether for all ancient mysteries. Here it has always been said that the soul is led to the threshold of death. It must descend into the elements; it must pass through the elements.

A student of esotericism must also pass through all of this today. But these experiences do not need to be passed through in this particular sequence. Earlier, the exercises that lead to these strongly felt experiences were carried out much more powerfully. They appeared in the soul with an enormous force, which a human being today would not be able to endure because our modern soul life has become much more differentiated.

The first experience, that of crossing the threshold of death, was experienced in the ancient mysteries in such a way that the students felt very momentarily the absence of the spirit from the body. They felt that their limbs were becoming lifeless, as with a corpse. Their bodies became as useless as a dead body. They felt that soul and spirit were no longer working within the body; they were outside. The entire material world, in which they lived, perceived, and experienced with their body, fell away from them and was no longer present. However, the true world, the real world of reality was hidden from them. Thus in this moment of death, the human being feels abandoned by God, by human beings, by the spiritual world, and the physical world. Wholly, completely abandoned! And a strong longing for that true world arises in the soul! But people feel that they cannot enter into this true world with the soul capacities that they have used until now. With their thinking, with their feeling, with their willing, they cannot begin to do anything.

All these experiences, students of esotericism also have today. They must also feel and experience strongly how the thinking that serves them when experiencing the physical plane is obtuse and useless for their striving for the spiritual; that another kind of thinking must be acquired. They must experience how their feeling is permeated by egotism, how with *this kind of feeling* they are pushed back from the spiritual world, and how their will is a hidden power that they must find. All of these experiences must be strongly felt. For an experience of the spiritual world, the soul looking on from outside the physical body must again and again experience the complete worthlessness of the thinking, feeling, and willing that serves only the physical world. Of course, along with this, a consciousness of the value of the physical world must also appear. There must be an awareness that this physical world is our school, and that only through a proper recognition of this value of the physical world are we able to come to the point of undergoing a spiritual development. Students must know that they must learn to regard the physical world and their physical bodies as tools for their soul and spiritual development. They must learn that they can really experience themselves outside of the physical world and their physical bodies in their true being, just as a manual laborer, when he uses his tools, feels himself to be outside of them. This feeling can go as far as the physical body's really dying—which can last for moment. But it is of the greatest importance that one notice what is really happening to one.

Then the second experience sets in; this is also an experience in one's feeling and knowing: descent into the lower worlds. Here we learn even further how to step back from ourselves. Previously we looked at our bodily nature. Now we also look upon our soul constitution from outside. And here a feeling of incredible shame rises within us. We are ashamed of our own unworthiness before the spiritual world. We learn to recognize that the capacities of our souls are gifts from the gods. And we realize that we have not used these divine gifts, which we should have used according to the intentions of the gods. We feel that all the egotism revealed in our emotions, drives, and passions has distanced our souls from the world of the gods. (We look down into a world of beings that have an intimate connection to human beings but are of a *subsensory* nature; and when we look into ourselves and perceive ourselves through our drives, instincts, and so forth, then we must suspect that the *subsensory* underlies them. Our drives, and so forth, are the effects of the work these beings do.) And if we have until now experienced only the body as distant, so now we experience what the soul used for egotism, which was thereby taken away from the spiritual world, as also moving away from us. Experiencing death, we often felt the body becoming like lead; now it is as if something foreign were coming into the body—we feel this especially strongly in our hands and arms. And the feeling of shame pours over us like a rush of lukewarm water, again and again. When we have learned, perhaps over a long period of time, to see into the underworld, which is our own soul-world, in which all the demonic beings live and weave; when we have intensely experienced the feeling of shame, then the third element appears: passage through the elements.

At this stage, the knowledge that a soul must have in order to find a path into the spiritual world without danger appears in the human soul. At first, the human being experiences there the reality of thoughts. We learn to recognize thoughts as living beings. In ordinary life it does not appear to be such a bad thing to do if we send evil thoughts to someone (thoughts of hatred, of envy, or lovelessness). We think that these are only thoughts. Now we learn that such thoughts are something worse than a shot with a deadly arrow on the physical plane. With imaginative pictures, we experience how these arrows bounce back so that they hit us. They touch our souls like a flame and imprint their stigma on us. We learn that we take up these stigmas into our karma, and we ourselves must compensate for them. On the other steps of the soul world there are also corresponding experiences for feeling and willing. (The human being learns the truth of the words: *The thoughts of the world live in my thinking. The forces of the world weave in my feeling. The beings of the world work in my willing.*)†

While meditating, the soul must live intensely in the given exercises; afterward, it must abide awhile for a few moments in the aftereffects of the meditation, and know at the same time that it is and lives in these aftereffects. Through all these experiences, centers of power are created within the astral body, whose work extends out to the circumference of the aura. There at the periphery of the aura, these forces from the centers of power meet with forces that stream into us from out of the spiritual world. Through this working outward from our own middle point, and working inward from outside, the organs of the astral body, the so-called lotus flowers, are formed. They bring it about that the purified astral body influences the etheric body, changing its configuration and making it independent of the physical body. In this way, the human being is given the ability to take further steps. At first we experience "beholding the sun at midnight" and then become acquainted with the great soul-world of the cosmos and the spiritual world that we find on the other side of the cosmos in the sphere of the zodiacal powers. And this expansion of self into these worlds is associated with an incredible feeling of blessedness.

RECORD E (Extract)

The ancients have always had a training that was similar to ours, up to a certain point, in relation to the experiences that a student has. At that time it progressed more quickly than now; it could be done in a few weeks. Now this is a self-initiation. Often we can carry out the same exercise for our entire lives with increasing intensity, and constantly have new experiences. What is important is that we pay close attention to the very subtle experiences that we have in our souls; very few of those present will have never experienced something like this. However, they are so weak, so fine that we do not notice them. Nevertheless, they characterize the progress made by a student. In *How to Know Higher Worlds*, many exercises are given that can gradually make one capable of experiencing the higher worlds on a path that is safe, without danger. However, means are given here through which one can progress even faster. The experiences in the ancient mysteries were: 1. Advancing to the threshold of the gate of death. 2. Descent into the underworld. 3. The fire-, water-, and air tests. 4. Beholding the sun at midnight and the encounter, as reality, with spiritual beings that lie hidden behind every material phenomenon.

Esoteric Lesson
STUTTGART, FEBRUARY 20, 1912

Record A: Manuscripts from Mathilda Scholl and Barbara Wolf; Record B: Manuscript from Alice Kinkel.

RECORD A

The evolution of the world and the evolution of the human being always go hand in hand. Those people who join an esoteric school must at the same time do justice to the age in which they live. However, because we connect ourselves with the eternal values of evolution through our esoteric development, there is something that has always been present and has an enduring significance for the student in the esoteric schools of all ages, even for the pre-Christian—for example, the Egyptian. These are words that present-day students, as well as students of ages past (in terms of their meaning), can allow to work on their souls. Such words from that time are as follows; when translated into our language they sound more or less like this.

I have come to the gate of death;
I have come to know the four elements;
I have seen the sun at midnight;
I have come close to the higher and lower gods;
I have returned to the external world.

What does it mean to say, "I have come to the gate of death," and so forth? In our meditations we gradually reach the point where we feel ourselves as double personalities. We feel that the "I" no longer belongs to what we have until now identified with: the physical body. When we die, it happens quite naturally that we no longer regard our body as belonging to us. But we must already have achieved this through training before we separate ourselves definitively from the body. If human beings had developed as the good gods intended, then they would have directed their bodies from outside. If, for example, we had wanted to travel from one city to another, then we would have directed our bodies there through a magical influence of the will from outside. The body would have been like a weight that belonged to us. We can illuminate this thought if we imagine that an inhabitant of Mars is suddenly placed on Earth, and the first human being whom he encounters carries a weight in each hand. The inhabitant of Mars might think, since he had never before seen a human being, that these two weights were growths on the human body. Thus have we grown together entirely too much with the physical body. Now if we properly train ourselves, we will increasingly get the feeling that the "I" is splitting, with one part directing the other from outside. As we increasingly come into contact with the highest creative beings with our elevated "I," which we should humbly feel as grace, it can happen that we increasingly identify this "I" with these high beings, for we are so permeated by ambition and vanity that we cannot even imagine it. Now there is a good means of working against this vanity.

How did the predecessors of humanity, the Elohim, appear on the Earth? They did not reflect themselves in their brilliancy, full of vanity. In the Bible we are told that they created, and that they then looked upon their deeds and saw that they were good. So, too, we should look upon the deeds of the "I," upon what our "I" has accomplished. Then we will see how little good is still to be found in all of our deeds. Take, for example, our handwriting. It is an expression of our "I," part of ourselves that we set forth outwardly. No one would be so vain as to find everything about his or her handwriting to be beautiful. And so with a little reflection, we could find many of our achievements, when examined more closely, to be very deficient.

What does it mean to say we have come to know the elements? The first element, in which the human being was created, was warmth. And actually, along with the evolution of the earth, it was intended that human beings should send streams of warmth into their bodies from outside. Summer warmth and winter cold, which they now as individual human beings experience in their bodies, they should have experienced as the "I" flowing toward them from outside. They should feel that this "I" is connected to all other human "I"s. The fact that warmth is now in us, has moved into our blood; this is Lucifer's deed.

The second element that we are intimately connected with is air. Actually we should have the feeling that we ourselves are the air that is outside of us; that with every breath we stream into the body with the air and enliven them it. Instead we feel air to be something that comes to us from outside; we send it back as something that is poisoned, as something that kills. And Ahriman comes forward to meet us in this dead air.

We identify ourselves only with the other two elements, the solid and the liquid in us; the physical body and blood. We experience them as we ourselves. However, we should identify ourselves as little as possible with our present personality, so that even if we come to know our earlier incarnations, we regard them only as passing stages. We should never say we have been this person or that person, for then we mix up the eternal "I" with our transitory "I."

* * *

Record B

Four sentences from the Egyptian initiation are given to you. The feelings associated with these stages an esotericist must penetrate even today.

I. I had to go through the gate of death. The experience is: feeling one's body like a weight that must be carried.

II. I had to come to know the elements.

III. I was allowed to behold the sun at midnight.

IV. I was very near the higher and lower gods.

Verse of the Egyptian Mysteries[†]

I have come to the gate of death;
I have come to know the four elements;
I have seen the sun at midnight;
I have come close to the lower and the higher gods;
I have returned to the outer world.
I went to the border of death;
I entered Proserpines' threshold.

And after I traveled through all the elements
I turned around and came back.

At midnight I saw the sun
With bright white light radiant.

I went to the lower and higher gods
From face to face and worshiped them
From the closest proximity.

> Ich ging bis zur Grenze des Todes
> Ich betrat Proserpinens Schwelle
>
> Und nachdem ich durch alle Elemente gefahren,
> Kehrte ich wiederum zurück
>
> Um Mitternacht sah ich die Sonne mit
> hellweissem Lichte flackern
>
> Vor die untern und obern Götter trat ich
> hin, von Angesicht zu Angesicht, und betete
> sie aus nächster Nähe an.

Verse of the Egyptian Mysteries in Note Book, Archive Nr. 263

Esoteric Lesson
STUTTGART, FEBRUARY 22, 1912

Record A: Manuscript from Barbara Wolf; Record B: Manuscript from Alice Kinkel.

RECORD A

With what we discussed the day before yesterday, it is above all important and necessary that an esotericist learn to feel these things, not merely to grasp them intellectually. However, before we discuss these things further, we want to mention still some things that are important and valuable for an esotericist.

When entering an esoteric stream it is entirely natural to ask how does one advance; how does one develop the soul upward? Here it is of the utmost importance that we stand firmly upon an esoteric centerpoint from which we can look out upon life, a center from which we allow ourselves to be irradiated. We should open ourselves with respect to the streams coming from the spiritual world that are appropriate for our time. There is absolutely no value in flirting with other routes to the spirit just because they appear theosophical to us; no value in engaging them superficially. This simply hinders our progress. It would be much better to attach ourselves to a more or less false route to the spirit if we thought that it would give us more, for we would then have from it what corresponds to ourselves. A true esotericist must look into life from his or her solid, unshakable standpoint with wakeful eyes, for this will always get more complicated. These complications are brought about by Luciferic beings that have remained behind in evolution since the Mystery of Golgotha; that is, they have not taken the consequences of this mystery into themselves. What is now happening in the spiritual world has a shocking effect on those who can see into it.

What Lucifer has brought us was actually good for us: that we entered into our physical and etheric bodies and did not remain hovering, for the "I" has thereby acquired the power of knowledge and memory. Memory is, indeed, something that also of course holds us back. However, without it, given the way we are stuck in our bodies, we could not manage; above all, we would not be able to distinguish between reality and illusion. Suppose we would think of someone whom we knew twenty years ago, and then approach this memory picture and greet it. This we would have to call a hallucination. But we would fall for this kind of hallucination if we took something that had been left behind, for something that was appropriate for our time. This is something that will frequently be the case in times not far from now. The Luciferic beings that remained behind since the Mystery of Golgotha have created a spearhead, so to speak, in certain souls. These are souls that the Luciferic beings overpowered after their last incarnation. These souls lived at the time of Tauler and Meister Eckhart in the thirteenth century. They belonged to the community of the Beghards.†

They are now attempting to confuse the hearts of human beings in the coming time; the means they are using is the old religions of Brahmanism and Buddhism. In the time when they were given, these were right for the ancient Indians; especially Brahmanism, which was a much more spiritual religion than Christianity is, even to this day. That Christianity is not more advanced is due to the fact that Europeans have, since the Middle Ages, allowed a certain opportunity to escape; that is, the opportunity to develop properly what was given to it. Above all, like a flood from China, a sublime spiritual culture will penetrate Europe and impress Europeans mightily, because precisely because of its advanced age, reaching all the way back to Atlantis, it is far superior to present-day Christianity. What has now happened in China† is perhaps externally politically of significance; however, an esotericist must consider a book by an outstanding Chinese writer, Ku Hung Ming, *China's Defense against European Ideas*, which has also been translated into German, as the expression of very far-reaching spiritual significance.† Ku Hung Ming is a significant thinker. What he says is not wrong; and yet there is much therein that an esotericist must consider. He says that Christian missionaries came to China in order to bring their Christianity into an ancient, lofty culture. Did they manage to do this? No. But something else came in its place. The missionaries brought Chinese culture back to Europe and, since the French Revolution approximately, Europe has become much more like China than it altogether suspects. This Chinese man knows full well that his people administer the memory of humanity, and that this fact makes a great impression upon the European. However, memory is, as stated, Lucifer's gift. Through him we have descended into the physical body. We must again rescind this deed of Lucifer's, but not think that it was not necessary.

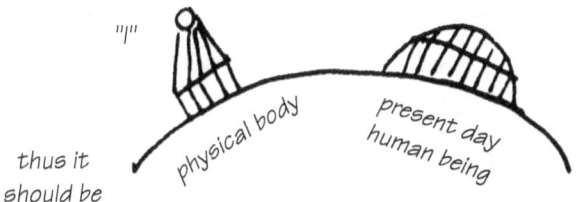

thus it should be

One could ask, why then did we have to descend? But that would be the same as if a man to whom one suggested that he should go to a particular place in order to experience something would answer that it would not be necessary, and that he would rather remain where he is. Then he would not have the experience. Likewise, we would never have achieved the consolidation of the "I" if we had not entered in this way into our physical body.

However, we should never regard it as more than an instrument. When, through meditation and concentration, we reach the point where we leave the body and see it lying before us, then of course the organs are not active. The eyes do not see; the ears do not hear. The body has the value of a plant, though a very highly developed plant. And as it lies there before us, we must say to ourselves that we must cease to speak of the "lower" physical body and the "lower" etheric body, for these two are miraculously structured in their organization. The physical body is a temple that the lower gods build for us; and all that is bad, faulty, and defective in it, we alone have caused. And when we, the inhabitants of this temple, then look upon ourselves, we become aware that we (that is, our spiritual part) have the form of a dragon, of a worm. There are many who imagine that they live selflessly only for their fellow human beings, but the clairvoyant sees with their jaws pushed forward and with the receding forehead of a worm, the sign of their egotism. Our souls still have this form of a worm, and the good gods have set the Guardian of the Threshold in front of it so that we do not see it all the time. Now we should undertake to bring this dragon transformed up to higher gods. This should be our constant work. When ancient Egyptians walked through the temple during their initiation, through the row of sphinxes, they said to themselves that this temple is a physical image of the perfect dwelling of God and that they have the task of achieving this divinity in order to live worthily in the temple of the body.

When leaving the body, the eyes lose the ability to see. They no longer see the physical sun, nor do they see what it illuminates. Instead, the human being illuminates the surroundings, perceives colors and sounds in the spiritual world. Our spiritual part increases its abilities. If one exaggerates the separation from the body, then of course the physical eyes can suffer. They no longer see things clearly, but surrounded by an aura. There is now in England even a certain instrument that can be used so that the eyes see the aura of things. However, this is directly dangerous for the eyes, and a healthy departure from the body does not need such practices.

Also ancient Atlanteans did not yet see things clearly. They did not need to see clearly because the sun was still veiled by thick masses of fog and mist. Toward the end of Atlantis, a giant colored circle filling the entire sky was to be seen, with a pale, veiled centerpoint.

In ancient Egypt during initiation, by means of physical substances, it was brought about that the students saw the sun through the earth, on the other side.

* * *

Record B

It has often been said that our present time is very important and also very critical. It is a time in which great spiritual currents stream down into our physical world. They are to serve by bringing a "new seed" to human beings through which their development will be able to move forward. At the same time, influences are streaming down that originate in the past, that made earlier development fruitful. As esotericists our task now should be to feel ourselves as in a centerpoint, as firmly standing in the new seed, and not to allow ourselves to be confused or swept away by any adjacent current.

Precisely in this moment a new spearhead, so to speak, has been formed. It is serving to strengthen the Luciferic influences that are already present. These are spirits not presently incarnated who were, however, followers of Johannes Tauler and Meister Eckhart, namely, the Beghards. They themselves belonged to a mystical stream and to many good things for their era. Now they send their impulses down from the spiritual world and, as such, create a powerful spearhead for Luciferic beings who remained behind at the Mystery of Golgotha. They had to remain behind in order to intervene in evolution again at a later date. We already know from earlier communications that Luciferic beings can also bring the good; from this point of view it must be pointed out that we must thank these beings for our memory, for all of our mental capacities. What would it be like if we were to forget all the incidents in our destiny, all the events of our youth and early adulthood, or if we saw them as taking place in the present? Then we would live in hallucinations; we would be confused within ourselves.

But this is what the retarded Luciferic spirits want to evoke in us: they want us to experience our memories of the past as something healthy and still existing in the present. If the teachings of the ancient Brahmans or of Buddhism, which fostered the evolution of humanity in their time, would now be conveyed to people still in the same form, it would be as if the memories in our souls had been transferred through time into the present. Then one would live in hallucinations. Esotericists should stand firmly centered, should not surrender to any of these streams, and especially not flirt with them, as all too often happens now when one wishes to "reconcile" all parties and hold together in a great brotherhood. Again and again, one hears that this or that personality spoke, wrote, or preached "so theosophically," or that this or that view or philosophy is permeated with theosophy. This only amounts to allowing oneself to be led astray, pulled away from one's center, in order to go along with another stream for a time. It would be better for such esotericists to continue for a time or for their entire lives with such partially good or partially wrong streams, rather than constantly to oscillate back and forth between this or that approach to the spirit.

One of the most characteristic things of our time is something that is happening at the moment in China. Furthermore, as strange as it may sound, it is the consequence of earlier attempts by Christian missionaries to bring Christianity to China. China still possesses a genuine Atlantean spiritual science that contains much greatness; however, it belongs to a concluded epoch out of which Chinese culture cannot lift itself. The consequence of missionaries going to China has not been the Christianization of China; but rather, the Europeans have become like the Chinese. The concepts and the ideas of the Chinese have flowed into the Europeans, and then been brought back to Europe; and they are now leading Europe into the culture of the Chinese, so that it has become a center of great confusion in concepts and worldviews.

The Chinese have the task of maintaining the memory of humanity. What they have preserved as spiritual treasures from the past, they should now show to humanity; all hindrances to this have been removed. It is not the task of the Chinese to distinguish between memory and hallucination; this is the task of Europeans. In the near future we will see that Europeans will be confused by these treasures, because they will want to introduce them as something new. (Compare, for example, *China's Defense against Europe* by Ku Hung Ming.)

And then when an outdated Buddhism and everything that has an oriental tint to it are also brought to Europe (and it is precisely what is most distant, the Orient, that exerts the greatest attraction to people), then error and confusion will reach a high point that we can hardly imagine. The new seed, which is just now emerging from Europe, which must be regarded as a seed, not as a full-grown fruit, forms a center-point that we can firmly cling to. All other streams must be decisively rejected as not belonging to this sprouting seed, with which our soul should unite its further development.

We should raise ourselves up with this spiritual stream, and then what we have often described will take place: the "I" will acquire two aspects; it will form a duality. The one aspect we will experience as bound to the earth, created out of earthly forces; we will experience it as separated from ourselves. We will experience this "I" as if it had become smaller. The other "I" we will experience as something greater than what we have experienced in ourselves until now. Then we will see our bodies outside of ourselves and will no longer be able to use our senses, even if they are still present. Sight, hearing, feeling, everything will have left the body, and yet the body lives, although it is only the life of a plant.

Then we will get the feeling that the body would be something very beautiful, if only we did not have to live in it. Our bodies have been perfectly formed even into the finest details; but we ourselves are responsible for making them into something inferior through our imperfections. When looking at things this way, we get the idea that what is outside of us as the body is similar to a dragon with gigantic jaws and a receding forehead; we realize that this is what we have made out of the work of the gods until now. The Guardian of the Threshold prevents us from seeing the gestalt of our self, but it is nevertheless always present.

We then learn to regard the higher part of our selves as the spiritual part that draws from itself the soul forces needed to fill itself with divine light. In ancient Atlantean times, the atmosphere was filled with so much fog and mist that the sun could not shine through the fog, and also the human being did not yet have eyes such as today's eyes to distinguish between objects. At first a gigantic, bright disc that filled the entire horizon and was permeated with color gradually pushed through the fog; according to how much light the disc radiated, the eyes were formed by the light. Thus the spiritual part of our being should become radiant and fill the spiritual environment around us with light in which the spiritual beings—the beings that we designate as spiritual hierarchies—then become visible. This is what the Egyptians called seeing the sun at midnight. For them, this required a special deed because they could not call it forth in the way described above. Rather, in order to see the sun through the earth on the other side, they had to be brought to it in the darkness of night. But today we fill ourselves with the spiritual sun and then radiate it out again with the organs that we could call spiritual eyes. The beings that we then see are higher gods, and that is what is called seeing the higher and lower gods.

One can injure one's physical eyes if one tries to train them too much to see suprasensory things. All the methods that are now coming primarily from England which are designed to lead one to see human auras by means of a certain artificial technique are injurious for physical eyes because they drive the etheric body out of the eyes. One can even become blind.

Esoteric Lesson
STUTTGART, FEBRUARY 23, 1912

Manuscript from Hulda Schouten-Deetz.

In the course of the last lectures we have learned that our entire existence is steered and guided by lofty beings, which work in their own particular way on the evolution of the world and our special human qualities. If we want to place ourselves in contact with them through concentration and meditation, we must fill ourselves with a feeling of humility that cannot be compared with the kind of humility we may well have in the course of daily life. When we connect ourselves with these high beings, who are also our teachers, our feeling of humility stands far above all human understanding. Only later do we acquire the ability to distinguish true beings from the forces that radiate out from within ourselves, and we can give a distinguishing marker that leads to a genuine insight of whether what is seen comes from a higher world or out of our own interior: We feel it in our hearts; a warmth and excitement streaming from the cosmos flows through the heart. For the heart is connected, on the one hand, with the zodiacal sign of Leo; and on the other hand, with the sun. And the warmth of these forces collaborates in spiritual vision.

What does it mean to be an esotericist?

In all phases of our earth existence we are situated in our karma, from which we can never escape because the consequences of our willing, our feeling, our thinking, and especially of our deeds, follow us irrevocably through all our incarnations, whether it be sooner or later. The guilt that we incur we must redeem on this earth, according to the circumstances in which we find ourselves in this incarnation. Divine guidance sees to this. Until we take our development into our own hands, everything proceeds according to regulated laws that nothing can accelerate. If we enter into an esoteric training, then something entirely different happens to us. We free ourselves from guidance; we take our development into our own hands; we become qualitatively different people. How? Everything that we regarded as worthy of our desire in the past now loses in large measure its value for us; our views and attitudes become different. We may see that earlier we behaved in ways that were hard and without compassion, and from now on our sense of responsibility becomes much more subtle; we will attempt to compensate for our incurred guilt in every way possible, even if it costs us great sacrifice inwardly and outwardly.

Through their daily repetition, the meditations and other exercises that are given to esotericists transform the etheric body, assuming they are done with right attitude; that is, if the percepts and images that appear inwardly are properly felt. Then the etheric body is transformed as it gradually separates from the physical body. Now when these exercises have been carried out for a long time with patience and devotion with one's whole being (however, this can be done each time for only a short period of time), then gradually and very gently, when we wake from sleep something wonderful makes itself noticed. This is something that we cannot express with words, for it is a very gentle feeling of an experience in the spiritual world from which we have just returned. After a process in time, we see colors appearing before us in which forms develop. In these forms, something entirely different from what we are accustomed to seeing comes to meet us. However, a warning must be given that we must not immediately consider these forms to be spiritual experiences, nor many other things that will rise up, and at the start of a spiritual development will be similar to things in our everyday environment. For our soul traits will very often be what appear radiating forth from our own souls.

Now an esoteric training by itself does not make a person any better; this must be expressly stated. No matter how highly developed an individual may be intellectually, or with moral virtues, there are still uncompensated, bad, immoral traits hiding in the soul, which are usually whitewashed over by conventional mores. The human being is actually worse than he or she is usually seen by others. During esoteric development, which we take in hand ourselves, our vices and bad habits inevitably come forward, and here esotericists must employ all their strength in order to conquer them. We call up our karma ourselves, and accelerate it through our development. May we well understand this! For we have entered upon a different path in life. We now have become comrades of our lofty spiritual guides, who alone until now have guided us; for we have now taken over the leadership ourselves, and also full responsibility for our spiritual evolution.

Now it is often said that it is nothing more than human egotism to want to develop faster than one's fellow human beings. But this is not the case. As soon as we become aware that we are of divine origin, and that we must work our way back to the origin of our existence, to our divinity; then it is even a sin of omission to say, "I will take my own sweet time. I do not wish to anticipate the divine; one day it will lead me to the goal." There is a great deal of arrogance in speaking in this way, for the gods have laid the seeds of our spiritual organs in us. As soon as we are conscious of this, it must become our duty not to let these forces lie fallow and wait for them to blossom in the general flow of evolution. We must take the unfolding of our spiritual organs in hand ourselves. We must not allow ourselves to be led, but rather become our own leaders. It is a difficult path. But this has nothing to do with egotism, for we are obligated to our leaders who have shown us the way so far already.

Let us now turn our thoughts again to the lofty being who has, especially, the present day under his protection. It is always a beneficial combination when an esoteric lesson is held on a Friday. This is because of the great influence that this being pours into our thoughts and feelings: (mantra) [Verse for the day.]

In the previous hour we discussed why we should become esotericists. Today I would like to tell you about the true significance of daily meditation. The meditations are tested and given to us by the Masters of Wisdom and Harmony of Feelings for esotericism. The force of these meditations is irrevocable when they are carried out in their true sense with sacred devotion. Shortly before falling asleep, we should use the meditations after we have banned all thoughts that connect us to daily life, with its joys and pleasures, with its cares and efforts. The meditation should be our last thought that we carry over into the other world, so that spiritual beings can unite with them.

We are immersed in their etheric body, they permeate us with their forces, so that we can receive from them new strength and fresh health for the coming day. How often do people unfortunately pass over into sleep with thoughts of all kinds of pleasures of everyday material life. These streams of thought produce vibrations that have the effect of pushing spiritual beings away. Human beings work in this way against their spiritual development, as well as against their health. Just as we sink into the spiritual atmosphere in the evening, so also in the morning upon awakening we should also not immediately take hold of all that filled our lives the previous day in terms of cares and burdens, struggles, desires, and passions. We should push all this away for a while and let our thoughts abide for a time in the regions from which we have just emerged. Here, too, after a longer or shorter exercise, we will feel how this also fosters our development, and not only for our inner being; for out of our eyes, out of our hands, the radiant power that has flowed into us will pass over into our deeds for the salvation of humanity.

Esoteric Lesson
MUNICH, FEBRUARY 26, 1912

Record A: Manuscript from Mathilde Scholl and Barbara Wolf; Record B: Manuscript from Alice Kinkel.

RECORD A

It is of course quite natural that our esoteric lectures in the course of the years are always becoming more complicated, in that they build upon those that have already been held. Since our esoteric movement is always growing, there are certain disadvantages that are thereby produced; above all, the fact that it is becoming increasingly widespread. The ideal would be to have a small group that constantly strives for greater deepening. Now we can work against superficiality if the newly joined members trustingly turn to the older members, who have been hearing these lectures for years, and hear from them what has been said. Altogether it would be good if some of those who expend so much loquaciousness for things of everyday life would rein it in, and instead think more about absorbing and spreading esoteric teachings in our circle. When so many of our members concentrate their trust so exclusively in one person (in the first instance in me) as more or less the karmic instrument for spreading these teachings—it is not right. The younger newcomers should trustingly turn to the older members with their questions concerning personal and daily life, and seek advice from me only concerning questions of esoteric development. Trust is a factor that plays a big role in the life of the lodge, and the ability to give advice grows with those who are asked for it. We also have many physicians in our movement whom I trust completely, as can be observed at any time. Our members could turn to them with many health questions. An especially intense esoteric life and work that can be considered a model is accomplished here at this locality. Of course, as a polarity, there also arise some disadvantages created, above all, by the arrival of those who do not realize how serious and sacred the esoteric life really is.

For those who have once devoted themselves to an esoteric life, it should be impossible for them to think the thought of ever leaving again for the sake of any external reason, for then they would prove how unserious and feeble their decision to join was from the outset. From the moment they become esotericists, many are able to manage their karma into a calm destiny so that they can place their meditations in the center of their lives. Others are met more by events that they cannot harmonize with an esoteric life, sometimes to such an extreme degree that their esoteric life suffers from it. The ideal, of course, would be for our entire life to be illuminated by our esoteric center, as if we always have our eyes on that center. Something that damages esoteric development a great deal is, above all, the unchecked, superficial, and therefore objectively false criticism that we often express among ourselves, or toward other people. I am not saying that it is wrong to express criticism, but it should always be related to a specific matter, and not to a person merely for the reason that we do not like that kind of person.

Our exercises are indeed apparently something very simple; nevertheless, they have an effect on us greater than anything else that we can encounter in life. What is their effect? Through these meditations we should loosen the etheric body from within and draw it out. One of these days, in our meditations, it will happen to us that we no longer see, hear, and feel. And this will happen through the loosening of the etheric body. There are many methods to bring out the etheric body, but those that are external and not based on meditation are injurious for our organs because the etheric body is "pushed away from the outside." For example, the etheric part of the eyes could be pushed away from them, and they suffer from this. Through meditative activity only so many forces are loosened, so that enough are always present to maintain the functions of life in the organs. When we arrive at this condition of not hearing, and so forth, we have left the physical body. Now many of us have carried out these exercises for years. Nevertheless, there are those who have not yet achieved this. Why is that?

Before departing the body, a discomforting feeling overcomes us, and the human being strives against that instinctively. There is nothing that a human being balks against as much as this resigning of the etheric body from the physical. Even just thinking about it hinders it. It is almost like a reflexive movement, that we immediately pull ourselves back again when this feeling overcomes us. We balk at this for a very specific reason. When, through sufficient intensity of meditation, students reach the point of leaving the body, it suddenly becomes clear to them just what a lofty, wonderful temple the body is with all its organs. When they then look at themselves, at what has left the physical, they see that they are an ugly worm, and this worm balks at leaving the physical body. That is what refuses to leave, because it is horrified by its own ugliness. Then it becomes clear to us how infinitely far we still have to go to attain perfection.

Through our meditations we receive power that should be poured from within outward. But one can hear many saying, "In my case, nothing is being poured." That is no wonder if we do our meditations lazily and not with sufficient intensity, and if many entirely everyday interests are placed higher than our esoteric work.

The first feeling we have when the etheric body is loosened is heaviness in the brain and in the entire physical body, so that we feel it to be a weight that does not belong to us. We experience this wonderful structure, which is the most highly developed part of us, as transitory and fragile. We have made it that way. Ever since old Saturn, it has been increasingly perfected by divine beings, and the Saturn and Sun forces that it retained from the past have been the up-building forces. However, we have also received something with the Moon forces, with the astral, and the forces of earth, the "I," the earthly self, which turns these forces outward in order to convey perceptions to the self through the sense organs. Now, in the course of esoteric training, people experience their senses as a destructive force, as a poison that is embedded in their organism. As the astral body and the "I" were integrated, so too must the nervous system, brain, and senses be transformed so that they can now receive from outside what streamed through them earlier (but then from inside toward the outer world). In this moment an understanding of death comes to the human being, the true cause of it, and this was called "standing at the gate of death" in the ancient mysteries.

The "I" should now make up for all the mistakes it has made and perfect all its bodies so that we can become true human beings. The expression "human being" is indeed not often used in the highest sense that actually underlies it. But esotericists should always see it as their highest striving—to make themselves into a human being.

So we should let everything that is imperfect die in the one whose name is so holy that we cannot mention it, in order to resurrect again in the perfect one, the Holy Spirit.

* * *

RECORD B

Concerning the four principles of Egyptian initiation.

I. Feel one's body as a weight that hangs on one, experience it as "becoming something" of the body.

II. An esotericist should not express superficial criticism. Esotericists must learn to remain silent and to trust all their older brothers and sisters. They should carry out their meditations diligently and faithfully. And what is the result of doing this?

1. Recognizing what one sees; the physical body as a temple and as a miraculous work of the gods.
2. Recognize one's self as an ugly worm that dwells in the body, making it impure.

Esoteric Lesson

MANNHEIM, MARCH 10, 1912

Record A: Manuscript from Alice Kinkel; Record B: Notes from Emma Klein.

RECORD A

Concerning Meditation

A fruit of meditation: getting a feeling that we strive for a connection with the beings of the higher hierarchies; this as a feeling of being taken up into higher worlds and as a feeling of arriving at the place where we originated. We experience warmth and life. The feeling of being taken up into the spiritual world must be warm and alive.

Everything, everything must become different for an esotericist: concepts, feelings, and knowledge must be transformed for an esotericist.

Concerning Egotism

It is Luciferic beings who have given us our memory. Those who are thrifty in physical life are bad profligates in the soul and spiritual realm. We should become sparing in these forces, and transform them into forces of vision. Self-knowledge alone can lead us to do this.

From morning to evening we selfishly misspend our feelings and experiences.

We must first pass through egotism in the soul-spiritual realm. Striving for entrance into the spiritual world presents for us the danger of our becoming egotistical in the physical world. For this reason, a proper training goes hand in hand with a moral and intellectual purification.

We must be clear that the impossible is demanded of us as esotericists, and that we are striving for the impossible. All striving is impossible, and being non-egotistical is also impossible!

Greed for knowledge and for progress is not proper for an esotericist, but rather a serious feeling of our duty to develop ourselves. The divine spirit placed powers in us that it developed without any contribution from us; those are passive powers. However, God also placed active powers in us that we ourselves must develop through deeds. And it is the greatest sin against the divine spirit not to develop these powers, which God placed in us for the benefit and salvation of human evolution and progress. And these powers are so strong in us that they can lead us into spiritual worlds, even if only after many years. For this reason we must not get impatient, but should say to ourselves, "I will wait, for I know that these powers do this, if only we are devoted in the right way to the spiritual world."

Auxiliary Exercises

The auxiliary exercises create for us the necessary characteristics for the physical plane, for here we need composure or imperturbability, control of thoughts, and so forth.

Then we will gradually have a compartment in our hearts, in our souls, in which we will keep what is our holiest, in which we are esotericists while we stand outside on the physical plane. It is obvious that this cannot happen without conflict. As esotericists we must become fighters.

Thoughts that attack us are beings from the spiritual world that flutter around us; the more we attempt to hold them at bay, the stronger they charge in toward us. We should not complain about this; no, "be happy that this is happening," one can say to the student. This represents success in meditation that shows that thoughts are a spiritual power. An esotericist needs courage, fearlessness, and faith.

* * *

RECORD B

The esoteric path is not only full of battles and thorns; rather, esotericists should and can permeate themselves with a fundamental feeling of blessedness concerning the fact that they have been taken up by higher powers into those regions from which we have all originated.

Those who meditate seriously find that they are disturbed by impressions and worries from everyday life, by conditions that intrude from the physical world. Many believe that they are thereby hindered in their higher development and for this reason advance too slowly. Actually this contact with real powers and beings in the physical world is a healing remedy of self-knowledge, and an ongoing opportunity to test the powers that have been achieved through spiritual knowledge.

Esoteric students must acquire a large measure of endurance and imperturbability; and learn to make subservient the powers that no one can dodge who wishes to fulfill his or her mission on earth: namely, the Luciferic powers. These powers have brought not only evil to humanity, but also the justified egotism of free, independent self-development.

Here esotericists should learn to protect themselves from the grim wastefulness of which we are all daily guilty when we give vent to our best inner forces in unnecessary feelings, in rage, envy, and worry. We should use these forces in justifiable egotism for our inner development. Instead of greed for spiritual knowledge, which is worthless, we should acquire a feeling of duty toward the higher powers, oneself, and the evolution of humanity, so that we say it is a sin against the Holy Spirit of Evolution if we do not offer everything to concentrate our inner forces in a frugal way, to perfect ourselves personally as much as possible. The greatest wastrel is a miserly cheapskate because he wastes his best forces with his greedy, worrisome thoughts; thus, he is excessively selfless in a useless way.

We must not permit this egotism in the realm of esotericism to be carried over into the realm of the exoteric. Here the demand for selflessness, the denial of one's own "I," remains standing. For this reason, all esotericists must be clear that they simply want the impossible, and therefore it is unavoidable that they wind up in a conflict and must fight. On the one hand, we must live in justified egotism of pure inwardness and regard meditation as the most hidden of the most holy essence of the soul, but then, on the other hand, we must also turn our attention to the outer world and work in a selfless way within it in order not to fall into unjustified egotism.

Here one can learn a lot from simple people who have an uncomplicated faith; they therefore face death with the confidant certainty that they will be taken up and connected with higher, eternal powers, while philosophers who have lived in one-sided thought-filled egotism face death with bitterness.

* * *

Esoteric Lesson
FRANKFURT, MARCH 10, 1912

Manuscript from Alice Kinkel.

>Concerning laziness in the face of karma;
>Observation of oneself and one's surroundings.
>Observing and guiding one's feelings.
>Purifying one's morality and intellectuality.
>Karmic connections = Revenge of spiritual beings.
>Endurance and imperturbability are to be practiced.

The most important part of our esoteric life is our meditations, through which we gradually work our way up into the spiritual world. So too is our attitude, and the way in which we should perform the meditations in connection with higher worlds and beings. Greed for spiritual knowledge must not be allowed to rule us. Rather the same mood should be present in which we carry our moral actions; for example, when we feel compassion or share someone's joy. Otherwise there is the great danger for us as esotericists that we lose our moral moorings in our exoteric lives, that we become worse than we were before. For this reason, auxiliary exercises are always given in conjunction with the actual meditations. They serve to educate, to consolidate us in intellectual and moral matters.

A further danger stalks esotericists in the course of their karma, on whose transformation and mastery they are working. Almost on a regular basis, the phenomenon appears here that those who are working intensely on a deepening of their souls become negligent with respect to external karmic events and conditions. In the life between death and rebirth, the karmic misdeeds with which esotericists burdened themselves in the past trigger a strong drive to balance them with karma. Thus they are placed in situations and in connection with personalities where they would have the possibility of fulfilling these karmic obligations.

In normal exoteric development, karma would slowly unfold or be worked out partially.

Now when students are too occupied with their esoteric development and do not pay enough attention to the external conditions that constitute their destiny, karma overtakes them. Then what would otherwise take place over years or in various incarnations, must now work itself out in a concentrated way through oppressive conflicts and great life difficulties. As this occurs, the students can be brought to the edge of despair and may also bring problems to their environment, drawing it into the karmic eruption. However, even in their simplest beginning exercises, they have the comfort that there are powers that also hold and support them. We can and should always bear this in mind.

* * *

Esoteric Lesson

BERLIN, MARCH 22, 1912

Record A: Anonymous Manuscript (Vreede Collection); Record B: Manuscript from Nelly Lichtenberg; Record C: Manuscript from Louise Clason.

RECORD A

Our esoteric exercises should bring us to imaginative knowledge. There are imaginations that in times not far behind us, relatively speaking, could be understood by every student without further explanation. Today such imaginations must be interpreted for us in understandable words because only very few esotericists would come upon the significance themselves. Now an imagination will be given here that is useful for all esotericists who have the feeling, despite their efforts, of not advancing far enough.

Students should imagine that their teacher or master is standing before them in the form of Moses (even if they have only an indefinite imagination of this personality), and that he then asks them, "So you want to know why then you have not come further on your esoteric path? I will tell you: It is because you worship the golden calf." After these words the student sees the golden calf next to Moses. Moses now causes fire to rise up out of the earth. The fire consumes the golden calf until it is powdery dust. This powder he throws onto clear water that is present, and gives the student this water mixed with powder to drink.

Not many centuries ago every esotericist could still have understood this picture. Now it needs to be explained in the following way.

If we go back in our memories, we come to the point when our memories stop and our I-consciousness had its start. What lies before is what we have made of ourselves in previous incarnations and have brought along with us into this incarnation. This is the golden calf that we worship without realizing it, our "sheath" nature.

In the place of the golden calf, students then place the picture of themselves as children who do not yet have any I-consciousness. They permeate themselves with the consciousness that what they feel as the "I" is nothing other than a Luciferic effect, for ordinary I-consciousness is based upon memory and memory is a Luciferic power, since it is Lucifer's task to bring the past over into the present. If we subtract from ourselves what we have as I-consciousness, there remains as a remnant what we have brought along from previous earth lives. It may appear difficult to have to imagine oneself in this way, but without such stern concepts we will not become prepared to encounter the Guardian of the Threshold.

Then the students really imagine how the fire burns the form of the child that they themselves were; meanwhile, they are only a little more grown, but fundamentally speaking, they are still this sheath nature that the child also was in, except that now the illusion of the "I" has been added. They see how the form has become powdery dust; and through this they should become very conscious of the fact that they should be indifferent to everything about these sheaths that is physical, etheric body, and astral body; indifferent to the pile of powder, as indifferent as clay is to a sculptor before he or she has made anything out of the clay. The physical body, the form, the external gestalt; the etheric body with its memories; the astral body with its sympathies and antipathies; all this must be thought away or thought of as a little pile of dust.

Perhaps we cannot transform this into practical life immediately. It is not intended that we should suddenly fling our arms around someone for whom we feel sympathy, but when we practice this exercise we should be able to reject all antipathy from ourselves.

And the dust is thrown into the pure water of divine substance, just as it was before the Luciferic power had worked into it. Thus should our sheath nature be sacrificed, as the divine substance returned. Esotericists also come to the insight that all this, which for them is only a little pile of dust, is nevertheless formed out of the spirit. The shape of the body was sculpted out of the spirit, the spirit made them into that which they now are as form. And that which the spirit has made out of us, we should again take into ourselves. We should drink again the water in which the dust was dissolved. Then we have it purified: after the golden calf burned, what became powder and was dissolved. When we do this, then at first, we will feel that a certain place in us becomes empty; it is the place where the "I" usually sits. We feel it becoming empty. Then one can either become a Buddhist, and enter a region for which a human being could feel him or herself worthy: into Nirvana, in a non-earthly sphere. Or one can arrive at a new consciousness of the Christ impulse, and feel this streaming into the place of the "I" that has become empty.

Christ could never have come to earth within the Hebrew people unless Moses had destroyed the golden calf and thrown it into water and given it to the people of Israel to drink.

It is not intended that students carry out this imagination daily, but rather every now and then after a certain period of time; for example, every three, or four, or six weeks. Fundamentally speaking it is only a clarification of our Rosicrucian verse.

* * *

RECORD B

Concerning the Golden Calf

Many esotericists think that they are not advancing on the esoteric path. They would like to be well versed† in their exercises, and do not know why they are hindered in their progress. Because it is difficult to capture in today's words and concepts what is to be said, I will now place an imagination before your souls that all mystery students had to experience. Imagine Moses as your teacher and master (the entire imagination as a vision)—Moses, who answers your question with a stern tone as to why you are not advancing faster, since you have such great longing to penetrate into the spiritual world (in silence one should expect the answer, which is very often not given in the sense in which the questioner intended it): "First you must burn the golden calf." In the same moment, imagine a golden calf placed next to Moses, then fire, which Moses calls forth from the earth, and that the golden calf is burning so that nothing remains except pulverized dust. Then imagine further that Moses stirs this dust into water and gives it to the meditating people to drink.

It has often been mentioned that human beings remember back only to a certain point in childhood. Our parents and siblings have told us what happened before this point in time, but we ourselves know nothing about it because the "I" was not yet in us, but rather worked from outside. Basically speaking, the "I" is just the sum of all previous memories. Therefore I am speaking of the time of your childhood that lies before your memory. Imagine how you were as a child, and put this child in the place of the golden calf. Then allow Moses again to call forth fire from the earth, which then burns and consumes the child. Although exoteric students in a time not too far in the past would have taken up such an imagination only with their feelings, today we must add an explanation in order to understand it. Much of what should now be said may sound harsh and wounding; but there need to be strong, gruesome pictures that call forth a strong reaction in the soul if we are to advance in our esoteric life.

There are four feelings that accompany these thoughts, which this imagination must call forth in our souls.

The first thought-feeling must be that we admit to ourselves that until now we really have worshipped the golden calf. Our own self as we have developed ourselves physically, this self is what we have been worshipping. Our memories of the past stand under the influence of Lucifer. What we call our memory we owe to Lucifer. Lucifer works in all that we have become, also through incarnations or through inheritance. If the purely spiritual is to once again attain dominion within us, our sheaths must be burned, must be pulverized to dust and ashes.

The second thought-feeling is that all that we see and feel of ourselves externally signifies nothing more than a little dust; and not the kind of dust from which something new can be formed; but rather like a little pile of dust lying on the street. This is how we should feel our personality. All sympathy and antipathy must stop. Indeed, I do not need to show this externally. I do not have to immediately embrace someone whom I do not particularly love! That would be a falsehood. Inwardly, though, we should greet everyone the same way.

Third, we should awaken the feeling within ourselves that everything around us is only maya. Our physical body and also our astral and etheric bodies are maya, or mere appearance; the purely spiritual that stands behind it is the "I." The nose that has grown with us is maya; the hand is maya. We only gain the correct standpoint when we think of them as something that really does not concern us, as an instrument like any other: a hammer, and so forth. Everything around us is maya, is a lie. And the picture we have of ourselves in childhood before memory begins is a double lie: first of all, everything is maya, and secondly, we cannot remember that time anyway. From this knowledge, that everything is maya, should come the certainty that a spiritual world stands behind everything, that everything significant about us has been formed in us by high spiritual personalities (beings).

And finally, the fourth thought-feeling should be this: everything that we have achieved in our previous incarnations also must be destroyed. Our own personality, our own "I," which has been totally pulverized to dust and entirely dissolved in water, we must drink. Then, of course, desolation and emptiness will arise in the soul, which longs to depart from the earthly into peace and rest, into Nirvana. A Buddhist remains standing here, but we know that the emptiness should be filled, and can be through the Christ impulse, which is our higher self, our higher "I" that should lead us up into the spiritual world again. This emptiness will always be recognized by a feeling of most devoted, deepest piety with respect to spiritual worlds. One should want nothing for oneself, but rather one should feel oneself as God's servant on earth, as a messenger from spiritual worlds.

Recall this story of the golden calf frequently; place it before your soul. If it had not occurred, then Christ Jesus could not have come forth from the Hebrew people. Not every day, but every three weeks for a quarter-hour; and not only two or three times and then think that is enough, but rather again and again remember this imagination. Then you will realize soon enough the cause of your not having advanced.

Esotericists on the path who want to turn back prove thereby their unworthiness and weakness. Such esotericists set themselves in contradiction to the feelings that filled their souls when they stepped onto the esoteric path. It is, nevertheless, better for them to turn back than to drag this falsehood through their entire lives.

* * *

Record C

Many will find that they are not really advancing in their meditations. Today I will give you a meditation that helps one to progress, when used frequently. Imagine the leader on the esoteric path in the form of Moses. He says to us, "You long to know why you are not advancing." He shows us the golden calf and says, "For this reason you are not advancing, because you worship the golden calf." He causes a fire to flame up around the golden calf and burn it up, then he grinds the ashes into dust, spreads them over the water, and then gives us this water to drink. Then he says, "Only now will you make progress."

Certain thoughts must arise in response to this story. We must remember back to childhood, to the time before our memory or our consciousness of self, which we owe to Lucifer, were present. All that we were at that time, before the onset of memory, was created by spiritual forces as a result of previous incarnations. There then appears before our inner eye, in place of the golden calf, the child that we ourselves were.

And the same thing happens: flames flare up and consume it in fire. It is ground to dust which is then strewn over water and given to us to drink. Moses then says to us with implacable sternness, "You yourself are the golden calf that you worship." Now recognize that the figure of the child (although you ultimately cannot imagine it for you do not know it, have never seen it) is maya, doubly maya. It is the kind of maya that is matter in every form that you meet it in the sense world; for that which holds matter together, the spiritual, you do not know. This is the case with respect to the etheric body and astral body, for that which you know about yourself is memory to you, and this is Lucifer, is maya. So too, is everything that is sympathy and antipathy, that you know about your own "I," yourself, maya.

All of this must be consumed in fire, must become nothing, if you want to recognize it. And you must become as indifferent to it as you are to the dust in the street that you walk by. When thus nothing remains of you more than a husk, and within a great emptiness, then you must fill it with the Christ being. That is what drinking the water means. When the dust is dissolved by the Christ being you will win back your sheaths; but each sheath must appear to you as something outside you;, an instrument only, like a hammer in your hand. You must be to yourself nothing more than an instrument for the work and deeds of the spiritual world.

* * *

Esoteric Lesson
HELSINKI (HELSINGFORS), APRIL 5, 1912

Notes from Else Kriecheldorff.

Purifying the blood: Achieves independence of mind.
Purifying lymph: Clear thoughts.
Purifying chyle: Noble feelings.
Purifying flow in nerves from the senses: Pure, honest intentions.

How we meditate is essential; what we meditate is less essential. The further we come, the greater the danger that impure spirits attempt to settle into us. There is an occult method to fight this. For a moment we must imagine the staff of Aaron (with a black and white snake wound around it).† Simply staring at this picture is, of course, not sufficient; on the other hand, we should not speculate about it for very long, since this would draw us out of the meditation. As we come further, the premature appearance of a feeling can become an obstacle. We can feel ourselves, so to speak, divided up into the very different beings that worked on us in earlier times.

We must very carefully protect ourselves from devoting ourselves to these feelings too soon. Again adversarial spirits interfere, spirits that want to draw us entirely to themselves; and instead of winding up in the world of the spirit, we land in the world of illusions. An effective occult means of fighting against this is the imagination of the black cross with seven red roses. From the cross (death) arises new life.

* * *

A person should read one book twenty-five times, rather than five books five times. When we lift ourselves up to the hierarchies we are taken hold of by them. In the final analysis, self-greed is developed unless love for all beings balances it out. When we are taken hold of, even by the best higher beings, we lose ourselves unless we develop courage and selflessness. Filled with and permeated by the Christ-principle, we can venture the jump over the abyss. Spiritual beings take hold of us and use us in order to work in the world, just as we use our eyes.

* * *

Something in the human being is drawn together and is hardened when thinking of the moon. One feels the spiritual working on one when looking at the sun. Sunrays are the deeds of high-standing spiritual beings. They come about (through deeds); that is, the effects are their deeds.

* * *

Development of the sixteen-petalled lotus flower (Distributed over the weekdays):†

1. The way in which one acquires ideas
2. Affects decisions
3. Speech must be rich in content
4. Regulating external actions
5. The arrangement of the whole
6. The striving of the human being
7. The striving to learn from life
8. Looking within ourselves

We must imagine the higher "I," or self, so that this, our higher self, observes our ordinary self as an object standing opposite us.

Esoteric Lesson

HELSINKI (HELSINGFORS), APRIL 14, 1912

Manuscript from an unknown person (Vreede Collection).

Those who begin with exoteric exercises should not expect that visions will immediately appear before them. It certainly could happen, but it is neither usual nor desirable. The normal course is that the feeling and thought world of the esoteric student should be brought first into harmony with the spiritual world. Only when this has happened, and the esoteric students feel in harmony with the ocean of the spiritual world, will they see figures of light arising out of this world, which are then formed into specific shapes.

However, it can happen that esotericists immediately begin to experience visions. These are then a consequence of their previous lives when they were either esotericists or were influenced by a religion that worked with ceremonies, rituals, or *cultus*, as was the case with all ancient religions. Then the visions are something atavistic and are a great danger because they appear with violence and overwhelm the esotericist, for they arose without the individual's involvement. For this reason it is better if they do not appear. Esotericists should rather pay attention to the changes that take place in their souls. Last time I already spoke about one of these changes: that through the exercises thoughts become so much more powerful and therefore influence other people so much more. For this reason, if they are not entirely pure and correct, they are taken away from us by the Guardian of the Threshold and we are led to unconsciousness, so that we do not thereby injure others and ourselves. The effects that come from the exercises will now be described in a somewhat different way.

The first is that thoughts become looser; that is, while earlier a specific thought would immediately follow a specific perception, and this thought was connected to another thought by itself, now this does not happen the same way. Esotericists do not feel so certain and are no longer as quick in their judgments and in the connections they make between thoughts. What earlier gave them certainty in their thoughts and judgments was what came from their education, from social conditions, environment; that is, from the angels, archangels, and spirits of personality, which work in all aspects of culture.

We are gradually being released from this guidance. Our angel, our leader, no longer inspires us directly and unconsciously with thoughts and judgments. However, if this loosening of thoughts for human beings goes too far, then it could become dangerous. For this reason, the Guardian of the Threshold intervenes and hinders the progress of this development. The means to prevent this, on the other hand, is the acquisition of a love of truth so absolute that not even in one's thoughts can anything arise that contains the possibility that it might be untrue.

The second effect that comes from the exercises concerns our feelings and will impulses. Esotericists also see these changing; they feel that they rule over these impulses less than before. If they were perhaps cautious in the past, they now sense how a feeling or a will impulse immediately arises in them in reaction to something that affects them. This too must not be allowed to go too far; if that happens, then for our sake the Guardian of the Threshold does not allow us to go on into the spiritual world.

The third effect is that the false attitudes that an esotericist can develop not only take hold of his or her soul, but also work into the physical body. If a perversity unconsciously continues to work in the ground of the soul, it becomes much more destructive than if it were to express itself in an illness that could be healed with physical means. For this reason, in these cases the Guardian of the Threshold assigns some minor illness to us, which we should regard as a sign, a warning, concerning what is working in our soul. In a well-guided esoteric development, this must not be allowed to become a serious illness; otherwise, the esotericist would be too strongly assaulted. In ancient times when souls were more robust, and only people with much inner strength and courage for life were accepted to become esoteric students, these dangers were also greater, and often became extreme. That is, the loosening of thoughts proceeded as far as madness, destruction; and the illnesses led to death. This is what is expressed in the tale from the ancient Hebrew mysteries, which was given to every esotericist as a warning: the tale of the four rabbis who sought to enter "the garden of joy." The first became mad, the second destroyed everything through his raving madness, the third died, and the fourth alone was admitted and entered the spiritual world.†

Esoteric Lesson

BERLIN, APRIL 24, 1912

Record A: Manuscript from Rudolf Meyer; Record B: Anonymous Manuscript (Vreede collection); Record C: Manuscript from Louise Clason; Record D: Manuscript from Nelly Lichtenberg.

RECORD A

In the previous lesson[†] an imagination was placed before our souls that released forces in our souls in its own way and can be a help to us on our esoteric path.

Today two inspiring thoughts are to be placed before your soul that can be effective in the same way. That is what is essential in such thoughts, such questions: that we allow them to rest awhile in our souls, that we allow them to speak to us without our touching them.

Exoterically we have spent enough time with these thoughts (admittedly in a very different sense), so that they have led people to the most impossible commentaries and disputations. Considered esoterically, they are a help for esoteric students.

The first of these inspiring thoughts is that of "the motherless human being," or better expressed, "the motherless being of a human being," which is called Adam in the ancient biblical text. All that comes to meet us as human beings is unthinkable without being born of a mother. The only motherless human being is Adam. Only the father-forces were at work in him. Of course, we must not imagine Adam as a physical-sensible being, for the physical conditions of today were not present at that time on planet earth when Jahveh created the first earth-being in his etheric body; and indeed he created him out of the substances of planet earth, just as this is indicated in the Bible. These substances are still today present in every human being, so that we can say Jahveh is also our father; and the planet is the mother of us all. The forces of the father then still continue to work in human beings; they are a force bound to the earth; a planetary force. They work in everything that is on the earth; thus also in human beings. It is not just the forces of the mother that continue to work on the child after conception, but also the forces of the father. They proceed from the earth, guided by the father to the child, and create up-building forces that are present in their strongest effects up to the thirty-third year of life.

Let us be clear. What actually happens when a new human being is born? The mother bears one part in herself, but the other part is suprasensory and invisible and is connected to the father. Put yourself meditatively into this thought of a motherless human being; try to take hold of this thought purely spiritually and place right next to it a second image: that of the fatherless Christ.

If the planetary forces coming from the father are predominantly [active] until the Mystery of Golgotha, then from this point in time onward the forces of the cosmos, the mother forces, are added. We know that this most important of all earthly events falls in the fourth cultural epoch of post-Atlantean times. Preceding it was the Egyptian cultural epoch, in which the Egyptian mysteries of the Isis *cultus* were cultivated in their highest perfection. The Egyptians revered the forces of nature that are expressed in all minerals, plants, and animals. But the Egyptian soul, full of sadness, full of the deepest sorrow, looked at the human being and said to itself that the human being was not actually conscious of these nature forces, for this reason the human being portrayed Isis as veiled, and it was said that no mortal was ever allowed to lift the veil in order to reach Isis. What does this mean? Nothing more than that the goddess did not dwell in the physical world, but rather in the astral world, and that only those who have stepped through the portal of death can recognize and know her.† No one alive could lift her veil. This means that the effects of the forces of Isis were not available to the living.

And what were these Isis forces? They were the pure forces of the mother, which before the Mystery of Golgotha were available to human beings only in the spiritual world; that is, when they had walked through the gate of death.

Knowledge of this was present in the Egyptian mysteries. Above the picture of Isis stood the words, "I am the I am, who I was, who I will be"; the same *"Ejeh asher ejeh"* that was once spoken to Moses from the burning bush. The Egyptian soul could only look with a foreshadowing perception toward the Mystery of Golgotha through which the pure mother-forces were to become active also for living human beings. Only when Christ Jesus, the fatherless human being, had united completely with the earth when he crossed the threshold of death, only from this time on can the pure forces of the mother (the forces from the cosmos) work within human beings on the earth. Let modern scholars smile when they look with their narrow-minded perspective at the animal worship of the Egyptians. We can only be filled with the deepest reverence, for we know that behind their worship was hidden the veneration of these nature forces that were closed to human beings. And with profound admiration we look at the lofty wisdom that lay under all these mysteries.

Let us ask what the effect is of these two forces in the human being. The forces of the father, which are from the earth, and are guided to the child through the detour of the father, work constructively bringing their forces until the thirty-third year. Although if the forces that strive downward, the forces of the mother, are already at work in the human being, the father-forces, nevertheless, are the stronger until this point in time. If only the forces that strive downward (the forces of Christ) would predominate in human beings, then they would not incarnate on the earth. If, on the other hand, only the forces that strive upward, the planetary forces, would predominate, then they would always live on the earth, then there would be no death.

That which was Isis in the Egyptian mysteries, this holy center of forces, is presented to us in Christianity as the Mary-Sophia of John's Gospel. The union of the rising and descending forces that occurred at the Mystery of Golgotha first made it possible that the human being can now also feel the mother-forces between birth and death. Christ Jesus could not have become any older than thirty three-years. From the point of view of occultists, at thirty-three years of age all human beings have actually reached the point that they are carrying their body as a corpse around with them. Of course, the effects of these forces and the changes they bring do not appear all at once, but rather occur gradually. Both (also the mother-forces) are in the human being from the start, but the father-forces predominate; that is, the constructive, up-building forces of the father.

In this time of the father-forces, we live life as it is karmically determined by our previous lives. However, from the time that the dying-down forces, the mother forces, predominate, we create through these spiritual forces what we will be able to live out only in the next life; that is, the karma of our next lifetime.

The father forces, or the constructive nature forces, work in us without our involvement; on the other hand, we ourselves must work and strive in the spiritual realm so that the mother forces become conscious within us. We must become conscious of these sublime, lofty forces, for they are the power that flows directly from Christ into us.

Again, as so often happens, the significance of the Rosicrucian verse is revealed to us in a *foreboding* of its depths: We are born out of the divine: *Ex Deo nascimur.* The power of Adam, of the motherless child, works in a constructive way to maintain the physical body; on the other hand, since the Mystery of Golgotha the fatherless human being is effective: Christ Jesus, the dying power, the power that leads to the dying of the physical body here on earth that awakens the spiritual life to the extent that we consciously devote ourselves to it. "In Christ we die"; that is, we die with all our physical concepts to the lower self that was built up in us during the time that the Adam forces were active in us. Thus the last sentence of the Rosicrucian verse is brought to a true experience: "In the Holy Spirit we are reborn."

* * *

Record B

An aid to understanding what was given here the last time† can be added. It consists of two mighty pictures, concerning which unfortunately there has been much debate in the evolution of humanity.

The first picture is that of the motherless human being. In the Bible it is indicated to us in the picture of Adam, who did indeed have a father but no mother. The father formed him out of the dust of the earth, that means out of forces that are contained in the earth. Thus there is something in every human being that is not visible, that is a system of forces that belongs to the earth, that is not directly given by the cooperation between the sexes or through inheritance; but rather, it is what the divine father gives to him or her on the detour path of the fatherly organism. Father and mother both give something suprasensory, except that what comes through the mother is bound to the organism of her body, while what comes through the father (on the detour through the fatherly organism) will come directly out of the forces of the earth. Only this last was present in Adam; he was the motherless human being. We have the opposite of this in the fatherless Christ, or Christ Jesus. Already in the third post-Atlantean epoch, which preceded the appearance of Christ, we find the figure of Isis, which reminds us of the appearance of the Madonna, but is nevertheless different. It is the veiled Isis, concerning whom the Egyptians felt: "No mortal has ever lifted her veil." That means during life no human being can reach what Isis expresses. She represents the spiritual forces that have not yet descended to the earth, which can only be found in spiritual worlds. Egyptians saw these heavenly forces at work in the kingdoms of nature around them (therefore, the worship of animals); but they knew that these forces worked only after death. Only then can human beings participate in these forces that belong to heaven. In the fourth post-Atlantean epoch, forces descended into humanity that had never before worked into a human being. And even if we cannot say that Sophia-Maria, the mother of Christ Jesus, was Isis; nevertheless, she represents Isis, because in her for the first time, and then in other people, heavenly forces worked on earth, which since that time unite with the fatherly forces coming from the earth with the help of the motherly organism. Thus, what the Egyptians felt would be reachable only after death has since that time come to earth. Thus has the kingdom of heaven come to earth, and the veil of Isis can be lifted through those who have the power of Christ within them. This is the resurrection of the third epoch in the fifth.

Theosophists can understand this if they pay attention to the dichotomy in human nature. There are two kinds of forces working in human nature: descending and ascending. If only the first kind existed in human beings, they would never be able to descend to earth; they would have to remain in the spiritual world. If only the ascending forces were in them, they would never be able to leave the physical world once they had arrived. (An example of the descending forces appearing alone is seen in the group souls of animals; for this reason, they cannot descend to the physical plane.) Both of these forces are at work in the human being, indeed, in such a way that at first the ascending forces predominate. This goes until approximately the thirty-third or thirty-fifth year, then the descending forces predominate. This is also the reason why Christ had to die in his thirty-third year: the descending forces worked in him; those of heaven that could no longer hold him on earth. The ascending forces were at work in Adam, but, of course, not these alone; so too, in the human being both forces are also present, but one kind of force predominates over the other. Thus at first in the evolution of humanity ascending forces are revealed in Adam, the earthly forces that are given to Adam from the divine Father; and then the descending forces in Christ, the fatherless human being. Until our thirty-third year we carry the forces of Adam in us; by the thirty-third year, we have developed everything that the earth can give us. Then we have everything within us that will be given back to the earth—fire. What we still develop after this, happens through the power of Christ, which constantly increases as our body deteriorates.

It is the Buddha-thought that wants to break the connection with the earth, that wants to seek heavenly forces in a sphere outside the earth. It is the Christ-thought that wants to experience these forces here on the earth. Thus we can feel that Adam must die in us so that Christ can live in us. This is expressed in another way by our verse:

> *Ex Deo nascimur.*
> *In Christo morimur.*
> *Per Spiritum Sanctum reviviscimus.*

* * *

Record C

Aside from the last exercise, or combined with it, there are two thoughts that can bring an esotericist further. One is the thought of motherless Adam, who was created by the divine Father-principle, by Jahveh. The forces that are the ascending forces, the forces that work in the physical body and come from the earth, the human being receives by means of a detour through the fatherly part of the body; these forces work until the middle of a person's life by building up the body, approximately until the thirty-fifth year. If human beings had only this power then they would never leave the earth at death. The other forces, which we get from our mother, come from the spiritual-soul world, from out of the cosmos, and these are the destructive forces. If these forces were the only forces working in us, we would never even be able to be born on the earth. This is the fatherless Christ. Before the Christian era these forces did not flow into humanity yet they worked on human beings only in the time between death and a new birth; they were present on earth only in the three lower kingdoms. This the Egyptians knew: that the Isis-power could certainly be found in the mineral, plant, and animal kingdoms. There they could be found, but not in human beings between birth and death. Hence the profound meaning of the Egyptian's animal gods. For the first time these forces flowed through the virgin Sophia-Maria into Jesus of Nazareth. For this reason, Jesus Christ had to die when he was thirty-three years old, because the destructive forces began to work, because the Adam forces were present in him in such a weakened state and the Christ-force was so strong that he could not stay on the earth any longer. We are born from God with the forces of Adam; we die in Christ, and we hope to one day be born again through the Holy Spirit.

* * *

Record D

Every Sunday at 9:00 am in the morning: In the spirit of Humanity I feel myself united with all esotericists.

Esoteric Lesson
COLOGNE, MAY 9, 1912

Record A: Notes from Marie Steiner; Record B; Manuscript from Alice Kinkel.

RECORD A

Through diligent work with esoteric exercises such as they are described in the book *How to Know Higher Worlds*† and other works, we attain progress in spiritual knowledge and an intensification of spiritual forces. However, we must observe various practical tips that further us.

A healthy state of exhaustion need not hinder us in concentrating and carrying out our meditations. On the contrary, nature here takes over some of the task because it dampens the external sense organs and reduces our ability to absorb things from the world of the senses. The goal is to see without the physical eyes, to hear without physical ears, and to think without a physical brain. We can illuminate and warm our being with the light-filled thoughts of meditation precisely in a state of physical exhaustion.

Abstinence from alcohol is necessary because it works from outside on the blood, interfering with our "I," which is unfolding its own activity in the blood. Meditation draws our spirit upward, loosens the connection with the physical body. Alcohol draws it down and binds it to the body.

Eating meat makes the spirit heavy with earth and binds it to the physical; it gives the body the opportunity to hang on to the spirit. Vegetarian food confronts the body with greater challenges, so it is busy and cannot hinder the spirit in its work.

What else is achieved through abstinence from meat, especially from eating fish?†

What is bad about eating meat is the enduring effect of causing pain to and killing animals. These martyred animals then return again in the form of beings that turn their power against the bodies of the descendants of those who once killed them. Bacteria are reincarnated animals that were tortured, killed, and eaten.†

Changes occur in esotericists through their exercises; these are changes that we must pay attention to if injury is to be avoided. There are four points that must be considered in this regard.

First of all, the intellect is changed; the train of thought becomes different; so too, judgment and memory. It becomes difficult for esotericists to explain to an ordinary person all the possible logical and everyday reasons for their actions. Such reasons are not at all necessary because in the decisive moment a true esotericist knows what is right to do. However, if we do not pull ourselves together, and if we neglect our exercise for thought control, then it can happen to us that our thoughts are confused.

There are immature people who force their esoteric development and achieve a certain power over other people, but at the last moment the bolt is slammed shut before they can instigate greater damage.

Second, our demeanor, the way in which we present ourselves, speak, and our gestures, become different. Here we must have ourselves under control, so that our nervous system does not get out of control and we start all kinds of things that are not allowed.

Third, the physical body must not be injured by a forced, greedy tempo in esoteric development; otherwise, in some cases an acute illness occurs, which is, however, curable and beneficial for the person involved. In the Hebrew mysteries there is a saying: Four seek the path through the gate of the temple, but only one gets through. Only one develops himself in a normal way, through especially consistent and patient action, and reaches the goal. The others who force their esoteric development are injured. From this we see the need for consistent execution of the auxiliary exercises that harmonize and consolidate the entire being of a human being. There is, in abundance, powerful content for meditations, especially in the Bible. There are, for example, the words spoken by God in the six days of creation in Genesis; the life of Moses with its many lofty moments, for example, the appearance of Yahweh in the burning bush†; the stories from the Gospels; the prologue to John's Gospel; and words such as "I am the Light of the World"†; and many others. Such an especially effective content is in Paul's first letter to Timothy, chapter 3, verse 16 in the following translation:

> *The mystery of God's path can be known.*
> *He who was manifested in the flesh,*
> *Whose being is, however, spiritual,*
> *Who is fully knowable to the angels only,*
> *Nevertheless, who could be preached to the nations,*
> *Who has life in the faith of the world,*
> *He is raised to the sphere of the Spirits of Wisdom.*

What the Bodhisattvas could give to humankind was inspired by the spirits of wisdom. The least of that which radiated from Christ came from the sphere of the hierarchy of the spirits of movement.† Christ himself stands above all the hierarchies—he belongs to the Trinity.

* * *

RECORD B

Through esoteric exercises we want to acquire progress in spiritual knowledge and an intensification of our spiritual forces. We must however, observe various practical indications that will further us in this esoteric striving.

> 1. Meditating with great exertion of will and concentration is made necessary by a healthy state of fatigue, which is suitable and useful for this purpose. Nature relieves us of having to carry out one part of the task, since it deadens the external sense organs and diminishes our ability to take up input from the sense world. The goal is, of course, to see without physical eyes, to hear without physical ears, and to think without a physical brain. It is precisely when we are in a state of exhaustion that we can illuminate and warm our being with light-filled thoughts in meditation.

2. Abstinence from alcohol is necessary because it works from the outside upon the "I," which lives in the blood where it expresses itself and unfolds itself. Meditation pulls the spirit upward and loosens the connection with the physical body. Alcohol pulls the spirit downward and hardens and fixes it in the physical body.
3. What effect does abstaining from eating meat, especially fish, have? What is bad about eating meat is the lasting effects of causing pain and of killing the animal. These martyred animals return again in the form of beings that turn their power against the bodies of the descendents of those who killed them. Bacteria are the reincarnated, tortured, killed, and eaten animals. Besides, eating meat makes the spirit "earth-heavy" and binds it to the physical, and gives the body the opportunity to hang on to the spirit. Vegetarian food places a greater demand upon the physical body, so that it is occupied and does not hinder the spirit.

Through the exercises there are changes that take place in esotericists in their entire being; they must pay attention to these changes or injury can result. There are four points that come into consideration:

1. There are changes that take place in the intellect; the train of thoughts becomes different, so too judgment and memory. It gets difficult for esotericists to explain their actions logically and with ordinary reason to everyday people. Such logical reasons are not at all necessary, because in the decisive moment esotericists know what the right thing to do is; they read it right out of the Akashic Chronicle, so to speak. If esotericists do not pull themselves together, if they are lazy in carrying out the thought control exercise, then it can happen to them that their thoughts get confused. There are immature people who force their esoteric development; however, at the decisive moment the gates are shut before they can do too much damage; then they become feeble-minded.
2. The attitude, the demeanor, the way in which they speak, gesture, and act becomes different with esotericists. Here they must have themselves in hand, so that the nervous system does

not break down, and then they do all kinds of impermissible things.
3. The physical body must not be allowed to be injured through a forced, greedy tempo in esoteric development; otherwise, in some circumstances an acute illness will appear, which will be curable and a warning to the one befallen. In the ancient Hebrew mysteries it was said: Four seek the way through the gate into the temple, but only one reaches it! Only the one who develops properly, through especially consistent and patient work, reaches the goal. Concerning the other three, who forced their esoteric development, the first becomes insane, the second wreaks moral devastation, and the third dies.

From this we see the necessity for consistent work on the auxiliary exercises, which harmonize and consolidate one's whole being.

There are valuable and powerful contents for meditations in abundance, especially in the Bible: for example, in the words of creation concerning the six days of creation in Genesis; or in the life of Moses with its many lofty moments, such as the appearance of Jahveh in the burning bush. The stories in the Gospels are also content for meditation: the beginning of John's Gospel or words such as "I am the light of the world," and many others. One such especially effective passage is found in First Timothy 3:16 in the following translation. Add it to your meditations.

> *The mystery of God's path can be known.*
> *He who was manifested in the flesh,*
> *Whose being is, however, spiritual,*
> *Who is fully knowable to the angels only,*
> *Nevertheless, who could be preached to the nations,*
> *Who has life in the faith of the world,*
> *He is raised to the sphere of the Spirits of Wisdom.*

What the Bodhisattvas could give to humanity was inspired by the spirits of wisdom. The least of what radiated from Christ came from the sphere of the hierarchy of the spirits of wisdom. Christ himself stands above all the hierarchies—he belongs to the Trinity.

So that all esotericists can find a connection to the esoteric teacher, and so that those who only seldom have an opportunity to hear and speak to Dr. Steiner can also participate, this was said:

Every Sunday morning at 9:00 a.m. you should meditate on the sentence: "In the spirit of humanity I feel myself united with all esotericists."

Esoteric Lesson
NORRKÖPING, MAY 30, 1912

Shorthand report from Franz Seiler.

Introductory words were spoken in memory of Frau Danielsson,† who had died a few months ago. There was an indication that her soul in the bright moments in the spiritual world felt united with those who strove for the same things; and that the streams of love sent to her from here provided her with these light-filled moments. It was said that she works in the interests of theosophical matters as an angel who creates a connection between the theosophists in the north and those in middle Europe.

1. The prayer of the day, Thursday, "Great encompassing spirit…"
2. (nothing entered)
3. Concerning the individual, concerning the feeling of shame.
4. Concerning the result that we should derive from this. We should regard all of this as concerning our own personality. Portrayal of our own being.
5. Concerning feeling one's own being as if a vessel filled with water were warmed by an inner point, and one felt this water in such a way as if one were feeling the water oneself.
6. How this warmth must then permeate every part of the human being.
7. The feelings that are to be connected with the exercises.
8. The breathing process is to be used as a support for the esoteric training, so too, the avoidance of alcohol and a vegetarian life.
9. (nothing entered)
10. Constantly growing of one's spiritual being; expansion over the cosmos.
11. (nothing entered)
12. Concerning the feeling of devotion and reverence.

13. (nothing entered)
14. Two forces.
15. …angel…demons.
16. …Christ.

1. How esoteric training proceeds. Concerning visions.
2. Symptoms that esoteric training is advancing correctly. Fear, instability, loss of ground under one's feet.
3. Feelings that must appear on the path. Feeling of shame…
4. Feelings that must not appear on the path. Egotism…
5. The opposing forces that a student must stand up to.

What must appear as a result of esoteric exercises

Those who carry out the exercises regularly and properly will sooner or later note that certain effects appear. Now, the effects can be either right or wrong. In order to judge which of these the case is, we look for certain symptoms or side effects. If these specific side effects appear, then the progress is proper; even if no visions, pictures, colors, or light-effects appear. Whether these first appear is karma. The teacher can only show the way, but not remove the hindrances.

It is often a hindrance to all progress precisely when a human soul wishes for visions and appearances. It is also a mistake for people to be satisfied with visions when they have them, and no longer to want to strive.

At first one feels that something has become alive within oneself. This feeling is as if we were in a vessel of water; as if in its middle there were a spring of warmth that flows through the water. We must then feel this warmth with our whole being.

Esoteric Lesson

OSLO (KRISTIANIA), JUNE 7, 1912

Record A: Manuscript from Vrauke Titringh; Record B: Notes from the collection of Elisabeth Vreede; Record C: Stenographic notes from Franz Seiler.

RECORD A

Why are you here? From whence comes the urge to know esoteric things? Approximately 4,000 years ago, that is, before the Mystery of Golgotha, the etheric body enlivened the physical body in such a way that there were forces left over, in such a way that not all the etheric body's forces were used to permeate the physical body. And one turned to esotericism with these extra forces; one turned to the spiritual worlds. Then about 3,000 years ago, all etheric bodies were sunk down into the physical body, especially in Greece; and those who were most highly developed in the physical realm felt the spiritual world to be like a kingdom of shadows. Now, however, the physical body no longer absorbs all the forces of the etheric body. It sends them back; it is withering, for we are more than half-way through earth evolution, and we can live only in the spiritual world through these forces that the physical body can no longer absorb.

And you who have felt this urge toward esotericism, for whom a purely physical life and knowledge is not enough, you have felt these unused forces within you; they have driven you to seek the esoteric life.

What is the difference between esoteric and exoteric? In exotericism we receive communications that are obtained from esotericism as nourishment for our souls. In esotericism we strive to see into the worlds from which these communications are obtained.

It is not merely communications that are given here, but also advice, which flows forth from spiritual inspiration. These are not merely words, concepts, ideals; but rather words, concepts, ideals that are permeated with life, with seeds of life that are implanted into our etheric forces and should blossom there; they are realities. They are tested again and again by those whom we call the Masters of Wisdom and Harmony of Feelings.

Esotericism is a source of life, of forces that flood through the world, and should also flow through us. For this reason Sundays at 9 [o'clock].†

When we begin our exercises, it is of the greatest importance that we first create inner peace. This can be achieved through patience. The only thing that we have to battle is the thought, "I am not yet achieving it." This thought we should reject as a temptation. No matter how long it takes, the time will come when the horizon of our thoughts is clear; if only we reject, with all the strength of which our will is capable, the thoughts and sense impressions that distract us. We must allow the meditations and symbols to live within us energetically and powerfully; we should not form thoughts about them, but experience them as an inner light. They must take hold of us with power, for they are taken from the unspeakable word that has the power to create. This is the *Mahavach* of the Indians; it is inspiration from the word that sounds through the spiritual world; it should shine in us like an inner sun. (Changes in our life situation.)

Then we must create an inner emptiness of everything that rises up out of memory. Even if it is theosophical content, it must be wiped away, suppressed, and we must only wait for what can rise up in our souls, either something entirely new that we never before suspected or heard or a living vision of occult facts that we received in exoteric life. What we are now told we could find out for ourselves, however, only after twenty-five incarnations. We have the duty to work together with the current state of human evolution as we shorten the path as much as possible.

* * *

RECORD B

What is imparted exoterically has been won esoterically. During esoteric gatherings advice can be given that can become sources of power for the human being.

Four thousand years ago there was still an excess of etheric forces that were not needed in the physical body. This excess of energy ended in the Roman-Greek age. Again, there is now a portion of our etheric forces that does not have access to our physical bodies—that is actually repelled by the physical body and from the physical world. In order to get access to this portion of the etheric body, we have our meditations, concentration, or contemplation as an advice-giver. This is very important. But no less important is the need also to develop our morality. For this purpose we have the auxiliary exercises. Those who faithfully practice them will notice that they begin to develop morality. What is involved is connecting the streams: the one that comes from outside with the one in one's own body.

The astral body is difficult to overcome, but it is possible. Patience is the only means of doing so. Our motto should be, "Steady drops hollow out the stone." Consistent, steady meditations conquer for us the spiritual world, sooner or later, according to our karma. At first our experience is very delicate, so that we barely notice it. Only when an exercise is frequently repeated does the experience gradually appear with greater power.

The urge to develop oneself is met through those who can give the teachings and the meditations. If we wanted to reject all that, and develop everything out of ourselves, then perhaps twenty to twenty-five incarnations would be necessary for this purpose.

The meditation on "the unrevealed light," which was spoken of in the lecture cycle, is important; even more important is the result that can then appear.[†] One drops the content of the meditation, empties oneself completely, and then waits to see what comes. Now we know that we will experience something new, although we already knew it. Theosophical teachings appear as if new; they become luminous and penetrate our hearts. We feel it like a sun radiating light.

Today any child can understand the Pythagorean Theorem, but to discover it required a Pythagoras. So receive with gratitude what can accelerate your development, what gives you an advantage.

* * *

RECORD C

1. Prayer of the day, Friday.
2. Concerning exoteric and esoteric communications. Many things are now also already imparted exoterically, which at first were imparted only esoterically. It [esoteric communication] lies in the way we use these things. The esoteric life must be conducted in such a way that it is kept free from all external influences. Everything that can give us cares and worries and all the sensory things that could flow into our meditation must be kept far from our consciousness.
3. Three things, three means are put into our hands that should bring us to esoteric experience: concentration, meditation, and contemplation. What should occupy us in the spirit during these exercises is given to us in certain sentences that have already been tested for a long time. They are not mere words, but are also forces.
4. [No entry]
5. Concerning the theosophical knowledge that we should acquire. We can read in detail about the way these esoteric exercises must be carried out in the books *How to Know Higher Worlds* and *Outline of Esoteric Science*.
6. Concerning the various members of the human being: physical body, etheric body, astral body, and "I." Until now, the etheric body has worked on the physical body. But in earlier times there were hidden forces placed in the etheric body, which not every human being has been able to use. There remain a large number of forces that can be found in the etheric body that have not been used. Then a time came when these forces had to find a use for higher development; and finally these forces are being weakened more and more all the time, so that a time will come when the physical body will no longer be able to be ... [word in manuscript illegible]. The physical body will gradually dry up; in future incarnations we will have available for our use only increasingly worse bodies.

7. The life forces held back earlier are now used for esoteric development. Without this earlier savings, which is now available to us, it would be impossible for us to spiritually ascend now.
8. [No entry]
9. [No entry]
10. Concerning the life forces that have been gathered together.
11. [No entry]
12. Concerning the significance of the words of meditation that have been given to us. They have been brought down from spiritual worlds and contain genuine spiritual forces, forces of inspiration. When we use them properly and allow them to work in us, they open in our souls the possibility of unfolding the power of inspiration.
13. Then the forces that we need for our development stream to us out of spiritual worlds.
14. The chief demand on us, indeed the first, is that we produce a mood in our souls of inner calm. With all our might we must strive to learn how to achieve this inner calm. Everything that comes into our souls from the external world must be kept far away. It is indeed difficult, but we must achieve it. For all the disturbances that come from the world: pictures, sounds, feelings, and sensations confuse the soul, so that the spiritual is not perceptible to us.
15. If we achieve inner peace, then the spiritual world is also opened for us. Spiritual forces are already at work in many of us, but we just don't know it, because we simply do not have this inner calmness of soul and attention.
16. However, if we do have it, then spiritual experiences will flow to us out of the spiritual world.
17. [No entry]
18. When we can then perceive these forces within us, then at first we will have in us a [word illegible] world.
19. This world is summed up and concentrated within us.
20. It must, however, be expanded constantly wider and wider.
21. Then we will recognize and perceive in the light, and in other appearances, forms, shapes, streams.

22. [No entry]
23. Goal
24. Example of Pythagoras with his Pythagorean Theorem. It required the entire genius of Pythagoras to discover the theorem. Today it is taught in all schools, and boys and girls understand it.
25. It is similar with esoteric tasks. There are things that are brought down from spiritual worlds, and if we use them we will advance in our development, even if we do not at first notice it. It is true that one could arrive at the same goal even without use of these resources, but then it would require several incarnations in order to reach the goal, which we can reach in a single lifetime.
26. Thus we have the obligation to use these resources in order then, once advanced in development, to be useful to humankind.
27. [No entry]
28. [No entry]
29. The repetition of the exercises is what is most important. "Steady drops hollow the stone." Even if it is very difficult at first, we will increasingly discover that one great day we complete the exercises, and the result of this we will have before us.
30. Unity with all esotericists. For this reason, every morning at 9 o'clock we should immerse ourselves in the thought, "In the spirit of humanity I am united with all esotericists of the world." In this way we achieve harmony with all and experience a significant inflow of power.
31. The Rosicrucian verse.
32. The Rosicrucian conclusion: *In the Spirit lies the seed of my body...*

Esoteric Lesson

OSLO (KRISTIANIA), JUNE 9, 1912

Record A: Notes from the collection of Elisabeth Vreede; Record B: Manuscript from Vrauke Titringh.

RECORD A

Last time the inner reasons were explained why one is in the school. Today we will speak more about the external conditions.

The very first characteristic that a person needs is honesty; the will to be true. That the Theosophical Society is an effluence from the teachings of the Masters of Wisdom and Harmony of Feelings does not need to be explained any further; this stands firm.[†] Time does not allow for an explanation of "why." The evolution of humanity simply calls for it. But faith in a master must never be obligatory. Those who conscientiously follow the path will definitely be led to him; at least to the concept, to the faith, to the knowledge that he exists. However, if this were a condition from the outset, then it would be a lie. The existence of the master should be recognized out of inner reason. The truth can already be found from what can be conveyed exoterically; and thus the path can be found from the exoteric teachings to esoteric teachings. Any esoteric teachings that would require faith (faith in the masters) is not an esoteric teaching.

Teaching, but not only teaching, should be given to students. They should discover forces in themselves, forces that are already present. They should learn how to use them; they simply do not know that they have them.

For what purpose does the school exist? Advice is given in order to move ahead more quickly and easily because humanity needs this. It is however, unavoidable that in so doing an appeal is made to people's egotism. For this reason we have the auxiliary exercises, to fight what is added to the substance of one's ego. If these exercises are neglected, then inevitably ambition and vanity will appear in the student. We should see these in ourselves.

When we are together we should always watch ourselves, but always ascribe honesty and conscientiousness to everyone else. We should not ascribe ambition or pride to those who stand up and present something, but rather start with ourselves. Those who praise others to high heaven injure themselves and the others. We should always remain sober, and allow only pure reason to speak. From what is given exoterically we should let the truth speak within us; we should experience the truth out of it. When people dedicate themselves with all their power to meditation then the ability to think and memory disappear. This should happen. But in everyday life they should work all the better.

As a consequence of improperly carried out meditations, megalomania may appear, or the illusion that others are afflicted by delusions of grandeur. Or also a reduction in one's memory or reasoning powers altogether can happen. To oppose this, one should strive for honesty as a matter of duty. We should observe ourselves, study theosophy, and strive not only to be truthful ourselves, but we should investigate the truth in all that comes to meet us.

There is an old Jewish story: four rabbis wanted to enter the "garden of paradise." The first becomes insane, that is, loses his mind; the second goes mad, that is, no longer acts with measured reason; the third dies, he succumbs to illness (this can never happen with our exercises); the fourth alone can enter the garden. He achieves the "love of nature" as a good consequence of his efforts. This is not intended to be on a majestic scale, such as is found with people who can enjoy only mighty seas or high mountains, which would correspond to a striving for sensation, but rather, we experience this love also with the small and insignificant things. Those things are also the work of the gods. They are happy with their surroundings and carried it down into the physical world in order to make human beings happy. Such feelings are also at work in human beings. Everything that is in the human being will come out one day and become manifest, even if only in a later incarnation.

One should never reveal anything of the previous incarnations of leading personalities within one hundred years of their last death; if it happens here or there, then only as information imparted to a

trusted smaller circle, but never publicly as A. B[esant] is now doing.†
Personally I (Dr. Steiner) would much rather say: everything is good
and true within the Theosophical Society; but that would not be in
keeping with my obligation to truthfulness. When one comes into
contact with occult sects, it is always possible that occult progress
occurs in that sect. But the question is, how does it enter the spiritual
world? On the correct path one becomes increasingly humble; one
becomes more and more modest.

All that has been said here, you should let work on your feelings.
You should not act the same way one acts when one is carrying out
busywork; you should not be "busy" in the search for truth, but be
able to calmly wait for it.

* * *

Record B

There are conditions that must be met for an esoteric life, which are
fundamental; there are means to an end, and one such is truth—
not only to be truthful, but to seek truth. When the Theosophical
Society was founded, it originally stood under a very favorable star.
The time had come when it was necessary for the knowledge that
earlier had been imparted to small circles only, and was obtained
from sources that are not accessible to all of humanity, to be made
accessible to all of humanity. It would lead too far to discuss the inner
reasons for this change. Thus those who took it upon themselves to
impart this knowledge were placed in an uncommonly difficult situation. They had to convey the impulses that flow from such sources
to the requirement of our age, which allows only knowledge that is
understandable to the common man or woman. That is, on the one
hand, they have to make accessible to everyone, knowledge that until
now was not accessible; and on the other hand, they must meet the
modern condition that knowledge be universally accessible to every
human being. The impulses were conveyed by means of the familiar
three fundamental principles.† Let us consider these. The principles
should be observed in such a way that no one in the entire world

should be excluded from this movement. The first principle fulfills this requirement. To form the seed [of a universal brotherhood of humanity] that recognizes the universal humanity of everyone without distinction of nationality, race, color, or sex. Today everyone can subscribe to this. And how could we understand our fellow human beings unless we deepened ourselves in their way of thinking, their faith? Hence, the second principle. But (someone will say) the third principle excludes one type of human being: namely, materialists. But is this really the case? You see, the most important principle that permeates our movement like a leitmotif is: no confession, no faith supersedes the truth. We should strive for truth; we should investigate it. Now, no human being who has honestly researched the occult world has ever rejected it; this has never happened. Also materialists, if they research it, will not do that. However, if they refuse to do this research, well, then they are not seeking any truth but rather opinion, confession, faith. Does this principle exclude anyone? No, because everyone will agree that we should strive for truth. In none of these principles is faith made into a precondition, not even faith in the source from which this movement has flowed, and at this hour is still flowing. As firmly as any knowledge can be rooted in a soul, just that firmly is the knowledge rooted that is indicated as the Masters of Wisdom and Harmony of Feelings. But each one of you is free to agree with this or to reject it. If you go through the esoteric school you will find the way to them. But I would encumber the way for you; I would place the greatest hindrances imaginable in your path, if I were to demand an unconditional faith in such masters as a precondition for entrance into this school.

The least deceptive sign that every esoteric school has rooted within it, which shows on their foreheads, is that it demands no faith of any kind, not even in the master. Aside from esoteric schools, the only one master accessible to all of humanity is Christ. And no faith is demanded of him, either; for that is a matter for the intimate private life of every human being, and is based upon … [text missing]†

And if you ever encounter a pseudo-esoteric school, then find out right away if any particular faith is required at the outset; and if this is the case, then know that it has nothing to do with the truth. I will say this with even more precision so that you are very clear about what I am saying. When you encounter such a school, it is not rooted in those whom we know as the Masters of Wisdom and Harmony of Feelings.

I have tried to find words to express something that could touch you in a certain way. I would like to keep distant from this school all those who approach it only out of personal authority. The day before yesterday we discussed the inner reasons why one becomes an esotericist. What should be the external reason that makes you into an esotericist? Not support from authority, but testing with reason. You are a part of humanity. You can thank human evolution, human culture, that you can think in an ordered fashion and draw conclusions. Those who have studied occult truths in exoteric books and tested them using their reasoning abilities and found them to be true and reasonable, those people come here with the trust that additional truth will also be shown them. And no one should enter here with any other assumptions. However, when people enter here, they tear themselves out of their ordinary connection with humanity. They separate themselves from the total course of humanity in order to significantly accelerate their development. This is, of course (let us be completely clear about it), an egotistical action, for which there will have to be compensation. But if a person says, "I do not want this egotistical action, I wish only to help, only to serve," is he or she acting any less egotistically? Or know how humanity, how the world is best helped? To speak this way is arrogance.

Here we should learn what is the best way for us to serve. You must only have faith in yourselves, that you already have within you the forces that you need to bring forth. You are not coming here in order to receive something, so that something can be given to you, but in order to bring forth what is already within you. We see this in the auxiliary exercises: Serenity, Positivity, and so forth. But your trust must not be a false trust. You certainly have the power, but you must say to yourselves that until now you have not used it, not observed it enough; now you will apply it always better and better. You will achieve the goal if you apply the means sufficiently. And you should not cross the threshold of this temple with arrogance and pride. It would not be the correct attitude for you to come expecting to receive something that others do not have, and only wanting to raise yourself above others. No, we should come in the spirit of humility, as we say to ourselves, "My weaknesses drive me here because my forces need a support that I find here. For this reason I cross the threshold." That would be the right attitude. For from the earliest times forward there has never been anything taught in an esoteric school that was not also taught in an exoteric context.

It corresponds entirely to the facts if I say, for example, that everything that is said here in the evenings hides occult forces that can lead human beings into the occult world, if what is said is processed in the soul with complete dedication and energy.† If people use all their energy to listen to these things not only as a theory, but to evaluate them practically, then they are esotericists. But because people think that they are too weak to do this, for this reason they seek support for their forces; seek advice and help in this esoteric school. Here one is helped to shorten the path.

One could ask, "How far should I surrender myself to this egotism? Where should I stop?" The gods will take care of this. They are good at showing us when "too much" arrives. They show us this first in the soul. For this reason self-observation is necessary, ongoing attention paid to oneself. If, for example, someone flies into a rage at his exercises, it will happen he also loses his memory for ordinary things in life. That this should happen is entirely correct; it must be so if something higher is to appear. But we should not let ourselves go, and have less memory and be less truthful than our fellow human beings. We should have much, much more memory, and be much, much, more truthful than our fellow human beings. It is not sufficient for us to remain as truthful as we were before; we must always be growing more truthful. We should fight for our memory. We must not say something later that we can say only because what happened earlier was covered over, or because we do not want to remember. And for this reason the auxiliary exercises are given; they should work to balance us.

Once again some advice. Watch out for vanity and ambition in yourself, and also in others. We are not strong enough to do everything by ourselves; we must help one another. Give no one a reason to be vain or to have ambition. Nourish joy and courage by allowing the goodness in others to come to the fore in the fullest measure, but do not give them blind trust that cannot be justified. Give no faith to any authority, but rather use your thinking reason to test. Many who have occupied leading positions have already failed when an appeal was made to their vanity; indeed, it is dangerous if they have even only an iota of vanity.

Esoteric Lesson
OSLO (KRISTIANIA), JUNE 11, 1912

Manuscript from Vrauke Titringh.

It has already become clear to you in the previous discussions that if you devote yourselves in an earnest and worthy fashion to your meditations, then certain effects will appear. And honest, conscientious self-observation is necessary if you want to notice certain consequences in a timely fashion. However, this self-observation must not be carried out in such a way that it degenerates into self-satisfaction; this is a great danger for an esotericist. The exercises will certainly have their effects, but if certain inclinations are already present in the constitution of your soul, such as arrogance, and so forth, then the meditations will have a deleterious effect on you. These inclinations are present in everyone, but in ordinary life, megalomania is soon corrected by external events. There we quickly notice that there is much that we cannot do, even though we may have imagined we could. In the occult life, these correcting perceptions do not show up as directly. Thus we must apply strict self-discipline in order to avoid the danger of arrogance.

The second danger consists of untruthfulnes, when reason and memory become worse and these finally degenerate into uncontrolled actions. The preventive measures against these evils are found in the auxiliary exercises, in the study of theosophy, and in the joy we find in nature. Willing, feeling, and thinking are strengthened by them. Through the study of theosophy one's thinking reason is exercised. For it is not enough to accept everything on authority and faith; this would bring about a complete loss of our reasoning capacity, and finally of our morality. Then we would be inclined to mollify our conscience with reference to, and ultimately deference to, authority. We should test everything using our reason, our thinking. This is why everything is cast in concepts and words that one can understand and that appeal to one's reason. Theosophy should be grounded in thinking.

Love of the beauty of nature. Enjoy small things. The materialistic people of today demand only sensational experiences, experiencing nature only when it appears as a majestic ocean or majestic mountains. You should be able to experience the beauty that can be found everywhere. Human beings for whom higher worlds have been opened should not close themselves off from the external world. They should not criticize nature without sympathy, but rather get to know it; they should attempt to understand it. Then every little animal can teach them something. A person should not say, "It is only maya!" The response to that person should be, "Yes, it is only maya, but maya of the gods—and that is beautiful!" Why can a human being today rejoice in a tree? Because the gods once rejoiced in what was in their surroundings. It would be very bad for the future if human beings were to walk apathetically through the world indifferent to it. They would leave behind a world without joy. Not only for themselves, but also for others, something will come forth in the future out of the joy that we feel for small things. Here it is true that all that is hidden will be revealed.

These three things should work in a healthy way on thinking, feeling, and willing. In ancient Hebrew mysticism the consequences of entrance into the Garden (of Paradise) were expressed in drastic terms.[†] In ancient times people were much more robust than today, and the exercises were also much more drastic than those customarily given to the nervous people of today. We must learn to suppress nervous anxiety, and therefore, also not shy away from hearing about the dangers of an esoteric schooling. The ancient Hebrews told of the four rabbis who entered the Garden (of Paradise): the first became insane, a megalomaniac; the second became wild and did crazy things; the third died. This is dramatically expressed to point out the bodily difficulties that can appear with esotericists as a consequence of moral and intellectual faults. This also occurs with ordinary people, but not so directly. But they do not know, for example, of the connection between lying and illness. Esotericists make their bodies much more receptive. In all illness and infirmity they should also see a warning from the gods that something is not in order; then they should be once again be attentive and careful. The human being should say only what is true, what has been tested. It is not sufficient to say, "I said it in good faith." That is not enough. Something else that esotericists should never use is the expression, "I can't help it." That is a denial of karma and helps not at all, because karma will hold sway. We should stand up for our deeds and improve them.

It would be easy to say, and certainly sensational to do so, that my school is inspired—just as it is, as a matter of fact—but that is no concern of the outer world. There we must appeal to reason, so that people understand what is said. For this reason we must write in such a way that it strikes the human understanding as reasonable. There is no use in claiming inspiration, or offering a young man's book to the world while proclaiming that it is inspired by a Master of Wisdom.[†]

If esotericists from other schools object that they also enter into other worlds, then we must be clear that it is not really very important what we see; rather, how we enter those worlds is significant. One can be a very lofty seer and yet see everything wrong. When esotericists from other schools hear this, they will, as so often happens, say ... [manuscript unclear]. But we must expose ourselves to this accusation because we must stand up for the truth.

Esoteric Lesson

MUNICH, SEPTEMBER 1, 1912

Record A: Manuscript from Barbara Wolf; Record B: Anonymous manuscript from the Vreede Collection; Record C: Manuscript from Alice Kinkel; Record D: Notes from the collection of Elisabeth Vreede; Record E: Notes from Bella Lang.

RECORD A

Esotericists must pay attention to many things that are entirely without significance for an exotericist. Thus they must constantly bear in mind that they can speak only of relative truth; that as an esotericist, one cannot speak of eternal truths at all. Our wishes constantly mix in with our striving; and we must say to ourselves that we always prefer to accept a truth that pleases us, rather than a truth that is unappealing to us. For example, the thought of immortality is, as such, much more appealing to most people than the idea that everything is over with death; thus for this reason alone they are more inclined to accept the idea of immortality as the truth. But esotericists must not do this. They should exclude their wishes, their personal feelings, and then carry out their research. Our meditations are given to us for this purpose, in which we should spiritually rest, as it were, upon a specific content of thought. It is not so important that we think through the meditation, rather we should allow our souls to rest within it. Then through this constant repetition our soul forces are strengthened.

The inclination to believe in absolute, eternal truths, and to defend them is a characteristic of our consciousness soul. Now it is possible that the consciousness soul gets the upper hand to such an extent that it no longer rules these thoughts, but rather is ruled by them and pours them out into the outer world. We have an expression for this in occultism: we refer to this kind of consciousness soul with these ideas as the "inner Sadducee." We all bear an inner Sadducee in us, and esotericists have the obligation to feel this and conduct themselves accordingly.† (For example, when Goethe (posthumously) was asked how one should interpret his work, he said: "Explain me out of my spirit, not with the same words that I spoke." Saint Martin (posthumously) once said, "I have many disciples; however, they usually spread my errors further.")

The intellectual soul, or mind soul, can also bear within it something like a second person; indeed, when a person wants to take a truth that has been personally recognized, and set it as a universally valid truth. People do this out of a certain feeling of shame because they do not want to say, "I have recognized this truth through this or that experience; it is therefore, for me a truth." They would rather set it forth as a universally valid truth. Occultism has a word for this: "Pharisee." The inner Pharisee is the intellectual soul that asserts its power in this direction. This inner obsession to convert personal truths into universal truths often results in hypocrisy and dishonesty.

In our inner striving for truth we can also allow the sentient soul to acquire too much sway. This happens in all those who would rather wallow in feelings, rather than take into themselves the teaching of the evolution of the world and inwardly digest this teaching. They would rather immerse themselves in a Tauler or another mystic of the Middle Ages, and decline everything else. Since the sentient soul is relatively distant from the consciousness soul, it does not express its mistakes in as unpleasant a manner as the consciousness soul does. Nevertheless, it is a mistake when esotericists turn away from everything that the external world can teach, in order to seek truth only in inner immersion. This way of allowing the sentient soul to predominate is called in esotericism the "inner Essene." Now, one could make the objection, "But an Essene is something good!" Certainly, he or she is; but the spiritual leader who founded this order actually knew at what location, at what time, and in what way it had to be instituted so that it would be something that could heal the world. This is the main thing to recognize in esoteric striving: which is the correct truth for the specific time in question. The Buddha knew this very well when he brought his teaching to India six hundred years before Christ. The same teaching transplanted to another time, does not have the same effect. All-important is the question: how is something to be made effective?

There are nodal points in the spiritual worlds at specific times, when from the highest worlds above us spiritual forces work down into the world that lies directly above us. Just such a time is now present, and the great initiates cannot pull these forces down from higher realms, only the Christ can do this through having passed through the Mystery of Golgotha. But the great initiates Buddha, Pythagoras, Zarathustra, and so forth, gather around Christ and allow themselves to be influenced by his forces; they do this whether or not they are incarnated in a physical body or are abiding in the spiritual world, and they work out of the spirit of Christ.

We should bring these three people who indwell us, the Sadducee, the Pharisee, and the Essene, into a harmonious relationship; for any one of them working alone is damaging. The Pharisee should serve the Sadducee; and these two together should serve the Essene. This one should rule over the two, but must not be allowed to rule alone. As esotericists we should really get a feeling for the fact that we have all three within us, for when we approach the Guardian of the Threshold we will feel them very clearly; we must leave them behind as something from the past that does not belong in the spiritual world. If it is objected that Essenes are very much concerned precisely with the spiritual world, then we must say that they are concerned with it in a way that is appropriate for them in the physical world. But their entire order was founded for the physical world, and for a specific point on the earth; and in spiritual worlds, an entirely different point of view serves as a starting point.

When we stand before God with these three deficiencies, which we feel as nakedness, then we have the feeling of shame as Adam and Eve had when they stood before God in their nakedness; therefore, we should aim to bring these three soul-traits into their proper balance.

For us, the spiritual world is surrounded by sheaths that we ourselves create, and that we must also remove through knowledge. But we do not find this knowledge through searching within ourselves. It can come to us when we allow a phenomenon of nature to work upon us with great intensity; for example, the sun slowly sinking into a quiet sea. Living with nature in the right way has an awakening and nurturing effect on esotericists. But they must not surrender to nature exclusively. On a sea voyage from Constantinople, Nicholas of Cusa had the most intense spiritual experiences.

The Master of Wisdom and Harmony of Feelings compressed help and support for us into a prayer like the ocean in a drop; this is possible in the spiritual, but of course, not in the physical. The master wishes for this prayer to be used continually as the conclusion of our esoteric lesson; it portrays all of evolution, the rise and fall of the human being.

In the spirit lay the seed of my body…

* * *

RECORD B

There are people who live as though locked within a certain mental horizon, within which they may be very much at home and are able to achieve significant things. Such people close themselves off, so to speak, from everything that might want to enter into the range of their mental horizon; or they reshape it so that it fits into their horizon. These are people who live primarily within the consciousness soul; in whom the consciousness soul greatly overwhelms the other members of the soul. Very active people, people with strong will belong to this group. The occultist has a name for such people: Sadducee.

Then there are people who would like to explain everything and would like to find everything explainable. Even when they act out of a strong drive to find the truth, such people easily come to a place in the end where they are not concerned with the truth. For there is no absolute truth. Truth is relative, changeable, and must accommodate itself to the spirit of the time, and to what is individual in an individual. Even if two people say the same thing, it may not be the same thing; and what is true today will not be true in exactly the same way tomorrow, or after months or years.

We will be able to speak about Goethe in the truest sense and see things in a way that most approximates his approach if we do not repeat the exact words he spoke as he had to express himself a hundred years ago, but rather if we speak in his spirit using his approach, as Goethe would himself speak in our entirely different time with its entirely changed conditions. On the other hand, those who hold to the exact words, to a rational explanation, weave themselves into thought systems and into concepts that are set for all time.

What is true for such people, what they have recognized as true and correct should, according to them, be true for everyone and should remain true for all times. Such people are ruled by the intellectual soul. For this kind of people an esotericist uses the expression: Pharisee.

Thus we have within us the Pharisee and the Sadducee, and we must realize that both of them work are at work, and must be at work, in each one of us, inasmuch as we are speaking of our work on the physical plane. What is important is that the Pharisee and Sadducee within us do not proliferate and get the upper hand over the other members of the soul. We see in the examples of Homer or even Shakespeare how this is to be understood. For example, doctors who have studied Homer carefully claim that Homer must actually have been a doctor. Or there are other people who are exceedingly interested in handmade crafts; they think that Homer must necessarily have been involved in some handcraft because what he reports concerning it is so incredibly accurate. Even Napoleon, the great field marshal genius, once expressed the opinion that Homer must have had great skill as a tactician and strategist, because the description of tactics in the *Iliad* is so competent and correct. Similar things could be said of Shakespeare. These writers knew how to subordinate their own opinions; they knew how to crawl into the essence of what they wanted to describe to such an extent that they could speak as a doctor, as a craftsman, as a field marshal to doctors, craftsmen, field marshals, and so forth.

Now there are other people who close themselves off in another fashion, and in doing so can, given certain circumstances, achieve significant things. Furthermore, they can be quite pleasant, dear people in their way. These are people who live entirely within their own feelings; who, like Johannes Tauler or Meister Eckhart, withdraw into their inner life and live entirely within it. Like hermits living in their own world within which they deeply, inwardly experience beautiful and sublime realities, and are also able to give something from themselves—something that is, however, in a certain way such that when others read or imagine it, it is no longer entirely the same thing. The way that they experience it and present it to the world is actually valid and entirely correct only for themselves. All those who are merely mystics and fuzzy-headed visionaries, but also significant poets of all ages, belong in this group. In our time also there are many artistic natures of this sort. In a certain sense, we could call this kind of inner experience precisely the fundamental artistic and aesthetic mood of sensitive people of our time. There are also many such natures among theosophists; natures who close themselves off, and in doing so, consider themselves to be someone special. This mood is also entirely understandable, for this kind of inner constitution comes from a preponderance of what should be the strongest within us, which we call the sentient soul. The esotericist characterizes such natures with the word: Essene.

You may be surprised by this because the school of the Essenes is something lofty and significant. It certainly is. It is entirely justified in fulfilling its great and sublime task in the physical world. But for those who are striving to enter the spiritual world, a more or less one-sided training, in the sense described as Essene, is just as dangerous for us as the excesses of the Pharisee or the Sadducee. The Pharisee and the Sadducee should not rule within us. The Essene should indeed rule over the Pharisee and the Sadducee; but in such a way that a proper mixture, a balance is brought about through the harmonizing forces of the sentient soul. Harmony of our inner soul forces can come about only when our willing and thinking are guided by our feeling, when they are permeated by properly balanced feelings. And we must always bear in mind that it is only in the physical world that we can work rightly through these soul forces. A soul constitution arrived at through the proper harmony of these forces can serve as a foundation for ascent into the spiritual world, but these soul forces themselves must remain with the Guardian of the Threshold.

The only thing that can remain in the spiritual world for us is what we have created in our higher self as manas. We take only our memory with us into the spiritual world; our lower self and all our other remaining lower members remain behind. When the lower members die away, there is, of course, an extract: a summary of the experiences and impressions from individual incarnations as a seed for a new form in the next incarnation, the causal body.

* * *

Record C

The forces that allow us to ascend into higher worlds are present in every soul, but they are bound up with the physical body. And for this reason, the forces of the higher bodies are bound up with the physical body because experiences must be had on the physical plane that cannot otherwise be had in any other world. They must be torn away from the physical body with forces from the higher bodies, and this happens through meditation. Spoken in esoteric terms, this means that the Sadducee in us must be overcome.

This is the consciousness soul that overwhelms the rest of the soul life; it seeks absolute truth even though on the physical plane, truth can be found only for a specific time, for a specific area. We must find truth in keeping with our time. Goethe was brought forward as an example. Dr. Steiner said: "Early on I experienced and saw how Goethe is now living in higher worlds, and how he wants to be interpreted, in order to bring to expression what he has to say. One is not allowed to use his words from the past in order to do this!"

It belongs to the secrets of the great initiates that they speak the right words at the right place at the right time. The great wisdom of Buddha consists of this, that he recognized the point in time of approximately 500 years before Christ as the right time for his teaching. What is important is how, where, and when certain things must be thought and done for the progress of humanity.

With greater clarity the occultist can now see the great initiates, who have achieved incredibly lofty heights of initiation, whether they are incarnated in physical bodies or they are living only in the spirit. We see them gathered around Christ in order for him to reveal to them, and for them to receive from him, what Christ has brought down from spiritual worlds from a height to which the initiates themselves could not have found their way. All of this occurs so that what is brought down can stream into humanity. Among these disciples of Christ are individualities such as Buddha, Krishna, Pythagoras, and so forth.

The intellectual or mind soul is the Pharisee in the human being that would do violence to the other parts of the soul; it causes us to accept as believable only that which we ourselves are fond of, and to be dishonest with ourselves.

The Essene in the human being is the excessive sentient soul that is one-sided and closed off in itself; it claims for itself an ascent into higher worlds and does not seek knowledge of, and a connection with, the cosmos. (Steiner mentioned sunrise and how differently it can be experienced by different human beings. He also mentioned Nicholas of Cusa and the awakening of the inner life.)

None of the three, neither the Sadducee, nor the Pharisee, nor the Essene, must be allowed to become the ruler; rather, each must become the servant of the others. Pharisee and Sadducee must both become servants of the Essene. The Essenes certainly knew that their lofty, magnificent order can be constructed only on the earthly plane; not even this order is appropriate in the spiritual world.

The feeling of shame as it began with Adam and Eve can overtake us; shame for the nakedness, concerning which we should be ashamed before God. When we pour this deep feeling of shame over our entire soul life, then a force will arise in us that teaches us to overcome the Sadducee, the Pharisee, and the Essene.

We must direct our attention to the feelings, to the inner processes, and what goes on in our inner life; this is necessary for our inner development.

It is important in meditation that we gather together all our fragmented soul forces through the meditation, into a point in the soul where all physical experience is excluded. Everything depends upon the intensity of the force that is developed, not upon the power of the thought.

All that esotericism gives us and would teach us is summarized in that which the Master of Wisdom has given us in the prayer:

In the Spirit lies the seed of my body…

Record D

The dominance of the consciousness soul in occultism is called the "inner Sadducee." It is seen when people have sharply outlined concepts of the truth; have little use for what is all-inclusive; and think that these concepts are unchangeable, as for example, scientific people who do not want to admit that every truth has its time and place.

The dominance of the intellectual soul is called the "inner Pharisee." This occurs when people experience a truth and then want to convince other people of its objective validity; when people think that what they have understood as truth for themselves must also hold true for others. Therefore, there is always in play a certain dishonesty toward oneself and others, whom we want to convince that what we have personally experienced is the only acceptable truth. Thus, this soul constitution always creates an impression of hypocrisy.

The dominance of the sentient soul is called "the Essene." Of course, the Essenes were an order that did good things in their time; nevertheless, we can speak of the "inner Essene" within the human being. This is the "exclusive-immersion-in-one's-own-soul"—"the withdrawal-from-others"—it is asceticism and waiting for revelation from higher world. In our time it would be an appeal to Tauler, Meister Eckhart, and other such mystics. The refusal to learn; the unwillingness to learn what is necessary for knowledge of higher worlds in the cosmos and in nature, this is what characterizes the inner Essene.

Everything that cannot stand up to the Guardian of the Threshold must inwardly be fought. Each one must serve the other two if we wish to become good esotericists. When truth is to be revealed then the where, how, and when is always important.

The greatness of Buddha consisted in this: that he gave his teaching in a certain age, at a certain place and in a certain way. If his teachings are repeated today, they are not correct; for usually it is the mistakes that still endure and are repeated. Every age has its own truths, or a specific form in which they are to be proclaimed for the progress and evolution of humanity.

* * *

RECORD D (Excerpts)

From all that has happened in these days we can understand that it is important to get away from our physical bodies. All human beings have the ability to do this; nevertheless, we see in everyday life that so few can actually do it. Why is this so? We are all in higher worlds in sleep; but in our daily consciousness we have no awareness of this. Life here conditions us so that our consciousness is occupied with the things of the physical world. Thus we do not notice the stream flowing deep within us. The forces are always present, but we do not notice them.

In what way is it possible to call forth this ability? The spiritual stream must become so strong in us through meditation that we can become conscious in these higher worlds. There we must not think of the various physical things or of our personal experiences. We must concentrate well and live only in this concentration. Here we can proceed from a certain thought, and then through this thought we can arrive at the correct mood.

The book *A Way to Self-Knowledge* is a means to achieve this.[†] Here we take a thought, develop it, and then the forces for meditation will come. But this happens in very different ways for different people.

People think that truth is the same for all times and for all beings; this is, however, false. If something is the truth for an era, it is not the truth for always. And if a truth is true for human beings, it is not true for all the other beings on the other planets. We see only a little of the truth, and the truth itself is only relative. This is the greatness of Buddha; that he came at the right time, to the right country, in order to give the right portion of the truth, which he could give. Later he moved to other places, indeed to another planet.[†]

[…]

We must not believe that the leader of the Essenes was like this or that, or that Jesus was like this or that. Certainly the leader of the Essenes taught his disciples only a certain part of the truth, the part that has to do with Christ—that he would come here to earth in a physical body. They had a specific mission to fulfill; and afterwards we hear nothing of the Essenes.

Esoteric Lesson

MUNICH, SEPTEMBER 20, 1912

Record A: Notes from Therese Walther; Record B: Manuscript from Mathilde Scholl and Barbara Wolf; Record C: Notes from Hendrika Hollenbach; Record D: Manuscript from Mathilde Scholl; Record E: Notes from Margareta Morgenstern.

RECORD A

It could appear that the current conflicts with the Theosophical Society must necessarily cause special difficulties for the esoteric life.† In view of what the external movement now makes necessary and in light of how the present time actually drives us to criticism, many souls can ask themselves how this criticism is to be reconciled with the development of positivity, which is a fundamental esoteric exercise required of all. In the course of this lesson we will discover how this is possible.

The way in which the esoteric life is now cultivated was not possible in earlier times. It was not possible then for a large number of students to sit together as happens with us now. And it is precisely this kind of esoteric life of the present age against which various powers now battle. Above all, the esoteric life must be taken seriously and with dignity. We must be very clear about how incredibly important is the step from the exoteric life into the esoteric life. Exoteric life must gradually appear to an esotericist in an entirely different light.

An example may help explain this. We can all remember back to childhood, to a time in which we played as children, and took this play seriously. Let us ask ourselves: If now, as adults, we wished to play with children, how would that take place? Certainly we could play with the children; perhaps even play better than they, because we could use our intellect for this purpose. But something essential would have to happen if we really wanted to be involved in the play: in order to do this, we would have to imagine ourselves into a different state of mind.

The relationship between esotericists and external life is very similar to that between an adult and the play of a child. When esotericists leave their spiritual exercises and enter into external, exoteric life, they will gradually learn to regard this external life as if they were adults who wanted to play with children. And just as adults must imagine themselves into another state of mind in order to play with children, so also do esotericists feel they must shift consciousness when transitioning into exoteric life. Esotericists do not become less capable, but rather more capable and competent in everyday life than was the case before entering into esotericism. Thus the transition from exoteric to esoteric life represents a unique moment in a human being's life; furthermore, the esoteric life cannot be taken seriously enough, nor can it be carried out with enough dignity.

Let us consider esoteric life a little more closely. We well know that changes in our soul life appear as a result of the exercises we have received, such as are described in the lectures held in Munich (August 1912).[†] These changes are of all kinds. Thus, the passions that a human being had earlier become stronger. Old inclinations, drives, and passions that we believed to have already overcome and set aside rise up again out of depths of soul, and assert themselves again with vehemence. Or esotericists do something, indeed often, without even thinking about it; something that before the start of their esoteric training they would have been ashamed of or would not even have done. Furthermore, sympathies and antipathies toward personalities become stronger than before; indeed, our entire soul life is powerfully stirred up. In short, people now begin to see how their souls are actually constituted; only now do they acquire true self-knowledge. For this reason, self-control and energetic self-discipline are indispensable for esoteric students.

The changes in one's soul life that appear after the start of an esoteric training, if it is carried through with patience and energy, could be something like the following. Experiences of a special sort do not necessarily have to appear immediately during or after the concentration exercises or meditation. It can certainly be the case that the exercises die away without anything special occurring, and the students calmly pursue their exoteric activities. There is one thing esoteric students must bear in mind and be very clear about; namely, that the first experiences can be very subtle and delicate, so fine and subtle that they can be noticed only by paying great attention. It could happen, for example, that esotericists during everyday activities suddenly have as a thought that seems to simply spring forth from their thought life and apparently does not belong in their everyday life—a thought that is concerned with their own being. If there is not sufficient attention present, then such a thought can flash past unnoticed. What is important and necessary is that we become attentive enough in order to notice such thoughts that drop into our ordinary consciousness, and that in so doing we become aware that thoughts (it could also be grotesque thoughts) appear in our soul without our ordinary waking consciousness of self being involved. We then discover that something is living behind our ordinary self, something concerning which until now we have known nothing; we learn that behind this self something is active that weaves thoughts. As we direct our attention more and more toward these thoughts that drop into our ordinary consciousness, they will appear with increasing frequency until finally much later they can be experienced at will. Then students see as if through a door that this weaving is altogether always present, that what we are accustomed to call the thought-body is constantly being woven. Without our being aware of it in our everyday life, work is constantly being done on our thought-body. Every student will one day come to experience this, if he or she is only patient and works energetically. However, we will not come to such experiences if we stop with our exercises. Hindrances in the outer as well as the inner life can cause us to suspend our further work and stop our exercises. On the one hand, difficulties in our outer life can arise that oppose our esoteric life; on the other hand, hindrances can arise out of weakness and lethargy that prevent progress in esoteric work. If students allow such hindrances to determine that the path will not be followed, then the fruits of their previous work remain in them, but they cannot progress further. Proper cultivation of the esoteric life does not allow such weakness to arise because it is precisely solidity, constancy, steadfastness, and patience that are more and more developed in the course of our esoteric striving. These traits prevent a resolve from being pushed aside or given up once it has been made.

If students continue the exercises that are given to them energetically and patiently, if after the course of the meditation they abide in quiet calmness in which their consciousness is entirely empty and they patiently wait to see whether something wants to be revealed from the spiritual world, then such steadfast and patient work will eventually lead to experiences out of the spiritual world. In doing this, the soul constitution with which the student receives revelations from the spiritual world is very important. The student should answer every thought, every experience from suprasensory realms with a feeling of gratitude toward the divine hierarchies. The student should always develop more of such feelings of gratitude, and they should be increasingly intense. The upright cultivation of these feelings eases the entrance of the revelations and brings one forward. We must already be grateful that we are permitted to do such exercises. Students must inwardly place themselves in a mood of prayer that makes them ready to receive revelations from the spiritual world. If an experience offers itself from the spiritual world, then students must say to themselves, and be clear about the fact, that something was bestowed upon them through grace from the spiritual world. If in this mood we look at all that has flowed into our exoteric and esoteric theosophical life here in Middle Europe during the last ten years, then we must become aware with overwhelming clarity that an abundance of spiritual truths have been handed over to us in course of this time through the grace of the masters. An incredible spiritual wealth has been entrusted to us during this time, and it is difficult for many souls to take in and hold together all of what has been said; for example, concerning the four Gospels. Indeed, and I say this taking complete responsibility, many souls behave in a negative way toward this spiritual wealth, or feel and even express a reluctance to accept it. Such behavior is understandable because we must admit that it is not easy to master these teachings. However, it is simply our task to achieve an increasingly encompassing understanding of Christ and to delve more and more deeply into the Mystery of Golgotha. All the wisdom of ages past, all the prophecies of Krishna and Elijah, have flowed into this understanding. For this reason, we must not slacken, but rather must pull ourselves together; willingly work together, learn; and again and again, learn. Page by page, we must study a lecture cycle and struggle through to an understanding; we must not allow ourselves to fall away.

Accordingly, our present difficult situation, seen esoterically, presents itself more or less as follows. It has often been pointed out, and we certainly know well enough, that the earth is a battleground for various powers. Recently, in Munich (lecture cycle of August 1912) we saw and heard once again in what ways the Luciferic and Ahrimanic powers can take possession of human beings.† They say to themselves, "There are lazy souls who do not want to cooperate with what has flowed down from spiritual worlds. We can start our work with these; we can catch these." Thus these beings take possession of such souls, and draw them away from the path by leading them into deception and error, and making them into instruments of their opposition. Our path, however, if we work diligently and do not slacken, is the straight line from Krishna (unless we want to go further back) through Buddha, Elijah, and John to Christ. We will be up to resisting the attacks of the adversarial powers, which are intended to stop esotericists in their striving, if we take the time, apply sufficient energy to our thinking, and make the effort to understand what is said concerning Christ and the event of Golgotha. But all those who slacken and do not want to come along, fall prey to the attack of the adversarial powers. These are those who show up as opponents to our movement and produce resistance; for some years we have noticed their numbers growing.

Now what esotericists must additionally cultivate in special measure is a feeling for the truth. Under no circumstances must anyone ever prevent us from speaking the truth freely and openly. Every attempt to bend the truth must again be atoned for at some time or another. It would be horrible if anyone were held back from speaking the truth because of the fundamental principle of brotherhood of the Theosophical Society, even if this truth is different from what is said by a personality who is revered by many. The advice of the masters is for us to remain in the Theosophical Society, in which, of course, all opinions can be represented. This is a given. But it is not permitted that something be spread concerning what we have said that is entirely different from what we actually said. This recently occurred in a theosophical periodical.† Something like a caricature of what was really said appears there. It is easy and lazy in this way to say, "What is said in Germany is not right. Christianity is not properly explained there. Direct your view to the near future and wait until the great teacher appears; he will explain everything to you." One can only respond to this by saying that if a great teacher is pointed out in this way, then he will certainly not come. It will be sufficient for an understanding of these phenomena to refer to the preconditions for the intervention of the Luciferic and Ahrimanic beings. We find these preconditions for the approach of these beings in the described behavior. And as a matter of fact, it is these enemy powers who have brought it about that something like what is described above can be said, and is said in the Theosophical Society; they are the ones who stand behind such words. After we have recognized this, if we then with a heavy heart, criticize in such a way that the love for this personality who is approaching us is not touched and is not diminished, then we will not go wrong, even if this personality has no understanding for our criticism and feels it to be an attack. It does not matter. If it is possible for us to agree on this: that we do not allow the love for this personality to suffer from this, if we tell the truth with a heavy heart, then we stand upright and we will be able to overcome the difficulties that stand against us.

Thus we have come to the point of understanding that if we hold together the exoteric and the esoteric and achieve an overview, this will result in a unity for us. We must attempt to achieve this overview in order to find a unity. Just as it is impossible to understand a symphony for someone who listens only to the individual tones and in this way finds at most "tone arabesques," and just as someone will have a proper understanding for a symphony who grasps and feels the movement of the entire body of tone as a unity, so too, we also know that we can nevertheless carry out and maintain our positivity exercises alongside the necessary exoteric criticism that is going on in our society if we can find the unified movement flowing through the events. Then we do not have to fear a weakening of our esoteric life, if we take what has been said to heart; rather, we can expect and hope for a strengthening.

But we must be careful not to allow any feelings of antipathy to mix into our dreams or into our holy meditations. If this happens then we must get them out. And we are learning to combine love and truth.

Thus we can see from the present situation in the Theosophical Society how behind everything in the sense world, there stands the suprasensory. This, along with many other things is contained in the verse of the masters:

In the spirit lies the seed of my body…

* * *

Record B

With all that is going on at the moment in the external theosophical movement, it is understandable if esotericists in the present time think their esoteric life could be thereby endangered. For all that we are now experiencing must, indeed, provoke criticism, and yet one of our most important exercises is positivity; that is, our effort to see the positive, the good in everything.

On the other hand, it should be said that esotericists must be clear about what is important here: how positivity is to be understood. I would like to discuss how an esotericist should altogether stand with respect to life. You will all be able to remember a time in your childhood when you played the games of childhood with full seriousness—when these games were all-important. If now as adults you see children playing, and actually play with them, you will immediately sense the difference in your feelings when you are now playing, compared with the games of your childhood. You will perhaps play better than the children, but that will be because you now stand *above* the game; you no longer invest all of your interest in it. Esotericists should relate themselves to everyday life in the same way that an adult is related to the games children play. The esoteric life should be the focus of earnestness and dignity in the souls of esotericists. They should always feel the limits clearly that separate them from their exoteric activities; otherwise, they are not true esotericists. For this reason they should carry out their exoteric deeds just as well as they did earlier; indeed, they may well execute them better, but they should always carry them out as something that they stand *above*.

They will gradually notice how the condition of their souls changes through their meditative life. If they do not notice, that is merely their fault, because they are not looking subtly enough in the right direction. Let us assume that an esotericist has carried out his morning meditation with true love, devotion, and energy; it was also possible for him to empty his mind thereafter, to open himself to the spiritual world, but he is forced to admit to himself that he has not experienced anything. Now it can happen that during the following exoteric activity (this can be as superficial as cleaning a room or folding laundry, and so forth), he suddenly has the feeling that he should be aware of his own thoughts; he should look into himself. Unless he gives in to this feeling, he will overlook an opportunity to make progress. If he gives in to this feeling, he will notice that thoughts rush through his mind that sometimes are very beautiful; sometimes they will seem grotesque to him; very often, indeed usually, they will quickly disappear from his memory. What is important here is to sense that something is thinking within us, independent of our own intellectual thoughts, something concerning which we can say, "It is not I that am thinking, but rather it is thinking in me."

Even if such thoughts mean little to us for the present, we can strengthen and nurture them through a feeling, through a feeling of gratitude toward the higher powers. Such moments can be as short as the twitch of an eye; it is sufficient for us to have noticed them. If after every moment of this kind we say, "I thank you, powers of the higher hierarchies, that you have allowed me to notice something like this"; then through this feeling of gratitude, of reverence, such moments will increase; moments in which higher worlds seek to reveal themselves to us. What in the beginning was dark and passed through our souls like dreams, we will be able to retain in our memory; eventually we will be able to voluntarily bring about such moments. Then it will gradually become clear to us that this thinking is always present in us, independent of our rational thought, independent of what approaches us from outside through life. For this reason, an esotericist can never say that external life hinders him or her from properly conducting an esoteric life. This always lies with us, with the mood that we create for ourselves. If we awaken in ourselves this feeling of gratitude, reverence, and awe (a feeling that we could call a mood of prayer) after every meditation, and become aware of the grace that we are receiving; if we feel the true beauty behind every enjoyment of nature, every glance of a rose, when hearing a symphony, then one day the spiritual worlds will open to us.

Until now it has never before in human evolution been possible for people to sit as you are here, next to each other, as an esoteric school; and the powers that set themselves against the Masters of Wisdom and Harmony of Feelings, the Luciferic and the Ahrimanic, try to attack esotericists especially on their weak sides. You will have noticed that before and during your meditation, your sympathies and antipathies that you bear for certain people, appear with a special strength; that desires and passions that you might have been ashamed of in earlier times now appear to you as not at all unjustified; that such character traits that earlier, especially in well brought up people, came to light only slightly, that they are not set free with elemental might. There is only one means of fighting this: self-discipline.

We will discuss these matters further on Sunday. Now we want to see if we can also apply what we heard to what is happening at the moment in the Theosophical Society. All that can now flow down out of the spiritual world with the permission of the Masters of Wisdom and Harmony of Feelings is such a wealth of wisdom. And what is given to us in terms of explanations of the Gospels and the Mystery of Golgotha is so deep and encompassing that a true esotericist must sacrifice much time, devotion, energy, and strength if he or she wishes to take up everything and penetrate it with understanding. It is understandable that some have fallen away, for we must learn, learn, and then learn again, in order to penetrate into these depths, and it is a test of the soul when we think that we cannot go any further.

Now there are lazy souls who do not *want* to learn; these are mastered by Luciferic powers who whisper to them that they, instead of learning, instead of seeking the straight path (and it passes through unceasing study from on the one hand, Krishna, and on the other, Elijah, through Buddha and Socrates to Christ) in order to find him they should prefer to wait for a world teacher, who will give them with two hands what they need so that they do not need to exert themselves.

In order not to fall into error, we must cultivate honesty as the highest, most holy good that we have; we must always cultivate truthfulness; never make any concession that sins against the truth. It is horrible and has severe consequences if esotericists twist the truth for the sake of brotherhood; if, in order not to irritate someone, they darken the truth even in the least, for they also damage the person to whom they are speaking. And if, with heavy heart, we must see that a human being whom we perhaps love, sins against the truth, then we must, nevertheless, remain with the truth we have recognized, no matter what consequences this might have for us. But there is one thing that we can do, and that should be the answer to the question posed at the beginning. Even if we must condemn the deeds of a person, we should never criticize the person him or herself, but rather love him or her. Whether or not we really love this person will be seen in the moments of our meditation. We should allow nothing of our sympathies and antipathies and our little worries to come over into the spiritual world. Then it will open for us and allow us to enter in the right way.

* * *

Record C

It would be thinkable that many of us today might become confused since the esoteric theosophical life brings so many difficulties with it, and so much negativity must be produced [this refers to the Alcyone affair], while otherwise the positive striving is stressed. Thus it could happen that some of us might not see clearly how we should respond to all this in our esoteric life. We must be conscious of the seriousness and the dignity of our esoteric striving. We can compare ourselves with adults who share with children their games. Children do everything with the greatest seriousness. They are completely lost in their games, while adults, although they may play much better than the children, experience everything from an entirely different point of view and are conscious that the game is something that does not touch their inner life. We must conduct our ordinary, everyday actions; we must stand in ordinary life, just as we stand as adults among children, even though this ordinary life is ever so important and significant and so much depends upon it.

If we faithfully and constantly carry out our exercises and really attempt to abide entirely in a higher consciousness during the time that we are devoted to our exercises, then we will notice that transformations occur in our soul life. It can happen during our meditations, or immediately afterward, that we feel ourselves in touch with something that originates in higher worlds. But it could happen differently. It can also happen that we sense nothing during our meditations, or even immediately after, during the serene calm that we have achieved at the end of our meditation—that nothing rises into our consciousness. But then later while we are going about our usual daily activities, it can happen that we suddenly feel the urge to divert our ordinary train of thought for a moment to think about ourselves. It can happen during the most ordinary activities, while moving a chair, for example, or when clearing the table, that we suddenly notice that within the brain a deeper life of thought shows itself behind our ordinary secular life of thought. For a brief, passing moment, we are now suddenly in touch with this deeper life of thought. Such moments are very important even if they are very short, especially in the beginning. If we could manage always to notice and retain these moments and to remain conscious of them, then we would reach the point where we can consciously come into contact with this deeper thought life when we want to. We feel that behind our ordinary, everyday life it is always present. We then become aware of the weaving in our thought-body; "it thinks in me," we can say, and that which is thought in us is revelation from the divine world.

Now we can also notice that in addition to the lofty and sublime thoughts that come to us, it can also happen that grotesque thoughts that do not fit with a mood of holiness arise within us. But when we realize that Luciferic and Ahrimanic beings also work in the spiritual world, this observation need not surprise us. However, in every case we must attempt to become conscious of what streams to us from the spiritual world in this way. And an ongoing welling-up, a rising up of feelings of gratitude toward the spiritual beings who wish to establish contact with us in our thinking, should rise up within our soul. In doing this, we should call forth a mood of prayer that should become an ongoing attitude of soul within us.

Those who arrive at such a consciousness will also notice that their sympathies and antipathies gradually become stronger. Something that in the past was only half-conscious is now strongly and clearly felt. It can happen that certain inclinations arise—even certain passions—but we are not ashamed of them, and do not even attempt to hide them; they are simply there. What is now needed is self-discipline, genuine esoteric discipline. More will be said about this the next time.

The only thing that can help us now [in the Alcyone crisis] is to cultivate our esoteric life harmoniously despite the external disharmony, to stand on the ground of truth. The truth must be said, even if with a heavy heart. For it would be something horrible for our movement if we did not tell the full, naked truth, in order to spare a personality; that would mean we would be placing something personal above the truth. In order for us not to experience any dissonance in our higher striving, the following is necessary. It is necessary that nothing of the severity or sharpness with which we must address the personalities involved and concerning whom we must speak the truth, none of this severity must penetrate into our esoteric life, whether it be in our meditations, or even in our dreams.

The truth must be said even if it is with heavy heart, but all the more should love rule in our esoteric life—love to those whom we must criticize or rebuke in the exoteric life. This is what is positive: love toward the personality, even when in external life now the negative must predominate. All esotericists will have to stand before difficult tests. We cannot feel enough the seriousness of what it means to be a striving esotericist, for much is demanded of us. All that is given us from the spiritual world as grace, we should accept as the content of our instruction. This requires unceasing effort: study, a desire to learn constantly, to immerse and deepen oneself more and more in what is given. No sacrifice is too great for us; effort, time, we must employ everything at our disposal. But not all are capable of this. A certain feeling of inertia or laziness can arise; the wish finally to not have to learn anything more now. This is understandable. Yet the Luciferic spirits can intervene precisely here. They use this inertia in people; they bring these people because of their fondness for comfort, to the point of no longer really wanting to study. So these people want only to look toward the coming world-teacher, who will then of course bestow everything upon them. Thus the Luciferic beings work in this way against the good gods. But, to be sure, no world-teacher will come to indulge the laziness of people.

The truth should be spoken as sharply and clearly as possible, but love should rule in the hearts of people. None of the exoteric disharmony must be allowed to slip into our meditation; it must be totally excluded.

* * *

Record D

It may appear to many esotericists, especially in the present time, as if their progress in the esoteric life were hindered by all that now approaches them in terms of the negativity that must call forth criticism. Thus it appears! For esotericists know that one of their main exercises is positivity. And so they ask themselves, how should I, in such a time as this, the present, when so much negativity approaches me, carry out this exercise? But this should not be the worry of an esotericist; but rather, how can I form my esoteric striving into something serious and worthy? Imagine the time when you were a child and played childish games, and that you now would again play with children when you have outgrown the age of children. You would play better than the children can play. You would place yourself right into the children's play, but with your present-day experience and soul constitution, you would be able to perform much better. It must be the same with esotericists when they take the step from exoteric life into esoteric life. They must regard exoteric life as something that no longer has the same significance as earlier. It must seem to them as if they are playing together with others, just as they might play with children. Esotericists can also work in exoteric life better than before.

We should certainly rejoice in the external world; we should enjoy nature in its revelations. Nevertheless, our state of mind, our soul-constitution, should be totally different, if we have stood for a while in esoteric life. If esotericists have devoted themselves with complete earnestness, with full intensity, to their meditations, then they will notice that a transformation of the soul has occurred; indeed, must occur. But many do not notice this themselves and think they have made no progress. Spiritual worlds shine into every meditation, and they can approach the meditator either during or immediately after the meditation. That is what occurs most frequently, and should occur. But it does not always happen this way. And in the moments in which esotericists achieve complete quiet in their souls, as is advised, and after meditation when they listen for the inflowing of spiritual worlds, they must often admit that they notice nothing of these spiritual worlds. However, if they continue working with patience, endurance, and with great effort, then spiritual worlds will approach them. The time comes for everyone who holds out.

But there is something else that can be noticed, which enters in either immediately after the meditation, or in the further course of the day. When we rise from our meditations in the morning and go to our usual daily activities (actions that are done every day; for example, moving a chair, entirely focused on our duties, and so forth), then the moment can suddenly come (it may last no longer than the blink of an eye); it can happen that, for a moment, we think of ourselves, if only in passing. Then the thought is forgotten. This is very important for the development of the soul. In this moment we are not thinking through the brain that we are bound to in the usual life of thought; but rather, our "I" thinks in us. We feel very clearly, "Here it is, thinking in me." We feel our "I-body," our thought-body. For this reason we should pay attention to such moments, for spiritual knowledge can appear in them. And the more often they occur, the more fruitful they are. And it is precisely this rushing-past and then quickly-forgotten thought that is proper. Everything that comes to us with great clarity, for example, visions that cannot then be forgotten, do not come from good powers. Genuine, true experiences come in a modest way, if I may be permitted to use this term with respect to lofty, sublime beings. Devils also approach us, and they show us clear visions. Inherited atavistic clairvoyance also appears in this way, but it is not what is right.

However, in addition to lofty, sublime thoughts, ordinary, even grotesque thoughts appear in our mind. And especially with advanced esotericists, it can happen that their vices are expanded without their even being ashamed of them. They are present; they cannot drive them away. It is also entirely natural; they must be present because they are in them. Precisely in the most holy moments of meditation, desires and passions approach us, of which we are not conscious in exoteric life, at least not in this strength. What helps here the most is esoteric self-discipline. We should practice being true in all the feelings of life. And we should also feel gratitude toward the great spiritual beings, the divine hierarchies. We should be thankful for everything that has been given to us through them (no matter how abstract it may seem), for everything that we think of as knowledge.

We should feel reverence and gratitude toward those beings that allow wisdom to flow into us from higher worlds. These feelings constitute true piety and have an especially beneficial effect upon the development of our souls, and above all, enable us to master the enemies of the soul: desires and passions. After every meditation, we should devote ourselves to these feelings of gratitude. There have not always been times in which the spiritual life could flow as well as just now. Esoteric associations, such as we have gathered here today, have not always existed.

The powers working against humanity want to prevent the spread of pure spiritual teachings and concepts. There are mighty beings at the forefront, and they are busily at work.

The fundamental preconditions for the purely spiritual esoteric life are truthfulness, studiousness, and endurance. For this reason we must be truthful in every moment of our lives. It belongs to this, that we not suppress the truth by not speaking up when a personality makes a mistake, merely because it is this personality. We are not allowed to be silent about something that we can recognize as error, that we must recognize as error. This would amount to suppressing the truth; this would be appalling, if we were to suppress the truth in this case.

There is something else we must pay attention to. This is the studiousness and endurance of the student already mentioned above. It can happen that some souls become too casual, that they no longer wish to take in the higher truths. A great deal of very intense work is required in order to hear, understand, and make our own, the newest esoteric research concerning the Mystery of Golgotha and what is said here concerning the Gospels, which relates to the Mystery of Golgotha. Page after page must be studied in order to understand the great truths that come to us; truths reaching from Krishna to Elijah, in order then to unite in the Christ impulse (which we have discussed in exoteric lectures).

Materialists and Bible critics are not our worst opponents; but rather, those who were once working with us to spread the teachings of theosophy, but who have become remiss in the way I have indicated. Luciferic powers gain access to people when casualness and laziness reign over the spiritual life. Every esotericist should make a sacrifice; he or she should sacrifice love of comfort and ease and the time required to fully grasp what is our task to proclaim: the Mystery of Golgotha.

Beginning ten years ago a spiritual impulse was given to middle Europe that can lead to clairvoyant sight, and for this reason we must approach this task with complete dedication.

We must not play like children. It would be abnormal if adults wanted to play with dolls or other children's toys. It is the same if esotericists do not take their meditations seriously enough, after they have once decided to go down the esoteric path. It can happen that esotericists leave the path after they have followed it awhile. This is often the result of external conditions. What they have worked to achieve remains with them; it is not lost. However, a true esotericist cannot ever leave the path again.

What do the adversarial powers say to indolent souls such as we have described? Do they say, "Work, so that you advance further?" No! They say, "Someone is coming who will give you everything; he will pour out all knowledge, all wisdom!" If one waits for him impatiently then he will certainly not come. If one observes entirely objectively what is now happening on the other side of this issue, one must say we cannot bring sympathy to meet what we have recognized as error on the physical plane. However, we are not permitted to bring feelings of sympathy and antipathy into our meditations; every aspect of those feelings must be silent. Now in the Theosophical Society, in which, according to the judgment of the Masters of Wisdom and Harmony of Feelings, we will remain, we must still be members; it is often said that everyone is entitled to his or her own opinion, that would be brotherly.

Everyone can have his or her own opinion; but it is not brotherly to allow an error to persist. And one cannot remain silent when untruth is written in theosophical periodicals, precisely where we are to proclaim the truth as our mission; we cannot remain silent when that is dragged down and distorted into a caricature.

It is still to be shown how we are to come to a feeling of positivity from all these events. We must feel love for those whom we must oppose outwardly. With a heavy heart, the master must say what he has to say; but in doing so, he has a feeling of love, even if it is not felt on the other side, where everything is even seen as an attack.

In our esoteric life, we must not suppress criticism, but learn to see situations and things objectively. These matters must be debated, but one must not become uncharitable toward one's opponents.

The best love is to look at the truth objectively, and to retain a warm feeling of love in one's heart. When we have developed in this way the feelings of love, of devotion to the spiritual worlds, courage to sacrifice, and endurance, then we will increasingly grow into the spiritual worlds, from which we originate. Then we will also increasingly come to understand the verse given to us by the masters:

In the spirit lay the seed of my body

* * *

Record E

It could seem that the esoteric life is really thwarted in this critical time. It seems as if the spiritual beings who are opposed to the course of our evolution, our striving, always want to become stronger. However, this does not always have to be the case, and it is not the case with those who are striving properly. You will certainly have often had the experience that nothing of any kind of suprasensory impressions appears, despite your greatest efforts and devotion to the meditations, despite your greatest efforts to allow a period of calm afterward in which all thoughts of external life are stilled. Then you go about your everyday life, immerse yourself fully in the challenges of the day; and then it can happen that a thought suddenly appears, fleetingly, like a dream that has nothing, nothing at all to do with the earthly activities that you are engaged in at that moment; like something suprasensory playing into your life. "It is thinking itself in me." This may be very brief and fleeting, and you can leave it unnoticed. But it is good and helpful for esotericists to pay attention to these opportunities in which something occurs like a weaving into their thought-body, into their self-body or ego-body; they should carefully, subtly pay attention, and then send a feeling of gratitude up to the higher hierarchies. This feeling of gratitude, which we should constantly be developing more intensely within us, can be extraordinarily beneficial for us. Furthermore, every time it has been possible for us to carry out a meditation, we should nurture this feeling of gratitude, and devotion, piety, and inner intensity. This should be the basic mood for our meditations with respect to the spiritual world.

If we learn to give increasing attention to the subtle appearance of thoughts in the middle of our everyday work, then these appearances will repeat more often. Our thought-body (?) [in the German] is then woven by spiritual beings more densely.

We should remember our childhood, and the childish games that we took so seriously back then. Let us imagine that for some particular reason, we were placed in a situation to take up again these childish games, and to play them with children. We would probably play the games better than the children, but we would probably not feel at home in this world of games. Thus an esotericist should be related to the external life in the same way.

This step from exotericist to esotericist we can never take too seriously, or overestimate the dignity involved. We should regard our everyday life and its daily tasks just as an adult regards the games of children. We feel and know that our true home lies in another world. We conduct all our daily business, but perhaps better than before. During our meditations we exclude the entirety of our external life; and with all external activities we feel that we are citizens of another world. Of course we will understand our task correctly only when we are simultaneously conscious of the fact that everything in the sensory world is the expression of something spiritual. For this reason we must not underestimate the sensory world, but rather value it properly.

Above all one thing must guide us: the love of truth. Nothing of our personal feelings should ever insinuate themselves into our meditation and concentration, not even in our dreams. And when we see that someone whom we love errs, this does not hinder us from loving his or her person more, but it must never, ever happen that the truth is crucified out of brotherly love. For leaving another person in error is certainly not love.

It is certainly true that in theosophy, everyone is entitled to his or her own opinion. It is permitted to everyone, and everyone should have an opinion. But there is one thing that a person must not do: misinterpret, distort, or consciously bring forth an untruth concerning the opinions and views of another. A person must not be permitted to do this—as it happened a few weeks ago in a theosophical periodical.

It was our mission and task, as commissioned by the spiritual powers that guide our movement, to awaken an understanding for the deep significance of the Mystery of Golgotha, here in middle Europe in our time.

It is understandable if someone becomes indolent, and no longer wants to obtain and study the insights and knowledge that flow from the spiritual world, but the reason for this lies in him- or herself. We must sacrifice for our knowledge; sacrifice the effort of thought, sacrifice will forces, and also sacrifice time; for we cannot acquire knowledge on the fly. We must always learn, learn, learn so that we are always becoming better at making our own what was permitted to be said out of esoteric wisdom, concerning the Mystery of Golgotha; what has been said in a straight line from the beginning.

Just this is our mission here in middle Europe, to constantly move forward in our understanding of the Mystery of Golgotha, where the forces of Elijah and Krishna have flowed together. If now we hear from the other side that hard work requiring great effort is not necessary for us to acquire knowledge of the Christ because the world-teacher is to come; that he will then strew around his wealth of wisdom, this is a concession to all those who are indolent and seek ease. This is allying with the adversarial elements of the spiritual world, which are opposed to the ascending path of human evolution. If we harbor such thoughts, then the world-teacher will certainly not come!

Even if in our meditations and exercises we sense no success for long, long periods of time, nevertheless, we should not become remiss, but rather with much patience, endurance, and energy we must strive; we must make ongoing efforts. The hour comes for everyone when he or she really "sees."

In the spirit lay the seed of my body...

Esoteric Lesson
BASEL, SEPTEMBER 22, 1912

Record A: Manuscript from Mathilde Scholl; Record B: Manuscript from Mathilde Scholl and Barbara Wolf; Record C: Notes from Hendrika Hollenbach; Record D: Notes from Margareta Morgenstern.

RECORD A

In the previous lesson, in the example of children playing, we have seen how esoteric students relate to the exoteric life after they have left the exoteric life for the esoteric; how they now play better than the children themselves, when they play the childish games again. They are better because, unlike the children, they do not relate to the game; but rather, they relate themselves to the children. The game is not important, but rather the attitude of the adults and their relationship to the children. Thus, it is also on the esoteric path. Here esoteric students enter upon a different relationship to their environment. They look at it with different eyes than before. From a certain point of view, they have outgrown their surroundings, and yet they understand it better. We should not lose our interest for the things of the outer world. Through an esoteric schooling it happens by itself that gradually we lose interest in what was of interest to us earlier.

Human beings are such that they tend to like one person more than others. They are, then, of course, more inclined to overlook or readily excuse the faults of those whom they like, than they are to excuse the faults of those whom they find antipathetic. This inclination must be transformed by esotericists. Their relationship to their fellow human beings must become more impersonal. This should not take place overnight; indeed, it would not even be right. It would thereby tear apart karmic connections. But very gradually they must reach the point where they want to help those who are unsympathetic to them. In this way, of course, we come to see the faults of people (even those whom we love) more clearly; but this does not damage anything because it will be balanced out again through the esoteric training.

Our soul constitution actually becomes different. Today we must look more closely at what happens to us in the moments when we allow our meditations to die away into the stillness. It is not the same thing for the spiritual world to play into our consciousness immediately after meditation or only later in daily life, as it is for so-called atavistic clairvoyance or clairaudience, or a mirroring of visions.

It is most valuable for our soul life if these incursions are very fleeting, and are easily forgotten. The main thing for esotericists is to learn to observe these events, training themselves to pay attention to these fleeting bursts of light from the spiritual world. Through esotericism our thinking becomes finer, more spiritual, and independent from the brain. Let us consider for a moment how the concepts of space and time play a role in human feeling. In the spiritual world, space and time are maya. The moment can arise for esoteric students when in the middle of exoteric life they suddenly have the feeling that it is not they who are thinking in this moment; but rather, that they are perceiving their thought-body—how thoughts are weaving and working in their thoughts. They will have the intense feeling, "Something is thinking (feeling, willing) in me." This weaving and working is always present, but in our unconscious; only in very special moments does it come to our consciousness. This thinking must constantly become finer, more spiritual, and independent from the brain; the feeling must awaken in us more and more that something spiritual is thinking, feeling, and willing in us. Now someone could ask if this isn't a contradiction, when we are sometimes told that we should receive everything in full consciousness; and now we hear that in our subconscious life thoughts are at work, our "I" is at work. Such questions are an aftereffect of brutal, present-day, logical thought; it is not only brutal to human beings but also brutal to thinking itself. However, esotericists must learn to think subtly; they must become aware that in the esoteric life everything is transformed.

In the life of the senses, we are conscious of three forces in our souls: feeling, thinking, and willing. We work with these three: sentient soul, intellectual soul, and consciousness soul. Upon entering higher worlds these three members of the soul become blurred; and yet, they are separated. There appears to be a contradiction here also. But you must know that these three soul members are altogether never entirely separated, although each one appears to exist for itself. All that we have in terms of desires, drives, and passions surges and wells up in the sentient soul. Now we must have one thing as a pole in opposition to our egoity. The powers that led the evolution of humanity in earlier times recognized this, and for this reason they placed fear into the human sentient soul. This is pointed out in the mystery play *The Guardian of the Threshold*.†

Human beings must have fear; otherwise, they would approach everything in order to have it for themselves, and in ancient times their egoity would have become too strong. The ancient pedagogues were also aware of this; thus, the telling of fairy tales and ghost stories constituted a factor in their education. Telling ghost stories to children is entirely excluded in modern pedagogy. However, to a certain extent this is necessary for the souls of children; to the extent that astonishment and wonder are called forth in the child's soul, because reverence and awe for the unknown are developed from this. A child who is never told about the unknown and about greatness can never develop devotion in later life. An esotericist must consciously transform fear into reverence, religious feeling, piety, devotion, and the ability to sacrifice. Upon entering the spiritual world fear must be transformed; for this reason it is good to cultivate it on the physical plane. However, if the experience of fear in a human being is exaggerated and the "I" (ego) is not strong enough to prevent it, then not only the soul, but also the body is taken hold of; then, for example, what we know as rabies can arise. This can always be attributed to a weak ego. When fear is combined with a weak ego, bodily forces are taken hold of. Thus the individual so afflicted is afraid of everything that is not coherently joined together; as for example, water (hydrophobia). They experience this quality of unconnectedness in water. This is an example of spiritual forces falsely influencing the soul and the body.

The basic condition for the intellectual soul is cleverness, which so often is thwarted by compassion. It is peculiar that precisely in the intellectual soul these two poles stand opposite each other. The intellect is so often foiled and influenced by compassion. Through our conscious meditations we should achieve the ability to imagine ourselves into other beings; that is, imagine compassion with other people's joy and suffering as though it were our own. We must arrive at the feeling that we are all one unity; and we must learn to feel that space and time are something separated, as was said at the beginning. We can make this clear with an example. A mother will feel the pain of her child very differently when it is a baby in her lap or a two or three year old, and then again entirely differently when the child is twenty years old. So too, the pain of one's own child is felt differently than the pain of another's. A mother will feel the pain altogether differently than others would feel the pain because the mother and the child form a unity, just as we are a piece of the unity of the spiritual world. And we see also that maya changes through time and space; and therefore the compassion felt in the soul changes.

It will often happen that we feel an enormous blessedness with such compassion. Nevertheless, we must not give ourselves over to this mood. This should become the predominate feeling only when we are free of the body; thus we should not feel it in the physical body but rather in meditation, and then enjoy the incredible blessedness of working creatively on the world together with higher beings.

This feeling of blessedness creates the greatest egotism; therefore, it is beneficial only through meditation. In our physical existence we should bear everything that our destiny brings us with calm composure, and learn to feel as if none of this really concerns us ourselves; we should learn to accept everything with poised serenity, as if our body were foreign to us. In the same way we are to awaken a feeling in ourselves, not that we have been specially chosen to make progress; but rather, we should rather rejoice in the progress others make, as if it were our own. From the point of view of the world's evolution, it matters not at all who is making the progress. For us the essential factor is the battle against and the transformation of egotism.

One pole of the consciousness soul is the feeling that can disconnect at will. The opposite pole, however, which extends down from the spiritual world, is conscience. This feeling restrains us when we want to do things that are not in accordance with the moral laws. We must allow ourselves to be guided and led by our conscience, and not according to the principles followed by a great statesman† in his actions. It was said that he appears to allow himself to be led by his horse; nevertheless, the statesman is doing the guiding as he wishes, and gives them both the direction.

We must be especially careful on the physical plane to develop our conscience in the proper way, for only what we have acquired can be taken into the spiritual world. But our conscience also is changed through our meditations. There is a step that is the most difficult for esotericists: "becoming conscienceless." However, here human beings must be especially highly advanced; everything must be cleared out of their sou. Vanity, ambition, these are the worst forces in the soul, and can always cause a person's downfall. They must be completely transformed.

To be "conscienceless" is when we feel free from the body, only in the sense of higher self-knowledge; then, to feel ourselves as a center for the reception of truths from the spiritual world. We must learn to lead a double life, to have the feeling that we are carrying our body around like a piece of wood. Esotericists must learn to feel that their entire body is an organ for thinking, feeling, and willing.

They must reach the point where they think not only with the brain, which is contained in the skull, but also with all the parts of the body, where, for example, their hands are a better organ for thinking than the brain. They must gradually spiritualize the physical world so that everything is, for them, only an instrument. They must become such that when they look at their hands, especially their etheric hands, they do not see them, just as they now see neither their brains nor their eyes.

Example: the ax in the hand. Just as we feel an ax to be something external, so too our hands must be experienced by us as something external, something that do not belong to us. We must be the driving factor that directs the hand as an instrument with which we are working. (The hand must be the driving factor with which we work—must be the driving spiritual element—and everything must become a unity.)

Our work on ourselves must bring everything beyond the bodily aspect; our work must spiritualize us so that we become like our archetype.

In the spirit lay the seed of my body...

* * *

Record B

Once again we would like to compare the behavior of an adult with respect to children's games to the behavior of an esotericist with respect to external life. Just as adults can play better than children because they approach the children's games with a different point of view, so also esotericists should, if possible, fulfill their daily tasks better because they allow the devotion and strength that their meditative life lends them to flow into those tasks.

What do they acquire then through meditation? They draw their three soul forces together to a point, so to speak, and concentrate them on the spiritual worlds, which then cause something to flow into each soul that is appropriate for that soul. The sentient soul, intellectual soul, and consciousness soul become even more related, and yet more separated, when they are lifted into the spiritual world. This is an apparent contradiction, but esotericists must accustom themselves to a logic more subtle than the one we encounter in modern, materialistic thinking, for that—modern logic—is brutal. For example, according to the usual logic, one could say that in esoteric lessons we are always told that we must never set aside our consciousness, our clear thinking; now, in the last lesson, we have heard that aside from this thinking we should develop something within us that thinks independently of our conscious thinking. This could appear as a contradiction. But the people who criticize in this way forget that something like this can be developed only through meditation; that it is something entirely different from esotericists' allowing thoughts and mental pictures unconsciously to rise up within them.

The powers that guide the evolution of the earth cause something to flow into the sentient soul in which our drives, desires, and passions surge—something that is very healing for human beings and without which they could not arrive at a proper relationship to their surroundings. Without fear, human beings would feel that an informal relationship with all things higher is appropriate; they would want to carry earthly democracy into the spiritual world. If they place the "I" over and against fear in the proper way, they transform it into reverence, into the piety we discussed the last time, and they will handle this feeling in the right way. There is a special case in which it can become dangerous: if the "I" or ego is extinguished in the sentient soul. This happens, for example, when human beings are afflicted by rabies. Then the feeling of fear grows into something monstrous, and people feel terror for everything that does not immediately have an effect on their senses; for example, water. Thus the fear of water that so often appears in cases of rabies.

Today people have an aversion to stimulating a fear of ghosts in children. In exaggerated amounts this is, of course, dangerous, but it is not damaging if children have a feeling that there is something weaving behind the world of invisible things. It is much more difficult for children to develop a feeling of reverence if they have never experienced this feeling through fairy tales. And adults' fear of children's fear of ghosts is really unnecessary.

Something different flows from the spiritual world into the intellectual soul. We think in the intellectual soul, of course; but the powers that guide the evolution of the earth add compassion, empathy, to this thinking. The forces that think in us, and awaken the ability to feel what other beings are feeling, are active in the same soul. For this reason we call it the intellectual- or mind-soul, hence these two names.†

Esotericists should develop especially this feeling of compassion. Until now, it has been absolutely colored by people's inclination toward or against other people. If something happens to someone whom we love, we feel it more strongly than if it were to happen to someone whom we do not love. However, we should not only share the happiness or the suffering of someone else; but also we should merge, as it were, with the suffering or the happiness. We should feel them as our own. If someone cuts a finger, then we should be cut in the finger as well, so to speak. There is a danger here also: we must not allow compassion to degenerate into a kind of blissfulness in which we wallow.

The gods who lead the earth's development have placed conscience into the consciousness soul. This is a force; indeed, it is the only force that is allowed to, and must, restrain the human "I," the ego. It works differently in esotericists. It is said of a famous statesman that his decisions and mode of action guide him like his horse, but actually his horse goes where the statesman guides him. Esotericists acquire the power to guide their conscience; and here there is great danger that esotericists become "conscienceless," and guide the horse, so to speak, wherever they wish. Our passions play a fateful role. If we allow ambition and vanity, these sticky companions of human evolution, to rise in us, they can have a very deleterious effect. They accompany the human being all the way up into the spiritual world.

In order to strengthen our sense of community, every one of us should send the following thought into the spiritual world every Sunday morning at 9:00 am: "In the spirit of humanity, I feel myself united with all esotericists."

* * *

Record C

We must take seriously the comparison of the relationship of esotericists to their surroundings with that of adults to children, in whose games they participate. Adults will not have a relationship to the toys such as exists for the children; rather, they will much more have a relationship to the children themselves. It is their interest in the children that brings them to the game. This must also be the case for esotericists. Their interest in their fellow human beings must bring it about that in ordinary life they do everything as well and exactly as possible, although their motive is different from that of exotericists.

We have pointed out that consciousness of a second life of thought in us will arise for those who practice their meditations earnestly. This is not a subconscious life of thought, because it is called forth by conscious exercise; that is, through the fact that a human being wants to become conscious of him or herself. We also said that this second consciousness is difficult to maintain in the first one, that everything that it brings us "rushes past." What is given us by the gods announces itself with modesty, whereas we must distrust that which comes to us in enduring visions. What is based upon atavistic vision can have a compulsory feeling accompanying it, but when we are prepared in the right way, what is given us by the gods never has this compelling character. It is always something fleeting and difficult to retain. We must become accustomed to a certain kind of subtlety in our thinking. We receive impressions through the sentient soul, intellectual soul, and consciousness soul. Fear is mixed in with our sentient soul. Without fear there would be no piety; with brutal egotism we would immediately want to become familiar with everything. What holds us back, what allows us to still have a sense for holiness, and recognize holiness in things or beings that we should hold ourselves back from, is a certain nuance of fear. This is good, and in our higher consciousness is increasingly transformed into awe, piety, humility, and reverence. The pole opposite to fear is the feeling for one's self, for the "I," which we should not lose.

The ability to share joy and suffering, compassion, is what is mixed in with the intellectual soul. Therefore, it has two names, intellectual soul and mind-soul.[†] In a higher consciousness, compassion with another means becoming one with the other. One no longer feels *with*, one *is* the other being. This pouring out of one's feelings in a higher consciousness has something about it that makes us feel blessed; we feel our own being spread out entirely in an all-encompassing being, who feels compassion and joy with all beings. However, this can become a danger for our usual exoteric life. For the experience of this blessedness can also become a higher kind of egotism. Thus, in the usual life of the intellect, a calm insight must form a balancing pole for compassion.

Our conscience lies in the consciousness soul. However, when entering a higher life, our conscience becomes such that we ourselves can determine the way in which it speaks, so that we do, indeed, follow it; but actually we are determining the path. If the moral feeling is not strongly enough schooled and developed in ordinary life, a lack of conscience can develop. For this reason we must stand firmly with respect to fundamental moral principles in our ordinary life; because conscience in higher worlds follows the will of the human being, and is determined by the will of the human being. This lack of conscience must be balanced by an opposite pole, which is a certain feeling of solidarity with all humanity. Our own personal and bodily well-being will become less and less important. Our body becomes as a kind of toy with which as an adult we play among children in life in order to be of use to our fellow human beings. But our astral body must also assume this role. Our own wishes, inclinations, sympathies, and antipathies should no longer appear important to us. We must learn to have a feeling of solidarity with all of humanity. Even if someone is not sympathetic to us, we must want to help with the greatest love; indeed, perhaps with even more love than if we felt sympathy for the person. In light of this, our own progress must no longer appear very important to us. We must, of course, do all we can to advance, but we must feel that it is entirely a matter of indifference for the evolution of humanity whether we have this or that specific ability. We must be able to rejoice over the progress of others as much as we would rejoice over our own progress. Only when we regard our bodies as something belonging to the external world will we be able to think with the entire body. As long as it is the case that we see the body as something that belongs to us, just so long will we be unable to use it as an instrument of knowledge. We must actually come to the point that, for example, we do not see our hand anymore at all; only then will it become the organ of thought that it can be. Thus we must more and more feel ourselves to be one with all of humanity and regard the body as a toy that we make use of in life in order to help our fellow human beings.

* * *

Record D

The day before yesterday we spoke of how we should relate ourselves to external life the way adults do to the games of children. An adult will play better than a child, out of love for the children, not for the toy. We must not think that the life of an ascetic monk would be the ideal that we should strive for. We should faithfully fulfill our daily obligations, and only in our meditations raise ourselves up entirely out of the everyday.

The first thing that we will experience as success in our meditations is a more subtle way of thinking. Materialistic thinking is brutal. We should pay attention to the weaving of our thoughts, to the "it is thinking in me," when it flashes up in our consciousness without any effort from our own "I-thoughts."

Now someone could say that this is a contradiction, that on the one hand I should pay attention and increase this unconscious weaving of thought within me, and on the other hand, I should constantly become more conscious of my thinking.

But such an objection only shows that it does not yet originate from subtle esoteric thinking (one must always pay attention to exactly what is said). What is meant is that when we meditate, these thoughts will find their way in as a result of meditation. A flashing up of thoughts in our exoteric life is not meant here. Divine powers insert themselves in this way chastely; we could say, modestly. So-called atavistic, inherited clairvoyance of exotericists is much less valuable. The devil reveals himself there in a turbulent way with powerful, vivid images. God reveals himself to esotericists in a delicate, modest, dream-like way.

As we ascend into spiritual worlds we want to experience ourselves more and more as threefold. The three elements are: sentient soul, intellectual soul, and consciousness soul. Here too there is an apparent contradiction; on the one hand, the three work more closely together, interweaving one another, while on the other hand, there is an intense isolation of each individual soul force.

Fear is something that must be present in the sentient soul if we are ever to arrive at true reverence, devotion, and piety, which we are to develop in the face of spiritual powers. When we love a rose or a human being then there is always some fear mixed in with the feeling of love. We do not wish to step too closely to the other; we need to maintain a certain distance with respect to them, a distance from what lies in them.

It is foolish for modern materialistic educators, for example, to want to eliminate entirely any fear of ghosts from the life of a child.

This fear of fear of ghosts is wrong. It is good for children to have a foreshadowing of the unknown; this prepares the ground for reverence. Of course, this must never be done in an exaggerated fashion; it must never go so far that fear gets the upper hand and the ego loses its hold on the sentient soul. In the spiritual realm madness appears, while in the physical it is, for example, rabies which appears with hydrophobia, because all that is matter-like is then experienced as unpleasant.

Compassion appears in the intellectual or mind soul (hence, its double name);[†] compassion is very often fought by the intellect, and vice-versa. An esotericist will constantly be developing more compassion, love for the entire world, and a joyful readiness to sacrifice. One wants to help; also to help especially those people that are unsympathetic to one. Not only should we feel joy with others, not only suffer with them; we should ourselves be the joy, ourselves be the suffering.

Then blessedness is experienced in the intellectual soul. The more bodily suffering and soul pain there is, the greater is the blessedness in the intellectual soul.

Conscience enters the consciousness soul. We are to develop it here on the physical plane, where it can be developed.

It has been said of a statesman that he only follows his horses; but they lead him wherever he wants to go. Thus it is with conscience. In the condition in which we are freed from the body, which we must achieve in order to live in the spiritual world, we must give our conscience its direction. Therefore, we need to have given it a proper direction here in the physical world.

Esotericists must always watch over themselves, over what wants to get the upper hand within them. In this way, from a lack of conscience, a higher conscience comes into the consciousness soul in the spiritual world. When we experience ourselves in the consciousness soul, we come to the feeling of being united with all of humanity.

Esoteric Lesson
BERLIN, NOVEMBER 8, 1912

Record A: Anonymous manuscript from the Vreede collection; Record B: Manuscript from Barbara Wolf; Record C: Manuscript from Louise Clason; Record D: Notes from Hendrika Hollenbach; Record E: Notes from Günther Wagner.

RECORD A

Even after long practice, many will have the feeling that they have not come any further in their experience of the spiritual world. Nevertheless, this can be due to an error. It can happen that we notice nothing during meditation, but afterward, when we turn to our usual daily activities and are not entirely lost in external work, it can happen that we suddenly have the feeling that now something is thinking in us! It can also happen often that we think that we have fallen asleep during our retrospective recollection of the day's events, but when we are again awake and attempt to remember what was going on within us during the time when we thought we were asleep, we will often discover that the retrospection was continued. It is very important to feel this. This is not a contradiction to what has always been said, that we must not attribute any value to what happens without our wakeful "I" without the presence of our conscious self. This is because when we recall it through our memory we embody it precisely into our "I," our self.

Those who have had such experiences can be permeated in special moments by the consciousness: "It thinks." It is not I who think, but rather it thinks. Indeed, *It is thinking me.* This is esoterically the same thing that is expressed exoterically in the words, "In your thinking live the thoughts of the world."

We can permeate ourselves with this thought, *it is thinking in me* every moment, even if only for seconds, when we are free in our daily life. We can permeate ourselves with the thought that the thoughts of the world, through their thinking, have created what otherwise appears to me as "I." But this thought must never appear without being accompanied by a certain feeling. People who stand in the world think that it is acceptable to think everything; esotericists know that there are certain thoughts that we are not permitted to think unless they are accompanied by a corresponding feeling. The feeling, or sensation, that should accompany *it is thinking in me* is that of reverence, piety, or religious feeling. Only when we connect this feeling with that thought do we think the thought in the right way. Esotericists should see it as their greatest sin for them to have the thought, *it is thinking in me*, without a feeling of piety.

Then a different consciousness can arise in esotericists that is connected with the words, "In your will, beings of the world are working." This can be changed in them to the thought: *It is weaving me, it works me / it creates me*.

How all the forces streamed together in order to bring about the human being, how the human being is put together out of the past and the future, all this lies in the words, "It creates me." But here too the thought must never be thought without being accompanied by a certain feeling: the feeling of reverence for the beings who create the human being.

What we have made out of ourselves through our karma collides with what the higher beings created. Human beings must never forget that whatever happens to them, they themselves have brought it about, just as they are the ones who close a door.

These are mighty mantras: *It thinks me* and *It creates me*. Those who are most advanced on the esoteric path were those who were able to unceasingly penetrate themselves the most with these words, *It thinks me* and *It creates me*, both always accompanied by the corresponding feelings.

Those who have practiced for years *It creates me*, will themselves receive something like a gift so that they will simultaneously feel the spiritual forces that are connected, for example, with rain; the forces that create the rain, and work in the rain; whenever external circumstances cause the words to be spoken, "It is raining."

There is yet another feeling that comes to those who develop themselves in this way; a feeling that is connected with the third, "In your feeling world-forces are weaving." This is the feeling, *It weaves me*.

And indeed in doing so we feel that just as the thoughts of the world think, so also the self, thus the higher self, is being woven by these forces of the world. For this reason the feeling that should always be associated with this thought is gratitude.

It is possible that the meditation of these words: *It thinks me, it weaves me, it creates me (that is, it works in me to bring me about)* combined with the feelings of piety, gratitude, and reverence, can replace all other meditations altogether, and by themselves can lead one into the spiritual world. (However, one must never think all three simultaneously together; rather, one after another.)

Nevertheless, we are given a great help through what we receive from theosophy, if we study what is said there concerning the Saturn, Sun, and Moon conditions; for then we can understand what the "it" is, in, *It thinks me.* Theosophy (anthroposophy) is this "it." Theosophy is the world-thoughts, which have thought me as "self." This casts yet another light upon our verse and the feelings that we should cultivate in conjunction with it. We are not always capable of these feelings of piety, gratitude or confidence, and reverence, which should accompany *Ex Deo nascimur – In Christo morimur – Per Spiritum Sanctum reviviscimus*. But we are using it in the right way only when we combine these feelings with the verse.

* * *

Record B

The experiences of an esotericist usually appear in a very subtle form. Therefore the greatest attention to the processes unfolding in one's soul is required. When the meditation is over, the meditators should drop it and make their consciousness, their souls, entirely empty; and wait quietly to see if anything, a message, some knowledge from the spiritual world, is being imparted to them. Then it can happen (often while engaged in entirely trivial activities of the day, when washing or getting dressed) that a feeling appears, such as, "What was that, that just happened? Was that a dream? That wasn't me!" Esotericists must learn to pay attention to such moments; to sense that there is something present in such moments; that is, outside or beyond the being and self that is known to them.

In life we often say, "I am thinking" Esotericists should learn to feel, *It is thinking me.* "It," the great, powerful "it" they should learn to understand. This is stated exoterically in the mystery drama *The Guardian of the Threshold.*† "In your thinking the thoughts of the world are living" is expressed esoterically as "it is thinking in me." It, the great, powerful spiritual-divine, it is thinking in me. Just as soon as esotericists have this thought, *it thinks me*, pass through their soul, the feeling that we associate with the word "piety" should rise within them. There is no greater sin (an esotericist must be aware of this) than to think the sentence *it thinks me* without simultaneously having the feeling of piety awaken within.

The second sentence is *it creates me (that is, it works in me to bring me about)*. Exoterically this is, "In your will is working the beings of the world." When speaking this sentence an esotericist should call up the feeling of reverence. (As obvious as it is that a fly flying against the eye belongs together with the defensive blink in response to the fly, just as obvious should it be that this sentence belongs together with the corresponding feeling.)

The third sentence is *It weaves me*; exoterically, "In your feeling the forces of the world are weaving." Esotericists are to feel the self as a part of divine-spiritual worlds; the self, which is of course, nothing more than something woven out of thoughts. A feeling of deepest, most intensive gratitude is to rise up within this: *It weaves me.* Altogether the soul of an esotericist should be filled with gratitude toward everything spiritual-divine, and to a special extent, when thinking this sentence, *it weaves me.*

Those who might have nothing more than this exercise, and who continually carry it out, could with its help grow into the spiritual world, in large measure. It is an exercise that everyone can do, even those who are busiest of all. Every free moment can be used for this purpose. For example, when closing a door we can have one of these sentences pass through our soul with the feeling appropriate to it. But, of course, always one thought only; not all three simultaneously at once.

The study of theosophy must join these exercises. There we discover everything about the earth and the being of human beings; how they have evolved through Saturn, Sun, and Moon evolutions. There we discover how we came about and were made into what we now are. With gratitude we observe the wonderful structure of the physical human body, which is the most perfect in all of creation. Thus esotericists must learn to feel what they have become without their own doing; and what the hierarchies have created for the human being, without the human being's having done anything on his or her own. And added to this they must learn to feel what they themselves have done, so that they have become precisely what they are today. Thus they can understand karma.

Thus these three sentences lead to a true understanding of our main verse: *E.D.N.*; *I.C.M.*; *P.S.S.R.*

We awaken in the morning and become conscious again of our physical body, which we have received from the Spirit of the Father: *E.D.N.* Thus we should awaken in the spiritual world after our death into what Christ through the Mystery of Golgotha has brought about for the spiritual world. *I.C.M.* (don't speak the name out loud). Then from this follows the *P.S.S.R.*, the resurrection in the Holy Spirit of Christ.

A human being who is not clairvoyant is unconscious before awakening. But a clairvoyant will never wake up without having previously prayed, "Thank you spiritual-divine worlds, that once again I am permitted to descend into the temple of my physical body."

The Bible has a saying that is spoken twice. And it means something different, depending upon what kind of being is speaking it. Lucifer once said, "You shall be as gods." That was not a blessing. The other time Christ said, "You shall be as gods."

* * *

Record C

In the course of our esoteric life, after meditating or between our daily activities, we should always see to it that we create a tranquil state in our soul. Then we will one day experience how something can stream into our soul out of the spiritual world that we are not ourselves thinking, but rather: "it is thinking in me." We will also find, while doing our retrospection in the evening, before it is ended, if we awaken a little while later, we find that we have continued our retrospection; that is, something is going on in our soul in which our consciousness is not participating. Our understanding of a certain passage from *The Guardian of the Threshold* must constantly be deepened: "In your thinking the thoughts of the world are living. In your feeling the powers of the world are weaving. In your will the beings of the world are at work." That is the exoteric version of three occult mantras, which can advance us in a very special way on the esoteric path.

The first is: *It thinks me*. However, it is not enough to have only these words live in our souls. Esotericists must strictly forbid themselves from allowing this thought into their souls without at the same time permeating their souls with a feeling of piety. The second is: *it creates me* (that is, *it works in me to bring me about*). This sentence must be experienced in such a way that we have the feeling that world beings are working from all sides, radiating inward into us and creating us. Then we hinder what they are doing with what we ourselves have created as our karma.

It creates me; we are allowed to think only with a feeling of great reverence. The third is: *It weaves me*. This sentence must always be connected with a feeling of deepest gratitude. These three sentences will help us to advance if we allow them to live in us in moments of calmness that we have created for ourselves in the course of the day. In the same way we should experience our central verse, *Ex Deo nascimur – In Christo morimur – Per Spiritum Sanctum reviviscimus.* Or the verse of explanation given to us by the masters:

In the spirit lay the seed of my body...

* * *

RECORD D

That it sometimes seems to us that we are not advancing is often due to the fact that we are not attentive enough. We must always make our souls entirely peaceful and empty *after* our meditations to attempt to catch what is coming to us from higher worlds. But it can also happen that *nothing* is revealed to us in such moments; but later in the day while getting dressed or washing after our exercises, it can suddenly happen that something passes through us, and we know that something is coming to us in a way that is different from our usual experience. We can feel it in such a way that we say: *It is thinking in me*. And this feeling of our own selves as if we were being thought by divine beings around us must always be accompanied by a strong feeling of piety. This leaving out of our own selves, and feeling ourselves in piety as a thought of divine beings can bring us very, very far in our esoteric life. In every free moment we can raise ourselves to this mantric verse, *"It thinks in me,"* which represents the esoteric form of "In my thinking the thoughts of the world are living." But this thought must never be in us without at the same time the presence of the feeling that belongs with it: deep piety.

In the same way we can then learn to feel the esoteric form of "In my will the beings of the world are working" in the mantra "it creates me" (that is, it works in me to bring me about). We can feel ourselves as created by higher beings whose work streams together in us from all sides. Conflicting with those streams we can feel our own karma, what we have made out of ourselves. A strong feeling of awe and reverence is created in us when we can really experience ourselves in the verse *it creates me* (that is, *it works in me to bring me about*). The consciousness, *it creates me*, must always by itself produce this mood of reverence.

And finally, we will be able to notice yet a third sentence, the esoteric form of "In my feeling the powers of the world are weaving"; *it is weaving me*. And this thought of ourselves being woven by the powers of the world must go together with a feeling of great gratitude.

Through these three mantric sentences, *It is thinking me; it creates me; it is weaving me*, the spiritual worlds can be opened to us, if we allow them to work on us again and again in connection with the feelings that belong to them. But we must also take up everything that is given to us in theosophical teachings. And if we ask ourselves what the theosophical teachings are, then we can say they are "it" because they are the thoughts of the world, and they form us also. And if we can experience all of this within ourselves always, this being torn loose from ourselves, in order to feel ourselves in the spiritual beings that form us, then we will understand more and more the words: *E.D.N.*; *I.C.M.* And in particularly graced moments we will also know in a hope-filled fashion: *P.S.S.R.* When we can experience our verse in this way, then we can know that moments of great grace have been bestowed upon us.

* * *

RECORD E

1. *It is thinking me* – in a pious mood
2. *It is weaving me* – in a mood of gratitude
3. *It creates me* – in a mood of reverence, in consideration of the fact that the karma we prepare ourselves opposes the true (destiny) divine will.

Exoterically:

1. "In your thinking the thoughts of the world are living."
2. "In your feeling the powers of the world are weaving."
3. "In your willing the powers of the world are at work."

Esoteric Lesson

HANOVER, NOVEMBER 19, 1912

Notes from Günther Wagner.

Those who join an esoteric school strive, of course, to get to higher worlds, but most of these people imagine the events that then occur differently than they frequently show themselves. Many regard the visionary life as most desirable and, indeed, it must also come about; however, a visionary life is not what is most important, a certain constitution of soul is most important. Just as soon as an esoteric training has begun, the human soul is transformed by the influence of the exercises that are given to the student, according to his or her individuality. And now it is a most important thing to observe exactly how such soul constitutions are affected in the finest and most subtle ways.

It has often been remarked how, after meditation, a meditator must allow total calmness to prevail in his or her soul. At first a meditation plays into the soul like a tone that slowly echoes away. Then this too must disappear from the meditator's mind. In order to receive the spiritual world, the human mind must become entirely, completely empty. We must practice this with patience and endurance. We must remain calm and still, even if we do not experience anything for a long time. We must be happy even to have achieved this calm.

Without at first recognizing it, in such moments, which are most fruitful for our development, we can experience something. We can have the feeling: now I have experienced something. It can appear to be only a dream. But experiences can come to an esotericist in yet other forms. After we have gotten up in the morning and turned to our everyday activities, it can happen that we suddenly have the feeling: now I have experienced something. We should pay the greatest attention to these moments, because after awhile another feeling will be added; we feel, "You yourself did not think this thought." It just rushed past, was immediately forgotten again; but it was there, we experienced it. Such an experience is very important. We should direct our attention toward it more and more. For in this moment we ourselves did not think, our ordinary "I" did not think; rather, that which did the thinking was the divine thought that goes through all times and eternity.

It is thinking me: the great world-thinking is thinking me. This is expressed exoterically in *The Guardian of the Threshold* as "In your thinking the thoughts of the world are thinking." Esoterically we say, *It is thinking me.* Allowing this mantric verse to pass through your mind repeatedly brings about a boundless strengthening for the soul. We can do this immediately after meditation or in the course of the day, in every hour of leisure wherever we may stand or go. But we must not allow these words to pass through our minds as a simple sentence; rather, we must fill our souls entirely with them and, at the same time, have a feeling of the deepest piety. Esotericists should make it a matter of duty never to say *"it is thinking me"* merely as a "sentence."

Now there is a second sentence that we can apply in the same way. Here we must look back at ourselves for a moment. When it comes to the blows of destiny that befall us, most people think about why it is that this particular event happened to them. An esotericist should always have the thought of reincarnation close at hand. We are, as a matter of fact, responsible for all that befalls us. If we allow this thought to live in us, then we will gradually be able to grasp karma; we will become conscious of the connections that exist between us and the divine, spiritual world, and how our destiny, our karma is created out of this unconscious background.

Here is the second mantric sentence that should live in our souls in the same way as the first one: *It creates me. (It works in me to bring me into existence.)* Expressed exoterically it is: "The beings of the world work in your will."

When allowing these thoughts to pass through our minds we should, at the same time, be feeling the most holy awe and reverence, the deepest devotion.

There is still a third sentence. If we allow this one also to work in us then we can also gradually reach the point where we feel the weaving of the divine hierarchies of the higher worlds in our soul-body.

(*The Soul's Probation*, First scene, Capesius) *It is weaving me.* This is the content of the third mantric sentence that we should allow to work in our soul in the same way as the first two sentences. With this sentence we should be feeling the greatest gratitude toward the lofty great spiritual beings. This sentence is expressed exoterically as, "In your feeling the powers of the world are weaving."

For example, in the meditation, *I rest in the divinity of the world…*†
we are not to feel our personal "I" but the divine "I." Of course, we cannot exclude the word "I," but we should feel the higher, expanded "I." The personal self, with which we live in our physical body, must end with death and pass over into our higher self. It dies into world-"I": the world-self — *I.C.M.*

There is yet another feeling we should have, the feeling of powerlessness; powerlessness with respect to the divine, spiritual world. We ourselves are not able to maintain our physical bodies through the night during sleep; we cannot prevent them from falling apart. We come from spiritual worlds, from which we originated, back into our physical body again upon awakening; spiritual forces maintain and form us: *E.D.N.* (Father principle).

In order to experience *E.D.N.* in the right way, we must fill ourselves with the thought that all that we are, in thinking, feeling, and willing, is given to us by God; He thinks in us, weaves in us, and works in us; we are born from Him: *E.D.N.*

During our lives through the incarnations, we have darkened this divine soul-being. We have surrounded ourselves with a world of visions that come from our own being, not from the divine beings of our origin. By means of esotericism we must reach the point that when we pass through the portal of death into the spiritual world, we have freed our own divine essential core from this darkness that has enveloped our entire being as a visionary cloud.

When we have achieved this, after death we find union with the spiritual being who flows though and permeates our cosmos, the Christ. We die into Christ: *I.C.M.* And in so doing, we receive the possibility of absorbing the pure cosmic forces that we need for the formation of a purer bodily nature for our next incarnation.

Our body is given to us from the forces of nature; we absorb these forces of the Father God into our being; we have come to the Father through the Christ; "The Father and I are one."† "No one comes to the Father except through me."†

The connection to the spiritual world that we can find already in the physical world through our connection to esotericism helps us to go this path. Thus we can take into our minds and into our morality the spiritual stream that flows to us from the spiritual world, and this is the Holy Spirit. *P.S.S.R.*

*

It thinks me: the descent of the spiritual archetype from the forces of the Father, which are found behind the zodiac.

It creates me: dying into the etheric body of Christ, who encompasses the zodiac and in the [...] [incomplete in the German text].

It weaves me: receive the new that is given us through Christ from the forces of the Father.

The same as in the exercise: *I am – it thinks – she feels – he wills.*†

Explanation of the various meditation exercises.

Esoteric Lesson
MUNICH, NOVEMBER 28, 1912

Manuscript from Mathilde Scholl and Barbara Wolf.

On the basis of esoteric experiences, it is incumbent upon me now to discuss the progress that we make through our exercises. There will be many who carry out their meditations correctly, who also can produce the proper calm after the meditation so that visions can enter their soul as a result of those meditations. Many people will do this for years, and will perhaps have the feeling that they are at exactly the same place now as when they started. And yet this is not the case. It must be said that a chief reason for this is found in the amount of attention applied to their soul life. This soul life is so delicately intimate that the attention required to perceive everything must also be very sharp.

After meditating as conscientiously and well as we can, we enter into our usual daily life; for example, washing and dressing, and our consciousness is devoted to these activities. Then it can happen that we suddenly have the feeling: I have just carried out my activities in an entirely mechanical way; my thoughts were elsewhere. And if we reflect back to what our thoughts were doing, then we can get at the same kind of feeling that we have with a gentle dream, as if we ourselves were not thinking, as if what passed though our minds had been doing the thinking. When we observe such occurrences we increasingly get the feeling that something is happening in us to which we could apply the mantric words: *It is thinking me.* If we think or say these words to ourselves at every opportunity in everyday life, we will become aware that they help us; they further us in our soul life. But there is one thing to which we must strictly adhere: when we say these words, even if we only think them, a feeling of piety will arise within us. We must attach this feeling to these words every time we say or think them. It would be wrong for someone not to say the words altogether, in order not to say them with the wrong mood of soul; rather, the union of reverence with these words must simply be practiced. We then get the feeling that what is thinking in us, is related to the "I," the self; that the lofty beings who created us are thinking in us. This should become clear to exotericists in the words of the mystery drama: "In your thinking the thoughts of the world are weaving."† For an esotericist this idea is expressed in the mantra: *It is thinking me.*

A second mantric expression that can help us when properly applied is: *It creates me. (It is at work in me to create me.)* We know that all the hierarchies work in and through us, that we would be nothing without them; for this reason it is good for us to become increasingly clear about the fact that we are entirely their work. And this lies in the mantric words: *It creates me. (It is at work in me to create me.)* We should think and speak these words with a feeling of holy devotion and awe filled reverence. In the *Bhagavad Gita*, that holy book, we have an image-filled description in the conversation between Krishna and Arjuna, to the effect that we should fulfill our prescribed duties, and yet keep awake a feeling for the work of God in our souls.† This is not pointed out in this way in any other holy book; nor in any Christian book, as it is in this lofty song. Krishna says there, "You should be a fighter, or a priest, or a merchant, and so forth, according to which caste you may belong. And you should carry out your tasks conscientiously, for your destiny has placed you in your work. Nevertheless, you with your 'I,' your self, should stand above your work and feel yourself united with the divine."

There is a third expression that results from the feeling that we must acquire when we are clear about the fact that forces stream into us from all of the universe: that we have our head from here, our members from there, all our organs from various places, and we also use them as directed and maintained from those places. We express this in the mantric words: *It weaves me.* And we should think and say this only with a profound feeling of gratitude.

Thus:
It is thinking me with piety,
It is creating me with devotion and awed reverence,
It is weaving me with gratitude.

This feeling of gratitude we can still increase and support if, when we return to our physical bodies in the morning, we say to ourselves, "I am returning to something that I have not woven for myself. I could not immerse myself in consciousness from an unconscious state unless you, O Spirit of the Father, had created this body for me, and I thank you for it with the greatest awe-filled reverence."

We can carry out our meditations in such a way that we get the feeling, I am not thinking them but rather *It is thinking me*. Just as, between birth and death, we plunge into our bodies in the morning in order to acquire consciousness, so too at death we must plunge into something in order to acquire consciousness, and that is Christ.

This is said to us in the verse: *Ex Deo nascimur* (mornings we are immersed into our bodies by the Spirit of the Father). *In Christo morimur* (at the gate of death we must be immersed into the Spirit of Christ). *Per Spiritum Sanctum reviviscimus* (in order to awaken in the Holy Spirit).

Esoteric Lesson

BERLIN, DECEMBER 16, 1912

Record A: Manuscript from Mathilde Scholl; Record B: Manuscript from Alice Kinkel.

Record A

In no other time has the battle against esoteric striving been as strong as it is now. Indeed, the battle against it was carried out in the past with fire and blood, but the battle was never as fierce as today. The brothers and sisters can contribute much to ameliorate this battle, which has been brought forth only by envy. You can do much if you speak of me *not* as a leader, as often happens at every opportunity. In your hearts of course you can have the certainty and know where you stand, but outwardly you should not speak of this matter.

In human life we can observe a certain periodicity, just as we perceive a periodicity in the outer world. For example, we have here a fact, an event in life. This event passes. Then a period of time passes, and this event is repeated.

o − O − O − O

We can see in this diagram before us that the circles become larger every time. In the ordinary lives of human beings, we can observe that people attempt to overcome ambition and vanity, laziness and love of comfort. In ordinary life we can already have achieved a certain victory over these faults, and then we advance a while further in life. Then, all at once, after we have undergone an esoteric development for a time, these faults stand before us anew; and as we can see from the diagram, to a much greater extent than before. Now we can attempt to overcome these faults again, until they come at us again in increasingly intense forms. We could also remain standing where we are, not overcome them; but then we would bring this vanity and so forth into esoteric life as a poison. A good means of overcoming these faults is the threefold power.[†]

When we get up in the morning, when the "I" and astral body slip again into the etheric body and physical body, our consciousness arises through the shock that accompanies this immersion. Without the etheric and physical bodies, there would be no consciousness present in this world. These two parts that we need for consciousness do not actually belong to us; we inherited them from our ancestors. Thus the thought can also occur to us when awakening that these parts that we have received as a gift could also one day be torn away from us. From this we can understand the words that the wise men and women always spoke in the morning, "I thank you, God, for making it possible for me to awaken again," and so forth. The Father God is the one who makes it possible for us to immerse ourselves in the morning into our physical bodies again. We have a power through speaking aloud the words, *"it weaves me,"* that allows us to feel this immersion into the physical body with gratitude. We have a very powerful mantra in these words. A great feeling of thankfulness must fill us with these words: *It weaves me.* Every time we speak them we have a great source of power. But they should not be spoken by anyone who cannot produce within him or herself a great feeling of thankfulness. Our first thought when we awaken every morning is a prayer of thankfulness to the Father God who makes it possible for us to return to our physical bodies.

But we still have more. When we have one life behind us, then something will encounter us in the spiritual world. Something different confronted us in the pre-Christian ages than in the time since Christ. This changed with time. Consciousness arises through the fact that a shock is experienced when we slip back into the physical body after being asleep. After death we do not have a physical body, and the "I" today (without this) still no consciousness. However, what maintains a consciousness for the "I" is the power of the Son, whom we can encounter in the spiritual world after death. Here too we have a powerful mantra. It is: *It creates me. (It works in me to bring me into existence)*. We should speak this with devotion and reverence, and thus maintain our consciousness between death and a new life.

But then it must also happen that we go over into spiritual worlds; that we wake again through the Holy Spirit, who leads us over. And here we have the mantra: *It thinks me*. This must be spoken with great piety. Thus we have hope, love, and faith.

The threefold love will then awaken in the human being: love for the truth, love of life, and the love of creating.

We frequently encounter the love of the truth. Love of life we encounter less often. Love of life will give every human being the proper attitude and placement with respect to other human beings. How can we love life rightly without loving other people? But surrendering to someone in everything out of passion does not mean that one is loving life. Love of life exists only when we do not allow injustice to persist out of our kindness; sometimes, out of love, we must not give in to everything. The third love, now this is very hard to find: the love of creating. We should love all making, doing, and creating. And how much do human beings turn against all that is creative! For example, when people find it a waste of time to create rooms such as these, which now surround us, thus they are opposed to creative love.†

What is it that hinders us in our love for truth? That is vanity! Who can still be vain who cultivates the love of truth? We must increasingly cultivate the love of truth. Through our love of life we develop compassion and the ability to empathize with all life. Egotism is melted by this love. Those who have the right love of life cannot abide in egotism. Love of making and creating, of what is creative, does away with all laziness, all love of comfort. Thus we can say, "I love the truth; I love life; I love what is creative." We can say, "I love the truth through the Father, who weaves in me. I love what is alive through the Son, who works in me. I love what is creative that thinks in me through the Holy Spirit." Or we can say, "We are born in God the Father. We die in Christ, and through the Holy Spirit we will again resurrect." *Ex Deo nascimur – In Christo morimur – Per Spiritum Sanctum reviviscimus.* We are born into this physical body through the Spirit of the Father; through the Son we die; and the Holy Spirit gives us the certainty of resurrection.

And so we now wish to speak the words that have been given us out of the truth:

In the spirit lay the seed of my body...

* * *

RECORD B

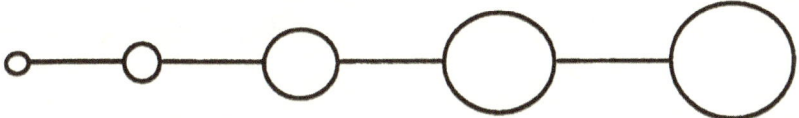

The law of periodicity, or movement in circles.
Concerning ambition and vanity, love of comfort, and laziness.

The law of periodicity, or movement in circles, exists for the larger world, and is determinative also for human beings.

Today we wish to speak of four traits that are to be found, more or less, in every human being: ambition, vanity, love of comfort, and laziness.

These traits appear periodically, and indeed each successive time with greater intensity, and must battled again and again.

It can happen that someone has defeated these traits for a time, has also worked very well esoterically for a period of time, and has also advanced. Now one thinks that he or she has overcome ambition and vanity, love of comfort and laziness, but then they suddenly appear again with increased power. The law of periodicity takes over. Now it is necessary to assert oneself over them with even greater strength. We must unceasingly watch over our soul; and this can happen successfully only if we take into ourselves an aspect of the Godhead, or the divine Trinity. These are the three aspects: the impulse from the Father God, the Son God, and the Holy Spirit.

Thus we have as the principle of the Father all that is creative, all that makes and does; all that has to do with waking and sleeping, falling asleep and waking up.

Upon waking we are dealing with what we find before us, what the principle of the Father has given us; that is, our physical and etheric bodies, and the fact that we become conscious within them when we are immersed in them upon awakening.

The principle of the Son is the principle of life; it is connected with life and death.

The impulse of the Holy Spirit is the impulse of truth and expresses itself in …(???) [missing in the German].

Thus we have the threefold love expressed in the three aspects of God:

1. The love of truth; those who have it, in them the Holy Spirit lives.
2. The love of all that is alive, compassion for all that lives; this is the principle of the Son.
3. Love for what is creative; in the Father.

This principle is the least well developed in humanity, and it must be said that all hatred and enmity comes from the fact that this principle is the most distant from human beings.

Three mantras are given for use: *it weaves me; it creates me; it thinks me.*

It thinks me; this is my angel in me.
It weaves me; the spirits of movement create us.
It creates me; the spirits of will send their forces down to us.

We should say the first mantra like a prayer upon awakening.

It weaves me; in these words the principle of the Father is living for us. These words can fill us with a feeling of gratitude.

It creates me; the principle of the Son. The feeling for this is reverence and devotion.

It thinks me; the Holy Spirit. The feeling of piety should permeate us here.

E.D.N.; I.C.M.; P.S.S.R.

1. Lazy and comfortable means that we do not love the creative principle.
2. Being egotistical means to lack love toward the life of the Son.
3. Not loving the truth means not loving the principle of the Holy Spirit.

The "I" dies in the spiritual world when we go through death; but if we immerse ourselves in the spiritual world in the Christ, then we will awaken in the Holy Spirit.

Thus the primal prayer of humanity is our Rosicrucian verse.

Ex Deo nascimur.
In Christo morimur.
Per Spiritum Sanctum reviviscimus.

* * *

Esoteric Lesson
ZURICH, DECEMBER 17, 1912

Manuscript from Alice Kinkel?

If we want to practice meditation then we must command ourselves to exclude everything from our thoughts and allow only the content of the meditation itself within our minds, our souls. Thereafter calmness of soul should rule; emptiness must enter our souls. Then we wait to see if something flows into our souls from the spiritual world; wait with patience and endurance. Then perhaps we will have the experience that feels like absent-mindedness—an experience like a dream that rushes past. We then have the feeling, "Something is thinking in me." "An angel touched me." "I lift myself into his kingdom."

As we relate to our thoughts, so an angel relates to the Holy Spirit. The Holy Spirit does not think as we do; but thinks, rather, in such a way that dispatches the angels through the world.

Such an experience is the first step into the spiritual world, and one should pay attention to it.

It thinks me, one should feel and experience with religious devotion.

Now we can further raise ourselves to what weaves through the world and enlivens the world as the divine principle; what we think in our existence. Here we have an experience like, *it weaves me.*

We thereby touch the edge of the skirt of beings whom we call the spirits of movement (dynamis).

Already in ordinary life we must immerse ourselves in something; we must bump against something in order to develop consciousness. We push against our physical bodies and awaken. After death we also push against something—against the substance of Christ! We must awaken in it; we must be immersed in it to acquire consciousness in the spiritual world in order not to spend our time there asleep.

However, having consciousness does not yet mean having I-consciousness, consciousness of self. We also have consciousness with the experience that something thought in us; but only when we remember what we have experienced, that something in us has thought, do we connect the experience with ourselves.

In this way, in death we lose the self, the "I"; as souls we plunge down dead in order to find ourselves and gradually become conscious in the substance of Christ.

Here we come to lofty beings that are foreboding to us; we characterize them as thrones, powers of will. Here the mantra is: *It creates me (it works in me to bring me into existence)*. The feeling in doing so is devotion and reverence.

When we have a clear moment in the spiritual world, we look down upon our body there below, but already a higher stage of seeing is required if we are to see it as in a mirror. At the start of such experiences, we see in a picture a coffin and a human being in it, or a bathtub filled with hot water, or we are standing in front of a door that does not open. All of these represent in pictures the physical body that will not let us in.

When we experience this picture, we are looking at our physical body there below, as we are born out of the divine-spiritual world. Then we can express this in the words:

Ex Deo nascimur.

If we imagine how we are immersed in the substance of Christ in order to die, then this is expressed:

In Christo morimur.

How we again rise up out of the rippling water and float in a delicate, fine body in the spiritual world is expressed:

Per Spiritum Sanctum reviviscimus.

EDITORIAL AND REFERENCE NOTES

GENERAL EDITORIAL NOTES

Concerning the documents used to compile this volume:
The title of this book, as well as most of the footnotes, come from the two German editors, Martina Maria Sam and Hella Wiesberger. Some footnotes were the work of the translator.

Most of the lesson notes, written from memory, have come to us in typewritten form; the rest are handwritten. In both categories the names of the note-takers are given. It was determined, however, that it is doubtful that the notes were always actually made by those who were named, since it is apparent that a lively exchange occurred between the participants. As a result there are several identical notes of the same lesson in various hands. Therefore, a handwritten or typed text that was either signed with a name or whose author could be determined may have been copied from the notes of another participant. This process of frequent copying from one another also explains why essentially identical reports of a lesson sometimes reveal minor deviations in the text.

Concerning the notes to the esoteric lessons:
For many lessons there exist several sets of notes. Some vary considerably from each other; some are a few sentences or paragraphs longer than others; some are only minimally different, by the use of other words or sentence structure. It was attempted to consider these various nuances in the following way:

1. If there are significant differences in several notes for the same lesson then they are given in full.

2. If the variations in several notes are minor but significant, they are referred to as "additional reports."

3. The relatively best set of notes for each lesson was placed at the beginning. Paragraphs from other sets of notes that enlarge on the subject or provide more details, but are essentially identical with the above, were excerpted and added to the first set. Since the authorship of almost all texts is so uncertain, the various versions are always designated only with A, B, C, and so forth. However, in the references for the text at the beginning of each lesson, it is indicated which handwritten notes were used.

Concerning the drawings in the text:
In the esoteric lessons, just as in the general lectures, Rudolf Steiner often made drawings on a blackboard. However, none of the original drawings was preserved. Hence, the drawings in the texts have been reproduced just as they were recorded by the individuals, as facsimiles wherever possible. In some cases, Rudolf Steiner's original sketches could be obtained from his notebooks.

Of the lessons collected in this volume, only a drawing from September 20, 1912, was published previously in: CW 264, *From the History and the Contents of the First Section of the Esoteric School from 1904 to 1914. Letters, Newsletters, Documents, and Lectures.*

Remarks concerning terms that recur in esoteric lessons:

My beloved sisters and brothers:
The lesson participants were always addressed in this way. This is known from several notes and from oral reports.

Race ... sub-race ... root-race ... main race ....
These were common terms in theosophical literature from the end of the nineteenth century and beginning of the twentieth. They referred to various large phases of the evolution of humanity. They were also used by Rudolf Steiner in the first years of his activity within the Theosophical Society. He gradually replaced the term "sub-race" with "cultural epoch" or "cultural period" and the term "root-race" with "main epoch." For example, compare the lectures in *The Apocalypse of John*, CW 104 from the year 1908 and his book *An Outline of Esoteric Science*, CW 13, which appeared around the turn of the year 1909–1910.

Esoteric schooling ... Exercises ... Meditations ... Auxiliary exercises:
These terms refer to various exercises given by Rudolf Steiner to his esoteric pupils. Further information concerning them can be found in: CW 264: *From the History and the Contents of the First Section of the Esoteric School from 1904 to 1914. Letters, Newsletters, Documents, and Lectures.* Valuable information is also to be found in: CW 268, *Soul-Exercises: Volume 2: Mantric Verses, 1903–1925;* CW 269 *Ritual Texts for the Celebration of the Free Christian Religious Lessons. The Collected Verses for Teachers at the Waldorf School;* CW 245, *Guidance in Esoteric Training.* Further information on the auxiliary exercises can be found in the chapter titled "Some Effects of Initiation," in his book *How to Know Higher Worlds.* (1904–1905) CW 10, and in the chapter titled "Knowledge of the Higher Worlds (Concerning Initiation)" in his book *An Outline of Esoteric Science,* CW 13.

Master... Masters of Wisdom and Harmony of Feelings
Rudolf Steiner is referring to highly developed individuals who are of the greatest significance for the evolution of humanity. "These sublime beings have already gone the path which the rest of humanity has still to tread. Now they work as the great "Masters of Wisdom and Harmony of the Feelings of Humanity." (From a letter of January 2, 1905, printed in *From The History and Contents of the First Section of the Esoteric School 1904 to 1914,* CW 264.

The spirits of time – archangelic epochs
In Rudolf Steiner's lectures there are repeated references to the seven archangels and their epochs of regency over history; the first mention is in the esoteric lessons. The names of the seven archangels and their individual connection to the seven planets, as well as the times of their regencies, can be traced back to Johannes Trithemius. In 1508 he published a mystical chronology in his treatise, *"Concerning the Seven Spirits or Angels,"* which, according to God, should rule the world. In the letter of dedication to Kaiser Karl Maximilian we read, "it is the belief of ancient wise people that the world be ruled according to the orders of God by subordinate spirits. From the beginning of the world the seven planets have been ruled by seven spirits, each of which rules the world for 354 years and 4 months (in the preface to the sixth book of *Polygraphie* four days and four hours are added). Thus the beginning of Michael's new age is given as November, 1879. It is this view, taken from the book of the old philosopher Menastor, which Trithemius mentions in the third book of his *Steganographie*." (Quoted from "Isidor Silbernagel, Johannes Trithemius." Regensburg 1885.)

Theosophy and Theosophical
Since Rudolf Steiner worked from 1902 to 1912–1913 as General Secretary of the German Section of the Theosophical Society, he used the technical terms common to that time, but always in the sense that he characterized in the introduction to the book *Theosophy*, published in 1904. "The highest to which we are able to look, we call the Divine, and we somehow must think of the highest destiny as being in connection with this Divinity. The wisdom, therefore, that reaches out beyond the sensory, and reveals to us our own being and with it our final goal, may well be called *divine wisdom* or *theosophy*. To the study of the spiritual processes in human life and in the cosmos, the term *spiritual science* may be given. When, as in this book, one extracts from this spiritual science those special results that have reference to the spiritual core of our human being, then the expression *theosophy* may be employed to designate this domain because it has been employed for centuries in this way."

After the separation from the Theosophical Society (1912–1913), Rudolf Steiner used the terms "anthroposophy" and "anthroposophically-oriented spiritual science."

Not I, but Christ in me.
This quote from Paul's letter to the Galatians (2:20): "I live, but not I; rather it is the Christ who lives in me," is frequently mentioned in the esoteric lessons, which is why it is listed here among the frequently occurring terms.

REFERENCE NOTES

Page 18, "...we can approach these spirits on each different day."
That is, every day has its own regent. See also the lesson of March 15, 1910.

Page 19, "...a longer pause would come next."
Mount Pelee is an active volcano on the West Indian island of Martinique, 1,397 meters high; its greatest known eruption in 1902 destroyed the city of Saint-Pierre with approximately 40,000 inhabitants.

Page 25, "It will have to 'glow in flaming red.'"
Presumably this refers to a passage in J. W. Goethe's *Natural Scientific Writings*, volume III (Berlin and Stuttgart 1884-1879), photographic reprint Dornach 1975) "Concerning a theory of color" (Vol. I). Didactic Part VI. Section: "The sensible and moral effects of color," Nr. 798. We read there: "The scarlet glass shows a well-illuminated landscape in a terrible light. So must be the color-tone spread out over the earth on the day of the last judgment."

Page 50, "This kind of phenomenon is genuine."
Another record of these notes includes here: "This is a sign that there is no illusion."

Page 52, "... and is related to higher spiritual things."
In another record we read here: "Indeed, we can be proud of correct, clear, logical thinking—but only if it is absolutely free of subjectivity."

Page 54, "... this is a sign that no illusion is present."
Whether the cancer symbol properly appears here is a question because it does not make sense in the context.

Page 78, "... a great difference lives in the soul when doing so."
In a record of these notes the following sentence is found additionally: "At the conclusion, the prayer was spoken leaving out the last three words; in its place a cross with a circle as a hand movement was repeated three times.

Page 91, "When we earnestly battle and strive without letting up."
In another record it reads "strive independently"

Page 97, "... because he had no time to concern himself with it."
It has not been possible to identify this man.

Page 97, "... published them as a book in America."
Presumably this is Max Hendel (1865-1919), who was at that time a representative of the American Theosophical Society. Under the name of Grashof (his

father's name), he had heard internal lectures by Rudolf Steiner and used them for his own publications. He is the founder of the community that characterized itself as Rosicrucian and was named "Lectorium Rosicrucianum."

Page 104, "...on behalf of those who entered the temple."
Plutarch, 50–120 A.D., was a Greek writer and historian. In his essay *Concerning the E at Delphi*, he says in point, "The letter *E* ... is an address to the god, and a greeting that together with the utterance thereof, puts the speaker in mind of the power of the deity. For the god addresses each one of us here, approaching him with the words 'know yourself.' We answer this with the word *E* (you are) and thereby bring to him the true, undying and sole property of himself, the predicate of existence." German version from the translation of Joh. Chr. Felix Baehr, quoted from "Greek Prose writers in a new translation" published by GLF. Tafel, E.N. by Osiander and G. Schwab, 145 Volumes. Volume 29 Plutarch's works, Stuttgart 1835.

Page 104, "The Delphic *E* is also the anchor of the Seleikids."
Presumably this should be "Seleucids," an Asiatic people in Babylon; also used as the name of their king.

Page 107, "... certain multitude whose leader is Samael."
Samael, Azazel, Azael, Mehazael: According to Agrippa of Nettesheim they are "four levels of evil spirits, destructive in the elements. (See Agrippa of Nettesheim, *De Occulta Philosophia: Three Books Concerning Magic*. Noerdlingen: Greno 1987. Second Book, chapter seven: "Concerning the number four and its leaders," p. 208.

Page 111, "... or the reversed retrospective of our meditations."
Steiner is here referring to the evening retrospective on the events of the day, which is done in reverse order, from the present backward to the start of the day.

Page 114, "... and the spirit of God hovered over the waters."
German editor's note: it should also be said that a Rosicrucian water verse circulated among the members of the esoteric school. The words are taken from the Rosicrucian writing *Secret Figures of the Rosicrucians from the Sixteenth and Seventeenth Centuries*.

Page 119, "... teach us the inner path and describe it in detail."
Meister Eckhart, 1260-1327, Dominican and mystic, taught in Paris, Strassburg, and Cologne; accused as a heretic. His best remembered works are his highly unusual sermons in the vernacular. See also the chapter on Eckhart in Rudolf Steiner's book *Mystics after Modernism* (1901) CW 7.

Johannes Tauler, 1300-1361, mystic, preacher in Strassburg, disciple of the "Unknown Man from the Highlands." See also the chapter on Tauler in Rudolf Steiner's book *Mystics at the Dawn of the Modern Age*" (1901) CW 7.

Miguel de Molinos, 1640-1697, Spanish mystic, who was sentenced to life imprisonment by Pope Innocent XI because of his book *Guida Spiritual*, (Rome 1675).

Page 120, "... on the island of Patmos he was caught up by the spirit."
Revelation 1:9.

Page 120, "... and from this point he had his visions."
In 1912 an astronomical-historical work on the Revelation of John by Nikolaus Morosow (born 1854) appeared in German translation titled *Revelation in Storm and Thunder*. (Petersburg 1907) It was published in German in 1912 with an introduction by Prof. Dr. Arthur Drews. Morosow arrives at the date of September 30, 395, for the star constellation contained in the Apocalypse. For this reason, he gives St. John Chrysostom, who was alive at that time, as the author of the Apocalypse. However, this does not explain, according to Arthur Drews, why numerous Christian writers before 395 refer to the Apocalypse.

Page 120, "We expressed this picture in one of the seven seals."
This refers to the seven seals that Rudolf Steiner designed for the Munich Congress of the Theosophical Society in 1907. The colored panels no longer exist. However, already in 1907 Rudolf Steiner published a folder of one-color reproductions of the seal and pillar images. The seals were then further developed by Clara Rettich, and placed in the house of the Stuttgart branch between the two-times-seven pillars. They are found in the collected works in the volume titled *Rosicrucianism Renewed: The Theosophical Congress of Whitsun 1907* (CW 284). One finds there two essays by Rudolf Steiner on the seals. (Lecture of September 16, 1907, "The Apocalyptic Seals" and the introduction to the folder with the 14 panels from October 1907. The motif discussed here is found on the fifth seal (Panel XI).

Page 127, "... the thought that we have killed the Christ."
Lecture from March 4, 1911, in Hanover contained in *The Mission of the New Christ Revelation*, CW 127.

Page 150, "... on Vulcan it will have become about as physical as our blood."
The terms "Jupiter" and "Venus" refer to the earth's planetary incarnations—not the planets currently orbiting the sun.

Page 160, "... health must be the same as it was before meditating."
Note in the record: "It can be noted here that certain disturbances in the sense of well-being of the one meditating certainly do enter, and that they are perceptible even into the physical body; yet these are not necessarily the result of a falsely carried out meditation. Rather, they prove to be the natural consequence of etheric and physical changes that occur within us. With such alterations in one's sense of well-being, the important thing is that one learns to deal with

them and bring them again into balance.

Page 163, "... that they learn to love lying and deception."
In another version the sentence follows here: "And it must be said that there is no way to help an esotericist against such self-incurred moral encumbrances."

Page 164, "... one's nightly experiences in the spiritual world."
In another record this sentence follows: "However, as much as possible, one must not have allowed entry to any other thought."

Page 170, "... we already considered in an exoteric public lecture."
Lecture in Munich on August 20, 1911 in *Wonders of the World, Trials of the Soul, Revelations of the Spirit*, CW 129.

Page 180, "'What is your name?' and they responded by saying, 'Legion.'"
Mark 5:9 and Luke 8:30.

Page 182, "Now I have received here a brochure ..."
This brochure has not yet been identified.

Page 186, "... doing so would bring as a result heavy karmic consequences."
Here we must bear in mind that this was said in the time before the First World War. The outbreak of the war led Rudolf Steiner to suspend the Esoteric School. However, in response to urgent requests from members of the School and the Anthroposophical Society, he continued to give esoteric advice. This led to attacks on him in a public publication (*Psychische Studien*, Volume XLIV, Leipzig) in the early summer of 1917, from followers who had become opponents. They accused him of giving meditations that were injurious. These slanders compelled him to declare to the membership of the Anthroposophical Society at various locations that he was forced to take the following measures: there would be no further private esoteric lessons, and everyone was released from their promise "not to speak about the content of their private conversation with him. Any members could convey to others, as much as he or she wanted, what occurred during such a private conversation. Nothing would be found that had to be hidden from the light of the general public." He firmly declared, "from now on everything should take place in the full light of the general public. If matters will grow in complete openness, then the ground will be taken out from under the slanderers. There is no longer any other method in the future. For this reason, as much as things depend upon me, in the future I will strive to the end that anthroposophically-oriented spiritual science unfolds in the future more and more in the full light of the public." (From a lecture held on May 11, 1917, in *The Spiritual Background of the First World War*, CW 174b; see also the lectures from May 13, 1917, in the same volume and from May 19, 1917, in *Middle Europe between East and West*, CW 174a.) In connection with the Munich lecture of May 19, 1917, he even declared in a personal conversation with Prof. Hans

Wohlbold, who had written a defense of Steiner in *Psychischen Studien*, the intention to have everything published for the public at large. (According to a written communication of Wohlbolds from May 12, 1949, to a member of the Rudolf Steiner Nachlassverwaltung.) This intention speaks for itself, even if it was not realized at that time.

Page 193, "... there where it is pale, as bright green."
The words "bright green" and "dark green" are reversed here. Compare with records B, C, D, and E.

Page 201, "The connecting link ..."
Record B has this word as "picture" or "image."

Page 202, "Praying in a mass of people is only group-blessedness."
Record E has this word as "quality of a group-soul."

Page 204, "The connecting link..."
Record B has this word as "picture."

Page 208, "... prayer in a Mass always brings a group-soul quality."
It is not clear here in this manuscript if "mass" (of people) or "Mass" (in church) is intended.

Page 208, "... does not have a beneficial effect on us; it causes brutality."
Presumably, the word "banality" is intended here. Compare with Record C.

Page 221, "'And their number is Legion!'"
Mark 5:9, "And Jesus asked him, 'What is your name?' He replied, 'My name is legion; for we are many.'"

Page 232, "... what as the creative power is active in the spirit."
The verse, "In the spirit lay the seed of my body..." is intended here.

Page 257, "The servant must not be greater than the Lord."
Reference to John's Gospel 13:16 and 15:20, and Matthew 10:24.

Page 257, "They should bring healing salvation through you."
This is a reference to "The Portal of Initiation" in *Four Mystery Dramas* (1910-1913) by Rudolf Steiner, CW 14.

Page 258, "...I have achieved certainty of being."
This is a reference to "The Portal of Initiation" in *Four Mystery Dramas*. In scene 9 the character Johannes is speaking.

Page 270, "... encounter with spiritual beings that are immediately present."

Compare: Rudolf Steiner's discussion in the lecture cycle *Egyptian Myths and Mysteries* (1908), CW 106, as well as in *The Mysteries of the East and of Christianity*, 4 lectures, Berlin, February 3-7, 1913, CW 144.

Page 274, "... as if drenched with lukewarm water."
The German editor suggests that the word the note taker heard and then wrote as *"durchleuchtet"* ("illuminated"), might actually have been *"durchfeuchtet,"* which sounds very similar to the written word, and was recorded in Record A in the sentence: "we feel ourselves to be entirely 'paralyzed,' and afterward we have the feeling as if lukewarm water were being poured all over us inwardly."

Page 280, "*The beings of the world work in my willing.*"
See: "The Probation of the Soul" (1911) in *The Four Mystery Dramas* (CW 14), first scene; and also "The Guardian of the Threshold," (1912), sixth scene.

Page 284, "Verse of the Egyptian Mysteries."
From *The Golden Ass* by Apuleius, this rhythmic version from Rudolf Steiner is in Note Book Archive Nr. 263.

Page 288, "They belonged to the community of the Beghards."
Beghards (also called Beguards or Beguins) and Beguines were Roman Catholic lay religious communities active in the thirteenth and fourteenth centuries, living in a loose semi-monastic community, but without formal vows. Coming from Flanders, they quickly spread into Germany. With time, heretical elements were revealed; above all, a kind of pantheistic mysticism. They were influenced by Albigensian teachings and by the Brethren of the Free Spirit, which flourished in and near Cologne around the same time. They were condemned as heretical, and in the course of time the persecution of these religious movements became systematic until they finally died out.

Page 288, "What has now happened in China ..."
On October 9, 1911, a military revolution took place in Hankou, China. As a consequence on December 31, 1911, a new republic with Juan Schikai was proclaimed. The Tsing Dynasty renounced the throne on the February 12, 1912.

Page 288, "... the expression of very far-reaching spiritual significance."
Ku Hung-Ming, *Chinas Verteidung gegen europäische Ideen,* Kritische Aufsätze, hrsg. Und mit einem Vorwort versehen von Alfons Paquet, Jena 1911.

Page 311, "They would like to be well versed ..."
Other versions say: "They believe they are well versed ..."

Page 316, "... black and white snake wound around it."
Presumably, this refers to the staff of Mercury (compare the lessons from

November 11, 1908, and March 3, 8, and 14, 1909 in CW 266/I). The staff of Aaron itself has an esoteric significance; compare: Exodus 7:10-12 and 8:12.

Page 317, "Development of the sixteen-petalled Lotus flower..."
Compare the chapter titled: "Concerning the Effects of Initiation" in *How to Know Higher Worlds* (1904/05), CW 10, in which the development of the sixteen-petalled lotus flower is described in detail, as well as "For the Days of the Week" in *Indications for an Esoteric Training. From the Contents of the Esoteric School.*

Page 320, "... the fourth alone was admitted and entered the spiritual world."
Concerning the 4 rabbis: In Rudolf Steiner's notebook Archive Nr. 505 there is the following note: "Garden of Joy. Rabbis in Talmud: 1. Died, 2. Lost his mind, 3. Wreaked devastation, 4. Mystic Rabbi Akiba went in peace in and out." Compare also the description found in Steiner's *Christianity as Mystical Fact* (1902), CW 8, Chapter: "The Gospels."

Page 321, "In the previous lesson..."
On March 22, 1912.

Page 322, "...the portal of death can recognize and know her."
In another version of this record the words are added: "or has been initiated."

Page 324, "An aid to understanding what was given here the last time..."
March 22, 1912.

Page 328, "*How to Know Higher Worlds* ..."
Also: *How to Attain Knowledge of the Higher Worlds* (1904/05), CW 10.

Page 328, "... through abstinence from meat, especially from eating fish?"
Compare with "Concerning Nourishment and Inner Development" in *Esoteric Lessons 1904-1909. From the Contents of The Esoteric School,* CW 266/I.

Page 329, "... reincarnated animals that were tortured, killed, and eaten."
More on this can be found in the lecture from April 17, 1912, in "Experiences of the Supersensible. The Three Paths of the Soul to Christ," CW 143.

Page 329, "... the appearance of Yahweh in the burning bush ..."
Exodus chapters three and four.

Page 330, "or words such as 'I am the Light of the World'"
John 8:12.

Page 330, "... the sphere of the hierarchy of the spirits of movement."
In Record B this reads "spirits of wisdom."

Page 334, "Introductory words were spoken in memory of Frau Danielsson."
Frieda Danielsson (1912). Member of the Swedish section of the Theosophical Society; wife of the farmer Daniel Danielsson on the farm Stathöga near Norrköping, where Rudolf Steiner had often stayed on his visits to the area; compare Marie Steiner's eulogy for Daniel Danielsson in the "News for Members" in the periodical "Das Goetheanum" Nr. 39/1940.

Page 337, "For this reason Sundays at 9 [o'clock]."
Compare with the notes from the lesson given on May 9, 1912.

Page 338, "...even more important is the result that can then appear."
Compare the lecture of June 5, 1912, in *Man in the Light of Occultism, Theosophy, and Philosophy* , CW 137.

Page 342, "... does not need to be explained any further; this stands firm."
Compare this to the lecture cycle: *The Occult Movement in the Nineteenth Century and Its Relationship to World Culture*, Dornach, October 10 to November 7, 1915, CW 254.

Page 344, "...but never publicly as A. B[esant] is now doing."
Compare this to the lecture of April 17, 1912 in *Experiences of the Supersensible. The Three Paths of the Soul to Christ*, CW 143.

Page 344, "...by means of the familiar three fundamental principles."
In the statutes of Theosophical Society Article 1 reads (charter) under point 3: "The purposes of the Theosophical Society are: First, To build the seed of a universal brotherhood, which should encompass all of humanity without distinction of race, creed, sex, caste or color. Secondly, The study of European and other literature, religions, and philosophies that belong to the East; and to foster sciences and to prove the significance of these studies. Thirdly, to study unexplained laws of nature and the psychic forces that sleep in human beings.

Page 345, "... private life of every human being, and is based upon…"
Here there is an omission in the notes.

Page 347, "... in the soul with complete dedication and energy."
Steiner is referring to the lectures he held for members of the society (*Man in the Light of Occultism, Theosophy and Philosophy*, CW 137.

Page 350, "... were expressed in drastic terms."
See reference above to p. 320 (lesson of April 14, 1912).

Page 351, "... that it is inspired by a Master of Wisdom."
This refers to the book by the fifteen-year-old Jiddu Krishnamurti (Alcyone), *At the Foot of the Masters*, Adyar, 1910 (Düsseldorf 1912).

Page 352, "... to feel this and conduct themselves accordingly."
Sadducees, Pharisees, Essenes are three Jewish groups. The Sadducees comprised, above all, the priest aristocracy. Although they were freer and more worldly in their attitude toward life than the Pharisees, nevertheless, in their teachings they were more rigid and stuck in the past. Thus they denied the possibility of the resurrection and immortality. The Pharisees fostered strict observance of the law and kept themselves apart from the "impure" masses. Many of the scribes belonged to this sect. They understood themselves to be protectors of the Old Testament ways. The Essenes formed their own communities away from civilization where they lived ascetically, often in poverty and celibacy. They had a secret teaching that was intended only for initiates. Concerning the Essenes, see Rudolf Steiner's discussion in his lectures *According to Matthew*, CW 123.

Page 361, "... *A Path to Self Knowledge* is a means to achieve this."
A Way of Self-Knowledge (1912), CW 16. Great Barrington, MA: SteinerBooks 2006.

Page 361, "Later he moved to other places, indeed to another planet."
More about this can be found in Rudolf Steiner's descriptions, for example, in his lecture on June 11, 1912, in *The Human Being in Light of Occultism, Theosophy, and Philosophy*, CW 137, as well as the lecture from December 18, 1912, in *Esoteric Christianity and the Spiritual Guidance of Humanity*, CW 130, as well as the lecture series "The Esoteric Significance of the Bhagavad-Gita," CW 146 in *The Bhagavad Gita and the West*, (Great Barrington, MA: SteinerBooks 2009).

Page 363, "... cause special difficulties for the esoteric life."
This refers to the differences that arose between Rudolf Steiner and Annie Besant based on their differing understandings of Christ. Although Rudolf Steiner from the beginning presented his insight that Christ would never again appear in a physical body, Annie Besant proclaimed from 1910-1911 onward that the Indian boy Jiddu Krishnamurti (Alcyone) was the bearer of a renewed incarnation of Christ. The order founded for this proclamation, "The Star of the East," which was intended to proclaim Krishnamurti as the "World-teacher," led to severe disagreements within the Theosophical Society; and finally to a dissolving of the German Section and the foundation of the "Anthroposophical Society." More about these events can be found in Eugene Levy's book *Mrs. Annie Besant und die Krisis in der Theosophischen Gesellschaft*, (Berlin 1913).

Page 364, "... described in the lectures held in Munich (August 1912)."
Initiation, Eternity, and the Present Moment. Concerning the Light of the Spirit and Darkness in Life, CW 138, Munich, August 25 to 31, 1912.

Page 367, "... Ahrimanic powers can take possession of human beings."
This refers to the lectures held in Munich. *Initiation, Eternity, and the Present*

Moment. Concerning the Light of the Spirit and Darkness in Life, CW 138, Munich, August 25 to 31, 1912, and to the performance of the first three mystery dramas, "The Portal of Initiation," "The Soul's Probation," and "The Guardian of the Threshold."

Page 368, "This recently occurred in a theosophical periodical."
It has not yet been possible to ascertain what periodical is being referred to here.

Page 385, "... mystery play *The Guardian of the Threshold*."
"The Guardian of the Threshold," (1912) in *The Four Mystery Dramas*, CW 14.

Page 387, "... principles followed by a great statesman ..."
It has not yet been possible to ascertain, to whom this is referring.

Page 389, "... the intellectual- or mind-soul, hence these two names."
In German these two names are *"Verstandesseele"* and *"Gemütseele."* In English the first is easily translated as "intellectual soul," while the second name presents difficulties because it means the part of our consciousness that thinks more with feelings. However, to call it "feeling soul" in English would leave out the essential thinking aspect of the German. Since the English word "mind" does include feelings, although the emphasis is on the rational aspect, the translator has chosen the term "mind soul" for *Gemütseele*.

Page 391, "... it has two names, intellectual soul and mind-soul."
See footnote to record B, above.

Page 394, "... the intellectual or mind soul (hence, its double name)..."
See footnote to Record B, above.

Page 398, "... the mystery drama, *The Guardian of the Threshold*."
"The Guardian of the Threshold" (1912) in *The Four Mystery Dramas*.

Page 405, "... in the meditation, *I rest in the divinity of the world* ..."
This is the second to last line in the mantra *"In the pure rays of the light."*

Page 406, "'The Father and I are one.'"
John 10:30.

Page 406, "'No one comes to the Father except through me.'"
John 14:6.

Page 406, "... *I am – it thinks – she feels – he wills.*"
More concerning this exercise can be found in *Soul Exercises Vol. 1, Meditations for the methodical development of higher powers of knowledge 1904-1924*, CW 267.

Page 408, "'In your thinking the thoughts of the world are weaving.'"
See: "The Soul's Probation" (1911) in the *Four Mystery Dramas*, first scene; and also "The Guardian of the Threshold" (1912), sixth scene.

Page 408, "... yet keep awake a feeling for the work of God in our souls."
Krishna says there: "You should be a fighter..." This is a summary of the meaning of the last part of the address of "the elevated one," (Krishna) in the eighteenth song of *The Bhagavad Gita*.

Page 411, "A good means of overcoming these faults is the threefold power."
This refers to the three mantric sentences to be discussed in the following.

Page 412, "... thus they are opposed to creative love."
The members of the Bern, Switzerland, branch moved into the branch's new quarters on February 9, 1912 in the "Wildchen Haus" at Marktgasse 9. "The rooms were discussed with Rudolf Steiner in detail; the colors of the walls as well as the chairs, the cabinets with the Rose Cross between the initials of the Rosicrucian verse ... and the speaker's podium with the seal of Jupiter; all the furniture was in dark blue. This was all specified by Rudolf Steiner, as well as the shape of the lamps and the exact measurements of the Rose Cross, and the zodiac in the small temple under the Rose Cross. Fraulein von Eckardstein carried out the corresponding work in painting and carving. Rudolf Steiner is said to have felt very comfortable in the room." From "The History of the Johannes Branch in Bern" by Richard Grob in *Mitteilungen aus dem anthroposophischen Leben in der Schweiz*, Nr. VI/1988.

RUDOLF STEINER'S COLLECTED WORKS

The German Edition of Rudolf Steiner's Collected Works (the Gesamtausgabe [GA] published by Rudolf Steiner Verlag, Dornach, Switzerland) presently runs to over 354 titles, organized either by type of work (written or spoken), chronology, audience (public or other), or subject (education, art, etc.). For ease of comparison, the Collected Works in English [CW] follows the German organization exactly. A complete listing of the CWs follows with literal translations of the German titles. Other than in the case of the books published in his lifetime, titles were rarely given by Rudolf Steiner himself, and were often provided by the editors of the German editions. The titles in English are not necessarily the same as the German; and, indeed, over the past seventy-five years have frequently been different, with the same book sometimes appearing under different titles.

For ease of identification and to avoid confusion, we suggest that readers looking for a title should do so by CW number. Because the work of creating the Collected Works of Rudolf Steiner is an ongoing process, with new titles being published every year, we have not indicated in this listing which books are presently available. To find out what titles in the Collected Works are currently in print, please check our website at www.steinerbooks.org, or write to SteinerBooks 610 Main Street, Great Barrington, MA 01230:

Written Work

CW 1	Goethe: Natural-Scientific Writings, Introduction, with Footnotes and Explanations in the text by Rudolf Steiner
CW 2	Outlines of an Epistemology of the Goethean World View, with Special Consideration of Schiller
CW 3	Truth and Science
CW 4	The Philosophy of Freedom
CW 4a	Documents to "The Philosophy of Freedom"
CW 5	Friedrich Nietzsche, A Fighter against His Own Time
CW 6	Goethe's Worldview
CW 6a	Now in CW 30
CW 7	Mysticism at the Dawn of Modern Spiritual Life and Its Relationship with Modern Worldviews
CW 8	Christianity as Mystical Fact and the Mysteries of Antiquity
CW 9	Theosophy: An Introduction into Supersensible World Knowledge and Human Purpose
CW 10	How Does One Attain Knowledge of Higher Worlds?
CW 11	From the Akasha-Chronicle
CW 12	Levels of Higher Knowledge

CW 13	Occult Science in Outline
CW 14	Four Mystery Dramas
CW 15	The Spiritual Guidance of the Individual and Humanity
CW 16	A Way to Human Self-Knowledge: Eight Meditations
CW 17	The Threshold of the Spiritual World. Aphoristic Comments
CW 18	The Riddles of Philosophy in Their History, Presented as an Outline
CW 19	Contained in CW 24
CW 20	The Riddles of the Human Being: Articulated and Unarticulated in the Thinking, Views and Opinions of a Series of German and Austrian Personalities
CW 21	The Riddles of the Soul
CW 22	Goethe's Spiritual Nature And Its Revelation In "Faust" and through the "Fairy Tale of the Snake and the Lily"
CW 23	The Central Points of the Social Question in the Necessities of Life in the Present and the Future
CW 24	Essays Concerning the Threefold Division of the Social Organism and the Period 1915-1921
CW 25	Cosmology, Religion and Philosophy
CW 26	Anthroposophical Leading Thoughts
CW 27	Fundamentals for Expansion of the Art of Healing according to Spiritual-Scientific Insights
CW 28	The Course of My Life
CW 29	Collected Essays on Dramaturgy, 1889-1900
CW 30	Methodical Foundations of Anthroposophy: Collected Essays on Philosophy, Natural Science, Aesthetics and Psychology, 1884-1901
CW 31	Collected Essays on Culture and Current Events, 1887-1901
CW 32	Collected Essays on Literature, 1884-1902
CW 33	Biographies and Biographical Sketches, 1894-1905
CW 34	Lucifer-Gnosis: Foundational Essays on Anthroposophy and Reports from the Periodicals "Lucifer" and "Lucifer-Gnosis," 1903-1908
CW 35	Philosophy and Anthroposophy: Collected Essays, 1904-1923
CW 36	The Goetheanum-Idea in the Middle of the Cultural Crisis of the Present: Collected Essays from the Periodical "Das Goetheanum," 1921-1925
CW 37	Now in CWs 260a and 251
CW 38	Letters, Vol. 1: 1881-1890
CW 39	Letters, Vol. 2: 1890-1925
CW 40	Truth-Wrought Words
CW 40a	Sayings, Poems and Mantras; Supplementary Volume
CW 42	Now in CWs 264-266

CW 43	Stage Adaptations
CW 44	On the Four Mystery Dramas. Sketches, Fragments and Paralipomena on the Four Mystery Dramas
CW 45	Anthroposophy: A Fragment from the Year 1910

Public Lectures

CW 51	On Philosophy, History and Literature
CW 52	Spiritual Teachings Concerning the Soul and Observation of the World
CW 53	The Origin and Goal of the Human Being
CW 54	The Riddles of the World and Anthroposophy
CW 55	Knowledge of the Supersensible in Our Times and Its Meaning for Life Today
CW 56	Knowledge of the Soul and of the Spirit
CW 57	Where and How Does One Find the Spirit?
CW 58	The Metamorphoses of the Soul Life. Paths of Soul Experiences: Part One
CW 59	The Metamorphoses of the Soul Life. Paths of Soul Experiences: Part Two
CW 60	The Answers of Spiritual Science to the Biggest Questions of Existence
CW 61	Human History in the Light of Spiritual Research
CW 62	Results of Spiritual Research
CW 63	Spiritual Science as a Treasure for Life
CW 64	Out of Destiny-Burdened Times
CW 65	Out of Central European Spiritual Life
CW 66	Spirit and Matter, Life and Death
CW 67	The Eternal in the Human Soul. Immortality and Freedom
CW 68	Public lectures in various cities, 1906-1918
CW 69	Public lectures in various cities, 1906-1918
CW 70	Public lectures in various cities, 1906-1918
CW 71	Public lectures in various cities, 1906-1918
CW 72	Freedom – Immortality – Social Life
CW 73	The Supplementing of the Modern Sciences through Anthroposophy
CW 73a	Specialized Fields of Knowledge and Anthroposophy
CW 74	The Philosophy of Thomas Aquinas
CW 75	Public lectures in various cities, 1906-1918
CW 76	The Fructifying Effect of Anthroposophy on Specialized Fields
CW 77a	The Task of Anthroposophy in Relation to Science and Life: The Darmstadt College Course
CW 77b	Art and Anthroposophy. The Goetheanum-Impulse

CW 78   Anthroposophy, Its Roots of Knowledge and Fruits for Life
CW 79   The Reality of the Higher Worlds
CW 80   Public lectures in various cities, 1922
CW 81   Renewal-Impulses for Culture and Science–Berlin College Course
CW 82   So that the Human Being Can Become a Complete Human Being
CW 83   Western and Eastern World-Contrast. Paths to Understanding It through Anthroposophy
CW 84   What Did the Goetheanum Intend and What Should Anthroposophy Do?

Lectures to the Members of the Anthroposophical Society

CW 88   Concerning the Astral World and Devachan
CW 89   Consciousness–Life–Form. Fundamental Principles of a Spiritual-Scientific Cosmology
CW 90   Participant Notes from the Lectures during the Years 1903-1905
CW 91   Participant Notes from the Lectures during the Years 1903-1905
CW 92   The Occult Truths of Ancient Myths and Sagas
CW 93   The Temple Legend and the Golden Legend
CW 93a   Fundamentals of Esotericism
CW 94   Cosmogony. Popular Occultism. The Gospel of John. The Theosophy in the Gospel of John
CW 95   At the Gates of Theosophy
CW 96   Origin-Impulses of Spiritual Science. Christian Esotericism in the Light of New Spirit-Knowledge
CW 97   The Christian Mystery
CW 98   Nature Beings and Spirit Beings – Their Effects in Our Visible World
CW 99   The Theosophy of the Rosicrucians
CW 100   Human Development and Christ-Knowledge
CW 101   Myths and Legends. Occult Signs and Symbols
CW 102   The Working into Human Beings by Spiritual Beings
CW 103   The Gospel of John
CW 104   The Apocalypse of John
CW 104a   From the Picture-Script of the Apocalypse of John
CW 105   Universe, Earth, the Human Being: Their Being and Development, as well as Their Reflection in the Connection between Egyptian Mythology and Modern Culture
CW 106   Egyptian Myths and Mysteries in Relation to the Active Spiritual Forces of the Present
CW 107   Spiritual-Scientific Knowledge of the Human Being
CW 108   Answering the Questions of Life and the World through Anthroposophy

CW 109   The Principle of Spiritual Economy in Connection with the Question of Reincarnation. An Aspect of the Spiritual Guidance of Humanity

CW 110   The Spiritual Hierarchies and Their Reflection in the Physical World. Zodiac, Planets and Cosmos

CW 111   Contained in 109

CW 112   The Gospel of John in Relation to the Three Other Gospels, Especially the Gospel of Luke

CW 113   The Orient in the Light of the Occident. The Children of Lucifer and the Brothers of Christ

CW 114   The Gospel of Luke

CW 115   Anthroposophy – Psychosophy – Pneumatosophy

CW 116   The Christ-Impulse and the Development of "I"- Consciousness

CW 117   The Deeper Secrets of the Development of Humanity in Light of the Gospels

CW 118   The Event of the Christ-Appearance in the Etheric World

CW 119   Macrocosm and Microcosm. The Large World and the Small World. Soul-Questions, Life-Questions, Spirit-Questions

CW 120   The Revelation of Karma

CW 121   The Mission of Individual Folk-Souls in Connection with Germanic-Nordic Mythology

CW 122   The Secrets of the Biblical Creation-Story. The Six-Day Work in the First Book of Moses

CW 123   The Gospel of Matthew

CW 124   Excursus in the Area of the Gospel of Mark

CW 125   Paths and Goals of the Spiritual Human Being. Life Questions in the Light of Spiritual Science

CW 126   Occult History. Esoteric Observations of the Karmic Relationships of Personalities and Events of World History

CW 127   The Mission of the New Spiritual Revelation. The Christ-Event as the Middle-Point of Earth Evolution

CW 128   An Occult Physiology

CW 129   Wonders of the World, Trials of the Soul, and Revelations of the Spirit

CW 130   Esoteric Christianity and the Spiritual Guidance of Humanity

CW 131   From Jesus to Christ

CW 132   Evolution from the View Point of the Truth

CW 133   The Earthly and the Cosmic Human Being

CW 134   The World of the Senses and the World of the Spirit

CW 135   Reincarnation and Karma and their Meaning for the Culture of the Present

CW 136   The Spiritual Beings in Celestial Bodies and the Realms of Nature

CW 137	The Human Being in the Light of Occultism, Theosophy and Philosophy
CW 138	On Initiation. On Eternity and the Passing Moment. On the Light of the Spirit and the Darkness of Life
CW 139	The Gospel of Mark
CW 140	Occult Investigation into the Life between Death and New Birth. The Living Interaction between Life and Death
CW 141	Life between Death and New Birth in Relationship to Cosmic Facts
CW 142	The Bhagavad Gita and the Letters of Paul
CW 143	Experiences of the Supersensible. Three Paths of the Soul to Christ
CW 144	The Mysteries of the East and of Christianity
CW 145	What Significance Does Occult Development of the Human Being Have for His Sheaths–Physical Body, Etheric Body, Astral Body, and Self?
CW 146	The Occult Foundations of the Bhagavad Gita
CW 147	The Secrets of the Threshold
CW 148	Out of Research in the Akasha: The Fifth Gospel
CW 149	Christ and the Spiritual World. Concerning the Search for the Holy Grail
CW 150	The World of the Spirit and Its Extension into Physical Existence; The Influence of the Dead in the World of the Living
CW 151	Human Thought and Cosmic Thought
CW 152	Preliminary Stages to the Mystery of Golgotha
CW 153	The Inner Being of the Human Being and Life Between Death and New Birth
CW 154	How does One Gain an Understanding of the Spiritual World? The Flowing in of Spiritual Impulses from out of the World of the Deceased
CW 155	Christ and the Human Soul. Concerning the Meaning of Life. Theosophical Morality. Anthroposophy and Christianity
CW 156	Occult Reading and Occult Hearing
CW 157	Human Destinies and the Destiny of Peoples
CW 157a	The Formation of Destiny and the Life after Death
CW 158	The Connection Between the Human Being and the Elemental World. Kalevala – Olaf Asteson – The Russian People – The World as the Result of the Influences of Equilibrium
CW 159	The Mystery of Death. The Nature and Significance of Middle Europe and the European Folk Spirits
CW 160	In CW 159
CW 161	Paths of Spiritual Knowledge and the Renewal of the Artistic Worldview
CW 162	Questions of Art and Life in Light of Spiritual Science

CW 163   Coincidence, Necessity and Providence. Imaginative Knowledge and the Processes after Death
CW 164   The Value of Thinking for a Knowledge That Satisfies the Human Being. The Relationship of Spiritual Science to Natural Science
CW 165   The Spiritual Unification of Humanity through the Christ-Impulse
CW 166   Necessity and Freedom in the Events of the World and in Human Action
CW 167   The Present and the Past in the Human Spirit
CW 168   The Connection between the Living and the Dead
CW 169   World-being and Selfhood
CW 170   The Riddle of the Human Being. The Spiritual Background of Human History. Cosmic and Human History, Vol. 1
CW 171   Inner Development-Impulses of Humanity. Goethe and the Crisis of the 19th Century. Cosmic and Human History, Vol. 2
CW 172   The Karma of the Vocation of the Human Being in Connection with Goethe's Life. Cosmic and Human History, Vol. 3
CW 173   Contemporary-Historical Considerations: The Karma of Untruthfulness, Part One. Cosmic and Human History, Vol. 4
CW 174   Contemporary-Historical Considerations: The Karma of Untruthfulness, Part Two. Cosmic and Human History, Vol. 5
CW 174a Middle Europe between East and West. Cosmic and Human History, Vol. 6
CW 174b The Spiritual Background of the First World War. Cosmic and Human History, Vol. 7
CW 175   Building Stones for an Understanding of the Mystery of Golgotha. Cosmic and Human Metamorphoses
CW 176   Truths of Evolution of the Individual and Humanity. The Karma of Materialism
CW 177   The Spiritual Background of the Outer World. The Fall of the Spirits of Darkness. Spiritual Beings and Their Effects, Vol. 1
CW 178   Individual Spiritual Beings and their Influence in the Soul of the Human Being. Spiritual Beings and their Effects, Vol. 2
CW 179   Spiritual Beings and Their Effects. Historical Necessity and Freedom. The Influences on Destiny from out of the World of the Dead. Spiritual Beings and Their Effects, Vol. 3
CW 180   Mystery Truths and Christmas Impulses. Ancient Myths and their Meaning. Spiritual Beings and Their Effects, Vol. 4
CW 181   Earthly Death and Cosmic Life. Anthroposophical Gifts for Life. Necessities of Consciousness for the Present and the Future.
CW 182   Death as Transformation of Life
CW 183   The Science of the Development of the Human Being
CW 184   The Polarity of Duration and Development in Human Life. The Cosmic Pre-History of Humanity

CW 185	Historical Symptomology
CW 185a	Historical-Developmental Foundations for Forming a Social Judgment
CW 186	The Fundamental Social Demands of Our Time–In Changed Situations
CW 187	How Can Humanity Find the Christ Again? The Threefold Shadow-Existence of our Time and the New Christ-Light
CW 188	Goetheanism, a Transformation-Impulse and Resurrection-Thought. Science of the Human Being and Science of Sociology
CW 189	The Social Question as a Question of Consciousness. The Spiritual Background of the Social Question, Vol. 1
CW 190	Impulses of the Past and the Future in Social Occurrences. The Spiritual Background of the Social Question, Vol. 2
CW 191	Social Understanding from Spiritual-Scientific Cognition. The Spiritual Background of the Social Question, Vol. 3
CW 192	Spiritual-Scientific Treatment of Social and Pedagogical Questions
CW 193	The Inner Aspect of the Social Riddle. Luciferic Past and Ahrimanic Future
CW 194	The Mission of Michael. The Revelation of the Actual Mysteries of the Human Being
CW 195	Cosmic New Year and the New Year Idea
CW 196	Spiritual and Social Transformations in the Development of Humanity
CW 197	Polarities in the Development of Humanity: West and East Materialism and Mysticism Knowledge and Belief
CW 198	Healing Factors for the Social Organism
CW 199	Spiritual Science as Knowledge of the Foundational Impulses of Social Formation
CW 200	The New Spirituality and the Christ-Experience of the 20th Century
CW 201	The Correspondences Between Microcosm and Macrocosm. The Human Being – A Hieroglyph of the Universe. The Human Being in Relationship with the Cosmos: 1
CW 202	The Bridge between the World-Spirituality and the Physical Aspect of the Human Being. The Search for the New Isis, the Divine Sophia. The Human Being in Relationship with the Cosmos: 2
CW 203	The Responsibility of Human Beings for the Development of the World through their Spiritual Connection with the Planet Earth and the World of the Stars. The Human Being in Relationship with the Cosmos: 3
CW 204	Perspectives of the Development of Humanity. The Materialistic Knowledge-Impulse and the Task of Anthroposophy. The Human Being in Relationship with the Cosmos: 4

Rudolf Steiner's Collected Works ✳ 441

CW 205   Human Development, World-Soul, and World-Spirit. Part One: The Human Being as a Being of Body and Soul in Relationship to the World. The Human Being in Relationship with the Cosmos: 5

CW 206   Human Development, World-Soul, and World-Spirit. Part Two: The Human Being as a Spiritual Being in the Process of Historical Development. The Human Being in Relationship with the Cosmos: 6

CW 207   Anthroposophy as Cosmosophy. Part One: Characteristic Features of the Human Being in the Earthly and the Cosmic Realms.   The Human Being in Relationship with the Cosmos: 7

CW 208   Anthroposophy as Cosmosophy. Part Two: The Forming of the Human Being as the Result of Cosmic Influence. The Human Being in Relationship with the Cosmos: 8

CW 209   Nordic and Central European Spiritual Impulses. The Festival of the Appearance of Christ. The Human Being in Relationship with the Cosmos: 9

CW 210   Old and New Methods of Initiation. Drama and Poetry in the Change of Consciousness in the Modern Age

CW 211   The Sun Mystery and the Mystery of Death and Resurrection. Exoteric and Esoteric Christianity

CW 212   Human Soul Life and Spiritual Striving in Connection with World and Earth Development

CW 213   Human Questions and World Answers

CW 214   The Mystery of the Trinity: The Human Being in Relationship to the Spiritual World in the Course of Time

CW 215   Philosophy, Cosmology, and Religion in Anthroposophy

CW 216   The Fundamental Impulses of the World-Historical Development of Humanity

CW 217   Spiritually Active Forces in the Coexistence of the Older and Younger Generations. Pedagogical Course for Youth

CW 217a Youth's Cognitive Task

CW 218   Spiritual Connections in the Forming of the Human Organism

CW 219   The Relationship of the World of the Stars to the Human Being, and of the Human Being to the World of the Stars. The Spiritual Communion of Humanity

CW 220   Living Knowledge of Nature. Intellectual Fall and Spiritual Redemption

CW 221   Earth-Knowing and Heaven-Insight

CW 222   The Imparting of Impulses to World-Historical Events through Spiritual Powers

CW 223   The Cycle of the Year as Breathing Process of the Earth and the Four Great Festival-Seasons. Anthroposophy and Human Heart (Gemüt)

CW 224	The Human Soul and its Connection with Divine-Spiritual Individualities. The Internalization of the Festivals of the Year
CW 225	Three Perspectives of Anthroposophy. Cultural Phenomena observed from a Spiritual-Scientific Perspective
CW 226	Human Being, Human Destiny, and World Development
CW 227	Initiation-Knowledge
CW 228	Science of Initiation and Knowledge of the Stars. The Human Being in the Past, the Present, and the Future from the Viewpoint of the Development of Consciousness
CW 229	The Experiencing of the Course of the Year in Four Cosmic Imaginations
CW 230	The Human Being as Harmony of the Creative, Building, and Formative World-Word
CW 231	The Supersensible Human Being, Understood Anthroposophically
CW 232	The Forming of the Mysteries
CW 233	World History Illuminated by Anthroposophy and as the Foundation for Knowledge of the Human Spirit
CW 233a	Mystery Sites of the Middle Ages: Rosicrucianism and the Modern Initiation-Principle. The Festival of Easter as Part of the History of the Mysteries of Humanity
CW 234	Anthroposophy. A Summary after 21 Years
CW 235	Esoteric Observations of Karmic Relationships in 6 Volumes, Vol. 1
CW 236	Esoteric Observations of Karmic Relationships in 6 Volumes, Vol. 2
CW 237	Esoteric Observations of Karmic Relationships in 6 Volumes, Vol. 3: The Karmic Relationships of the Anthroposophical Movement
CW 238	Esoteric Observations of Karmic Relationships in 6 Volumes, Vol. 4: The Spiritual Life of the Present in Relationship to the Anthroposophical Movement
CW 239	Esoteric Observations of Karmic Relationships in 6 Volumes, Vol. 5
CW 240	Esoteric Observations of Karmic Relationships in 6 Volumes, Vol. 6
CW 243	The Consciousness of the Initiate
CW 245	Instructions for an Esoteric Schooling
CW 250	The Building-Up of the Anthroposophical Society. From the Beginning to the Outbreak of the First World War
CW 251	The History of the Goetheanum Building-Association
CW 252	Life in the Anthroposophical Society from the First World War to the Burning of the First Goetheanum
CW 253	The Problems of Living Together in the Anthroposophical Society. On the Dornach Crisis of 1915. With Highlights on Swedenborg's Clairvoyance, the Views of Freudian Psychoanalysts, and the Concept of Love in Relation to Mysticism

CW 254	The Occult Movement in the 19th Century and Its Relationship to World Culture. Significant Points from the Exoteric Cultural Life around the Middle of the 19th Century
CW 255	Rudolf Steiner during the First World War
CW 255a	Anthroposophy and the Reformation of Society. On the History of the Threefold Movement
CW 255b	Anthroposophy and Its Opponents, 1919-1921
CW 256	How Can the Anthroposophical Movement Be Financed?
CW 256a	Futurum, Inc. / International Laboratories, Inc.
CW 256b	The Coming Day, Inc.
CW 257	Anthroposophical Community-Building
CW 258	The History of and Conditions for the Anthroposophical Movement in Relationship to the Anthroposophical Society. A Stimulus to Self-Contemplation
CW 259	The Year of Destiny 1923 in the History of the Anthroposophical Society. From the Burning of the Goetheanum to the Christmas Conference
CW 260	The Christmas Conference for the Founding of the General Anthroposophical Society
CW 260a	The Constitution of the General Anthroposophical Society and the School for Spiritual Science. The Rebuilding of the Goetheanum
CW 261	Our Dead. Addresses, Words of Remembrance, and Meditative Verses, 1906-1924
CW 262	Rudolf Steiner and Marie Steiner-von Sivers: Correspondence and Documents, 1901-1925
CW 263/1	Rudolf Steiner and Edith Maryon: Correspondence: Letters, Verses, Sketches, 1912-1924
CW 264	On the History and the Contents of the First Section of the Esoteric School from 1904 to 1914. Letters, Newsletters, Documents, Lectures
CW 265	On the History and Out of the Contents of the Ritual-Knowledge Section of the Esoteric School from 1904 to 1914. Documents, and Lectures from the Years 1906 to 1914, as well as on New Approaches to Ritual-Knowledge Work in the Years 1921-1924
CW 266/1	From the Contents of the Esoteric Lessons. Volume 1: 1904-1909. Notes from Memory of Participants. Meditation texts from the notes of Rudolf Steiner
CW 266/2	From the Contents of the Esoteric Lessons. Volume 2: 1910-1912. Notes from Memory of Participants
CW 266/3	From the Contents of the Esoteric Lessons. Volume 3: 1913, 1914 and 1920-1923. Notes from Memory of Participants. Meditation texts from the notes of Rudolf Steiner

CW 267	Soul-Exercises: Vol. 1: Exercises with Word and Image Meditations for the Methodological Development of Higher Powers of Knowledge, 1904-1924
CW 268	Soul-Exercises: Vol. 2: Mantric Verses, 1903-1925
CW 269	Ritual Texts for the Celebration of the Free Christian Religious Instruction. The Collected Verses for Teachers and Students of the Waldorf School
CW 270	Esoteric Instructions for the First Class of the School for Spiritual Science at the Goetheanum 1924, 4 Volumes
CW 271	Art and Knowledge of Art. Foundations of a New Aesthetic
CW 272	Spiritual-Scientific Commentary on Goethe's "Faust" in Two Volumes. Vol. 1: Faust, the Striving Human Being
CW 273	Spiritual-Scientific Commentary on Goethe's "Faust" in Two Volumes. Vol. 2: The Faust-Problem
CW 274	Addresses for the Christmas Plays from the Old Folk Traditions
CW 275	Art in the Light of Mystery-Wisdom
CW 276	The Artistic in Its Mission in the World. The Genius of Language. The World of the Self-Revealing Radiant Appearances – Anthroposophy and Art. Anthroposophy and Poetry
CW 277	Eurythmy. The Revelation of the Speaking Soul
CW 277a	The Origin and Development of Eurythmy
CW 278	Eurythmy as Visible Song
CW 279	Eurythmy as Visible Speech
CW 280	The Method and Nature of Speech Formation
CW 281	The Art of Recitation and Declamation
CW 282	Speech Formation and Dramatic Art
CW 283	The Nature of Things Musical and the Experience of Tone in the Human Being
CW284/285	Images of Occult Seals and Pillars. The Munich Congress of Whitsun 1907 and Its Consequences
CW 286	Paths to a New Style of Architecture. "And the Building Becomes Human"
CW 287	The Building at Dornach as a Symbol of Historical Becoming and an Artistic Transformation Impulse
CW 288	Style-Forms in the Living Organic
CW 289	The Building-Idea of the Goetheanum: Lectures with Slides from the Years 1920-1921
CW 290	The Building-Idea of the Goetheanum: Lectures with Slides from the Years 1920-1921
CW 291	The Nature of Colors
CW 291a	Knowledge of Colors. Supplementary Volume to "The Nature of Colors"
CW 292	Art History as Image of Inner Spiritual Impulses

CW 293	General Knowledge of the Human Being as the Foundation of Pedagogy
CW 294	The Art of Education, Methodology and Didactics
CW 295	The Art of Education: Seminar Discussions and Lectures on Lesson Planning
CW 296	The Question of Education as a Social Question
CW 297	The Idea and Practice of the Waldorf School
CW 297a	Education for Life: Self-Education and the Practice of Pedagogy
CW 298	Rudolf Steiner in the Waldorf School
CW 299	Spiritual-Scientific Observations on Speech
CW 300a	Conferences with the Teachers of the Free Waldorf School in Stuttgart, 1919 to 1924, in 3 Volumes, Vol. 1
CW 300b	Conferences with the Teachers of the Free Waldorf School in Stuttgart, 1919 to 1924, in 3 Volumes, Vol. 2
CW 300c	Conferences with the Teachers of the Free Waldorf School in Stuttgart, 1919 to 1924, in 3 Volumes, Vol. 3
CW 301	The Renewal of the Pedagogical-Didactical Art through Spiritual Science
CW 302	Knowledge of the Human Being and the Forming of Class Lessons
CW 302a	Education and Teaching out of a Knowledge of the Human Being
CW 303	The Healthy Development of the Human Being
CW 304	Methods of Education and Teaching Based on Anthroposophy
CW 304a	Anthroposophical Knowledge of the Human Being and Pedagogy
CW 305	The Soul-Spiritual Foundational Forces of the Art of Education. Spiritual Values in Education and Social Life
CW 306	Pedagogical Praxis from the Viewpoint of a Spiritual-Scientific Knowledge of the Human Being. The Education of the Child and Young Human Beings
CW 307	The Spiritual Life of the Present and Education
CW 308	The Method of Teaching and the Life-Requirements for Teaching
CW 309	Anthroposophical Pedagogy and Its Prerequisites
CW 310	The Pedagogical Value of a Knowledge of the Human Being and the Cultural Value of Pedagogy
CW 311	The Art of Education Out of an Understanding of the Being of Humanity
CW 312	Spiritual Science and Medicine
CW 313	Spiritual-Scientific Viewpoints on Therapy
CW 314	Physiology and Therapy Based on Spiritual Science
CW 315	Curative Eurythmy
CW 316	Meditative Observations and Instructions for a Deepening of the Art of Healing
CW 317	The Curative Education Course
CW 318	The Working Together of Doctors and Pastors

CW 319 Anthroposophical Knowledge of the Human Being and Medicine
CW 320 Spiritual-Scientific Impulses for the Development of Physics 1: The First Natural-Scientific Course: Light, Color, Tone, Mass, Electricity, Magnetism
CW 321 Spiritual-Scientific Impulses for the Development of Physics 2: The Second Natural-Scientific Course: Warmth at the Border of Positive and Negative Materiality
CW 322 The Borders of the Knowledge of Nature
CW 323 The Relationship of the various Natural-Scientific Fields to Astronomy
CW 324 Nature Observation, Mathematics, and Scientific Experimentation and Results from the Viewpoint of Anthroposophy
CW 324a The Fourth Dimension in Mathematics and Reality
CW 325 Natural Science and the World-Historical Development of Humanity since Ancient Times
CW 326 The Moment of the Coming Into Being of Natural Science in World History and Its Development Since Then
CW 327 Spiritual-Scientific Foundations for Success in Farming. The Agricultural Course
CW 328 The Social Question
CW 329 The Liberation of the Human Being as the Foundation for a New Social Form
CW 330 The Renewal of the Social Organism
CW 331 Work-Council and Socialization
CW 332 The Alliance for Threefolding and the Total Reform of Society. The Council on Culture and the Liberation of the Spiritual Life
CW 332a The Social Future
CW 333 Freedom of Thought and Social Forces
CW 334 From the Unified State to the Threefold Social Organism
CW 335 The Crisis of the Present and the Path to Healthy Thinking
CW 336 The Great Questions of the Times and Anthroposophical Spiritual Knowledge
CW 337a Social Ideas, Social Reality, Social Practice, Vol. 1: Question-and- Answer Evenings and Study Evenings of the Alliance for the Threefold Social Organism in Stuttgart, 1919-1920
CW 337b Social Ideas, Social Realities, Social Practice, Vol. 2: Discussion Evenings of the Swiss Alliance for the Threefold Social Organism
CW 338 How Does One Work on Behalf of the Impulse for the Threefold Social Organism?
CW 339 Anthroposophy, Threefold Social Organism, and the Art of Public Speaking
CW 340 The National-Economics Course. The Tasks of a New Science of Economics, Volume 1

CW 341	The National-Economics Seminar. The Tasks of a New Science of Economics, Volume 2
CW 342	Lectures and Courses on Christian Religious Work, Vol. 1: Anthroposophical Foundations for a Renewed Christian Religious Working
CW 343	Lectures and Courses on Christian Religious Work, Vol. 2: Spiritual Knowledge – Religious Feeling – Cultic Doing
CW 344	Lectures and Courses on Christian Religious Work, Vol. 3: Lectures at the Founding of the Christian Community
CW 345	Lectures and Courses on Christian Religious Work, Vol. 4: Concerning the Nature of the Working Word
CW 346	Lectures and Courses on Christian Religious Work, Vol. 5: The Apocalypse and the Working of the Priest
CW 347	The Knowledge of the Nature of the Human Being According to Body, Soul and Spirit. On Earlier Conditions of the Earth
CW 348	On Health and Illness. Foundations of a Spiritual-Scientific Doctrine of the Senses
CW 349	On the Life of Human Being and of the Earth. On the Nature of Christianity
CW 350	Rhythms in the Cosmos and in the Human Being. How Does One Come To See the Spiritual World?
CW 351	The Human Being and the World. The Influence of the Spirit in Nature. On the Nature of Bees
CW 352	Nature and the Human Being Observed Spiritual-Scientifically
CW 353	The History of Humanity and the World-Views of the Folk Cultures
CW 354	The Creation of the World and the Human Being. Life on Earth and the Influence of the Stars

SIGNIFICANT EVENTS IN THE LIFE OF RUDOLF STEINER

1829: June 23: birth of Johann Steiner (1829-1910)—Rudolf Steiner's father—in Geras, Lower Austria.

1834: May 8: birth of Franciska Blie (1834-1918)—Rudolf Steiner's mother—in Horn, Lower Austria. "My father and mother were both children of the glorious Lower Austrian forest district north of the Danube."

1860: May 16: marriage of Johann Steiner and Franciska Blie.

1861: February 25: birth of *Rudolf Joseph Lorenz Steiner* in Kraljevec, Croatia, near the border with Hungary, where Johann Steiner works as a telegrapher for the South Austria Railroad. Rudolf Steiner is baptized two days later, February 27, the date usually given as his birthday.

1862: Summer: the family moves to Mödling, Lower Austria.

1863: The family moves to Pottschach, Lower Austria, near the Styrian border, where Johann Steiner becomes stationmaster. "The view stretched to the mountains...majestic peaks in the distance and the sweet charm of nature in the immediate surroundings."

1864: November 15: birth of Rudolf Steiner's sister, Leopoldine (d. November 1, 1927). She will become a seamstress and live with her parents for the rest of her life.

1866: July 28: birth of Rudolf Steiner's deaf-mute brother, Gustav (d. May 1, 1941).

1867: Rudolf Steiner enters the village school. Following a disagreement between his father and the schoolmaster, whose wife falsely accused the boy of causing a commotion, Rudolf Steiner is taken out of school and taught at home.

1868: A critical experience. Unknown to the family, an aunt dies in a distant town. Sitting in the station waiting room, Rudolf Steiner sees her "form," which speaks to him, asking for help. "Beginning with this experience, a new soul life began in the boy, one in which not only the outer trees and mountains spoke to him, but also the worlds that lay behind them. From this moment on, the boy began to live with the spirits of nature...."

1869: The family moves to the peaceful, rural village of Neudorfl, near Wiener-Neustadt in present-day Hungary. Rudolf Steiner attends the village school. Because of the "unorthodoxy" of his writing and spelling, he has to do "extra lessons."

1870: Through a book lent to him by his tutor, he discovers geometry: "To grasp something purely in the spirit brought me inner happiness. I know that I first learned happiness through geometry." The same tutor allows him to draw, while other students still struggle with their reading and writing. "An artistic element" thus enters his education.

1871: Though his parents are not religious, Rudolf Steiner becomes a "church child," a favorite of the priest, who was "an exceptional character." "Up to the age of ten or eleven, among those I came to know, he was far and away the most significant." Among other things, he introduces Steiner to Copernican, heliocentric cosmology. As an altar boy, Rudolf Steiner serves at Masses, funerals, and Corpus Christi processions. At year's end, after an incident in which he escapes a thrashing, his father forbids him to go to church.

1872: Rudolf Steiner transfers to grammar school in Wiener-Neustadt, a five-mile walk from home, which must be done in all weathers.

1873-75: Through his teachers and on his own, Rudolf Steiner has many wonderful experiences with science and mathematics. Outside school, he teaches himself analytic geometry, trigonometry, differential equations, and calculus.

1876: Rudolf Steiner begins tutoring other students. He learns bookbinding from his father. He also teaches himself stenography.

1877: Rudolf Steiner discovers Kant's *Critique of Pure Reason*, which he reads and rereads. He also discovers and reads von Rotteck's *World History*.

1878: He studies extensively in contemporary psychology and philosophy.

1879: Rudolf Steiner graduates from high school with honors. His father is transferred to Inzersdorf, near Vienna. He uses his first visit to Vienna "to purchase a great number of philosophy books"—Kant, Fichte, Schelling, and Hegel, as well as numerous histories of philosophy. His aim: to find a path from the "I" to nature.

October 1879-1883: Rudolf Steiner attends the Technical College in Vienna—to study mathematics, chemistry, physics, mineralogy, botany, zoology, biology, geology, and mechanics—with a scholarship. He also attends lectures in history and literature, while avidly reading philosophy on his own. His two favorite professors are Karl Julius Schröer (German language and literature) and Edmund Reitlinger (physics). He also audits lectures by Robert Zimmerman on aesthetics and Franz Brentano on philosophy. During this year he begins his friendship with Moritz Zitter (1861-1921), who will help support him financially when he is in Berlin.

1880: Rudolf Steiner attends lectures on Schiller and Goethe by Karl Julius Schröer, who becomes his mentor. Also "through a remarkable combination of circumstances," he meets Felix Koguzki, an "herb gatherer" and healer, who could "see deeply into the secrets of nature." Rudolf Steiner will meet and study with this "emissary of the Master" throughout his time in Vienna.

1881: January: "… I didn't sleep a wink. I was busy with philosophical problems until about 12:30 a.m. Then, finally, I threw myself down on my couch. All my striving during the previous year had been to research whether the following statement by Schelling was true or not: *Within everyone dwells a secret, marvelous capacity to draw back from the stream of time—out of the self clothed in all that comes to us from outside—into our innermost being and there, in the immutable form of the Eternal, to look into ourselves.* I believe, and I am still quite certain of it, that I discovered this capacity in myself; I had long had an inkling of it. Now the whole of idealist philosophy stood before me in modified form. What's a sleepless night compared to that!"

Rudolf Steiner begins communicating with leading thinkers of the day, who send him books in return, which he reads eagerly.

July: "I am not one of those who dives into the day like an animal in human form. I pursue a quite specific goal, an idealistic aim—knowledge of the truth! This cannot be done offhandedly. It requires the greatest striving in the world, free of all egotism, and equally of all resignation."

August: Steiner puts down on paper for the first time thoughts for a "Philosophy of Freedom." "The striving for the absolute: this human yearning is freedom." He also seeks to outline a "peasant philosophy," describing what the worldview of a "peasant"—one who lives close to the earth and the old ways—really is.

1881-1882: Felix Koguzki, the herb gatherer, reveals himself to be the envoy of another, higher initiatory personality, who instructs Rudolf Steiner to penetrate Fichte's philosophy and to master modern scientific thinking as a preparation for right entry into the spirit. This "Master" also teaches him the double (evolutionary and involutionary) nature of time.

1882: Through the offices of Karl Julius Schröer, Rudolf Steiner is asked by Joseph Kurschner to edit Goethe's scientific works for the *Deutschen National-Literatur* edition. He writes "A Possible Critique of Atomistic Concepts" and sends it to Friedrich Theodore Vischer.

1883: Rudolf Steiner completes his college studies and begins work on the Goethe project.

1884: First volume of Goethe's *Scientific Writings* (CW 1) appears (March). He lectures on Goethe and Lessing, and Goethe's approach to science. In July, he enters the household of Ladislaus and Pauline Specht as tutor to the four Specht boys. He will live there until 1890. At this time, he meets Josef Breuer (1842-1925), the coauthor with Sigmund Freud of *Studies in Hysteria*, who is the Specht family doctor.

1885: While continuing to edit Goethe's writings, Rudolf Steiner reads deeply in contemporary philosophy (Edouard von Hartmann, Johannes Volkelt, and Richard Wahle, among others).

1886: May: Rudolf Steiner sends Kurschner the manuscript of *Outlines of Goethe's Theory of Knowledge* (CW 2), which appears in October, and which he sends out widely. He also meets the poet Marie Eugenie Delle Grazie and writes "Nature and Our Ideals" for her. He attends her salon, where he meets many priests, theologians, and philosophers, who will become his friends. Meanwhile, the director of the Goethe Archive in Weimar requests his collaboration with the *Sophien* edition of Goethe's works, particularly the writings on color.

1887: At the beginning of the year, Rudolf Steiner is very sick. As the year progresses and his health improves, he becomes increasingly "a man of letters," lecturing, writing essays, and taking part in Austrian cultural life. In August-September, the second volume of Goethe's *Scientific Writings* appears.

1888: January-July: Rudolf Steiner assumes editorship of the "German Weekly" (*Deutsche Wochenschrift*). He begins lecturing more intensively, giving, for example, a lecture titled "Goethe as Father of a New Aesthetics." He meets and becomes soul friends with Friedrich Eckstein (1861-1939), a vegetarian, philosopher of symbolism, alchemist, and musician, who will introduce him to various spiritual currents (including theosophy) and with whom he will meditate and interpret esoteric and alchemical texts.

1889: Rudolf Steiner first reads Nietzsche (*Beyond Good and Evil*). He encounters Theosophy again and learns of Madame Blavatsky in the Theosophical circle around Marie Lang (1858-1934). Here he also meets well-known figures of Austrian life, as well as esoteric figures like the occultist Franz Hartman and Karl Leinigen-Billigen (translator of C.G. Harrison's *The Transcendental Universe*.) During this period, Steiner first reads A.P. Sinnett's *Esoteric Buddhism* and Mabel Collins's *Light on the Path*. He also begins traveling, visiting Budapest, Weimar, and Berlin (where he meets philosopher Edouard von Hartman).

1890: Rudolf Steiner finishes volume 3 of Goethe's scientific writings. He begins his doctoral dissertation, which will become *Truth and Science* (CW 3). He also meets the poet and feminist Rosa Mayreder (1858-1938), with whom he can exchange his most intimate thoughts. In September, Rudolf Steiner moves to Weimar to work in the Goethe-Schiller Archive.

1891: Volume 3 of the Kurschner edition of Goethe appears. Meanwhile, Rudolf Steiner edits Goethe's studies in mineralogy and scientific writings for the *Sophien* edition. He meets Ludwig Laistner of the Cotta Publishing Company, who asks for a book on the basic question of metaphysics. From this will result, ultimately, *The Philosophy of Freedom* (CW 4), which will be published not by Cotta but by Emil Felber. In October, Rudolf Steiner takes the oral exam for a doctorate in philosophy, mathematics, and mechanics at Rostock University, receiving his doctorate on the twenty-sixth. In November, he gives his first lecture on Goethe's "Fairy Tale" in Vienna.

1892: Rudolf Steiner continues work at the Goethe-Schiller Archive and on his *Philosophy of Freedom*. *Truth and Science*, his doctoral dissertation, is published. Steiner undertakes to write introductions to books on Schopenhauer and Jean Paul for Cotta. At year's end, he finds lodging with Anna Eunike, née Schulz (1853-1911), a widow with four daughters and a son. He also develops a friendship with Otto Erich Hartleben (1864-1905) with whom he shares literary interests.

1893: Rudolf Steiner begins his habit of producing many reviews and articles. In March, he gives a lecture titled "Hypnotism, with Reference to Spiritism." In September, volume 4 of the Kurschner edition is completed. In November, *The Philosophy of Freedom* appears. This year, too, he meets John Henry Mackay (1864-1933), the anarchist, and Max Stirner, a scholar and biographer.

1894: Rudolf Steiner meets Elisabeth Förster Nietzsche, the philosopher's sister, and begins to read Nietzsche in earnest, beginning with the as yet unpublished *Antichrist*. He also meets Ernst Haeckel (1834-1919). In the fall, he begins to write *Nietzsche, A Fighter against His Time* (CW 5).

1895: May, *Nietzsche, A Fighter against His Time* appears.

1896: January 22: Rudolf Steiner sees Friedrich Nietzsche for the first and only time. Moves between the Nietzsche and the Goethe-Schiller Archives, where he completes his work before year's end. He falls out with Elisabeth Förster Nietzsche, thus ending his association with the Nietzsche Archive.

1897: Rudolf Steiner finishes the manuscript of *Goethe's Worldview* (CW 6). He moves to Berlin with Anna Eunike and begins editorship of the *Magazin fur Literatur*. From now on, Steiner will write countless reviews, literary and philosophical articles, and so on. He begins lecturing at the "Free Literary Society." In September, he attends the Zionist Congress in Basel. He sides with Dreyfus in the Dreyfus affair.

1898: Rudolf Steiner is very active as an editor in the political, artistic, and theatrical life of Berlin. He becomes friendly with John Henry Mackay and poet Ludwig Jacobowski (1868-1900). He joins Jacobowski's circle of writers, artists, and scientists—"The Coming Ones" (*Die Kommenden*)—and contributes lectures to the group until 1903. He also lectures at the "League for College Pedagogy." He writes an article for Goethe's sesquicentennial, "Goethe's Secret Revelation," on the "Fairy Tale of the Green Snake and the Beautiful Lily."

1898-99: "This was a trying time for my soul as I looked at Christianity.... I was able to progress only by contemplating, by means of spiritual perception, the evolution of Christianity.... Conscious knowledge of real Christianity began to dawn in me around the turn of the century. This seed continued to develop. My soul trial occurred shortly before the beginning of the twentieth century. It was decisive for my soul's development that I stood spiritually before the Mystery of Golgotha in a deep and solemn celebration of knowledge."

1899: Rudolf Steiner begins teaching and giving lectures and lecture cycles at the Workers' College, founded by Wilhelm Liebknecht (1826-1900). He will continue to do so until 1904. Writes: *Literature and Spiritual Life in the Nineteenth Century; Individualism in Philosophy; Haeckel and His Opponents; Poetry in the Present;* and begins what will become (fifteen years later). *The Riddles of Philosophy* (CW 18). He also meets many artists and writers, including Käthe Kollwitz, Stefan

Zweig, and Rainer Maria Rilke. On October 31, he marries Anna Eunike.

1900: "I thought that the turn of the century must bring humanity a new light. It seemed to me that the separation of human thinking and willing from the spirit had peaked. A turn or reversal of direction in human evolution seemed to me a necessity." Rudolf Steiner finishes *World and Life Views in the Nineteenth Century* (the second part of what will become *The Riddles of Philosophy*) and dedicates it to Ernst Haeckel. It is published in March. He continues lecturing at *Die Kommenden*, whose leadership he assumes after the death of Jacobowski. Also, he gives the Gutenberg Jubilee lecture before 7,000 typesetters and printers. In September, Rudolf Steiner is invited by Count and Countess Brockdorff to lecture in the Theosophical Library. His first lecture is on Nietzsche. His second lecture is titled "Goethe's Secret Revelation." October 6, he begins a lecture cycle on the mystics that will become *Mystics after Modernism* (CW 7). November-December: "Marie von Sivers appears in the audience...." Also in November, Steiner gives his first lecture at the Giordano Bruno Bund (where he will continue to lecture until May, 1905). He speaks on Bruno and modern Rome, focusing on the importance of the philosophy of Thomas Aquinas as monism.

1901: In continual financial straits, Rudolf Steiner's early friends Moritz Zitter and Rosa Mayreder help support him. In October, he begins the lecture cycle *Christianity as Mystical Fact* (CW 8) at the Theosophical Library. In November, he gives his first "Theosophical lecture" on Goethe's "Fairy Tale" in Hamburg at the invitation of Wilhelm Hubbe-Schleiden. He also attends a tea to celebrate the founding of the Theosophical Society at Count and Countess Brockdorff's. He gives a lecture cycle, "From Buddha to Christ," for the circle of the *Kommenden*. November 17, Marie von Sivers asks Rudolf Steiner if Theosophy does not need a Western-Christian spiritual movement (to complement Theosophy's Eastern emphasis). "The question was posed. Now, following spiritual laws, I could begin to give an answer...." In December, Rudolf Steiner writes his first article for a Theosophical publication. At year's end, the Brockdorffs and possibly Wilhelm Hubbe-Schleiden ask Rudolf Steiner to join the Theosophical Society and undertake the leadership of the German Section. Rudolf Steiner agrees, on the condition that Marie von Sivers (then in Italy) work with him.

1902: Beginning in January, Rudolf Steiner attends the opening of the Workers' School in Spandau with Rosa Luxemberg (1870-1919). January 17, Rudolf Steiner joins the Theosophical Society. In April, he is asked to become general secretary of the German Section of the Theosophical Society, and works on preparations for its founding. In July, he visits London for a Theosophical congress. He meets Bertram

Keightly, G.R.S. Mead, A.P. Sinnett, and Annie Besant, among others. In September, *Christianity as Mystical Fact* appears. In October, Rudolf Steiner gives his first public lecture on theosophy ("Monism and Theosophy") to about three hundred people at the Giordano Bruno Bund. On October 19-21, the German Section of the Theosophical Society has its first meeting; Rudolf Steiner is the general secretary, and Annie Besant attends. Steiner lectures on practical karma studies. On October 23, Annie Besant inducts Rudolf Steiner into the Esoteric School of the Theosophical Society. On October 25, Steiner begins a weekly series of lectures: "The Field of Theosophy." During this year, Rudolf Steiner also first meets Ita Wegman (1876-1943), who will become his close collaborator in his final years.

1903: Rudolf Steiner holds about 300 lectures and seminars. In May, the first issue of the periodical *Luzifer* appears. In June, Rudolf Steiner visits London for the first meeting of the Federation of the European Sections of the Theosophical Society, where he meets Colonel Olcott. He begins to write *Theosophy* (CW 9).

1904: Rudolf Steiner continues lecturing at the Workers' College and elsewhere (about 90 lectures), while lecturing intensively all over Germany among Theosophists (about a 140 lectures). In February, he meets Carl Unger (1878-1929), who will become a member of the board of the Anthroposophical Society (1913). In March, he meets Michael Bauer (1871-1929), a Christian mystic, who will also be on the board. In May, *Theosophy* appears, with the dedication: "To the spirit of Giordano Bruno." Rudolf Steiner and Marie von Sivers visit London for meetings with Annie Besant. June: Rudolf Steiner and Marie von Sivers attend the meeting of the Federation of European Sections of the Theosophical Society in Amsterdam. In July, Steiner begins the articles in *Luzifer-Gnosis* that will become *How to Know Higher Worlds* (CW 10) and *Cosmic Memory* (CW 11). In September, Annie Besant visits Germany. In December, Steiner lectures on Freemasonry. He mentions the High Grade Masonry derived from John Yarker and represented by Theodore Reuss and Karl Kellner as a blank slate "into which a good image could be placed."

1905: This year, Steiner ends his non-Theosophical lecturing activity. Supported by Marie von Sivers, his Theosophical lecturing—both in public and in the Theosophical Society—increases significantly: "The German Theosophical Movement is of exceptional importance." Steiner recommends reading, among others, Fichte, Jacob Boehme, and Angelus Silesius. He begins to introduce Christian themes into Theosophy. He also begins to work with doctors (Felix Peipers and Ludwig Noll). In July, he is in London for the Federation of European Sections, where he attends a lecture by Annie Besant: "I have seldom seen Mrs. Besant speak in so inward and heartfelt a manner...." "Through Mrs. Besant I have found the way to H.P. Blavatsky."

September to October, he gives a course of thirty-one lectures for a small group of esoteric students. In October, the annual meeting of the German Section of the Theosophical Society, which still remains very small, takes place. Rudolf Steiner reports membership has risen from 121 to 377 members. In November, seeking to establish esoteric "continuity," Rudolf Steiner and Marie von Sivers participate in a "Memphis-Misraim" Masonic ceremony. They pay forty-five marks for membership. "Yesterday, you saw how little remains of former esoteric institutions." "We are dealing only with a 'framework'... for the present, nothing lies behind it. The occult powers have completely withdrawn."

1906: Expansion of Theosophical work. Rudolf Steiner gives about 245 lectures, only 44 of which take place in Berlin. Cycles are given in Paris, Leipzig, Stuttgart, and Munich. Esoteric work also intensifies. Rudolf Steiner begins writing *An Outline of Esoteric Science* (CW 13). In January, Rudolf Steiner receives permission (a patent) from the Great Orient of the Scottish A & A Thirty-Three Degree Rite of the Order of the Ancient Freemasons of the Memphis-Misraim Rite to direct a chapter under the name "Mystica Aeterna." This will become the "Cognitive Cultic Section" (also called "Misraim Service") of the Esoteric School. (See: *From the History and Contents of the Cognitive Cultic Section* (CW 264). During this time, Steiner also meets Albert Schweitzer. In May, he is in Paris, where he visits Edouard Schuré. Many Russians attend his lectures (including Konstantin Balmont, Dimitri Mereszkovski, Zinaida Hippius, and Maximilian Woloshin). He attends the General Meeting of the European Federation of the Theosophical Society, at which Col. Olcott is present for the last time. He spends the year's end in Venice and Rome, where he writes and works on his translation of H.P. Blavatsky's *Key to Theosophy.*

1907: Further expansion of the German Theosophical Movement according to the Rosicrucian directive to "introduce spirit into the world"—in education, in social questions, in art, and in science. In February, Col. Olcott dies in Adyar. Before he dies, Olcott indicates that "the Masters" wish Annie Besant to succeed him: much politicking ensues. Rudolf Steiner supports Besant's candidacy. April-May: preparations for the Congress of the Federation of European Sections of the Theosophical Society—the great, watershed Whitsun "Munich Congress," attended by Annie Besant and others. Steiner decides to separate Eastern and Western (Christian-Rosicrucian) esoteric schools. He takes his esoteric school out of the Theosophical Society (Besant and Rudolf Steiner are "in harmony" on this). Steiner makes his first lecture tours to Austria and Hungary. That summer, he is in Italy. In September, he visits Edouard Schuré, who will write the introduction to the French edition of *Christianity as Mystical Fact* in Barr, Alsace. Rudolf Steiner writes the autobiographical statement known as the "Barr Document." In *Luzifer–Gnosis*, "The Education of the Child" appears.

1908: The movement grows (membership: 1150). Lecturing expands. Steiner makes his first extended lecture tour to Holland and Scandinavia, as well as visits to Naples and Sicily. Themes: St. John's Gospel, the Apocalypse, Egypt, science, philosophy, and logic. *Luzifer-Gnosis* ceases publication. In Berlin, Marie von Sivers (with Johanna Mücke (1864-1949) forms the *Philosophisch-Theosophisch* (after 1915 *Philosophisch-Anthroposophisch*) *Verlag* to publish Steiner's work. Steiner gives lecture cycles titled *The Gospel of St. John* (CW 103) and *The Apocalypse* (104).

1909: *An Outline of Esoteric Science* appears. Lecturing and travel continues. Rudolf Steiner's spiritual research expands to include the polarity of Lucifer and Ahriman; the work of great individualities in history; the Maitreya Buddha and the Bodhisattvas; spiritual economy (CW 109); the work of the spiritual hierarchies in heaven and on Earth (CW 110). He also deepens and intensifies his research into the Gospels, giving lectures on the Gospel of St. Luke (CW 114) with the first mention of two Jesus children. Meets and becomes friends with Christian Morgenstern (1871-1914). In April, he lays the foundation stone for the Malsch model—the building that will lead to the first Goetheanum. In May, the International Congress of the Federation of European Sections of the Theosophical Society takes place in Budapest. Rudolf Steiner receives the Subba Row medal for *How to Know Higher Worlds*. During this time, Charles W. Leadbeater discovers Jiddu Krishnamurti (1895-1986) and proclaims him the future "world teacher," the bearer of the Maitreya Buddha and the "reappearing Christ." In October, Steiner delivers seminal lectures on "anthroposophy," which he will try, unsuccessfully, to rework over the next years into the unfinished work, *Anthroposophy (A Fragment)* (CW 45).

1910: New themes: *The Reappearance of Christ in the Etheric* (CW 118); *The Fifth Gospel; The Mission of Folk Souls* (CW 121); *Occult History* (CW 126); the evolving development of etheric cognitive capacities. Rudolf Steiner continues his Gospel research with *The Gospel of St. Matthew* (CW 123). In January, his father dies. In April, he takes a month-long trip to Italy, including Rome, Monte Cassino, and Sicily. He also visits Scandinavia again. July-August, he writes the first mystery drama, *The Portal of Initiation* (CW 14). In November, he gives "psychosophy" lectures. In December, he submits "On the Psychological Foundations and Epistemological Framework of Theosophy" to the International Philosophical Congress in Bologna.

1911: The crisis in the Theosophical Society deepens. In January, "The Order of the Rising Sun," which will soon become "The Order of the Star in the East," is founded for the coming world teacher, Krishnamurti. At the same time, Marie von Sivers, Rudolf Steiner's coworker, falls ill. Fewer lectures are given, but important new ground is broken. In Prague, in March, Steiner meets Franz Kafka (1883-1924) and Hugo Bergmann (1883-1975). In April, he delivers his paper to the

Philosophical Congress. He writes the second mystery drama, *The Soul's Probation* (CW 14). Also, while Marie von Sivers is convalescing, Rudolf Steiner begins work on *Calendar 1912/1913*, which will contain the "Calendar of the Soul" meditations. On March 19, Anna (Eunike) Steiner dies. In September, Rudolf Steiner visits Einsiedeln, birthplace of Paracelsus. In December, Friedrich Rittelmeyer, future founder of the Christian Community, meets Rudolf Steiner. The *Johannes-Bauverein*, the "building committee," which would lead to the first Goetheanum (first planned for Munich), is also founded, and a preliminary committee for the founding of an independent association is created that, in the following year, will become the Anthroposophical Society. Important lecture cycles include *Occult Physiology* (CW 128); *Wonders of the World* (CW 129); *From Jesus to Christ* (CW 131). Other themes: esoteric Christianity; Christian Rosenkreutz; the spiritual guidance of humanity; the sense world and the world of the spirit.

1912: Despite the ongoing, now increasing crisis in the Theosophical Society, much is accomplished: *Calendar 1912/1913* is published; eurythmy is created; both the third mystery drama, *The Guardian of the Threshold* (CW 14) and *A Way of Self-Knowledge* (CW 16) are written. New (or renewed) themes included life between death and rebirth and karma and reincarnation. Other lecture cycles: *Spiritual Beings in the Heavenly Bodies and the Kingdoms of Nature* (CW 136); *The Human Being in the Light of Occultism, Theosophy, and Philosophy* (CW 137); *The Gospel of St. Mark* (CW 139); and *The Bhagavad Gita and the Epistles of Paul* (CW 142). On May 8, Rudolf Steiner celebrates White Lotus Day, H.P. Blavatsky's death day, which he had faithfully observed for the past decade, for the last time. In August, Rudolf Steiner suggests the "independent association" be called the "Anthroposophical Society." In September, the first eurythmy course takes place. In October, Rudolf Steiner declines recognition of a Theosophical Society lodge dedicated to the Star of the East and decides to expel all Theosophical Society members belonging to the order. Also, with Marie von Sivers, he first visits Dornach, near Basel, Switzerland, and they stand on the hill where the Goetheanum will be. In November, a Theosophical Society lodge is opened by direct mandate from Adyar (Annie Besant). In December, a meeting of the German section occurs at which it is decided that belonging to the Order of the Star of the East is incompatible with membership in the Theosophical Society. December 28: informal founding of the Anthroposophical Society in Berlin.

1913: Expulsion of the German section from the Theosophical Society. February 2-3: Foundation meeting of the Anthroposophical Society. Board members include: Marie von Sivers, Michael Bauer, and Carl Unger. September 20: Laying of the foundation stone for the *Johannes Bau* (Goetheanum) in Dornach. Building begins immediately. The third mystery drama, *The Soul's Awakening* (CW 14), is completed.

Also: *The Threshold of the Spiritual World* (CW 147). Lecture cycles include: *The Bhagavad Gita and the Epistles of Paul* and *The Esoteric Meaning of the Bhagavad Gita* (CW 146), which the Russian philosopher Nikolai Berdyaev attends; *The Mysteries of the East and of Christianity* (CW 144); *The Effects of Esoteric Development* (CW 145); and *The Fifth Gospel* (CW 148). In May, Rudolf Steiner is in London and Paris, where anthroposophical work continues.

1914: Building continues on the *Johannes Bau* (Goetheanum) in Dornach, with artists and coworkers from seventeen nations. The general assembly of the Anthroposophical Society takes place. In May, Rudolf Steiner visits Paris, as well as Chartres Cathedral. June 28: assassination in Sarajevo ("Now the catastrophe has happened!"). August 1: War is declared. Rudolf Steiner returns to Germany from Dornach—he will travel back and forth. He writes the last chapter of *The Riddles of Philosophy*. Lecture cycles include: *Human and Cosmic Thought* (CW 151); *Inner Being of Humanity between Death and a New Birth* (CW 153); *Occult Reading and Occult Hearing* (CW 156). December 24: marriage of Rudolf Steiner and Marie von Sivers.

1915: Building continues. Life after death becomes a major theme, also art. Writes: *Thoughts during a Time of War* (CW 24). Lectures include: *The Secret of Death* (CW 159); *The Uniting of Humanity through the Christ Impulse* (CW 165).

1916: Rudolf Steiner begins work with Edith Maryon (1872-1924) on the sculpture "The Representative of Humanity" ("The Group"—Christ, Lucifer, and Ahriman). He also works with the alchemist Alexander von Bernus on the quarterly *Das Reich*. He writes *The Riddle of Humanity* (CW 20). Lectures include: *Necessity and Freedom in World History and Human Action* (CW 166); *Past and Present in the Human Spirit* (CW 167); *The Karma of Vocation* (CW 172); *The Karma of Untruthfulness* (CW 173).

1917: Russian Revolution. The U.S. enters the war. Building continues. Rudolf Steiner delineates the idea of the "threefold nature of the human being" (in a public lecture March 15) and the "threefold nature of the social organism" (hammered out in May-June with the help of Otto von Lerchenfeld and Ludwig Polzer-Hoditz in the form of two documents titled *Memoranda*, which were distributed in high places). August-September: Rudolf Steiner writes *The Riddles of the Soul* (CW 20). Also: commentary on "The Chemical Wedding of Christian Rosenkreutz" for Alexander Bernus (*Das Reich*). Lectures include: *The Karma of Materialism* (CW 176); *The Spiritual Background of the Outer World: The Fall of the Spirits of Darkness* (CW 177).

1918: March 18: peace treaty of Brest-Litovsk—"Now everything will truly enter chaos! What is needed is cultural renewal." June: Rudolf Steiner visits Karlstein (Grail) Castle outside Prague. Lecture cycle: *From Symptom to Reality in Modern History* (CW 185). In mid-November,

Emil Molt, of the Waldorf-Astoria Cigarette Company, has the idea of founding a school for his workers' children.

1919: Focus on the threefold social organism: tireless travel, countless lectures, meetings, and publications. At the same time, a new public stage of Anthroposophy emerges as cultural renewal begins. The coming years will see initiatives in pedagogy, medicine, pharmacology, and agriculture. January 27: threefold meeting: " We must first of all, with the money we have, found free schools that can bring people what they need." February: first public eurythmy performance in Zurich. Also: "Appeal to the German People" (CW 24), circulated March 6 as a newspaper insert. In April, *Toward Social Renewal* (CW 23)—"perhaps the most widely read of all books on politics appearing since the war"—appears. Rudolf Steiner is asked to undertake the "direction and leadership" of the school founded by the Waldorf-Astoria Company. Rudolf Steiner begins to talk about the "renewal" of education. May 30: a building is selected and purchased for the future Waldorf School. August-September, Rudolf Steiner gives a lecture course for Waldorf teachers, *The Foundations of Human Experience (Study of Man)* (CW 293). September 7: Opening of the first Waldorf School. December (into January): first science course, the *Light Course* (CW 320).

1920: The Waldorf School flourishes. New threefold initiatives. Founding of limited companies *Der Kommenden Tag* and *Futurum A.G.* to infuse spiritual values into the economic realm. Rudolf Steiner also focuses on the sciences. Lectures: *Introducing Anthroposophical Medicine* (CW 312); *The Warmth Course* (CW 321); *The Boundaries of Natural Science* (CW 322); *The Redemption of Thinking* (CW 74). February: Johannes Werner Klein—later a cofounder of the Christian Community—asks Rudolf Steiner about the possibility of a "religious renewal," a "Johannine church." In March, Rudolf Steiner gives the first course for doctors and medical students. In April, a divinity student asks Rudolf Steiner a second time about the possibility of religious renewal. September 27-October 16: anthroposophical "university course." December: lectures titled *The Search for the New Isis* (CW 202).

1921: Rudolf Steiner continues his intensive work on cultural renewal, including the uphill battle for the threefold social order. "University" arts, scientific, theological, and medical courses include: *The Astronomy Course* (CW 323); *Observation, Mathematics, and Scientific Experiment* (CW 324); the *Second Medical Course* (CW 313); *Color*. In June and September-October, Rudolf Steiner also gives the first two "priests' courses" (CW 342 and 343). The "youth movement" gains momentum. Magazines are founded: *Die Drei* (January), and—under the editorship of Albert Steffen (1884-1963)—the weekly, *Das Goetheanum* (August). In February-March, Rudolf Steiner takes his first trip outside Germany since the war (Holland). On April 7, Steiner receives a letter regarding "religious renewal," and May 22-23, he agrees to address the question in a practical way. In June, the Klinical-Therapeutic Institute opens in Arlesheim under the direction of Dr. Ita Wegman. In August, the Chemical-Pharmaceutical Laboratory opens in Arlesheim (Oskar Schmiedel and Ita Wegman, directors). The Clinical Therapeutic Institute is inaugurated in Stuttgart (Dr. Ludwig Noll, director); also the Research Laboratory in Dornach (Ehrenfried Pfeiffer and Gunther Wachsmuth, directors). In November-December, Rudolf Steiner visits Norway.

1922: The first half of the year involves very active public lecturing (thousands attend); in the second half, Rudolf Steiner begins to withdraw and turn toward the Society—"The Society is asleep." It is "too weak" to do what is asked of it. The businesses—*Die Kommenden Tag* and *Futura A.G.*—fail. In January, with the help of an agent, Steiner undertakes a twelve-city German tour, accompanied by eurythmy performances. In two weeks he speaks to more than 2,000 people. In April, he gives a "university course" in The Hague. He also visits England. In June, he is in Vienna for the East-West Congress. In August-September, he is back in England for the Oxford Conference on Education. Returning to Dornach, he gives the lectures *Philosophy, Cosmology, and Religion* (CW 215), and gives the third priest's course (CW 344). On September 16, The Christian Community is founded. In October-November, Steiner is in Holland and England. He also speaks to the youth: *The Youth Course* (CW 217). In December, Steiner gives lectures titled *The Origins of Natural Science* (CW 326), and *Humanity and the World of Stars: The Spiritual Communion of Humanity* (CW 219). December 31: Fire at the Goetheanum, which is destroyed.

1923: Despite the fire, Rudolf Steiner continues his work unabated. A very hard year. Internal dispersion, dissension, and apathy abound. There is conflict—between old and new visions—within the society. A wake-up call is needed, and Rudolf Steiner responds with renewed lecturing vitality. His focus: the spiritual context of human life; initiation science; the course of the year; and community building. As a foundation for an artistic school, he creates a series of pastel sketches. Lecture cycles: *The Anthroposophical Movement; Initiation Science* (CW 227) (in England at the Penmaenmawr Summer School); *The Four Seasons and the Archangels* (CW 229); *Harmony of the Creative Word* (CW 230); *The Supersensible Human* (CW 231), given in Holland for the founding of the Dutch society. On November 10, in response to the failed Hitler-Ludendorf putsch in Munich, Steiner closes his Berlin residence and moves the *Philosophisch-Anthroposophisch Verlag* (Press) to Dornach. On December 9, Steiner begins the serialization of his *Autobiography: The Course of My Life* (CW 28) in *Das Goetheanum*. It will continue to appear weekly, without a break, until his death. Late December-early January: Rudolf Steiner refounds the Anthroposophical Society (about 12,000 members internationally) and takes over its leadership. The new board members are: Marie Steiner, Ita Wegman, Albert Steffen, Elizabeth Vreede, and Guenther Wachsmuth. (See *The Christmas Meeting for the Founding of the General Anthroposophical Society* (CW 260). Accompanying lectures: *Mystery Knowledge and Mystery Centers* (CW 232); *World History in the Light of Anthroposophy* (CW 233). December 25: the Foundation Stone is laid (in the hearts of members) in the form of the "Foundation Stone Meditation."

1924: January 1: having founded the Anthroposophical Society and taken over its leadership, Rudolf Steiner has the task of "reforming" it. The process begins with a weekly newssheet ("What's Happening in the Anthroposophical Society") in which Rudolf Steiner's "Letters to Members" and "Anthroposophical Leading Thoughts" appear (CW 26). The next step is the creation of a new esoteric class, the "first class" of the "University of Spiritual Science" (which was to have been followed, had Rudolf Steiner lived longer, by two more advanced classes). Then comes a new language for Anthroposophy—practical, phenomenological, and direct; and Rudolf Steiner creates the model for the second Goetheanum. He begins the series of extensive "karma" lectures (CW 235-40); and finally, responding to needs, he creates two new initiatives: biodynamic agriculture and curative education. After the middle of the year, rumors begin to circulate regarding Steiner's health. Lectures: January-February, *Anthroposophy* (CW 234); February: *Tone Eurythmy* (CW 278); June: *The Agriculture Course* (CW 327); June-July: Speech [?] Eurythmy (CW 279); *Curative Education* (CW 317); August: (England, "Second International Summer School"), *Initiation Consciousness: True and False Paths in Spiritual Investigation* (CW 243); September: *Pastoral Medicine* (CW 318). On September 26, for the first time, Rudolf Steiner cancels a lecture. On September 28, he gives his last lecture. On September 29, he withdraws to his studio in the carpenter's shop; now he is definitively ill. Cared for by Ita Wegman, he continues working, however, and writing the weekly installments of his *Autobiography* and *Letters to the Members/Leading Thoughts* (CW 26).

1925: Rudolf Steiner, while continuing to work, continues to weaken. He finishes *Extending Practical Medicine* (CW 27) with Ita Wegman.
On March 30, around ten in the morning, Rudolf Steiner dies.

INDEX

abandonment, 62
absentmindedness, 177, 416
Adam, 321-322, 324-327
   Adam and Eve, 354, 359
   as motherless human being, 321-322, 324-325, 327
agoraphobia, 194, 206-207
Ahazel. *See* Mehazael
Ahriman, 58, 61, 64, 68, 72, 80, 87, 117, 122-123, 130, 284
ahrimanic, 126, 143, 367-368, 371, 374
Akashic Chronicle, 79, 84, 149, 189, 331
alcohol, 101, 328, 331, 334
Alcyone affair, 372, 374
ambition, 103, 157, 160-161, 165, 167, 171, 283, 342-343, 347-348, 387, 390, 410, 413
animal kingdom, 37, 43, 45-46, 197, 200, 202, 204, 228, 322, 327
Anthroposophy. *See* spiritual science
antipathetic/antipathy, 156, 159, 163, 167, 310, 312, 314, 364, 369, 371-372, 374, 379, 383, 392
apathy, 58, 218, 224, 251
Apocalypse, 120
Archai. *See also* Hierarchies, Archai
   as primal beings, 31, 33, 35
archetypal/archetype, 2-3, 18, 75,77, 80, 82, 85-86, 190, 197, 219, 387
Arjuna, 408
arrogance, 18-20, 31, 33, 45, 52, 54, 103, 143-144, 165, 195, 227, 297, 346, 349
astral, 22, 38, 78, 83-84, 100, 114, 137, 143, 171, 174, 177, 180, 221, 301, 322
   astral maya, 117. *See also* Lucifer
astral body, 21-22, 37, 46, 48, 51-52, 90-92, 97, 100, 107-108, 110-113, 119, 123, 125, 149-151, 155, 159, 162, 165, 168, 170-172, 174, 176-177, 179-181, 210-211, 213, 215-217, 275, 277, 281, 301, 310, 312, 314, 338-339, 392, 411
   as body of knowledge, 150, 153
   as cognition body, 150
   purified, 275, 277, 281
   thread connection, 171
art/artistic, 16, 91, 115, 152, 196, 204, 255, 258, 260, 357
Atlantean/Atlantis, 147, 219, 233, 235-236, 288, 290, 292-293
Atma, 87
aura, 41, 151, 201, 203, 272, 275, 277, 281, 290, 294
awe/awe-filled, 46, 127, 131, 371, 391, 401, 404, 408-409
Azael, 221, 223-224, 226, 230,-231 250-251, 253, 268
Azazel, 107-108, 210, 211, 213-218 220, 223, 226, 230, 250, 253, 268

backbone, 95
bacteria, as reincarnated animals (martyrs), 329, 331
balance, 30, 33, 57, 60, 67, 69, 84, 118, 161, 226, 307, 316, 347, 357, 383
Baptism in the Jordan, 178, 237-238
bearing fruit, 26
Beghards, 288, 291
Besant, Annie, 344
Bhagavad Gita, 408
black cross, 25, 28-29, 74-75, 77, 79, 316
   change color to white, 28, 36, 77, 79
black magic/magician, 123
blasphemy, 93, 101
blessedness, 158, 162, 166, 224, 275, 277, 281, 305, 386, 391, 394
bliss/blissfulness, 6-8, 126, 130, 155, 162, 389
blood/circulation, 106, 110, 150,

209, 212, 214-215, 217, 228, 284, 328, 331
Bodhisattvas, 330, 332
Brahmanism, 288, 291
breathing process, 334
bridge (over the river Jordan), 234-235, 238
brotherly love, 381
Buddha, 253-354, 358-361, 367, 372
Buddhi, 87
Buddhism, 288, 291-292, 311, 313, 326
burning up (in shame), 124, 128, 130-131

calmness of soul, 416
causal body (new form), 358
Chinese culture, 289, 292
Christ, 20, 22, 27-29, 40-41, 46, 50, 52-54, 56-60, 62, 64-72, 80, 86, 121, 123, 127, 130, 137, 145, 151, 153, 172, 177, 193, 196-197, 199, 201-202, 206, 234-238, 252, 265, 311, 313, 315, 323-325, 330, 332-333, 335, 345, 353-354, 358-359, 362, 366-367, 372, 382, 399, 405-406, 409, 411, 415-417
  as Ahura Mazdao, 27
  Christ event, 55, 68, 202, 204
  Christ impulse, 89, 123, 311, 313, 378
  Christ power, 29, 86, 178
  Christ principle, 27, 40, 145, 148, 317
  Christ spirit, 41
  Christ thought, 326
  death in Christ (in us), 86, 127, 137, 172,
  as earth's planetary spirit, 27-29
  etheric aura, 41
  etheric body, 29, 406
  as fatherless Christ, 322-323, 327
  forces, 323
  gives inner balance, 60
  as great Spirit of the Sun, 145
  I am the Light of the World, 329-330, 332
  Light of Christ, 152-153
  as love, 123
  relation of Christ, 234
  sacrifice of Christ, 205
  as Savior, 104
  as the Son, 411-413, 415
  substance of Christ, 151, 178, 205, 417
Christian/Christianity, 62, 66, 69, 101, 104, 115, 234, 288, 292, 323, 327, 368, 408
  exoteric, 27
Christ-bearer, 197, 201
Chrysostom, John, 120
colors, 57, 73-74, 76, 78, 80-82, 84, 290, 296, 335
  black, 25, 28-29, 74, 77
  blue, 24, 79, 115, 170, 193, 195, 198, 201, 203-205, 221, 225
  color disk (circle), 290, 293
  complementary, 28, 36, 82, 195, 198, 201, 203, 205, 221
  green, 28-29, 36, 79, 170, 193, 195, 198, 201, 203-205, 221, 225
  red, 24-26, 28, 73, 75-76, 79-80, 82-84, 193, 195, 198, 201, 203, 205, 221, 225
    flaming-red, 25-26
    reddish lilac, 221
  violet, 24, 73, 80, 82-84
  violet-red, 203
  white, 28, 36, 77, 79
  yellow, 79, 170
community, sense of, 390
clairaudience, 384
clairvoyance/clairvoyant, 49, 101, 107, 137, 153-158, 160, 171, 183, 186, 188, 190, 201, 203-204, 210, 213, 215, 217, 224, 226, 228, 249, 289, 378, 399
  ancient/atavistic, 89, 377, 384, 391, 393
  clairvoyant consciousness, 156, 158-159, 161
Clason, Louise, 149, 154, 192, 209, 219, 233, 254, 309, 321, 395
cleverness, 385
compassion, 136, 140, 183, 255, 257, 273, 296, 307, 385-386, 389, 391, 394, 412
concentration, 13, 52, 54, 97, 99-101,

217, 229, 232, 240, 244, 247, 252, 254, 264, 289, 295, 330, 338-339, 361, 364, 381, 388
conscience, 349, 386-387, 390-392, 394
conscienceless, 387, 390
conscientious/conscientiousness, 97, 117, 342-343, 349
contemplate/contemplation, 199, 338-339
consciousness, 16, 40, 42-43, 49, 77, 80, 99, 115, 119, 143, 153, 163, 166, 180, 192, 204, 207, 209-210, 230-231, 235, 239, 244-245, 250, 257-258, 267, 276, 279, 309, 314, 339, 361, 364-366, 373-374, 384, 388, 390, 393, 395-397, 400, 409, 411-412, 416
  higher, 115, 373, 391
  self-consciousness, 35, 47, 194-195
consciousness soul, 352-353, 355, 358, 360, 384, 386, 388, 390-391, 393-394
constellations, 120, 125, 129
cosmic/cosmos, 56, 151, 162, 166-167, 178, 189, 195, 235-238, 249, 251, 256, 259, 272, 275, 277, 281, 295, 322-323, 327, 334, 359-360, 405
cosmos of wisdom, 122
counter image, 114
courage, 133, 136, 140
Creation, the, 329, 332
criticize/criticism, 261-262, 300, 363, 368-369, 372, 374-375, 379

Danielsson, Frau, 334
deceit/deceitfulness, 156, 159
Delphi temple, 103
delusions of grandeur, 343
descent into underground, 270, 273-274, 276-279, 281-282, 284-285
destiny, 12, 39, 85-86, 101, 156, 160, 225-226, 291, 300, 308, 386, 402, 404, 408
desires/drives/passions, 22, 74, 84-85, 91-92, 126-127, 130, 155, 159, 162, 167, 219-220, 249, 255, 257, 279, 298, 364, 371, 377, 385, 388

destructive forces, 233, 235-237, 249, 327
devachan/devachanic, 11, 14, 110, 137, 220, 223
devotion, 13, 79, 99, 172, 221, 223, 265-266, 268, 296-297, 334, 370-371, 380, 385, 388, 393, 404, 408, 412, 414, 416-417
dignity, 364
dishonesty, 157, 170, 215, 218
dispassionateness, 202, 221
doppelgänger (double), 210, 230, 241-242, 245-249, 254-255, 257-258
  as division of personality, 245, 248
  as second "I," 241
doubt, 16-17, 119-120, 129
double. *See* doppelgänger
dove, with olive branch, 74, 77, 80, 82, 84
dragon, 289-290, 293
drowning (spiritual), 108, 124, 126, 128-129, 131, 211, 214, 216-217, 230, 251, 268
Druid mysteries, 38, 40

East, the (spiritual), 67, 70-71, 73, 76, 78, 80-81, 83
Eckhart, Meister, 119, 288, 291, 356, 360
ecstasy, 38, 40
egoity, 385
egotism/egotistical, 13, 51, 55, 70, 77, 79-80, 82, 85-87, 89, 92-93, 106-107, 115, 121, 126-127, 130, 132, 136, 140, 144-146, 157, 163, 184, 193-194, 196, 199, 202, 207, 209-210, 212, 215-216, 218, 227, 244-245, 248, 253, 257, 262, 266, 279-280, 290, 297, 303, 305-306, 335, 342, 346-347, 386, 391, 412, 415
  justified egotism, 305
Egyptian mysteries, 38, 40, 270, 273, 276, 278, 282, 322-323
elements (air, earth, fire, water), 37, 135-137, 139-141, 270, 275-276, 283-284
elemental world, 136-141, 275
Elias, 234-235
Elijah, 234-235, 366-367, 372, 378, 382

Elohim. *See* Hierarchies, Elohim/Elusiai (Spirits of Form)
empathize/empathy, 389, 412
enlightenment, 29
enmity, 414
envy. *See* jealousy
Essene (inner), 353-354, 357, 359-360
Essene (the sect), 357, 359-360, 362
ethers
   chemical, 108, 211, 214, 216-217
   light, 210, 213, 215, 217
   warmth, 106, 209, 212, 215, 217
ether-spheres, 51
etheric, 22, 51-52, 55-56, 87, 95, 99-100, 147, 157, 160, 163, 165, 172, 177, 196, 199, 336, 338, 387
   etheric maya, 117. *See also* Ahriman
etheric body, 21-22, 31-32, 36-37, 41, 44-46, 48, 52, 56, 90, 92, 95-101, 106-108, 110-113, 118-119, 125, 129, 150, 155-156, 158-160, 162-171, 174-176, 178-179, 188, 195, 198, 204-205, 209-217, 220, 226, 254, 256, 259-260, 272, 275, 277, 287, 289, 294, 296, 298, 300-301, 310, 312, 314, 336, 338-339, 411, 414
   loosening of, 46, 95-99
etherization of the blood, 172
Ex Deo nascimur, 40, 53, 56, 75, 77, 81, 86, 91-92, 101-102, 115, 121, 127, 130, 145, 151, 172, 205, 252, 265, 324, 326, 397, 399-400, 402, 405, 409, 412, 415, 417

fairy tales/ghosts, 385, 389, 393-394
faith, 17, 82, 133, 157, 161, 164, 168, 236, 241, 304, 306, 330, 342, 345, 348-349, 351
   blind-faith, 168, 177, 241
fall into sin, 153
fanaticism, 32, 34-36
The Father and I are One, 406
father-forces, 321-325, 327
   work until 33rd year (in human), 322-323, 326-327
Father-principle (divine), 321, 327, 405, 414

falsehood. *See* lies (untruth)
fear, 23, 26, 40, 75, 77, 86, 89, 119, 207, 239, 243, 385, 388-389, 391, 393-394
fearlessness, 133, 136, 140, 243, 246, 304
feeblemindedness, 220, 225, 331
feeling, 10, 14, 18, 20, 23-26, 28, 35, 46, 52, 54, 58-60, 66, 68, 75-76, 87, 89, 92, 101, 106-107, 109, 114, 118, 121, 126, 129, 131-132, 134-136, 138, 143-144, 155, 157, 159-160, 163, 165, 172, 175, 185, 190, 194, 196-197, 200-206, 209-210, 212-215, 223, 226, 230, 251-252, 254, 256, 258-260, 263-265, 270-271, 274, 276, 279-281, 293, 295, 297, 301, 303, 307, 309, 312-313, 316, 318-319, 334-335, 340, 343-344, 352-353, 356, 359, 366, 369-370, 377, 379-381, 384, 386, 389, 391, 395-404, 407-409, 411
feeling of warmth, 200-201, 204, 209-210, 212, 215
fertilization, 24-25
fog (to overcome), 126, 128, 130
forces (in human nature)
   ascending, 326-327
   descending, 326-327
forces of ascent, 236
freedom, 19, 22, 38, 150, 153, 234, 236, 240
French Revolution, 289
front bone (series of lotus flowers), 95, 97, 100
Fugger-Gloett, Amalie, 21, 89, 118

gate of death, 264-266, 274, 281-282,
   as threshold of death, 270-271, 276-278, 285
Genesis, book of, 329, 332
germinating, 25, 43
gestalt, 293, 310
ghosts. *See* fairy tales/ghosts
Gnostics, 104
God (Father), 8, 20, 25, 28, 52-54, 61, 63, 70, 75, 77-78, 82, 85-86, 89, 91, 114, 119, 144, 150, 172, 190, 195, 197, 200, 202, 204, 206, 219, 221, 234-235, 238-241,

243-245, 249, 256, 259, 265, 274, 276, 278, 290, 304, 313, 326-327, 329-330, 332, 354, 359, 393, 399, 405-406, 408-409, 411-413
we are born from Him, 405, 409
Godhead, 89, 133, 144, 197, 200, 413
godliness, 10, 61-62, 65, 68, 70
light of, 61
He thinks, weaves, works in us, 405
gods. *See* Hierarchies, as gods
Goethe, 25-26, 228, 352, 355-356, 358
going through the elements, 272, 275-276, 284-285
Golden Calf, 309, 311-314
as sheath of nature, 309-310, 312
Golgotha, 27, 119, 152, 178, 206, 222, 235, 367
grace, 49, 163, 195, 283, 366, 371, 374, 402
gratitude, 25, 54, 101, 260, 377, 380, 397-402, 405, 408-409, 414
group soul, 194, 207, 326
guardian angel, 144-145, 148, 319
my angel in me, 414
as good angel, 147
as inner impulse, 144
Guardian of the Threshold, 117, 290, 293, 310, 318, 354, 357, 360

habit, 21
hallucination, 288, 291-292
hand, as organ of thought, 387, 392
harmonious/harmony, 329, 332, 354, 357, 374
hatred, 414
heart/circulation, 50, 53-54, 229, 295, 304, 338
forces, 54
Leo (lion), zodiacal sign, 50, 54, 295
shining star, 229
Hebrew mysteries, 319-320, 329, 332
hierarchical beings, 2, 13, 27, 45, 47-48, 51-54, 104-106, 109-113, 117, 132, 136, 138, 140-141, 168, 172, 174-176, 178-179, 188-189, 194-195, 197, 200, 202, 204-

205, 209, 212-213, 215, 228-229, 239, 243, 246-247, 270, 294-295, 297-298, 303, 305, 307, 313, 316-317, 330, 333, 366, 370, 374, 377, 380, 396, 398-399, 401, 405, 408
as gods, 13, 15, 19-20, 40, 44, 91, 93, 101, 112, 150-151, 153, 163, 197, 202, 204, 206-207, 229-230, 234, 279, 282, 284-285, 289-290, 293, 343, 347, 350, 375, 391
human hierarchy, 111-113
hierarchies
2nd, Angeloi (spirits of life), 136, 140, 143, 147, 156, 159, 168, 170, 174, 177, 179, 197, 200, 202, 204, 206, 264, 319, 330, 332, 334-335, 416
3rd, Archangeloi (spirits of fire), 123, 136-137, 140, 168, 170, 174, 177, 179, 197, 200, 202, 204, 206, 319
4th, Archai/Primal Beginnings (spirits of personality), 31, 33, 35, 137, 140-141, 168, 170, 174, 176-177, 179, 197, 200, 202, 204, 206, 319
5th, Elohim/Exusiai (spirits of form), 31, 33, 36, 168, 170-171, 177-179, 185, 190, 228
6th, Dynamis (spirits of movement), 31, 34, 168, 177, 185, 188, 190, 228, 330, 414, 416
7th, Kyriotetes (spirits of wisdom), 31, 36-37, 168, 177, 330, 332-333
8th, Thrones (spirits of will), 137, 140-141, 168, 177, 414, 416
9th, Cherubim (spirits of harmony), 168, 177-178
10th, Seraphim (spirits of universal love), 168, 177-178
holiness, 391
Hollenbach, Hendrika, 363, 383, 395
hollowness (sense of), 126, 129
Holy Spirit, 53, 102, 115, 127, 130, 137, 198, 201-202, 206, 235, 265, 302, 324, 327, 399, 406, 409,

412-413, 415-416
  as Holy Spirit of Evolution, 305
  impulse of, 414
  as individualized, 115
  principle of, 415
  resurrection in, 399, 412
  world-thoughts of, 202, 205, 397, 402
Homer, 356
  Iliad, 356
honesty, 342-343, 372
hope, love, and faith, 412
Hubbe-Schleiden, 11, 87
Hübner, Emilie, 94
humility, 21, 32, 82, 126, 130, 143-144, 147, 165, 221, 295, 347, 391
hydrophobia, 385, 394
Hypoborean, 243
hypochondria, 31-32, 34, 36
hypocrisy, 353, 360

"I" (ego), 9, 22, 30, 33-34, 36-38, 46, 48, 51-52, 56, 63-64, 74, 84-85, 87, 89-92, 108, 115, 119, 123-125, 128, 140, 149, 165, 168-169, 171-172, 174, 178-181, 183, 186-187, 189, 211, 216-217, 228, 240, 343-244, 247, 261, 263, 266-267, 282-283, 287, 289, 293, 301-302, 305, 310-314, 328, 331, 339, 342, 384-385, 389-391, 395, 408, 411, 415, 417
  dissolution of ego, 38
  divine "I," 405
  ego-hood, 261
  elevated "I," 283
  eternal self, 220, 284
  higher "I" (self), 46, 75, 226, 257, 313, 317, 358, 397
  "I"-thoughts ("I" thinking in us), 376, 393, 395-397
  as self, 2, 22, 30, 33, 38, 46, 82, 107, 115, 125, 130, 140-141, 181, 189, 228, 240, 243-244, 247, 261, 263, 266-267, 293, 301, 312, 395, 397-398, 405, 408, 417
  spiritual "I," 75
  transitory "I," 284

  true "I," 77
  world-"I," 405
  "I"-being, 243
  "I"-body, 376, 380
  "I"- consciousness, 115, 194, 257-258, 309-310, 416
I am the way, the truth and the life, 62, 65-67, 69-71
illness, 31, 45, 91, 98, 103, 200, 220, 222, 225, 231, 319, 329, 332, 350
illusion. *See* maya
illusions of personality, 16-17
imagination/imaginative, 82, 113, 118, 136, 140, 144, 183-184, 187, 190, 192, 195, 198, 203, 205, 222, 225-226, 241, 274, 280, 309, 311-313, 321
Imagination (stage of), 184, 187, 190, 241
immortality, 226, 352
imperturbability, 304-305, 307
In Christo morimur, 41, 53, 56, 81, 91, 101, 121, 126, 130, 151, 153, 177, 205, 265, 326, 397, 399-400, 402, 405, 409, 412, 415, 417
In _____ morimur, 75, 77-78, 86, 92, 101-102, 131, 137, 145, 252, 399
incorporation, 10
indifference, 215, 217, 221
individuality, 123, 207, 226, 403
initiation, 115, 358
  Christian, 221, 224, 226-227
  Druid, 38, 40
  Egyptian, 38, 40, 284, 290, 302
  Rosicrucian, 38
  self-initiation, 281
insanity, 32
inspire/inspiration, 81, 118, 136, 144-145, 321, 336-337, 340, 351
Inspiration (stage of), 184, 187, 190
instability, 120
  as camouflaged, 120
intellectual (mind) soul, 353, 356, 359-360, 384-385, 388-389, 391, 393-394
intuition, 140, 144
Intuition (stage of), 184, 187, 190
Isis, 322, 325

spiritual forces of, 322, 325, 327
It weaves me, it thinks me, it creates me, 396-398, 400-402, 404, 406-409, 411-412, 414-416

Jahveh. *See* Yahweh
Jesus of Nazareth, 67, 205, 327, 362
  two Jesus children, 173
jealousy (envy), 106, 210, 212, 214, 249, 305, 410
John the Evangelist, 120, 124, 126, 128-129, 367
  September 30, 395 A.D., 120, 125-126, 129-130
  writer of the Apocalypse, 120, 124, 126, 128, 130
John, St., gospel of, 220, 323, 329, 332
  Mary-Sophia, 323
Jupiter (epoch), 123, 150-151, 152
Jupiter (planet), 7, 145
  spirit of, 28

Kabbalistic, 212
kamaloca, 155, 159, 162, 166
karma/karmic, 48, 58, 63, 67, 75, 80, 85, 106, 140, 146-147, 157, 161, 163, 186, 189, 202-203, 209, 212, 215, 219-221, 223-226, 231, 233, 235-237, 251-253, 261, 268, 274, 277, 295, 297, 299-300, 307-308, 324, 335, 338, 351, 383, 396, 399-402, 404
  world-karma, 75, 80
kingdom of shadows, 336
Kinkel, Alice, 30, 57, 89, 92, 122, 124, 132, 142, 154, 192, 233, 261, 282, 287, 299, 303, 307, 328, 352, 410
Klein, Emma, 303
Kriecheldorff, Else, 316
Krishna, 359, 366-367, 372, 378, 382, 408
Ku Hung Ming
  China's Defense Against European Ideas, 288, 292

Lang, Bella, 352
language, 60

larynx, 73, 81, 83
Legion (our name is), 221, 223
lemniscate, 136, 139
Lemuria/Lemurian epoch, 150, 197, 200, 202, 206, 219, 222, 243
Lichtenberg, Nelly, 57, 73, 103, 124, 134, 149, 309, 321
lies (untruths), 107, 156, 159-160, 163, 165, 210-213, 215-218, 226, 250, 253, 268, 313, 342, 350
light, 9-10, 24-25, 27, 29, 34, 40-41, 56, 58, 61, 64, 66-68, 70, 113-115, 142, 147, 151, 155, 159, 172, 182, 184, 186-190, 192, 241, 244-245, 247, 252, 254, 256, 259, 272, 293-294, 330, 340
  inner light, 337
  light-effects, 330, 334-335
  light-filled, 334
  spiritual, 56, 65, 188
Logos (Word), 185-186, 189-191
Lord's Prayer, 12, 14, 18, 111
lotus flowers, 95, 97, 100, 110, 112-113, 275, 277, 281
  16-petal, 317
love, 9-10, 25, 29, 31-34, 41, 58-59, 62, 66, 69, 76, 79, 91, 122-123, 190, 194, 196, 199, 202, 204-205, 207, 255, 257-258, 263-264, 266, 312, 316, 334, 343, 368-369, 372, 374-375, 379, 381, 383, 389, 392-394, 412, 415
  brotherly love, 381
  love of creating (creative), 412, 414
  love of God, 190
  love of life, 412, 414
  love of nature, 349
  love of truth, 319, 381, 412, 414
  pure, 29, 41, 61-62, 65, 68, 70, 72, 182, 189
  spiritual, 78
  true love, 257, 370
Lucifer, 19-20, 59, 61, 64-65, 80, 83, 87, 117, 122-123, 130, 150, 153, 234, 284, 287, 289, 310, 312, 314, 399
luciferic, 19-20, 22, 106-107, 126, 132, 143, 147, 152-153, 183, 191, 209-210, 212, 214-215, 217, 230,

235, 246, 248-249, 251-253, 255, 268, 287, 291, 305, 310, 367-368, 371, 374-375, 378

Madonna, 325
Maha Aya, 87, 103-104
manas, 87, 358
Mars, 21, 52
Martin, Saint, 353
Mary-Sophia, 323, 325, 327
Masters of Wisdom and Harmony of Feelings, 12, 18, 22, 28, 32, 40, 45, 79, 90, 131, 143, 145, 154, 156, 158, 160-161, 164, 173, 186, 209, 211, 216, 228, 265, 297, 337, 342, 345-346, 351, 355, 360, 371, 379
materialism/materialistic, 37, 39, 89, 99, 126, 130, 220, 222, 225, 251, 345, 350, 378, 388, 393
maya (illusion), 18-20, 23-24, 26, 28, 42, 49-50, 53, 61, 64, 68, 70, 87, 106, 109, 111, 134, 157, 160, 184-185, 187-190, 192, 195-196, 198-199, 201, 203-204, 207, 221, 224, 226-229, 233-234, 236, 239-240, 242-247, 251-252, 269, 288, 310, 312-314, 316, 343, 350, 384, 386
  great non-existence, 103-104
  reversed maya, 184
meat, abstaining from eating, 328, 331
meditate/meditation, 11-14, 18, 20, 24-25, 27, 29-30, 38, 40-41, 43, 48-55, 58, 60-62, 65, 67-72, 76, 79, 81, 95-97, 99-100, 108-110, 112-114, 117-118, 122, 128, 132-134, 138, 140, 142, 144, 146, 148,
153-160, 162-167, 169, 171, 175-176, 178-179, 182-184, 186, 189, 194, 204, 206, 211, 216-217, 220-221, 223, 226-227, 229-230, 235-236, 240-241, 244, 247, 251-252, 254, 256, 258-262, 264-265, 267, 271, 275, 277-278, 289, 295-297, 300-305, 307, 314, 316, 322, 328-331, 333, 337-340, 343, 349, 352, 358-359, 361, 364, 366, 369-371, 373-374, 376-377, 379-381, 384, 386-388, 393, 395, 397, 399, 401, 403-404, 407, 409, 416
meditations/verses, 2-10, 14, 18, 21, 27, 30, 32, 43, 45, 51, 53, 55, 58-59, 61, 65, 68, 70, 75, 77-78, 81, 92, 101-102, 108, 114-115, 127-128, 142, 145, 152, 158, 169, 172-173, 175, 182, 205, 326, 330, 332, 400, 415
megalomania, 343, 349-350
Mehazael, 220, 224, 226, 231, 251, 253, 268
melancholic, 108
memory, 56, 92, 111, 132, 261, 267, 288-289, 291-292, 309-310, 312-314, 331, 337, 343, 347, 349, 358, 370, 395
  as Lucifer's gift, 289, 312
mental pictures, 24-25, 43, 110, 153, 165
Mercury (alchemical), 114
Mercury (planet), 6, 32
  spiritual, 167
mesmerizing, 194, 196, 199
Meyer, Rudolph, 219, 255, 270, 321
mineral kingdom, 37, 43, 45, 194, 197, 200, 202, 204, 228, 322, 327
mirror image/mirroring, 92, 109, 140, 156, 159, 163, 188, 190, 192, 196, 199, 221, 227, 384, 417
modesty, 391
Molinos, 119
Moon (old, stage of earthly evolution), 9, 20-22, 122-123, 172, 178, 233, 235, 240, 243, 246-247, 399
moon (planet)
  forces, 301, 317
moral/morality, 17, 46, 48, 62, 132, 157, 160, 183, 188, 190, 221, 296, 303, 307, 332, 338, 349-350, 386, 391, 406
Morgenstern, Margareta, 57, 73, 363, 383
Moses, 178, 309-312, 314, 322, 329
mother-forces, 322-325
Muller, Johannes, 224-225
music of the spheres, 110
Mystery of Golgotha, 64, 151, 171,

197, 201, 219, 233-236, 287, 291, 322-324, 336, 354, 366, 371, 378, 381-382, 399

nakedness, our, 354, 359
Napoleon, 356
nature, 19
  enjoyment of, 354, 360, 371
negativity, 372, 375
Neo-Buddhism, 121
nervous system, 210, 213, 215, 217, 301, 329, 332
Nicholas of Cusa, 355
Noah's Ark, 74, 76
No one comes to the Father except through me, 406
non-egotistical, 75, 132
Not I but Christ in me, 41, 127, 130, 145, 148, 151, 178, 198, 201
nothingness, 89

observation, 307, 374
  self-observation, 347, 349
occult imprisonment, 126, 130

passage through the elements, 270, 273-277, 280-282
Paul, St. (Pauline), 41, 127, 130, 145, 148, 178, 330
  first letter to Timothy, 330, 332
patience, 12, 14, 82, 85, 117, 219, 252, 258, 261, 296, 337-338, 364-365, 376, 382, 403, 416
Per Spiritum Sanctum revivisimus, 40-41, 53, 56, 75, 78, 81, 91-92, 102, 127, 130, 145, 172, 205, 252, 265, 326, 397, 399-400, 402, 406, 409, 412, 415, 417
periodicity, 410, 413
  as movement in circles, 413
personality, 144-145, 147, 243, 282, 284, 307, 309, 313, 334, 364, 368, 374, 378
perversity, 319
Pharisee (inner), 353-354, 356-357, 359-360
pictures, mental, 60, 82, 85, 146, 149, 153, 162, 165, 183-184, 190, 247, 280, 335, 340, 388
pious/piety, 73, 80, 82, 377, 380, 385, 389, 391, 393, 396-398, 400-402, 404, 407, 412, 415
pineal gland, 172
plant kingdom, 37, 45, 194, 197, 200, 202, 204, 228, 322, 327
planetary forces, 321-322
Plutarch, 103
Poeppig, Fred, 106, 154, 192
poise, 202
Polarean (epoch), 243
positivity, 363, 368-369, 375, 379
post-Atlantean cultural epochs
  3rd, (Babylonian/Chaldean/Egyptian), 322, 325
  4th, (Greco-Roman), 322, 338
  7th, (American), 95
powerlessness, 405
powers, human
  active, 304
  passive, 304
prayer, 18, 21, 49, 55, 103, 194, 196, 206, 232, 355, 366, 399, 414
  communal, 194
  in Mass, 207
  mood of prayer, 371, 374
  prayer of thanksgiving, 411
prejudice, 17, 21, 46, 161
pride, 33, 52, 54, 143
propaganda, 173-174
Proserpine, 285
purifying, 316
Pythagorean Theorem, 338, 341
Pythagoras, 338, 341, 354, 359

rabies, 385, 389, 394
reason, 234, 342-343, 346, 349
red roses, 25, 28, 36, 75, 77, 79, 150
  seven red roses, 316
reincarnation, 174, 181, 272, 404
resurrection of the 3rd epoch (in the 5th), 325
reverence, 21, 28, 46, 52, 54, 127, 131, 144, 221, 323, 334, 370-371, 377, 385, 389, 391, 393-394, 396-398, 400-402, 404, 407-409, 412, 414, 417
reversal of time sequence, 111-112
rhythmically, 117
rituals (*cultus*), 318, 322
Roesel, Artur, 154, 169

Rose Cross, 28-29, 36, 74-75, 77, 79, 85, 150, 252
Rosicrucian, 38, 53, 66, 75, 82, 86, 92, 96, 122, 125, 127, 129, 135, 137, 142, 152, 172, 178, 202, 271, 276, 278, 311, 324, 341
   mysteries, 92, 257-258
   schools, 120, 124, 128

sacrifice, 3, 5, 172, 255, 257, 371, 375, 378-379, 382, 385, 394
Sadducee (inner), 352, 354-360
salamanders (fire spirits), 213, 217
Samael, 107, 212-213, 215, 217, 220, 223, 226, 230, 246, 248-250, 253, 255, 268
Saturn (old, stage of earthly evolution), 22, 77, 110, 137, 140-141, 151, 153, 172, 240, 243, 246-247, 301, 399
Saturn (planet), 2
   forces, 301
Scholl, Mathilde, 18, 21, 23, 27, 30, 37, 40, 43, 89, 99, 118, 154, 192, 228, 239, 282, 299, 363, 383, 407, 410
Schouten-Deetz, Hulda, 16, 295
Schubert, Günther, 268
Scourging, 221, 224, 226-227
seeds (germs), 10, 12-13, 15, 25, 35, 50, 53, 59, 76-77, 108, 111, 128, 130, 137, 146, 152, 158, 162, 173, 178, 191, 204-205, 211, 216, 257, 265, 291, 293, 297, 336, 341, 345, 355, 358, 360, 369, 379, 382, 388, 400, 413
Seiler, Franz, 233
Seleikids, 104
self-discipline, 371, 374, 377
self-forgetfulness, 49, 51
self-greed, 316
self-knowledge, 303, 305
selfless/selflessness, 32, 62, 75, 79, 106, 194, 196, 207, 209, 212, 216, 255, 257, 289, 303, 305, 316
sentient soul, 44, 353, 357, 359-360, 384-385, 388-389, 391, 393
serve/service, 346
seven seals, 120, 125, 129
Shakespeare, 111, 356

shame, 25-26, 28, 274, 279-280, 334-335, 354, 359
sheath nature. *See* Golden Calf
Socrates, 372
solidarity. *See* unity
solitude, 193, 196, 199, 202, 206-207, 254-256, 258-260, 262-263, 265-266
Son, principle of (divine), 414
Sophia-Maria. *See* John, St, gospel of, Mary-Sophia
sorrow, 75, 126, 262, 322
sound, 58, 74, 76, 78-82, 109, 185-186, 192, 229, 299, 340
spirit of darkness, 32
spirit of devotion, 35
spirit of the Earth, 43-44, 151
spirit of fire, 50, 54, 137
spirit of good attitude, 35
spirit of heaviness, 31-36
spirit of light, 31-36
spirit self, 150, 152
spirit of truth, 35
spiritual beings. *See* hierarchical beings
spiritual science (Anthroposophy), 161, 176, 251, 397
   Atlantean, possessed by China, 292
springing to life, dying away, 12-14, 24-25
squawking of the ravens, 73, 76, 78, 80-81, 84
staff of Aaron, 316
steadfastness, 140
steady drops hollow the stone, 109, 111, 117, 119, 134, 138, 338, 341
Steiner, Marie, 9, 103, 328
Steiner, Rudolf
   The Christian Mystery, 142
   "The Education of the Child," 28
   Freemasonry and Ritual Work, 142
   "Guardian of the Threshold," 385, 398, 400, 404, 408
   How to Know Higher Worlds, 203, 281, 328, 339
   An Outline of Esoteric Science, 137, 180, 339
   The Way Self-Knowledge, 361
   "The Soul's Probation," 405
   Theosophy, 203

Wonders of the World Trials of the Soul and Revelations of the Spirit, 154, 179
strength, 10, 12, 23, 49, 56, 77, 91, 120, 193-194, 196, 206-207, 244, 258, 371, 377, 388
Stryczek, Paula, 51, 124, 134
sub-sensory, 135-136, 138, 140-141, 280
suffering, 75, 87, 128, 130, 150, 153, 193-195, 202, 207, 224, 229, 386, 389, 391, 394
sulfur, 114
Sun, 3, 11-14, 27, 50, 54, 64, 145-146, 237
  inner, 337
  spiritual, 147, 224, 294
Sun (old, stage of earthly evolution), 22, 123, 137, 172, 177, 228, 233, 240, 243, 246-247, 399
  condition, 22
  forces, 301, 317
sun at midnight, beholding, 270, 273, 275, 277, 281-282, 284-285, 294
superstition, 16-17, 157
sympathy, 156, 163, 167, 252, 310, 312, 314, 350, 364, 371-372, 374, 379, 392
symphony, 368, 371
talkativeness, 256, 259-260, 266
Tauler, Johannes, 119, 288, 291, 353, 356, 360
thankfulness, 256, 260, 411
theosophy/theosophical, 12, 14, 16, 18, 21-23, 37, 42, 52, 88, 91, 96-98, 100, 103, 109-110, 118-121, 125-126, 129, 134, 138, 149-153, 174, 179, 184, 195, 197, 200, 202, 204, 210, 220, 239, 242, 251, 253, 287, 292, 325, 334, 337, 339, 343, 349, 357, 366, 368-369, 372, 378-379, 381, 397, 399, 402
Theosophical Society, 342, 344, 363, 367-369, 371, 379
thinking/thoughts, 10, 15, 22, 28, 43, 45-46, 52, 54, 58, 60, 64, 66-67, 70-71, 74, 78, 83, 92-93, 99-101, 107, 110-113, 117, 123, 126-127, 129, 133-134, 143, 146, 155, 157-158, 160-161, 165-166, 173-174, 177, 183-184, 186, 196-199, 202-204, 206, 211, 216, 221, 223, 229, 231, 241, 247, 250-251, 256, 261, 263-266, 272, 274, 277, 279-280, 297-298, 300, 304, 306, 312, 318-319, 321-322, 329, 331, 337, 345, 348-349, 352, 355, 359, 361, 365, 367, 370, 373-374, 376-377, 380, 382, 384, 388-390, 392-393, 395-398, 400-404, 407-408, 411, 416-417
  loosening of, 318-319
  pure thinking, 61, 202
  thinking in me, 376, 393, 395-397, 400-401, 403-404, 406-409, 412, 416
Thought thinks the thought, 111-113
thought-arrows, 272, 274, 277, 280
thought-body, 365, 373, 376, 380, 384
  as "I"-body, 376, 380
thoughts as living beings, 280, 304
thinking, feeling, willing, 37, 48, 86, 101, 117, 126, 171, 174, 271, 278-279, 295, 349-350, 357, 384, 387, 402, 405
Titringh, Vrauke, 270, 336, 342, 349
Timothy I, book of, 330, 332
tones, 58, 79
transform/transformation, 46, 48-49, 53, 68, 76, 82, 132, 164, 183, 192-193, 237, 251, 257-258, 265, 301, 303, 310, 373, 376, 383-384, 386-387, 389, 391, 403
Tree of Knowledge, 150
Tree of Life, 150
Trinity, the, 330, 333, 413
trust, 29, 85, 346-347
truth, 25, 29, 57, 59-62, 64-67, 69-72, 78, 83-84, 90, 100, 107, 127, 144, 147, 152, 156, 160, 164, 173-174, 187, 192, 195, 198, 200, 207, 210, 214-215, 228, 251, 265, 342-344, 346-347, 351-353, 355, 358, 360-362, 367-368, 372, 374-375, 378-379, 381, 415

absolute, 358
truth/truthfulness, 12, 14, 44, 147, 228-229, 232, 234, 344, 372, 377
turning inside out, 203

ugliness, as beauty, 193, 196, 199, 204-205
unity, 386-387, 392
   with esotericists and humanity, 341, 390, 394
Universal love of humanity, 69, 71-72
unrevealed light, 338
Unspeakable name (of God), 63-64, 67, 70-71, 76, 79, 83, 86, 96, 337
   the sound (tone), 67-69
   Mahavach, 337
untruth, 144, 215, 250
untruthfulness, 107, 156, 161, 165, 171, 210, 215-217, 230, 349
uprightness, 189

vain/vanity, 20, 31, 33, 52, 54-55, 103, 146, 161, 167, 283, 342, 347-348, 387, 390, 410-413
vegetarian, 73, 83, 101, 329, 331, 334
veil/veiled, 79, 124-125, 128, 165, 210, 234, 243, 246, 290, 322, 325
   Isis's veil, 322, 325
Venus (epoch), 123, 150
Virgo, constellation, 120, 125, 129
visions, 42, 224, 318, 335, 337, 377, 391, 405
   atavistic, 318
   visionary cloud, 405
vowels, lack of, 76, 79-80, 81, 83
Vreede, Elisabeth, 11, 27, 30, 37, 40, 43, 48, 57, 73, 95, 134, 142, 154, 169, 182, 192, 209, 219, 239, 249, 270, 309, 318, 321, 336, 342, 252, 395
Vulcan (epoch), 150

Wagner, Günther, 23, 57, 73, 97, 109, 134, 142, 149, 154, 169, 182, 192, 209, 239, 249, 255, 270, 395, 403
walking in the lower-world, 271
walking, speaking, understanding (thinking), 57, 60, 63, 67, 69-71
Walther, Therese, 233, 363
Wandrey, Camilla, 57, 73, 103, 109, 209, 219, 239, 255, 270
warmth, 56, 59, 61, 64-65, 68-70, 72, 106-107, 110, 190, 197-198, 200-201, 204, 209-210, 212, 260, 283, 295, 303, 334-335
wastefulness, 305
water, 114-115
water permeated by light, 114
weaves in me, 396-398, 400-402, 404-406, 408, 411, 416
will, 9-10, 52, 55, 66, 100, 122-123, 160, 252, 267, 274, 276, 279, 282, 319, 330, 337, 355, 382, 392, 396, 398, 400-402
willing, 9, 126, 130, 280, 384
wisdom, 10, 19, 32, 60, 66, 93, 113, 115, 122-123, 142, 151, 189, 202, 323, 358, 366, 371, 377, 379, 382
withered, 74
Wolf, Barbara, 37, 40, 43, 51, 89, 99, 118, 154, 182, 192, 228, 261, 282, 287, 299, 352, 363, 383, 395, 407
Word, the creative, 81, 86.
   See also Logos (Word)
words, primal, 229
world of light (spiritual), 244
world order, 268
world-forces, 396-397
world-thoughts, 397
   as theosophy, 397, 402
worldviews, 16, 31, 292
wrinkles, 155, 159, 167

Yahweh, 321, 327, 329
Yahweh-Christ, 178
You shall be as gods, 399

Zarathustra (Zoroaster), 27, 29, 236, 354
Zoroaster. *See* Zarathustra
zodiac, 50, 104, 281, 406

www.ingramcontent.com/pod-product-compliance
Lightning Source LLC
Chambersburg PA
CBHW030559230426
43661CB00053B/1774